Volume 26

Advances in
Librarianship

Volume 26

Advances in
Librarianship

Edited by

Frederick C. Lynden

Rockefeller Library
Brown University
Providence, Rhode Island

Academic Press
An imprint of Elsevier Science
Amsterdam   Boston   London   New York   Oxford   Paris   San Diego
San Francisco   Singapore   Sydney   Tokyo

Academic Press
An imprint of Elsevier Science
525 B Street, Suite 1900, San Diego, California 92101-4495, USA
http://www.academicpress.com

Academic Press
84 Theobald's Road, London WC1X 8RR, UK
http://www.academicpress.com

International Standard Book Number: 0-12-024626-0

PRINTED IN THE UNITED STATES OF AMERICA
02   03   04   05   06   07   MB   9   8   7   6   5   4   3   2   1

Contents

Swedish Libraries 2001: An Increased Role in the Education Society While Adjusting to Harder Economics and Technology   83
Mats G. Lindquist

The Humanities Computing Center and Library Collaboration in New Scholarly Communication Processes   91
Jennifer Vinopal

International MARC: Past, Present, and Future   127
Sally H. McCallum

Contributors

Numbers in parentheses indicate the pages on which the authors' contributions begin.

Nancy Allen (43), Penrose Library, University of Denver, Denver, Colorado 80208

Liz Bishoff (43), Penrose Library, University of Denver, Denver, Colorado 80208

Mary M. Case (1), ARL Office of Scholarly Communication, Washington, DC 20036

Mark T. Day (231), Indiana University Libraries, Bloomington, Indiana 47405

Robin D. Gross (29), Electronic Frontier Foundation, San Francisco, California 94103

Michael G. Jackson (299), Rockefeller Library, Brown University, Providence, Rhode Island 02912–9101

Diane Kresh (149), Library of Congress, Washington, DC 20540-4000

Mats G. Lindquist (83), Göteborg University Library, Economics Library, 40520 Göteborg, Sweden

Sally H. McCallum (127), MARC Standards Office, Library of Congress, Washington, DC 20540

John V. Richardson, Jr., (175), UCLA Department of Information Studies, Los Angeles, California 90095–1520

Jennifer Vinopal (91), Humanities Reference, Bobst Library, New York University, New York, New York 10012

Preface

As in the previous volume, the predominant theme of Volume 26 of *Advances in Librarianship* is the advance of technology in libraries. This volume focuses, in eight of its ten papers, on how libraries have been changed by electronic communication of information and knowledge. From the approach of SPARC (the Scholarly Publishing and Academic Resources Coalition) that is creating new scholarship venues electronically, to an in-depth treatment of the limitations of the Digital Millennium Copyright Act for electronic publishing, the volume examines how technology is affecting libraries. Use of technology has resulted in new collaboration and cooperation by libraries and museums in the United States in providing electronic access to the American cultural heritage, and technology has allowed a similar approach in Sweden for combining services of all libraries to offer electronic access to their cultural resources. Another technology paper presents a comprehensive examination of steps required to involve humanities faculty and the library collaboratively in producing, distributing, and accessing scholarship in machine-readable form. Two more technology papers by authors from the de facto American national library, the Library of Congress (LC), examine issues of importance to libraries in the Digital Age. The first paper from LC looks at the development of MARC 21 in providing electronic access to collections, and how it is being increasingly used internationally. Finally, the second paper describes the newest experiment in reference taking place at LC, the Collaborative Digital Reference Service (CDRS) that brings reference and information services to patrons via the Internet wherever they live.

This volume not only covers digital trends but also looks at issues of significance to librarians today in the areas of reference and management in its last three papers. The first reference paper concerns public service and surveys, in an extensive article, how reference departments in libraries have responded to reference queries during the past century and how this process has been improved and refined. The management paper is a comprehensive bibliometric study of management literature showing how research in this area has affected library publications and practices. This paper can be of great use to anyone looking for the core articles on managing organizations and libraries.

The second reference paper takes a critical look at the issues involved in serring patrons at the reference desk 24 hours 7 days a week, and surveys the literature on this topical theme.

The volume's first paper is by Mary Case, Director of the Office of Scholarly Communication in the Association of Research Libraries. Entitled "Igniting Change in Scholarly Communication: SPARC, Its Past, Present, and Future," this paper chronicles the development of the Scholarly Publishing and Academic Resources Coalition which was formed in 1998 in response to the exorbitant costs of scientific journals produced by scholarly scientific technical publishers. In 1998, SPARC began to offer a choice to research libraries in the form of lower cost scientific and technical journals published with the support of societies such as the American Chemical Society. SPARC is relying more and more on newly created nonprofit electronic journals and databases as alternative forms of scholarly resources. Ms. Case's paper speaks about the progress of the effort, and its future programs.

The second paper, by Robin Gross, Staff Attorney of the Electronic Frontier Foundation and Director of the Campaign for Audiovisual Free Expression (CAFE), critiques a central element in the new electronic environment, the Digital Millennium Copyright Act (DMCA). This paper, the "Digital Millennium Copyright Act's Impact on Freedom of Expression, Science, and Innovation" speaks of the dangers to free speech and scientific inquiry of the anticircumvention provisions of DMCA. Ms. Gross looks at a number of cases and shows how libraries as well as average citizens are being threatened as media giants use the DMCA to curtail free speech. Librarians can have an effect if they participate in political efforts to change the DMCA. Advances in electronic librarianship will be constrained by DMCA provisions unless they are either modified or eliminated.

In the third paper, "Collaborative Digitization: Libraries and Museums Working Together," Nancy Allen, Dean of Denver University Library, and Liz Bishoff, Project Director of the Colorado Digitization Project, report on the joint efforts of libraries and museums to convert their collections into electronic form. The first part of the article describes the history and nature of collaboration, examining success stories and how government has encouraged and supported digitization programs. Special emphasis is placed on the Colorado Digitization Project in which both authors participated. Later the article addresses international cooperation of libraries and museums, and issues of metadata and interoperability, scanning, rights and legal issues, digital archiving, and cooperative funding. The article shows the overall benefits of collaboration when digitizing collections.

Mats Lindquist, Director of the Economics Library, Göteborg University, is the author of the fourth paper, "Swedish Libraries 2001: An Increased Role in the Education Society While Adjusting to Harder Economics and

Technology." This paper also describes how technological developments, along with economic hardships and an interest in lifelong learning, have increased the role of libraries in Swedish society. According to the Swedish Library Law of 1997, (a) libraries must make their collections available free of charge to all types of users and (b) libraries of all types (public, academic, special) must cooperate. Lindquist describes the digital revolution in Swedish libraries and points out that in the future there will a "continuous convergence in form and technology for library, archive, and museum materials. . . ."

In the fifth paper, Jennifer Vinopal, Librarian for French and Italian Language and Coordinator of the Studio for Digital Projects Research, examines in detail how to integrate Humanities Computing Centers into libraries. The title of her article, "The Humanities Computing Center and Library Collaboration in New Scholarly Communication Processes," describes her focus. Ms. Vinopal, in the preparation of her paper, interviewed six professionals in the area of scholarly computing. Their expertise will be of value to any library planning to add a humanities computing component to library activities. Ms. Vinopal points out that the library needs to "involve itself in efforts (both on-campus and off) to partner with scholars and other information professionals to focus on activities that have not traditionally been part of the academic library's concern . . ." such as creation of electronic files in the humanities.

The sixth paper, "International MARC: Past, Present, and Future" by Sally H. McCallum, Chief of the Network Development and MARC Standards Office of the Library of Congress, speaks about the origins, history, and remarkable impact of the MARC format on the library environment. Her article gives technical details about the MARC format and its development in the United States and internationally, and analyzes different national standards showing the importance of one international standard for bibliographic records. Sally McCallum describes factors for MARC 21 adoption focusing on consistently applied maintenance and broad participation in its development. She shows how MARC 21 is becoming the de facto international standard. McCallum speaks, in her conclusion, about the future implications for using IFLA's Functional Requirements for Bibliographic Records (FRBR) and cataloging rules combined with the MARC format for enhancing bibliographic search results for users.

Diane Kresh, Director of Public Services, Library of Congress, writes in the seventh paper, "High Touch or High Tech: The Collaborative Digital Reference Service as a Model for the Future of Reference," about a major new digital reference experiment. Ms. Kresh looks at how the digital environment, specifically the Internet, has made possible instantaneous communication on a worldwide basis. The LC experiment makes use of these capabilities. Members exchange questions and answers via e-mail and the diverse character of libraries is used to obtain the best answers. Currently, the members of the Collaborative Digital Reference Service (CDRS) comprise 17 libraries (including the Library of Congress) spread over 15 time zones. CDRS has two components: questions and answers, and archived answers for future use. Quality control is applied as well. Participation in CDRS has value to member libraries through access to other collections, reaching out to new patrons who may not visit the library, and offering extended service to local patrons. Kresh sees CDRS as fulfilling library service values.

In the eighth paper, Dr. John V. Richardson, Professor of Information Studies, UCLA Department of Information Studies, shows how responses to the reference query by library reference services have changed over the past century. His paper, "The Current State of Research on Reference Transactions," traces research on the "reference (i.e., question asking and answering) process." Richardson's survey is chronological, beginning with the late 19th and early 20th century and discussing each decade from the 1930s to the 1990s. He points out that this paper should be of interest to those who wish to build a "testable model of the reference transaction." For example, one can learn from this survey such information as the traits important to success in reference work; the role of question negotiation; psychological factors at work in the successful reference transaction; the reference core titles for library science programs; and the types of tools most used in responding to reference questions.

In the ninth paper, Mark T. Day, Reference Librarian, Indiana University Libraries, does a bibliometric study entitled "Discourse Fashions in Library Administration and Information Management: A Critical History and Bibliometric Analysis." Day looks at managerial literature in the library science field and outside the library. His analysis shows that management literature inside and outside libraries follows bibliometric theory by coming "from a few high-impact journals located in the most influential subdisciplines." Through bibliometric analysis he comes to a number of conclusions: contemporary communication in library science is now dominated by the literature of information science and the information society; library management trends are dependent for ". . . innovative ideas on idea entrepreneurship external . . ." to libraries; and quality management is a trend which has been adopted heavily by libraries. Day's paper is a thorough analysis of management "fashions" in libraries.

The volume's tenth and last paper, entitled "A Rush to Serve: Digital Reference Service and the Commitment to 24/7," by Michael G. Jackson, Reference Librarian, Brown University, examines in depth one of the latest trends to digitize reference service and then offer it twenty-four hours a day, seven days a week. He looks at the pro's and con's of whether a librarian should be on call 24 hours a day and 7 days a week. He urges a more thorough assessment of what is really happening, i.e., are there needs which are not being fulfilled? He also asks excellent questions about the needs for such services, but concludes that one cannot simply discourage such an idea without carefully measuring and assessing what kind of reference service is now being offered and what is required.

I hope that this year's volume presents information that will be of great value to practicing librarians, researchers, and students because it was created by real experts in the field. I am especially grateful to my colleagues, the members of the Editorial Board, who worked together to prepare this volume. I would also like to thank my wife, Irina, for her constant encouragement and support. I dedicate this volume to our two daughters, Madeleine in the United States, teaching fourth-graders, and Olga in Russia, studying public relations. Both of them appreciate books and learning.

Frederick C. Lynden
Editor, *Advances in Librarianship*

Igniting Change in Scholarly Communication: SPARC, Its Past, Present, and Future

Mary M. Case
Office of Scholarly Communication
Association of Research Libraries
Washington, DC 20036

Scholarly communication can be defined as the process by which scholars and scientists conduct their research and make the results of their work known. Encompassing both formal and informal means, scholarly communication is critical to the advancement of knowledge and a scholar's career. In the formal process of publishing, researchers, building on the works of others, write up their findings and give them essentially without charge to publishers. In turn, publishers manage the peer-review process, provide editorial improvements, and distribute the work widely through inclusion in scientific journals. The journals are then purchased by libraries which organize, provide access to, and preserve them for future generations of scientists.

Evidence has accumulated over the past 15 years that this system is in crisis and is badly in need of repair. Libraries were the first to experience the effects of the breakdown as they struggled to keep up with the exploding volume and cost of journals in science, technology, and medicine. As the unit cost of serials in major research libraries soared, libraries were forced to cancel millions of dollars worth of subscriptions. At the same time, scientists, eager to exploit the potential of the networked digital environment, have been hindered by the inability to efficiently search and access distributed, proprietary information resources.

This paper will explore the success of an initiative—SPARC, the Scholarly Publishing and Academic Resources Coalition—launched by the library community to begin to address the scholarly communication crisis. Understanding that libraries are but one stakeholder in scholarly communication, SPARC was designed to build partnerships with scholarly publishers and scientists in its efforts to create change. This particular paper, however, will address the issues and the progress of SPARC through the perspective of libraries.

ADVANCES IN LIBRARIANSHIP, VOL. 26
0065-2830/02 $89.95

I. The Crisis in Scholarly Communication

Librarians were the first to experience the consequences of a breakdown in the scholarly communication system. For the past 15 years, their ability to build collections in support of the teaching and research needs of their faculties has been severely impaired by an increasingly evident dysfunction in the journals marketplace.

Data collected by the Association of Research Libraries (ARL) (2001), a membership organization of more than 120 of the largest research libraries in North America, reveal that the unit cost paid by research libraries for serials increased by 226% between 1986 and 2000. (In comparison, over the same time period, the consumer price index increased by 57%.) With serials costs increasing at 8.8% a year, and library materials budgets increasing at only 6.7% a year, libraries simply could not sustain their purchasing power. Even though the typical research library spent almost 3 times more on serials in 2000 than in 1986, the number of serial titles purchased declined by 7%. Even more dramatically, as libraries diverted resources to support journal subscriptions, book purchases declined by 17%. Based on 1986 acquisition levels, this figure represents more than 6000 monograph volumes a year not purchased by the typical research library. With such a drastic erosion in the market for books, publishers had no choice but to raise prices. By 2000, the unit cost of books had increased 66% over 1986 costs.

The overall high prices and significant price increases of journals have been traced to titles in science, technology, and medicine (STM). Price increases in these areas have averaged from 9 to 13% a year over at least the past decade (Albee and Dingley, 2000). Studies over the years have led librarians to believe that at least a part of the cause of the high prices in the STM disciplines is the increasing commercialization of science publishing. Data consistently show that the cost-per-unit of content, the cost-per-citation, and the cost-per-use of commercially produced journals are higher than those of journals produced by society and not-for-profit organizations. Studies in physics (Barschall, 1988; Barschall and Arrington, 1988), economics (Bergstrom, 2001), agriculture (Cornell University, 1998), biomedicine (McCabe, 1999), and the recent Wisconsin studies (1999) in chemistry, economics, physics, and neuroscience have all borne out these conclusions. For example, McCabe's data show that in 1998, the not-for-profit biomedical publishers were providing, for 40% of the price of the commercially produced journals, one-and-a-half times the information at four times the quality as measured by the number of citations recorded that year. McCabe's data also show that not only are commercially produced publications more expensive, but commercial publishers in the biosciences are producing seven times more journal titles than publishers in the not-for-profit sector.

In addition to this market dominance, commercial publishers are seeking to expand their market share through mergers and acquisitions. The purchase of individual titles from societies and independent editorial boards increases the number of titles under commercial ownership, while the purchase of other companies consolidates more and more content into the hands of fewer and fewer firms. Both these practices have been shown to exacerbate already high price increases (McCabe, 2000). One of the most significant recent mergers was the purchase in 2001 of Harcourt General by Reed Elsevier. This transaction brought more than 400 additional STM titles under the control of Elsevier Science, already the largest publisher of science journals in the world with its sizable portfolio of about 1200 titles. Although the economic impact of mergers is of great concern, there are equally grave implications of more and more scientific information being owned exclusively by a single company. Major content owners, such as Reed Elsevier, have aggressively lobbied for database legislation, UCITA, and restrictions on the educational use of copyrighted digital works.

If there are not significant changes in the trends that have emerged over the past 15 years, the next 20 will be increasingly dire. Projecting the ARL trend lines out 20 years shows that by 2020, the typical research library will be paying $1632 for a journal subscription and $107 for a monograph compared to $267 and $47, respectively, in 1999 ("Journal costs," 2000). Such a library would continue to lose purchasing power, buying only 13,700 serials and 15,048 monographs—16% fewer serials compared to 1986 and 54% fewer monographs. With the economy currently struggling and library budgets under siege, the actual results could be far worse.

Over the last 15 years, libraries have undertaken a number of strategies to cope with the continuing increase in journal prices. They reduced dramatically the purchase of monographs, asked their administrations for special budget increases, and when these were not enough, canceled millions of dollars worth of serials. Libraries also turned to document delivery services and developed strategies to improve interlibrary lending performance. They sought to reinvigorate cooperative collection development programs. More recently, site licensing of electronic resources has helped eliminate the need for duplicate print subscriptions. Consortial arrangements are reducing unit costs at individual institutions, distributing rising costs across a wider range of libraries. Although all of these strategies can help local institutions better manage their budgets, none of them have changed the underlying dynamics of the scholarly communication system.

Scholarly communication is a process through which scholars share their findings with colleagues and claim precedent for their ideas. In the sciences, in exchange for wide dissemination of their work and the ability to build on the work of others, faculty willingly give away the results of their intellectual effort to publishers for no direct financial remuneration. Their reward comes from contributing to the advancement of knowledge, building a reputation within their fields, and receiving promotion and tenure from their institutions. Scientists trust that the publishers to whom they give their work are operating in their best interests, intent on furthering scholarship through wide distribution of research results.

This arrangement worked well for a long time. Publishers helped shape the disciplines by collecting manuscripts in specific fields, managing the peer-review process, and marketing and selling subscriptions. During the 1960s, however, the Institute for Scientific Information (ISI) introduced a system for tracking citations in scientific journals (Guédon, 2001). To make this task manageable, ISI formalized the notion of a core list of journals that were deemed important enough to be covered in a citation index. As the index evolved, journals were ranked according to impact factor (the average number of citations per average article per year). Scientists found themselves rated by the journals in which they published and libraries by the titles to which they subscribed. As publishers recognized the earnings potential of a constant supply of free content for journals identified as "must have" for libraries, they were able to raise prices higher and higher. Librarians, who had taken over responsibility from faculty for selecting library materials, did all they could to protect the journals budgets. As a result, faculty soon lost touch with the prices of the journals in their field. Very quickly, a concept meant to be a practical solution to the overwhelming problem of tracking citations from a potentially limitless number of titles became a tool for creating a class of "must-have at any price" journals.

Librarians had hoped, perhaps naively, that the introduction of electronic technologies would bring efficiencies to journals publishing. Reduced production costs could be passed on to customers in the form of reduced subscription prices. Many primary journal publishers, however, have yet to reengineer their entire operations. Electronic versions of their journals are produced as add-ons, at the end of the print process. As a result, those added costs are passed on to the subscriber. Though a number of small publishers and independent editorial boards are producing electronic journals with print output at very low cost, there is no reason to believe that libraries will soon be the beneficiaries of cost savings passed on by the large commercial companies. If any cost savings are generated, they will benefit the shareholders.

In the meantime, scientists themselves have adopted technology for use in gathering and manipulating data. They now desire to communicate sophisticated digital works to their colleagues and to conduct their research efficiently across vast archives of related resources. The current system of publishing, in which content is owned by private interests and is accessible only from proprietary servers for a fee, limits the scientist's ability to exploit the power of the network to advance knowledge. Efforts to address these issues (for example, the development of PubMed Central by the National Institutes of Health and the Public Library of Science petition) by encouraging publishers to make their content freely available on public archives after a certain interval after publication have met with great resistance from publishers who fear a loss of control over the integrity of their content and the loss of subscription and advertising revenues. PubMed Central is a digital archive of life sciences journal literature managed by the National Center for Biotechnology Information at the U.S. National Library of Medicine. Access to PubMed Central is free and unrestricted. Participation in PubMed Central is voluntary and journal articles can be deposited by publishers at any time. For more information, see http://www.pubmedcentral.nih.gov.

The Public Library of Science is a grassroots initiative of life scientists created to encourage publishers to deposit their journals in central archives, such as PubMed Central, within 6 months of publication. These scientists believe that information from multiple sources stored in a common format in central repositories can significantly enhance their ability to search across collections, manipulate data, and develop tools to integrate the literature with a variety of other information resources. While more than 29,000 scientists from around the world have signed a petition not to publish in, review or edit for, or subscribe to publications that do not submit their content to a central repository, publishers have been slow to respond. The key leaders of the Public Library of Science movement are now developing their own nonprofit scientific publisher. For more information, see http://www.publiclibraryofscience.org.

The current system of scholarly communication, then, is not only economically unsustainable; it no longer meets the needs of the scientists themselves—those for whom the system exists.

II. A Search for Solutions

In 1988, at the request of ARL, the Economic Consulting Services Inc. (ECS) (1989) undertook a study of trends in average subscription prices and publisher costs from 1973 to 1987. The study compared the price per page over time of a statistically valid sample of approximately 160 journal titles published by four major commercial publishers (Elsevier, Pergamon, Plenum, and Springer-Verlag) with an estimated index of publishing costs over the same time period. The study concluded that the price-per-page of the journals exceeded the growth in costs by 2.6 to 6.7 percentage points a year. To illustrate the impact of these differentials on publisher profits, the report (p. 1) gave the following example:

> Suppose the publishers were just breaking even in 1973, that is, their costs of publishing serials were equal to the prices which they were charging. Then assuming a price–cost growth rate differential as estimated, publisher profit ratios (the difference between price and cost divided by cost) in 1987 would be between 40% and 137%.

The ECS concluded (p. 21) that "If such estimated rates of growth are reasonably accurate, then the library community would benefit greatly from such measures as the encouragement of new entrants into the business of serials publishing, and the introduction of a program to stimulate greater competition among publishers by injecting a routine of competitive bidding for publishing contracts of titles whose ownership is not controlled by the publishers."

In a companion piece to the ECS study, a contract report by Ann Okerson (1989) defined the causes of the "serials crisis" and proposed a set of actions to confront the problems. The report concluded (p. 43) that "the distribution of a substantial portion of academic research results through commercial publishers at prices several times those charged by the not-for-profit sector is at the heart of the serials crisis." The report went on to note (p. 43) that:

> Satisfactory, affordable channels for traditional serials publication already exist. For example, there are reasonably priced commercial serials publishers. Many of the non-profit learned societies are already substantial publishers. University presses could substantially expand their role in serials publishing. . . . The serials currently produced by these organizations are significantly less expensive than those from the commercial publishers, even though they may increase in price at similar rates. Several analyses of the "impact" of serials, in terms of the readership achieved per dollar, show that those produced by non-commercial sources have a higher impact than commercial titles.

Among the recommendations in the report was one centered on introducing competition (p. 42): "ARL should strongly advocate the transfer of publication of research results from serials produced by commercial publishers to existing non-commercial channels. ARL should specifically encourage the creation of innovative non-profit alternatives to traditional commercial publishers."

Over the next several years, ARL directed great energy to engaging stakeholders beyond the library community, such as societies, university presses, and university administrators, in the discussions of the scholarly communication crisis. The Association of American Universities (AAU) formed a series of task forces to address key issues related to research libraries. The Task Force on a National Strategy for Managing Scientific and Technological Information took up, as its name suggests, the issues related to scholarly journals publishing. In its report (Association of American Universities, 1994), the Task Force called for competition, but this time competition facilitated through electronic publishing. The recommendation stated (p. 55) that the community should "introduce more competition and cost-based pricing into the marketplace for STI by encouraging a mix of commercial and not-for-profit organizations to engage in electronic publication of the results of scientific research."

As a result of the work of the task force, ARL proposed several projects over the next few years intended to address the crisis in scholarly publishing. These were rejected in turn as too narrow or too broad or not directed at the appropriate leverage point in the system. Reaching consensus among the membership on a single strategy seemed less and less likely. In the meantime, prices continued to climb. Finally, in May of 1997, at an ARL membership meeting, Ken Frazier, Director of Libraries at the University of Wisconsin, Madison, proposed a way forward. He suggested that perhaps consensus was not needed, that action on the part of some libraries could begin to make a difference. He suggested further that if 100 institutions would be willing to contribute $10,000 each there would be $1 million to fund 10 startup electronic journals to compete head-to-head with the most expensive scientific and technical titles. While competition may not be the only or even the most effective solution to the crisis in scholarly publishing, several studies suggested that it was at least a reasonable place to start. He invited interested colleagues to join him in developing this project.

III. A Brief History of SPARC

A. Early Development: 1997–98

While Frazier's proposal to create 10 e-journals received little comment at the business meeting, it generated lively discussion in the hallways. A month later, when a meeting was held during the annual ALA conference for interested ARL members, representatives from 45 libraries attended. As a result of the meeting, a working group of library directors was formed to work with ARL staff to develop an action plan. Several meetings of the working group were held via conference call during the summer and fall. By October of 1997, the project had been christened SPARC, the Scholarly Publishing & Academic Resources Coalition, and approved by the ARL Board of Directors as an official ARL project. In its announcement of the formation of SPARC ("ARL Promotes Competition," 1997), ARL described its mission as "a catalyst for change through the creation of a more competitive marketplace for research information" and noted that SPARC would "promote academic values of access to information for research and teaching and encourage innovative uses of technology to improve scholarly communication."

In the early development of SPARC, several key decisions had to be made to determine its scope of action. It was clear that the main goal of SPARC was to reduce the price of STM journals. Based on the several analyses of the journals crisis, the SPARC founders believed that introducing direct head-to-head competition with high-priced titles would be the most effective strategy for achieving this goal. But would SPARC itself be the publisher and actually fund and distribute the competing journals? Or would it provide development funds to established publishers who would launch the new titles?

The SPARC working group quickly rejected the notion of SPARC becoming a publisher. Many able and sympathetic publishers already existed. Moreover, SPARC did not yet have name recognition. SPARC-supported titles would need to develop prestige quickly to attract editors, authors, and readers, as well as subscribers. Although prestige necessarily takes time to establish, the working group members believed that partnering with traditional scholarly societies and university presses known for their high-quality publications could help speed the process along. In addition, working with prestigious partners would help SPARC establish its own reputation. But what incentives would encourage existing publishers to take on this risky proposition?

Many working-group members indicated their willingness to contribute substantial amounts of money to SPARC to provide incentives to publishers in the form of development funds. Early conversations with some potential partners, however, revealed that, at least for traditional publishers, what was desired most was libraries' subscription dollars. The publishers were willing to absorb the up-front development costs if they could be assured that libraries would subscribe early on to the new titles. This would ensure wide visibility from the beginning, reduce the amount of time publishers would need to recover their investments, and avoid possible entanglements that could result from external funding arrangements. Hence the evolution of SPARC's incentive plan for publishers: a commitment that SPARC member libraries would subscribe to SPARC partner journals as long as the titles fit into their collections profile.

With some initial decisions made, the Working Group recognized the need to retain a consultant to develop a business plan and to hire a project manager. The Working Group, with the approval of the ARL Executive Committee, invited ARL members in January 1998 to become Founding Members of SPARC. By the May ARL membership meeting, 76 libraries had joined, contributing $5000 each. In the meantime, the ARL Board appointed a formal Steering Committee to guide SPARC development while maintaining the larger Working Group to help provide strategic direction and act as a sounding board. Members of the Steering Committee were Margo Crist (University of Massachusetts, Amherst), Fred Heath (Texas A&M University), Paul Kobulnicky (University of Connecticut), Carla Stoffle

(University of Arizona), Gloria Werner (UCLA), and Ken Frazier, Chair. The Working Group continued to meet with potential partners, developed a communications plan, and began recruitment for a SPARC director.

In mid-June, Richard Johnson, formerly Vice President of Planning and Development at the Congressional Information Service where he worked for 20 years, was hired as the new SPARC Enterprise Director. Johnson was on board in time to participate in the press briefing at the end of June announcing the first SPARC partnership, an agreement with the American Chemical Society (ACS) to publish one new journal each year for the next 3 years. ACS reported that the first title, tentatively called *Organic Chemistry Letters*, would be launched in summer 1999 at an initial subscription price of $2300 and would compete directly with *Tetrahedron Letters*, an Elsevier Science title that cost $8000 at the time. Several key journals, including *Nature*, *Science*, the *Chronicle of Higher Education*, *Chemical & Engineering News*, *Library Journal*, and *Publishers' Weekly*, covered the story.

Before the end of the year, SPARC signed two additional agreements, one with the Royal Society of Chemistry and another with Michael Rosenzweig and *Evolutionary Ecology Research*. The story of Rosenzweig, a professor of ecology and evolutionary biology at the University of Arizona who abandoned the journal he helped create to start a competing title, captured the attention of the *New York Times* which ran a story on SPARC and Professor Rosenzweig in its December 8, 1998, issue (Yoon, 1998). The *Times* called Professor Rosenzweig the "poster child of the movement" and reported that "although the battle is being fought over subscription prices, what is really at stake . . . is the scientific process itself." This coverage by the *Times* inspired many of Professor Rosenzweig's colleagues to understand that they, too, had the power to address concerns with their own journals. Several of SPARC's subsequent partnerships resulted from journal editors reading the *Times* story.

As a result of an October 1997 press release announcing the development of SPARC, ARL was contacted by nonmember libraries from both the United States and abroad expressing their enthusiastic support and interest in participating. The SPARC Working Group, concerned about diverting energy to recruit and service a large and diverse member base, decided to move cautiously. But interest continued to build. In late June 1998, SPARC invited non-ARL library directors to a briefing on SPARC's progress and explored with them possible membership models. The directors made it clear that they were very excited by the potential of SPARC and desired to support SPARC as fully as possible. They particularly wanted the opportunity to join SPARC as Founding Members. By late July, SPARC announced a new set of membership categories and invited institutions from the international academic and research community to join. By the end of 1998, SPARC had 115

Founding Members. Today, SPARC has more than 200 full, consortia, and supporting members.

In addition to attracting an international library membership base, SPARC has attracted support from major academic and library organizations. In 1997, the Association of American Universities, the Association of American University Presses, and the Big 12 Chief Academic Officers expressed their support for SPARC as an important strategy in ensuring a robust international research environment. In 1998, the Canadian Association of Research Libraries/Association des bibliothèques de recherche du Canada (CARL/ABRC), the Association of College and Research Libraries (ACRL), the Standing Conference of National and University Libraries (SCONUL) (United Kingdom and Ireland), and the Conference of Directors of Research Libraries (Denmark) all announced their support of SPARC goals. During 1999, the Council of Australian University Librarians, the Medical Library Association, and the Association of Academic Health Sciences Libraries added their endorsements, along with the National Association of State Universities and Land Grant Colleges. Subsequently, the Association of Universities and Colleges of Canada, the Australian Vice-Chancellors' Committee, the Joint Information Systems Committee (JISC) (United Kingdom), and the Committee of New Zealand University Librarians also offered their support of SPARC. The endorsements of these key organizations have helped build awareness of and support for SPARC among a broad array of librarians, publishers, and academic administrators the world over.

B. Maturation: 1999

During 1999, SPARC continued to receive numerous inquiries from potential partners. As the evaluation of these requests proceeded, however, two significant new programs were announced. The first, the Scientific Communities Initiative (SCI), offered over $500,000 in grants to digital ventures with promise to transform scientific publishing. Through the SCI program, SPARC hoped to stimulate the creation of new university-based information community projects. SPARC viewed the development of discipline-based communities by universities in partnership with professional societies an important new model for both meeting the needs of scientists and transforming scholarly communication.

SPARC announced its SCI competitive grant program in March 1999. It received 54 initial introductory letters from grant-seekers; 13 were invited to submit formal proposals. The 12 proposals that were received were evaluated by a formal peer-review process managed for SPARC by the American Institute of Biological Sciences Scientific Peer Advisory and Review Services Department. The SPARC Steering Committee served as the final decision-makers. The three winners of the SCI grants—Columbia's *Earthscape*, MIT's *CogNet*, and the California Digital Library's *eScholarship*—were announced publicly at the SPARC Membership meeting in October. Obviously, with limited funds available, many worthy projects could not be funded. But with the initial planning already spurred by the application process, several organizations went on to implement their projects, including the University of Arizona Library's *Journal of Insect Science* and Cornell University Library's *Project Euclid*.

The second significant new program announced in 1999 was *BioOne*. One of the most exciting and potentially far-reaching of SPARC projects, *BioOne* was conceived as an opportunity for societies, libraries, and the private sector to collaborate in building an electronic aggregation of leading research journals in the biological, ecological, and environmental sciences—journals then published in print by the member societies of the American Institute of Biological Sciences (AIBS). *BioOne* would offer these small societies the means to ensure visibility in the electronic environment and maintain financial viability, without the need to contract with a commercial publisher. *BioOne* would be developed in a unique collaboration of AIBS, Allen Press, the Big 12 Plus Libraries Consortium (now the Greater Western Library Alliance), the University of Kansas, and SPARC.

The basic premise of *BioOne* was to offer small undercapitalized societies—most of whom published in print only—incentives to license their content for inclusion in an aggregated database. *BioOne* provided text conversion, SGML coding, hosting, linking, and archiving for no out-of-pocket expenses. Costs would be deducted from the revenue share earmarked for return to the societies. As an added incentive, *BioOne* would provide access to marketing and sales resources that the societies would be unable to afford on their own, as well as access to library consortia dollars. *BioOne's* business plan called for 50% of the revenues from sales to be returned to the societies based on individual journal's relative size and use. The other 50% would go to cover the cost of operating *BioOne*. To allay societies' concerns over the possible loss of print revenues, *BioOne* offered a special reimbursement program during the initial phase to protect societies from above-average cancellations of institutional print subscriptions.

SPARC members were instrumental in providing financial support for the development of *BioOne*. In summer, SPARC requested its members to apply a portion of their 1999 purchase commitment toward Charter support of *BioOne*. In return, supporters would receive a credit of 115% against future *BioOne* subscription fees. In addition, for colleges and universities that were able, SPARC encouraged contributions beyond the Charter Support fee in return for recognition as a *BioOne* "Sponsoring Organization." Almost $660,000 was raised from SPARC members by the end of the year.

The development of *BioOne* required a substantial investment in time and in-kind contributions from each of the partners. A Working Group representing each of the Founding Organizations operated as a *de facto* management team. The Working Group developed the business model and created the revenue-sharing plan, drafted an agreement for society participation, held extensive discussions with AIBS societies, drafted a license agreement for library subscribers, developed a detailed technology plan, and negotiated arms-length contractor agreements with Allen Press and the University of Kansas for production and technology services. In addition to its efforts in soliciting development financing, SPARC took a leading role in business planning, marketing/communications, and international market development. *BioOne* signed exclusive marketing and distribution agreements with Amigos for North America and OCLC for the international market. In return, both organizations made significant financial contributions to the development of *BioOne*.

In early 2000, *BioOne* was incorporated in the District of Columbia and appointed its first Board of Directors. In July, it was granted 501c(3) tax-exempt nonprofit status. Heather Joseph, a 10-year veteran of electronic scholarly publishing in both the nonprofit and commercial sectors, was appointed President and COO of BioOne in August. *BioOne* launched on schedule in April 2001 with 40 journals from 29 societies.

The early SPARC working group was adamant that SPARC be lean and agile. SPARC's focus was to be on developing partnerships and projects, not on issues of governance or membership. During 1999, however, as SPARC added 25 new members and two new staff, it reached a level of maturity that required a bit more formal structure. The appointed SPARC Steering Committee that had guided SPARC since early 1998 decided that it should replace itself with a democratically elected body that would ensure a mechanism for continually renewing its leadership. A new Steering Committee consisting of 7 members with staggered terms was elected in the fall to take office in January 2000. At its first meeting, the new Steering Committee elected Ken Frazier, University of Wisconsin, to serve as chair. Other members elected included Karyle Butcher (Oregon State University), Ray English (Oberlin College), Fred Heath (Texas A&M), Sarah Michalak (University of Utah), James Neal (Johns Hopkins University), and Carla Stoffle (University of Arizona). Ernie Ingles (University of Alberta) was appointed as an ex officio member and liaison to SPARC's substantial Canadian membership.

SPARC held its first membership meeting, "Opportunities for Scholarly Communications: Crafting New Models," in October 1999. This was the first opportunity for SPARC members and partners to come together. The 2-day event drew approximately 225 attendees and was centered on an advocacy training session geared to the needs of SPARC members interested in conveying to their faculty solutions to the scholarly communications crisis. Members also welcomed the opportunity to meet and talk with SPARC partners. The timing was exactly right for this event: it helped to build a sense of community and excitement around SPARC. But given the extensive amount of staff and financial resources required by the meeting, SPARC decided not to make the membership meeting a regular event, but to look to alternative opportunities for keeping members informed of SPARC developments.

C. Communication: 2000

In addition to continuing intensive efforts to develop *BioOne*, in 2000 SPARC expanded its advocacy and educational programs, announced several new partnerships, and created a new international membership category.

SPARC's leaders always saw communications as an essential component of the SPARC program. Faculty who understand the context of scholarly publishing and are reconnected with the reality of journal prices are more likely to support the efforts of new titles through editing, submitting, and reviewing. This is essential to the success of creating viable alternative publications. An effective communications program is also essential to alert SPARC members to new partnerships and to identify new partnership opportunities. SPARC's initial efforts focused on developing an active and far-reaching media program which has been very successful in achieving regular coverage from *Science* and *Nature*, the *Chronicle of Higher Education*, *Library Journal*, *Professional Publishing Report*, and *Information Today*. Articles have also appeared in the *New York Times*, the *Economist*, the *Times Higher Education Supplement* (United Kingdom), *Le Monde*, *Frankfurter Allgemeine Zeitung*, *Technology Ireland*, *Academe*, *D-Lib Magazine*, *Chemical & Engineering News*, and *Lingua Franca*, to name a few, and many campus-based newsletters and magazines.

In 2000, SPARC's communication efforts expanded to include development and promotion of an advocacy campaign called *Create Change*, a collaboration between SPARC, the Association of Research Libraries' Office of Scholarly Communication, and the Association of College & Research Libraries (ACRL). The Create Change campaign includes print and Web resources designed to aid faculty and librarians in learning about and advocating changes in scholarly communication.

Working with ACRL, in 2000 SPARC instituted a semiannual SPARC Forum, which takes place at the conferences of the American Library Association (ALA). Each SPARC Forum presents new partners and others, along with updates on current projects, with ample opportunity for discussion and questions. These meetings are open to all ALA attendees and have generally attracted large audiences. These fora are one cost-effective way of keeping the library community and SPARC members up-to-date on SPARC progress.

SPARC finalized agreements with several additional partners during 2000. These included *Geometry & Topology*, published by the Mathematics Institute at the University of Warwick, England; *IEEE Sensors Journal* by the Institute of Electronics and Electrical Engineers; and *Geochemical Transactions* from the Royal Society of Chemistry. SPARC also provided support for *Project Euclid*, a joint project of the Cornell University Library and Duke University Press.

During 2000, membership, particularly from non-ARL libraries, continued to grow. So did interest from libraries outside of North America unable to afford the membership fee and purchase commitment. In response, SPARC introduced in April a new International Supporting Member category. This category allows non–North American institutions to join SPARC for U.S. $1000 per year with no purchase commitment. SPARC's international membership grew as a result of this new category to six non–North American members by the end of 2000.

D. Evaluation: 2001

During 2001, while implementing several new partnerships and launching *BioOne*, SPARC Europe, and *Declaring Independence*, SPARC also undertook an evaluation of its programs, surveyed its members, and reviewed its strategies for the future.

There were multiple signs in 2001 that SPARC's programs were having a significant impact in the journals marketplace. SPARC partner *Organic Letters* made news during the summer with word that it had surpassed *Tetrahedron Letters*, its main commercial competitor, in impact factor. According to the 2000 *ISI Journal Citation Reports* (2001), *Organic Letters* was #7 among organic chemistry titles while *Tetrahedron Letters* was #13. *Evolutionary Ecology*, the Wolters Kluwer title with which the SPARC partner title *Evolutionary Ecology Research* competes, reduced both its price and the number of issues per volume for 2001 as it continued to struggle to attract editors and authors. In addition, 40 editorial board members of the *Machine Learning Journal*, published by Wolters Kluwer, resigned in protest of that journal's policies and costs and announced their support of the SPARC partner title *Journal of Machine Learning Research*. In a letter to the community (Jordan, 2001), the editorial board stated that they "see little benefit accruing to our community from a mechanism that ensures revenue for a third party by restricting the communication channel between authors and readers."

It is clear that SPARC's message is penetrating the scientific community. In fact, echoes of SPARC's message were recently found in promotional material from a commercial publisher (*Blackwell Publishing News*, 2001) that noted that "On average, [our] journals cost just 25% of those published by the largest commercial publisher." It went on to report that "a high proportion of the income from our journals publishing is returned to academic research via the societies for whom we publish." It is perhaps a victory of sorts when established players in the commercial sector seek to align themselves with the library community values that SPARC is promoting.

Despite the successes that SPARC is experiencing through its partnerships and public relations efforts, its member survey conducted in the spring of 2001 revealed that it is only beginning to have an impact on its member institutions. The survey was sent to more than 200 SPARC members in April and 119 usable responses were received. The survey revealed that libraries have been slow both to add new titles and to cancel the competition. In addition, only about a third of the respondents have begun any sort of campus campaign to educate librarians and faculty about scholarly communication issues, but another third say they plan to. The results of the member survey provided important background for the SPARC Steering Committee's Strategic Planning meeting held in late June. The survey results and the strategic planning session will be discussed in more detail later.

In response to growing interest in SPARC from European libraries, SPARC proposed the creation of a SPARC Europe to facilitate competition in the European scientific journals marketplace and introduce advocacy initiatives tailored to the European research and library communities. The proposal was enthusiastically received and a meeting with representatives from the Consortium of University Research Libraries (CURL), SCONUL, LIBER, UKB, and JISC was held in early 2001. This group arranged for a public meeting in London and, with wide support, set up a working group to move the initiative ahead. As a result, several national organizations and institutions in Europe committed to the startup of SPARC Europe. LIBER, the principal association of the major research libraries of Europe, will serve as the umbrella organization. Startup financial support has been received from CURL, JISC, SCONUL, and the UKB, the Netherlands research libraries cooperative, in collaboration with IWI, the SURF Foundation program for innovation in scientific information supply. These organizations have guaranteed 2 years of basic operational funding for SPARC Europe. In addition, fees from current European SPARC members have been transferred to SPARC Europe. Recruitment for a Director of SPARC Europe is underway. The development of SPARC Europe propelled interest in Japan where a proposal for development of a similar initiative in Japan or Asia will be explored in 2002.

Over the past couple of years, the SPARC Steering Committee encouraged SPARC staff to focus their efforts on identifying editorial boards of existing high-priced commercial titles interested in exploring alternative publishers. An important centerpiece of this effort is the *Declaring Independence* Initiative launched by SPARC in collaboration with the Triangle Research Libraries Network in January 2001. *Declaring Independence* encourages journal editorial boards to evaluate their current journals and, if warranted, either work with the publisher to make changes or move the editorial board to an alternative publisher.

IV. SPARC Publisher Partnership Programs

As its partnership projects have developed over the past several years, SPARC has categorized its efforts into three programmatic areas: SPARC Alternatives, SPARC Leading Edge, and SPARC Scientific Communities.

A. SPARC Alternatives

SPARC is most closely identified with its Alternatives Program. SPARC Alternatives are the titles that compete directly with high-priced STM journals. The first partnership in this category was that with the American Chemical Society, which agreed to introduce three new competitive titles over 3 years. *Organic Letters*, the first of these, began publication in July 1999. *Organic Letters* competes with *Tetrahedron Letters*, a $9036 title (2001 subscription price) published by Elsevier Science. ACS, one of the largest professional societies in the world and highly respected for its quality publications program, was able to attract three Nobel laureates and 21 members of the National Academy of Sciences to its new editorial board. Two hundred and fifty articles were posted on the *Organic Letters* Web site and more than 500 manuscripts were submitted in its first 100 days (J. P. Ochs, personal communication, March 5, 2001).

A 2001 subscription to *Organic Letters* cost $2438. The business plan calls for a fully competitive journal offering 65–70% of the content at 25% of the price of *Tetrahedron Letters*. The effects of this new offering have already been felt. The average price increase for *Tetrahedron Letters* for several years had been about 15%. For 2000, just after *Organic Letters* was introduced, the price increase of *Tetrahedron Letters* was only 3%; in 2001 it was 2%. For 2000, the average price increase across all of the Elsevier Science titles was 7.5% and for 2001 it was 6.5%. If the price of *Tetrahedron Letters* had continued to increase at the rate of 15%, it would have cost $12,070 in 2001. Subscribers have saved more than $3000 each as a result of competition. Even if the title had increased at the more modest average rate of the Elsevier Science titles for 2000 (7.5%) and 2001 (6.5%), subscribers would have paid over $800 more for *Tetrahedron Letters* in 2001.

On a cost per article basis, *Organic Letters* published 1081 articles in 2000 at a cost of $2.13 per article. *Tetrahedron Letters* published 2197 articles at a cost of $4.03 per article. *Organic Letters* has also been able to attract authors away from *Tetrahedron Letters*. In 1999, *Tetrahedron Letters* published 9% fewer articles than it did in 1998; in 2000, it published 8% fewer articles than it did in 1999.

As noted before and even more significantly, *Organic Letters* debuted in its citation rankings at #7 out of 48 journals in Organic Chemistry (*ISI*, 2001), well ahead of *Tetrahedron Letters* at #13. According to the 2000 *ISI Journal Citation Reports*, *Organic Letters* had an impact factor of 3.367, while *Tetrahedron Letters* had an impact factor of 2.558. Moreover, when considering journals that publish more than 100 articles annually, *Organic Letters* rises to #2, just below the *Journal of Organic Chemistry*, another ACS publication. In its May 12, 2001, issue, the *Economist* ("Journal Wars," 2001) called *Organic Letters* a "credible competitor."

The second ACS SPARC Alternative, *Crystal Growth and Design*, was introduced in 2001. Priced at $1600, it competes with the *Journal of Crystal Growth*, an Elsevier Science title priced at $8657 for 2001.

Another high-profile SPARC Alternative is *Evolutionary Ecology Research* (*EER*), as mentioned earlier, a title founded by Michael Rosenzweig, a professor of ecology and evolutionary biology at the University of Arizona. In the mid-1980s, Rosenzweig founded and edited *Evolutionary Ecology* with Chapman & Hall (Rosenzweig, 2000). The title was subsequently bought and sold, most recently in 1998 to Wolters Kluwer. During these years, the journal's price increased by an average of 19% a year. Fed up by the price increases and the refusal of the publishers to take their concerns seriously, the entire editorial board resigned. In January 1999, they launched their own independent journal published by a new corporation created by Rosenzweig. A subscription to *EER* was priced at $305, less than half of the cost of the original title ($800).

Apparently, authors had no qualms submitting their papers to a new journal edited by respected scholars in the field. In fact, 90% of the authors withdrew their papers from *Evolutionary Ecology* when the editorial board resigned. As a result, at the end of 2000, *EER* had published 16 issues while the original title published only 6. Still struggling to attract papers, Kluwer reduced the price of *Evolutionary Ecology* to $560 for 2001. *EER* was quickly picked up by the major indexes, surmounting yet another hurdle that faces new publications. And, most significantly, *EER* broke even in its first year. SPARC played a significant role in generating publicity about and, more importantly, subscriptions to *EER*. *EER* is another example of how a new title can quickly become a true competitor.

EER debuted in the 2000 journal citation rankings (*ISI*, 2001) at #45 out of the 100 titles in ecology with an impact factor of 1.127. *Evolutionary Ecology* was ranked #31 with its impact factor slipping more than 15% from 2.087 in 1999 to 1.762 in 2000.

SPARC has a number of other titles in the Alternatives program. These include *PhysChemComm*, an electronic-only physical chemistry letters journal, and *Geochemical Transactions*, both published by the Royal Society of Chemistry. *PhysChemComm* is an alternative to *Chemical Physics Letters*, and *Geochemical Transactions* is an alternative to *Organic Geochemistry*, both Elsevier Science titles. *Geometry & Topology*, a title that is free of charge on the Web with print archival versions available for a fee, is an alternative to *Topology*, an Elsevier Science title. The *IEEE Sensors Journal* offers a $395 alternative to Elsevier's *Sensors and Actuators, A and B*, almost $5000 in 2001. *Theory & Practice of Logic Programming* (*TPLP*) is a journal founded by an entire editorial board who resigned from the *Journal of Logic and Algebraic Programming* after unsuccessful negotiations with Elsevier Science. *TPLP* is published by Cambridge University Press and is the official journal of the Association for Logic Programming.

More recent partnership titles include *Algebraic & Geometric Topology* (*AGT*), a free online journal published by the Institute of Mathematics at the University of Warwick. *AGT* is an alternative to *Topology and Its Applications* published by Elsevier. The *Journal of Machine Learning Research* (*JMLR*), a computer science publication, is an alternative to *Machine Learning*, published by Kluwer. JMLR is published by JMLR, Inc., in partnership with the MIT Press. JMLR offers two electronic versions: a free site maintained by JMLR, Inc., and a paid electronic edition available on the CatchWord Service. The paid version provides additional features including linking to abstracting and indexing services, archiving, and mirror sites around the world. Quarterly paid print editions are also available from MIT Press.

A number of other partnerships are currently under negotiation.

B. SPARC Leading Edge

To support the development of new models in scholarly publishing, SPARC has created a "Leading Edge" program to publicize the efforts of ventures that use technology to obtain competitive advantage or introduce innovative business models. Titles in this program include the *New Journal of Physics*, the *Internet Journal of Chemistry*, *Documenta Mathematica*, and the *Journal of Insect Science*.

The *New Journal of Physics (NJP)*, jointly sponsored by the Institute of Physics (U.K.) and the German Physical Society, is experimenting with making articles available at no charge on the Web and financing production through the charging of fees to authors whose articles are accepted for publication. That fee is currently $500. In order to encourage faculty to consider publishing in the *NJP*, a few libraries have offered to pay the fee for their faculty members.

The *Internet Journal of Chemistry* is experimenting with attracting authors by offering them the opportunity to exploit the power of the Internet. This electronic-only journal was created by an independent group of chemists in the United States, the United Kingdom, and Germany. It offers the ability to include full 3-D structures of molecules, color images, movies, animation, and large data sets. It also allows readers to manipulate spectra. Institutional subscriptions to the journal cost $289.

Documenta Mathematica is a free Web-based journal published by faculty at the University of Bielefeld in Germany since 1996. A printed volume is published at the end of each year. Authors retain copyright to articles published in the journal and institutional users are authorized to download the articles for local access and storage.

The most recent Leading Edge title is the *Journal of Insect Science (JIS)*, a free Web-based journal begun by a former editor of a commercial title and published by the University of Arizona Library. *JIS* is the first SPARC partner journal to be published by a university library. *JIS* editor Henry Hagedorn, Department of Entomology, University of Arizona, resigned as editor of the *Archives of Insect Biochemistry and Physiology* because of concerns regarding price and access policies. The *Journal of Insect Science* allows copyright to be retained by authors, with limited rights for *JIS* to maintain the articles online and in archives. *JIS* debuted in March 2001.

Under the auspices of the Leading Edge program, SPARC also supports the Open Archives Initiative (OAI), an effort to develop standards to link distributed electronic archives. SPARC views the development of institutional and disciplinary e-archives as an important strategic direction for the future of scholarly communication. To this end, SPARC helped underwrite one of the first meetings of the technical experts running e-print servers, held in Santa Fe in October 1999, to discuss issues regarding interoperability. During 2001, SPARC organized a session at the spring CNI meeting featuring institutions that are working to implement e-print services and the metadata harvesting protocol in the hopes of encouraging others to follow suit. SPARC also helped underwrite a portion of the costs of a spring OAI meeting in Geneva.

C. SPARC Scientific Communities

Another important program area for SPARC is the Scientific Communities. These projects are intended to support broad-scale aggregations of scientific content around the needs of specific communities of interest. Through these projects, SPARC encourages collaboration among scientists, their societies, and academic institutions. The Scientific Communities program helps to build capacity within the not-for-profit sector—an important SPARC goal— by encouraging academic institutions to develop electronic publishing skills and infrastructure, and seeks to reduce the sale of journal titles by providing small societies and independent journals alternative academic partners for moving into the electronic environment.

Several Scientific Communities projects have received support from SPARC. These include *eScholarship* from the California Digital Library, Columbia's *Earthscape*, and MIT's *CogNet*. The goal of California's *eScholarship* project is to create an infrastructure for the management of digitally-based scholarly information. *eScholarship* will include archives of e-prints, tools that support submission, peer-review, discovery and access, and use of scholarship, and a commitment to preservation and archiving. Columbia's *Earthscape* is a collaboration among Columbia University's press, libraries, and academic computing services. The project integrates earth sciences research, teaching, and public policy resources. MIT *CogNet* is an electronic community for researchers in cognitive and brain sciences that includes a searchable, full-text library of major reference works, monographs, journals, and conference proceedings, virtual poster sessions, job postings, and threaded discussion groups. All three of these projects received funding from SPARC in a competitive awards process.

Project Euclid is yet another SPARC Scientific Communities partnership. It is a joint venture between the Cornell University Library and the Duke University Press. *Project Euclid* provides an infrastructure for independent journals in theoretical and applied mathematics and statistics to publish on the Web. The *Euclid* site will support the entire range of scholars' output from preprints to peer-reviewed articles and will provide journal editors with a toolkit to manage their editorial and peer-review processes. Project Euclid currently supports eight titles online with another four in process.

One of the most ambitious projects in the Scientific Communities program is *BioOne*, discussed in some detail earlier. As indicated, *BioOne* is a nonprofit, Web-based aggregation of peer-reviewed articles from dozens of leading journals in adjacent areas of biological, environmental, and ecological sciences. *BioOne* was officially launched in April 2001 and currently provides access to 46 titles from 38 publishers. *BioOne* includes the current volumes plus one or two back years of each title. Access is provided through institutional site licenses. Fees for academic institutions are based on institution type and size where size is determined by student FTE counts. A price cap is included for large institutions.

An initial goal of *BioOne* was to create an aggregation that would meet the needs of library consortia at the same time as expanding the market for societies' journals. Both to reach that particular market and to keep operational costs as low as possible, *BioOne* contracted with Amigos Library Services to license *BioOne* within North America. In the 9 months since its launch, *BioOne* negotiated agreements with 15 consortia and university systems. *BioOne* also entered into an agreement with OCLC to serve as *BioOne*'s international distributor. As of mid-December 2001, *BioOne* had 328 subscribing institutions serving more than 2.8 million FTEs.

V. SPARC Communication and Advocacy

From the very beginning, communication has been a critical component of the SPARC agenda. As noted previously, the need for faculty to understand their role in the scholarly communication crisis and to believe in their ability to help create change is essential to the success of SPARC, let alone to the success of any new title. Just as important is the role of the librarian who selects materials and serves as a critical link to the faculty. Both groups need to be informed and SPARC has devised multiple strategies to reach them.

One of the greatest successes of SPARC has been its ability to keep the scholarly journals issue in the mainstream press. Over 115 articles, as recorded on the SPARC "In the News" Web page, have covered SPARC in such publications as the *New York Times*, *Science*, *Nature*, and the *Chronicle of Higher Education*. SPARC has developed contacts with key reporters, places stories, issues frequent press releases, and responds quickly to requests for information or articles. This aggressive media program provides scientists and librarians with a tangible representation of the magnitude of the dysfunctions in scholarly communication. Indeed, every appearance of the name SPARC in the press is a reminder that the problems persist.

SPARC staff, steering committee members, and partners travel extensively to speak at local, regional, and international meetings and conferences. In addition, the SPARC speakers bureau aids numerous institutions in arranging speakers for campus scholarly communication symposia.

SPARC has developed a number of communication channels to update members and interested parties. The SPARC e-news is a bimonthly newsletter distributed to more than 1500 SPARC members, supporters, and the media. This newsletter allows SPARC to alert members to new partners, as well as to innovative developments in disciplinary areas of scholarly publishing not currently supported in the SPARC partnership programs. It also includes an Industry News section that provides analysis of current trends in the scholarly publishing marketplace. SPARC maintains a comprehensive Web site to which new resources are continually added.

As noted earlier, SPARC hosts a semiannual Forum at ALA's summer and winter conferences. Each Forum presents new issues and is organized thematically on a topic of interest to the library community. SPARC also exhibits at conferences, such as ALA, IFLA, and ACRL.

As previously meationed, SPARC's communications efforts expanded in 2000 to include development of the advocacy campaign, *Create Change*, cosponsored by SPARC, the Association of Research Libraries' Office of Scholarly Communication, and ACRL. The *Create Change* campaign includes print and Web resources designed to aid faculty and librarians in learning about and advocating changes in scholarly communication. The Web site includes descriptive information on scholarly communications issues with supporting data, advocacy planning tools for librarians, and sample letters and copyright agreements for faculty. The site also includes a database of the editors of the 100 most expensive journals. The site was launched in May 2000. The campaign also includes a printed *Create Change* brochure which is available for purchase and distribution. In addition, the *Create Change* partners encourage organizations to adapt the brochure to local conditions. For example, the Board of Regents of the State of Iowa created a local version; SPARC worked with the Canadian Association of Research Libraries to create French and English versions with statistics relevant to the Canadian library marketplace; and CURL has consulted with SPARC on a U.K. version. Efforts are underway to establish similar collaborations in other countries.

Create Change was followed by *Declaring Independence*, an important project directed at faculty editors. *Declaring Independence* provides journal editors with the tools to assess whether the business practices and policies of their publishers are allowing their journals to serve best the needs of their disciplines. *Declaring Independence* is a handbook available both in print and online. The handbook was mailed by SPARC to editorial board members of high-priced journals and distributed by library staff to editors as part of their scholarly communications campus outreach activities. The handbook is currently being translated into German, and as the SPARC Europe network grows, SPARC will look to opportunities for further adoption.

A companion piece to *Declaring Independence* will be a Web resource tentatively titled *Gaining Independence*. This project is intended to aid institutions and small, society-based publishing ventures in developing effective startup business plans. It will help these willing partners build competitive and viable services more quickly by learning from the experience of others. For those organizations that desire more extensive help, SPARC will be offering a fee-based consulting service.

VI. Issues: Is There an Alternative?

The power of SPARC's Alternatives program rests on the pledge to publishers that SPARC members will subscribe to these new competitive titles. While the purchase commitment is one of the greatest attractions of SPARC for publishers, it is one of the most controversial parts of SPARC's program for some of its members. In essence, SPARC's alternatives program is creating new titles that members are expected to buy (or is contributing to journal proliferation, as some would say). The founders of SPARC recognized that changing the system would require investment by libraries. Although they hoped that university administrators would provide special allocations to support SPARC fees and purchase commitments, in many cases funds are likely coming from already overstretched collections budgets. Theoretically, libraries should cancel the existing high-priced journals to free up funds to purchase SPARC titles. As competition works, the high-priced titles should lose authors to the new titles and should ultimately be forced to lower their prices or at least curtail their price increases. As valuable content is lost, the titles will become more vulnerable to cancellation. But this takes time.

In addition, as the number of new SPARC alternatives grows, it may be possible for libraries to cancel only a few of the competitors to be able to recoup their investment in SPARC titles. In 2001, the 10 commercial titles with which SPARC alternatives compete head-to-head cost a total of over $40,000. The 10 SPARC titles cost a total of just over $5200. The cancellation of only a few of the established titles would easily pay for the SPARC titles.

But the SPARC Members Survey has revealed that adding and canceling journal titles is not as straightforward a process as the SPARC founders had hoped. Librarians responding to the survey indicated that they were reluctant to add a new title until it had established itself or had been requested by a faculty member. Some reported that by policy they were adding no new journal titles at all or they were purchasing only electronic titles. Others noted that if the title was published by a society, they were waiting to see if the journal would be included in the society's package. *Organic Letters* and *Evolutionary Ecology Research* were the exceptions with over 90% subscribing to *Organic Letters* and over 80% to *EER*.

Very few libraries indicated that they planned to cancel the competition. Some noted that they had in fact cancelled the competitor in years past, but were now receiving it as a part of a consortia deal. For others, because of the "big deal" (that is, an agreement where the library is given online access to all of a publisher's titles for some increment over the total print subscription price), cancellation was not an option. This particular comment appeared frequently in the survey responses.

While the survey did have the positive effect of bringing SPARC supported titles to the attention of some members, it made absolutely clear that capturing cost reductions from the introduction of competitive alternatives is a slow, expensive, and risky process.

As alluded to previously, one of the most persistent criticisms of SPARC's Alternative's Program—from all quarters—has been that it is proliferating journals and increasing costs. Obviously, it has taken time to demonstrate that even if cancellations are not possible, overall costs can be reduced; that is, the cumulative cost of the old and new journals may be lower than the old journal alone. But evidence does now exist. For example:

- If *Tetrahedron Letters* had continued on the price increase trajectory it was on in 1995–98 (+15% per year), it would cost $12,000 today. But that steep trajectory immediately flattened with the launch of *Organic Letters* and today a library can subscribe to *both* titles for $11,500.
- Kluwer's price drop on *Evolutionary Ecology* (*EE*) for 2001 means that a library can now buy the print editions of both *EE* (at $467) and *Evolutionary Ecology Research* (at $272) for $38 less than the old price of the Kluwer title.
- Several SPARC journals that are available free compete against Elsevier titles. Given Elsevier's newfound moderation in pricing, one could argue that libraries now get both journals for less than they would have paid without competition.

Although some complain that SPARC has contributed to journal proliferation, SPARC's modest number of partnerships have in reality had little impact on this phenomenon. This complaint is perhaps a reflection instead of the very significant impact SPARC has had on the public discussion of scholarly communication issues. The publicity around SPARC has clearly resulted in a strong market "push back" leading to constrained prices by publishers and broader engagement with the issues by all stakeholder groups.

Nevertheless, the issues raised and the modest impact on members' budgets thus far led the SPARC Steering Committee to ask whether there were new opportunities that might offer libraries and their institutions a greater degree of leverage and strategic impact. As it looks to the future, how can SPARC continue to capitalize on the strength of its message and expand its impact on the marketplace?

VII. The Future of SPARC

The SPARC Steering Committee met in strategic planning sessions during the summer of 2001. From these meetings, a number of themes emerged that will help shape SPARC's strategies over the next 3 years. Key among them is the recognition that large-scale aggregations of information are replacing journals as the fundamental economic unit of scholarly publishing. At the same time, real potential for transforming the system may come from freeing individual articles from the branding of journals. Even more importantly, a few institutions are beginning to take a more active role in providing the infrastructure to aggregate the content produced by their faculties, laying the groundwork for the development of new models of scholarly repositories and services.

Based on these emerging trends, the findings of the Member Survey, and the issues raised by the Alternatives Program, the Steering Committee recommended that SPARC focus its efforts on the new realities of the market. Hence, SPARC will direct greater support to initiatives that address larger aggregations of content. In particular, it will encourage and facilitate the creation of discipline and institutional servers. To advance this goal, SPARC may organize, support, and publicize discipline server projects and promote development of institutional intellectual property policies necessary for implementation.

At the same time, the Steering Committee recognized that when scholars take action and assert control of scholarly communication, they must have concrete options. Regardless of the long-term future of the journal, it is the format with which scholars today engage with the issues. SPARC resources, therefore, must to some extent continue to support new journals. SPARC will focus, however, on scholar-led initiatives in which editorial boards are "declaring independence," addressing important emerging fields, developing innovative value-added models, experimenting with new economic models, or offering transformational opportunities.

Based on other recommendations of the Steering Committee, SPARC will now support projects in the humanities and social sciences. In addition, it will build new partnerships to help reach vital stakeholder groups, a broader range of institutions, and a larger number of individuals with education and advocacy programs.

At this point, SPARC envisions a long-term future in which scholarly and scientific research is available to users through a loosely federated array of institutional and disciplinary repositories, hosted by universities, societies, and consortia. SPARC's goal over the next few years is to encourage and facilitate efforts that have the potential to move scholarly publishing toward this vision.

It is clear that the current system of scholarly communication must change, not only for economic reasons, but because the system is no longer meeting the needs of the scholars themselves. The potential for efficient research, sophisticated analyses, and broad dissemination can only be realized through transformation. SPARC has an important role to play in that process.

References

Albee, B., and Dingley, B. (2000). U.S. periodicals prices—2000. *American Libraries* **31**, 78–82.
ARL promotes competition in scholarly publishing. Press Release. Association of Research Libraries, Washington, DC, October 24, 1997.
Association of American Universities (1994). A national strategy for managing scientific and technological information. In *Reports of the AAU Task Forces*, pp. 43–98. Association of Research Libraries, Washington, DC.
Association of Research Libraries (ARL) (2001). *ARL Statistics 1999–2000*. ARL, Washington, DC.
Barschall, H. H. (1988). The cost-effectiveness of physics journals. *Physics Today* **41**, 56–59.
Barschall, H. H., and Arrington, J. R. (1988). Cost of physics journals: A survey. *Bulletin of the American Physical Society* **33**, 143–147.
Bergstrom, T. C. (2001). Free labor for costly journals? http://www.econ.ucsb.edu/~tedb/Journals/jeppdf.pdf
Blackwell Publishing News (2001). **5**, 1.
Cornell University (1998). *Journal Price Study: Core Agricultural and Biological Journals*. Faculty Taskforce, College of Agriculture and Life Sciences, Albert R. Mann Library, Cornell University, Ithaca, NY.
Economic Consulting Services Inc. (1989). A study of trends in average prices and costs of certain serials over time. In *Report of the ARL Serials Prices Project*. Association of Research Libraries, Washington, DC.
Guédon, Jean Claude (2001). *In Oldenburg's Long Shadow: Librarians, Research Scientists, Publishers, and the Control of Scientific Publishing*. Association of Research Libraries, Washington, DC.
ISI Journal Citation Reports, 2000 Science Edition (2001). ISI, Philadelphia, PA.
Jordan, M. (2001). Leading ML researchers issue statement of support for JMLR. October 8, 2001. http://www.ai.mit.edu/projects/jmlr/statement.html
Journal costs: Current trends and future scenarios for 2020 (2000). *ARL: A Bimonthly Report on Research Library Issues and Actions from ARL, CNI, and SPARC* **210**, 10–11.
Journal Wars (2001). *Economist*, May 12, 2001.
McCabe, M. J. (1999). The impact of publisher mergers on journal prices: An update. *ARL: A Bimonthly Report on Research Library Issues and Actions from ARL, CNI, and SPARC* **207**, 1–5.
McCabe, M. J. (2000). Academic journal pricing and market power: A portfolio approach. Paper presented at the 2000 American Economic Association Conference, Boston, MA.
Okerson, A. (1989). Of making many books there is no end: Report on serial prices for the Association of Research Libraries. In *Report of the ARL Serials Prices Project*. Association of Research Libraries, Washington, DC.

Rosenzweig, M. L. (2000). *Protecting Access to Scholarship: We Are the Solution.* http://www
.evolutionary-ecology.com/citizen/spring00speech.pdf

University of Wisconsin—Madison Libraries (1999). *Measuring the Cost-Effectiveness of Journals: Ten Years After Barschall.* University of Wisconsin—Madison Libraries, Madison, WI.
http://www.library.wisc.edu/projects/glsdo/cost.html

Yoon, C. K. (1998). Soaring prices spur a revolt in scientific publishing. *New York Times,*
December 8, 1998, p. D2.

Digital Millennium Copyright Act's Impact on Freedom of Expression, Science, and Innovation

Robin D. Gross
Electronic Frontier Foundation
San Francisco, California 94103

This paper describes a new and alarming challenge to libraries' use of electronic materials. Librarians must be made aware of how media companies are using the DMCA in a campaign to profit from electronic controls on media which do not permit either the fair use or first sale doctrines, thus harming both libraries and the average citizen. Further, these companies are encouraging criminal penalties for those who challenge these controls. In the future, libraries must ally with foundations such as the EFF (Electronic Frontier Foundation) to both educate the public and challenge these actions with court cases; otherwise many of the advances libraries have made may be lost.

I. Digital Millennium Copyright Act (DMCA) of 1998

A. DMCA Outlaws Circumvention with Little Exception

The Digital Millennium Copyright Act (DMCA) was passed by the U.S. Congress by a voice vote in 1998. Although the law was passed under the Copyright Statute,[1] it truly is not copyright legislation, but rather technology legislation. Controversial on many issues, the DMCA's anticircumvention provisions have been subject to most of the criticism against the statute's sweeping new prohibitions.

The DMCA created a new ban on the act of circumventing technological protection measures or "digital locks" that control access to a copyrighted work.[2] The statute also outlawed making or providing tools, including in-

---

[1] Title 17 of the U.S. Code is known as the "Copyright Act."
[2] 17 USC §1201 (a)(1)(A).

ADVANCES IN LIBRARIANSHIP, VOL. 26

formation and software, that circumvent access or use controls for digital works.[3] Despite the multitude of lawful reasons a person might need to bypass use controls, the statute only creates a handful of narrowly crafted exemptions to the general ban on circumvention. Unfortunately, however, no one has been able to rely upon any of the exemptions in court. The U.S. Library of Congress has also exempted two limited circumstances under which one may be allowed to circumvent the digital locks controlling a work's use.[4]

B. DMCA Ban Is Broader Than WIPO Called For

While DMCA proponents claim that the statute was enacted to implement the United State's treaty obligations under the World Intellectual Property Organization (WIPO), during the Congressional hearings on DMCA, Clinton Administration officials admitted during testimony that the anticircumvention provisions of Section 1201 went further than were required by the treaties.[5] Signatory countries to WIPO are only required to "provide adequate legal protection and effective legal remedies." Scholars have noted that U.S. copyright law already contained adequate legal protections and legal remedies to meet the U.S. treaty requirements even without enacting the DMCA.[6] The legal theories of both contributory and vicarious copyright infringement were enough to stop Napster and would have met our treaty obligations as well without the need for DMCA's anticircumvention provisions.

C. Use of Technological Protection Systems Dramatically Shifts Copyright Bargain

The introduction of new digital technology dramatically shifts the copyright bargain, tipping the balance in favor of copyright holders at the expense of

---

[3] 17 USC §1201 (a)(2) and (b)(1).

[4] 17 USC §1201 (a)(1)(B).

[5] See WIPO Copyright Treaties Implementation Act; and Online Copyright Liability Limitation Act: Hearing on H.R. 2281 and H.R. 2280 Before the House SubComm. On Courts and Intellectual Prop., 105th Cong. 62 (1997) (congressional testimony of Asst. Sec of Commerce and Commissioner of Patents and Trademarks Bruce A. Lehman):

Mr. Boucher: Within the confines of the treaty and its legal requirements, assuming that we ratify it, could we meet those requirements by adopting a conduct oriented approach as opposed to a device oriented approach?

Mr. Lehman: In my personal view, the answer is yes.

Mr. Boucher: All right. So the answer is yes, we could adopt a conduct oriented approach and be in compliance with the treaty.

[6] Pamela Samuelson, *SYMPOSIUM: Intellectual Property and the Digital Economy: Why the Anti-Circumvention Regulations Need to Be Revised*, 14 Berkeley Tech. L.J. 519 (Spring, 1999).

the public. Historically, copyright struck a balance, or "bargain," between the competing legitimate interests of authors and the public to use creative expression. For a limited period of time, copyright law grants authors the right to control reproduction, distribution, adaptation, and public perform-ance or display with respect to a work.[7] In exchange for a government-created monopoly to exploit a particular work, the public receives rights as well. The public's side of the copyright bargain includes the public domain, where all works are designed to wind up. Fair use rights are another important part of the public's side of the copyright bargain, as are first sale privileges and private performances.[8]

Digital technology permits either side of the copyright bargain to use it to the disadvantage of the other side. Both sides of the copyright bargain deserve respect. Copyright imposes responsibilities as well as rights upon both authors and the public. It is simply not fair for one side to take all the benefit and accept none of the responsibility of the copyright bargain. This applies equally to both authors and the public. The public must ensure that authors are economically rewarded for their creative gifts, and authors must ensure that the public is able to retain its rights and abilities to use and access creative expression. But these digital locks are designed to respect only one side of the copyright bargain, with publishers taking all the privileges from the government-created monopoly, with none of the responsibilities—such as ensuring fair use and contributing to the public domain, since works stay locked up under the total control of the copyright holder forever.

II. DMCA Enforcement: Legal Cases

A. DeCSS: *Universal City Studios et al. v. Corley (2600 magazine)*[9]

An ingenious 15-year-old Norwegian boy purchased a DVD movie while on vacation in France. When he returned home his DVD would not play on the DVD player that was built in another part of the world. The movie studios encode DVD movies with "region code restrictions" that prevent the movies from playing on DVD players that are built in another region of the world. The movie studios build these region code playing restrictions into the movies to control the flow of the films in order to maximize their profits for worldwide DVD sales and rentals. Jon Johansen, being the clever and curious teenager that he was, thought he might try to solve the problem of his

---

[7]17 USC §106. Exclusive rights in copyrighted works.
[8]17 USC §107, §109, §117, §202.
[9]*Universal City Studios et al. v. Corley (2600 Magazine)*, 273 F.3d 429 (2nd Cir. 2001).

nonfunctioning DVD, with the tools in his head. But he had no idea of the firestorm he started.

By taking apart the DVD technology and independently figuring out how it works, Jon and two other individuals created DeCSS as part of an effort to build a DVD player for the Linux operating system. Jon simply wanted to be able to watch his DVD movies on his computer the same way that Microsoft Windows users can. LiVid (Linux Video), an open-source development group, set out to build such an independent DVD player for Linux users. Aiding the LiVid project in its effort, in October 1999 Jon published DeCSS, computer code that descrambles the encryption of the studios' Content Scrambling System (CSS). CSS controls access to the data that comprises the movie stored on a DVD, a necessary step to viewing it.

The publication of DeCSS created quite an uproar among major Hollywood studios, embarrassed about how weak and vulnerable their CSS system had proved to be. On December 27, 1999, the movie studios' newly created licensing entity, DVD-CCA, filed a lawsuit in California state court requesting an injunction banning the speech of 521 individuals located throughout the world. On the theory of trade secret misappropriation, the judge granted a preliminary injunction and ordered Web publishers to remove DeCSS computer code from their Internet sites. Represented by the Electronic Frontier Foundation and the First Amendment Project, an appeals court in California in November 2001 overturned the lower court's injunction against DeCSS publication based on the First Amendment rights of Web speakers who come across information in the public domain and simply want to republish it.[10]

In the fall of 1999, *2600 Magazine* had been covering the story since news of Jon's software innovation hit the Web, as did many news publications at the time. Emmanuel Goldstein, the editor-in-chief of the magazine, had covered computer security and related news items for more than 20 years. As part of Goldstein's coverage of the DeCSS controversy, he included the code on the magazine's Web site, so readers could discover for themselves the functionality and social value of DeCSS. Good journalism provides references to the original material under discussion so readers are able to make up their own mind on issues.

With a new federal law on the books outlawing the dissemination of information that could help gain access to a copyrighted work, eight of the largest movie studios sued *2600 Magazine* and immediately obtained an injunction banning the journalist from publishing DeCSS. Hollywood argued DeCSS is a "circumvention device" in violation of the DMCA's anti-dissemination measures. After trial, the court also ordered the Web publisher to remove from his Web publication all references in the form of hyperlinks

[10]*DVD Copy Control Ass'n v. Bunner*, 113 Cal.Rptr.2d 338 Cal.App. 6 Dist., 2001.

to other Web sites where DeCSS can be found. After the 2nd Circuit Court of Appeals upheld the lower court's ruling in November 2001,[11] the Electronic Frontier Foundation filed a petition for en banc review to the 2nd Circuit Court of Appeals based on the decision's poor treatment of the First Amendment rights of *2600 Magazine*.

DeCSS is necessary for individuals to exercise their fair use rights with DVD movies since copying is disabled. DVD movies and the players are designed by the studios to prevent any copying of the movie; both analog and digital copying are prevented by the CSS system. For example, any student who needs to copy a snippet from the DVD movie *Schindler's List* to include in a school multimedia project on the Holocaust would need to use DeCSS to make that lawful fair use. Any parent who wants to make a backup copy of the film to play on the kids' bedroom VCR would need DeCSS to do so. Parents who want to be able to fast-forward through the salacious commercials for soon-to-be-released movies, but are prevented from doing so by the CSS system, would need DeCSS also. Despite the long list of substantial noninfringing uses for this software and its importance in assisting others to exercise their lawful rights with DVDs, the court banned the dissemination of this code under the DMCA.

In its ruling, the 2nd Circuit upheld the ban against *2600 Magazine* from publishing the code because of its fear of the speed and ease with which information can travel on the Internet. Despite the U.S. Supreme Court's clear guidance on the treatment of Internet speech in 1997's *ACLU v. Reno*, which found Internet speech to be worthy of the highest protection since it is the most participatory form of communication yet developed, the 2nd Circuit gave Internet speech less protection than traditional speech for that same reason.[12]

While the court recognized that computer code is creative expression, worthy of First Amendment protection, it also found that, because the code is functional and the danger it poses is so great, Congress can ban it. The appeals court also upheld the journalist's ban on linking to the controversial information. Other publications, such as the *New York Times, Washington Post, San Jose Mercury News,* and *Wired News,* who also linked to DeCSS code would be liable under the court's reasoning.

The public's fair use rights were significantly curtailed under the 2nd Circuit's treatment of the fair use doctrine under the DMCA. Despite the U.S. Supreme Court's indication that fair use was the breathing space required to prevent copyright from conflicting with the First Amendment, the appellate court renounced any constitutional underpinning behind the

---

[11]273 F.3d 429 (2nd Cir. 2001).
[12]*Reno v. American Civil Liberties Union,* 521 U.S. 844, 970 (1997).

doctrine. The court admonished those dissatisfied with the DMCA to take their complaint to Congress.

In January 2002, the Norwegian Economic Crime Unit (OKOKRIM) indicted Jon Johansen at the request of the MPAA,[13] who filed an official complaint against the teenager for his role in creating DeCSS software. Johansen could face 2 years in prison for violating Norwegian Criminal Code 145(2), which outlaws breaking the security system of another to gain access to records one is not entitled to access. In the past, this law has always been used to prosecute individuals who break into another's bank or phone company records. Hollywood has convinced Norwegian prosecutors to extend this law for the first time to punish an individual for accessing his own property.

The DeCSS case highlights an important point which is often overlooked in the digital copyright debate. When I buy a DVD, who owns it? If I own it, if I have paid for the right to view the movie on the DVD, how are the studios using the DMCA to prevent me? The studios own the copyright in the movie, but the copy of the movie on the DVD and the DVD itself belong to me and are my private property. How can it be illegal for me to access my own property?

The studios are using their public performance right to claim rights to control all use, all "experiencing," of a particular work. While copyright holders are given control over public performances of their works, the private performances of works have always belonged to the public. In the privacy of one's own home, the studios want to control what one can do with one's own property. As a result, the studios will have control over the expression of an idea. This is a tremendous and unprecedented shift in the balance of rights away from the public in favor of the copyright holder. While crying "Piracy!" in crowded courtrooms, the studios are stealthily usurping the private performance rights of individuals who buy and lawfully own DVD movies and other types of intellectual property.

B. *U.S. v. Skylarov & Elcomsoft*[14]

In July 2001, the first criminal charges were filed under the DMCA against 26-year-old Russian computer programmer Dmitry Skylarov for exposing

---

[13]MPA's & DVD-CCA's Official Complaint (in Norwegian) to OKOKRIM requesting prosecution: http://www.eff.org/IP/DeCSS_prosecutions/Johansen_DeCSS_case/20000104_dvdcca_no_prosecutor_letter.no.pdf

English translation: http://www.eff.org/IP/DeCSS_prosecutions/Johansen_DeCSS_case/20000104_dvdcca_no_prosecutor_letter.en.html

[14]U.S. Dist. Court for Northern District Case No. CR 01-2-138 RMW.

the insecurities of Adobe's electronic-book software. While a graduate student at Moscow University, Dmitry wrote software that can read Adobe e-books. He used part of his thesis project on an employment project with the software company Elcomsoft.

The software that Dmitry wrote and Elcomsoft offered from its Web site is important for assisting people to simply view their e-books in unsupported ways. Adobe e-book technology gives publishers total control over what an individual can do with an e-book. Technology is enabling publishers to turn traditional rights into "product features" that can be disabled at the whim of the publisher. Because Adobe allows publishers to disable fair use, Dmitry's software is needed in order to make fair use or other uses that are not preauthorized by the copyright holder. This software was useful to blind people for its text-to-speech functionality that reads the e-book aloud. Someone who wants to read their e-book on a laptop or computer other than the one it was originally downloaded to would need to bypass the publisher's restrictions to do so. Anyone who needs to lawfully print or copy a page of an e-book against a publisher's restrictions needs this software.

Upon learning of the software's creation, the California-based software company Adobe filed a complaint with the Federal Bureau of Investigation (FBI) and informed the investigators of Dmitry's upcoming speech at a major technical conference in Las Vegas where he had been invited to lecture about the vulnerabilities of Adobe's e-book viewer software.

On his way back to the airport to return home to Russia after his lecture, the FBI arrested Dmitry and charged him with disseminating information that could help someone access a copyrighted work under the DMCA's anticircumvention measures. Because Elcomsoft sold the software from its Web site, the DMCA's criminal penalties had been triggered as it was done "willfully" and for "commercial advantage or financial gain." Dmitry was jailed for 6 weeks as a flight risk before his release on bail. In August 2001, both Dmitry and Elcomsoft were indicted on five counts of trafficking and conspiracy to traffic in a copyright circumvention device. If convicted on the first offense, the penalties are up to 5 years in prison and a $500,000 fine. On the second offense, a conviction can earn 10 years in prison and a $1,000,000 fine.[15]

Such harsh penalties for writing software with legitimate uses created a public outcry and an embarrassing international incident for the United States and Adobe, and eventually led to Dmitry's release. Hundreds of citizens organized protests all over the globe to express outrage at Dmitry's arrest under the DMCA. The Electronic Frontier Foundation met with and convinced Adobe to withdraw its support for Dmitry's prosecution and met with U.S. attorneys to request dismissal of the criminal DMCA charges. After

[15]17 USC §1204.

months of letter-writing campaigns and protests at U.S. embassies, federal buildings, and congressional offices, the Department of Justice finally announced it would drop all charges against Dimitry Skylarov, and he was free to go home in late December 2001.[16] The public simply was unwilling to allow this young father of two to spend the next 25 years in prison for writing software that reads books.

C. Felten et al. v. RIAA et al.[17]

Since the DMCA had just proven itself so successful in silencing the critics of the U.S. movie studios, the recording industry quickly cited the powerful new weapon in a threat letter sent to a Princeton University professor Edward Felten and his research team.[18]

In the fall of 2000, the noted computer scientist, Felten, and his research team participated in the "SDMI Hack Challenge," the recording industry's open invitation to defeat the technology designed to control uses of digital music. While the recording industry claimed that this technology would protect the interests of the public and the world's musicians, the scientists who studied it discovered it would likely be defeated upon its introduction into the market.

When the researchers attempted to publish a scholarly paper on the lessons of their experience at a U.S. technical conference in April 2001, the threat of litigation from the multibillion-dollar recording industry forced the researchers to pull the paper and presentation at the last minute. Not until after the scientists and the Electronic Frontier Foundation filed an affirmative law suit in federal court asking for a declaration of law that the scientists had a freedom of speech right to publish their paper did the recording industry back down and withdraw earlier threats of litigation.

Although the paper was finally presented at a technical conference in Washington, DC, in August of 2001, the industry remains unwilling to commit to refraining from future prosecution of the scientists for other papers they are currently working on related to their study of the SDMI technology.

The fear of DMCA litigation among researchers who study certain encryption technologies continues to grow, driving this important scientific research underground or overseas. Scientists must run risk of prosecution in

---

[16]See press release from the U.S. Attorney's Office for the Northern District of California, regarding a deal to not prosecute Dmitry Skylarov. (Dec. 13, 2001):
http://www.eff.org/Intellectual_property/DMCA/US_v_Skylarov/20011213_usatty_pr.html
[17]U.S. DC-NJ Case No. CV 01-2669 GEB.
[18]http://www.eff.org/sc/felten/20010409_riaa_sdmi_letter.html

order to find out if their research falls outside the bounds of DMCA's information prohibitions.

While the DMCA does contain a few narrowly crafted exemptions that permit circumvention in a few circumstances, these exemptions have proven useless to most scientists in the course of their work, leaving them vulnerable to prosecution. Specifically, the exemption for reverse-engineering purposes only applies to computer programs (not DVDs) and can be used solely for interoperability purposes.[19] The encryption research exemption only permits research after asking permission and forbids publishing the information.[20] And this exemption only applies to the ban on copy control tools (not access tools), so it would not help most researchers because the two functions are often combined in the same technology. The exemption for security testing only applies if the information is used solely to promote the security of the owner of the computer system and scientists are forbidden from publishing their results.[21] There is an exemption for libraries, but it only applies to the ban on the act of circumvention in certain circumstances.[22] And since no one is permitted to make or provide libraries with the tools needed to circumvent, libraries will have to employ cryptographers in order to access works the law entitles them to access.

III. DMCA's Impact on Freedom of Expression

A. Fair Use Rights in Theory Only

The DMCA is creating a shockingly dangerous impact on freedom of expression in the digital age. Hollywood has successfully convinced Congress that a copy-enabled public is too dangerous to be trusted. In its zeal to stamp out infringement, it has also outlawed a substantial amount of lawful speech as well. Since the DMCA outlaws all tools that are needed in order to exercise one's fair use rights in the digital environment, Congress has effectively outlawed fair use privileges without ever having said so.

B. Technology Gives Publishers Total Control over Works

Technology grants publishers something that both copyright law and the First Amendment specifically guard against—total control over the experi-

---

[19] 17 USC §1201 (f).
[20] 17 USC §1201 (g).
[21] 17 USC §1201 (j).
[22] 17 USC §1201 (d).

encing of a creative work. Such excessive control over the expression of an idea signals danger to anyone who is concerned about freedom of expression.

C. Usurpation of Private Performance Right by Studios

Hollywood is using the legal muscle behind the DMCA to create a new "private performance" right. Since copyright holders are only granted the right to control public performances of a work, the individual's private experience of a work has always been outside of their control. But now, through the new power of technology, publishers are able to control all uses of a work, thereby controlling the private experience of a work, without regard for the limitations to a copyright holder's power.

D. Public Domain Disappears

Ironically, although copyright was originally designed as the ideal mechanism for creating a rich and vibrant public domain, the DMCA prevents works from ever reaching their intended target. Even though public domain movies are released on DVDs—in an encrypted, copy-restricted format—any tool or information that would help one gain access to that public-domain movie is strictly forbidden by the DMCA. Consequently, the pubic domain, much like fair use, exists only in theory under the DMCA.

E. Linking Ban: Journalists' Freedom of Speech Rights Curtailed

Something unprecedented in traditional space, the DMCA has been used to silence a journalist from providing truthful information on where data can be found. Imagine if the *New York Times* were forbidden from publishing the location of a suspected crime, out of fear people would go there to commit crime. But because it is cyberspace and judges and politicians are largely strangers to technology, there is an urge to regulate it into control.

IV. DMCA's Impact on Science and Innovation

A. DMCA Stifles Scientific Research

Since its enaction in 1998, and particularly after its initial enforcement had begun, the DMCA has hampered science and innovation: in the United States, where the DMCA is law, but also abroad, where the threat of its broad prohibitions is felt just as strongly.

Scientists report a stifling of research into certain technologies since the DMCA was passed. Several foreign scientists have issued statements indicating that they are afraid to travel to the United States, since some research they have done or a computer program they have written that might help someone access a work could find its way to the United States subjecting the scientist to liability under the DMCA.[23] Technical conferences are moving overseas, since organizers and the speakers risk violating the criminal provisions of the DMCA, since they charge a fee.[24] In the fall of 2001, Russia's Ministry of Foreign Affairs issued a travel advisory warning its citizens, particularly computer programmers, about the dangers of traveling to the United States since the DMCA was enacted into law.[25]

B. DMCA Weakens Public Security

DMCA weakens public security because scientists can no longer test the security of a system to learn if it is vulnerable to attack. Since the DMCA is used to prevent the public from obtaining the truth about the vulnerabilities of the security systems, scientists refer to it as the "Snake Oil Protection Act." Through the tool of censorship, the studios leave the public with hobbled technology and weakened public security. Bank records, telephones, electricity, medical records, e-mail communications, etc., all depend upon the highest of security to ensure people are able to protect themselves in an electronic world. Since a law was passed making it illegal to test security systems, only the crooks learn which systems are vulnerable.

C. DMCA Stifles Innovation and Creates Monopoly

The DMCA is a powerful tool in the hands of the Hollywood studios, who are using it to dictate technology design choices. Hollywood depends on its copyright powers to leverage control over a new technology and consumer electronics. Through its many lawsuits, the industry is attempting to force

---

[23]See Legal Declaration of Dutch Cryptographer Niels Ferguson (Aug. 13, 2001) http://www.eff.org/sc/felten/20010813_ferguson_decl.html

See Legal Declaration of Alan Cox (Aug. 13, 2001) http://www.eff.org/sc/felten/20010813_cox_decl.html

"Digital Copyright Act Harms Research" by Richard Smith of Privacy Foundation http://www.privacyfoundation.org/commentary/tipsheet.asp?id=47&action=0

[24]Knight, Will, Computer scientists boycott U.S. over digital copyright law. *New Scientist*, July 6, 2001. http://www.newscientist.com/news/news.jsp?id=ns99991063

[25]Lee, Jennifer B., Travel advisory for Russian programmers. *New York Times*, Sept. 10, 2001.

software developers to beg Hollywood for permission each time before they may build products that can play or otherwise interact with their content. This would be the equivalent of allowing book publishers to control photocopy. The DMCA effectively creates monopoly control over playing technology, eliminating any competition for devices that read that content. This obsession with controlling content will grossly stifle innovation and chill freedom of expression for everyone.

D. DMCA Outlaws Technology Rather Than Criminal Behavior

A major flaw of the DMCA is that it attempts to outlaw technology rather than criminal behavior. It bans all devices and information that can circumvent without regard to whether the circumvention itself is lawful. No one suggests society should jail the employees of Xerox, even though we know those copy machines are used to violate copyrights. We do not seriously consider jailing the employees of Smith & Wesson, even though we know guns are used to kill people. Software should be treated no differently from other multiuse technologies, whether guns, knives, or cars, which can be used for both lawful and unlawful purposes. We do not outlaw the technology altogether even though we know some will use it for unlawful purposes.

V. Conclusion: A Plea for Balance in Copyright: Repeal DMCA's Anticircumvention Provisions

There is no question that the DMCA tips copyright's delicate balance too far in favor of the media industry at the expense of the public's rights to creative expression. Although copyright law intentionally places limits on a copyright holder's right to control the uses of a work, the DMCA gives complete control to the copyright holder over all uses of a work, trampling on the freedom of speech rights of individuals.

History has taught that every time a new technology comes out (piano rolls, radio, VCR, MP3 players), the media industry has reacted by claiming that because the technology is new and better than what has existed in the past, it poses too great a danger to their ability to profit to be allowed in the hands of the public. Yet in each case, the courts have prevented the industry from outlawing the technology and the industry has found a way to profit from the new opportunities brought on by the new technology.

In the zeal to prevent infringement, Hollywood has used DMCA to silence a substantial amount of lawful speech as well. DMCA has been used to squelch the research of a Princeton professor about weaknesses in the recording industry's controls for digital music; to gag a journalist who published information about the movie studios' encryption system for DVDs; to prosecute a competitor for creating software that can interoperate with Adobe e-books; and to criminally charge a teenager for daring to participate in an effort to create a DVD player for the Linux operating system that could compete with Hollywood's monopoly on DVD players while offering more consumer-friendly features. In none of these cases has anyone been accused of copyright infringement, yet the DMCA is unquestioningly chilling speech and research.

In 1998, Hollywood asked Congress for the DMCA, promising it would be used only as a "shield" against infringement. But now that it is law, Hollywood wields the DMCA as a powerful "sword" to prevent competition, disable fair-use rights, control information distribution, and censor data about technologies' vulnerabilities.

As Congress and the courts have proven sympathetic to the glamor and money behind Hollywood and shown little regard for the public's rights under copyright and our society's commitment to freedom of expression, the public must take matters into its own hands and call for reform in copyright. The anticircumvention provisions of the DMCA simply go too far and must be repealed to restore balance in copyright. Otherwise, we will usher in the Digital Millennium Dark Ages.

References

Recommended Reading

Band, J., and Isshiki, T. (1999). The new anti-circumvention provision in the copyright act: A flawed first step. *Cyberspace Law* **3**, 2.

Benkler, Y. (1999). Free as the air to common use: First Amendment constraints on the enclosure of the public domain. *New York University Law Review* **74**, 354.

Lessig, L. (1999). *Code: and Other Laws of Cyberspace*. Basic Books, New York.

Lessig, L. (2001). *The Future of Ideas: The Fate of the Commons in a Connected World*. Random House, New York.

Litman, J. (2001). *Digital Copyright*. Prometheus, Amherst.

Samuelson, P. (1999). Why the anti-circumvention regulations need to be revised. *Berkeley Technology Law Review* **14**, 519.

Samuelson, P. (1996). The copyright grab. *Wired* **134**.

Vaidhyanathan, S. (2001). *Copyrights and Copywrongs: The Rise of Intellectual Property and How It Threatens Creativity*. New York University Press, New York.

Legal Cases

Sony Corp. of America v. Universal City Studios, Inc., 464 U.S. 417, 104 S.Ct. 774 (1984).

Universal City Studios et al. v. Corley (2600 Magazine), 273 F.3d 429 (2nd Cir. 2001).

DVD Copy Control Ass'n v. Bunner, 113 Cal.Rptr.2d 338 Cal.App. 6 Dist., 2001.

MGM Studios et al. v. Grokster, Music City, Consumer Empowerment/FastTrack CV # 01-8541-SVW filed in United States District Court for the Central District of California in Los Angeles on Oct. 2, 2001.

Harper & Row Publishers, Inc. v. Nation Enterprises, 471 U.S. 539, 105 S.Ct. 2218 (1985).

Campbell v. Acuff-Rose Music, Inc., 510 U.S. 569, 114 S.Ct. 1164 (1994).

Reno v. ACLU, 521 U.S. 844 (1997).

Collaborative Digitization: Libraries and Museums Working Together

Nancy Allen and Liz Bishoff
Penrose Library
University of Denver
Denver, Colorado 80208

Libraries and museums share common purposes as cultural heritage institutions working for the public good, but they have very different traditions of collaboration and have, over the years, developed different organizational and professional practices. In this article, we will outline the ways libraries and museums have been collaborating in the complex process of creating digital collections of primary resource material, beginning with collaboration within each type of organization, and leading to a rich array, on an international basis, of collaboration among cultural heritage institutions—libraries, museums, archives, and historical societies.

I. The Development of Library Collaboration

The libraries of North America have extensive multitype library collaboration experience. Libraries work together in academic–public library partnerships, public-school library programs, regional consortiums for technology support, and dozens of other combinations for general cost sharing or specific project purposes. This collaboration occurs even though each library is quite clear about its primary clientele and its mission within its primary communities. Libraries have collaborated for a variety of reasons, including the availability of funding for collaborative activity. Federal funding since the passage of the Library Services and Construction Act (LSCA) has provided incentives for such collaborative projects from the mid-1970s to 1995 through state libraries. In 1996, the LSCA was replaced by the Library Services and Technology Act (LSTA), which shifted focus from public libraries to all libraries and from construction to technology initiatives as well as interlibrary cooperation programs. The newly formed Institute for Museum and Library Services (IMLS) (http://www.imls.gov) administers the LSTA

ADVANCES IN LIBRARIANSHIP, VOL. 26

process. Further, the most basic of all library functions, organization of library material, has since 1967 been supported by a growing library collaborative called OCLC, Online Computer Library Center, Inc. (http://www.oclc.org). Through the sharing of cataloging records, libraries have reduced expenses, have been able to build resource sharing and interlibrary lending networks, and have recently branched out into new arenas of shared cataloging, such as the cataloging of Web sites and other digital objects through the new OCLC service CORC (Collaborative Online Resource Catalog) (http://www.oclc.org/corc). On the regional level, OCLC services and other consortial services are available to libraries on a low-cost membership basis through the OCLC regional networks (http://oclc.org/contacts/regional/usnetworks.shtm), such as AMIGOS, SOLINET, and BCR. In the mid-1970s the research library community created the Research Libraries Group (RLG) (http://www.rlg.org), which provided for the specific cooperative cataloging initiatives of the community. As with OCLC, the members of RLG developed a shared catalog, the Research Library Information Network (RLIN), which supported interlibrary loan, preservation management, and access to special collections through specialized programmatic initiatives.

During the 1960s and 1970s many states developed public library systems that supported local resource sharing and collaboration for public libraries. In the mid-1970s these systems began expansion to include nonpublic libraries. Today more than 10 states[1] have multitype regional library systems. These collaborations support interlibrary loan activities among the members and offer training and continuing education, technical support, bulk-purchase arrangements for supplies or equipment, and more recently group licensing services for online resources. These collaboratives offered all libraries a means of lowering costs and engaging in resource sharing through interlibrary lending to support local and primary client needs. These systems reinforced the fact that no library stands alone in its effort to meet its mission. Collaboration is deeply engrained in the function and financial structure of public and academic libraries in the United States and Canada, and with the increasingly international growth of OCLC, this dependency on library cooperation and collaboration is growing worldwide.

In the academic library community, the growth of consortia and the growth of consortial programs is notable, especially the development of regional academic and multitype library consortia. Some of these are growing far beyond the traditional geographic limits of a driving-distance-based definition of resource sharing. One example of this is the "Big Twelve Plus"

[1]Examples are California, Colorado, Florida, Illinois, Kansas, Massachusetts, Michigan, Minnesota, New Jersey, New York, and Ohio.

library consortium, which changed its name to the "Greater Western Library Alliance" to reflect its expansion beyond the members of the Big Twelve athletic conference (http://www.big12plus.org).[2] Technologies supporting the sharing of collections (fax, scanning, and Internet delivery) are the basis of such widely dispersed consortia that used to focus on the courier van schedule. In the 1990s the large collaboratives, OCLC and RLG, expanded their emphasis into other countries and international regions around the world.

Because the managers, executive officers, and staff of consortium offices are engaged in similar work, the somewhat obvious result has happened. In 1997, a new library consortium was created: the International Coalition of Library Consortia (ICOLC).[3]

Finally Dr. Joyce Ray, Director, Library Program IMLS, notes that the number of collaborative grants awarded across all the IMLS grant programs has grown significantly in the past few years. In 1998, 41% of the grant recipients were collaborative projects. In 1999 that grew to 50%; 54% of the projects were collaboratives in 2000; and, in the most recent round of awards, 55% were collaboratives. This growth is most important in that it has occurred across all areas, not just those that require collaboration.[4]

II. Library Collaboration and Digitization

Despite all this "togetherness" it is still not generally the case that a collaborative approach to digitization is a library's first choice, or first strategy. Barriers or perceived barriers to library collaboration around digitization persist.

---

[2]See the press release about the expansion of this consortium at http://www.big12plus.org/pressreleases/newname.htm.

[3]"The International Coalition of Library Consortia (ICOLC) first met informally as the Consortium of Consortia (COC) in 1997. The Coalition continues to be an informal, self-organized group comprising (as of September 2000) nearly 150 library consortia from around the world. The Coalition serves primarily higher education institutions by facilitating discussion among consortia on issues of common interest. At times during the year, ICOLC may conduct meetings dedicated to keeping participating consortia informed about new electronic information resources, pricing practices of electronic providers and vendors, and other issues of importance to directors and governing boards of consortia. During these sessions, the Coalition meets with members of the information provider community, providing a forum for them to discuss their offerings and to engage in dialog with consortial leaders about issues of mutual concern" (http://www.library.yale.edu/consortia/).

[4]Phone conversation between Joyce Ray and Liz Bishoff, August 24, 2001. Ray also presented this data to the September 15, 2000, meeting of the National Commission for Library and Information Services and the National Museum Board. The only program requiring collaboration is the National Leadership Grant Program for Museum–Library Collaboration.

One significant issue relates to the widely perceived failure of genuine collaboration involving shared ownership of collections. There are well-known efforts to organize selection responsibilities among research libraries, such as the Farmington Plan, which involved more than 60 members of the Association of Research Libraries from the late 1940s to the 1960s. However, once a library has acquired something, even if the reason for acquisition relates to a larger and coordinated scheme of national or international collection management, the item is regarded by the library with a proprietary attitude. Pride in collections and collection effort and the long-term creation of distinctive sets of resources in a discipline are both essential elements of collection strength in research libraries. And further, there have been few successful programs of shared consortial funding for primary resources or expensive published resources in regional consortia,[5] with the Center for Research Libraries (http://wwwcrl.uchicago.edu/) persisting as the best single example of member-based shared purchasing and access.

With this deeply ingrained attitude regarding the ownership of significant collections being based primarily on independent funding and purchase of collections, it is probably only natural that research libraries tend to seek funding for digitization of their own valuable primary resources rather than taking a collaborative approach to the development of digital, multi-institutional collections online. When looking through the Association of Research Libraries directory of digitization projects, the Digital Initiatives Database (http://www.arl.org/did/), it is notable that most of the projects there represent digitization undertaken by a single library based on that library's collections. Of the 414 listings, about 400 of them are single-library projects. Although many collaborative projects are not listed in the ARL directory,[6] this still illustrates that while collaboration is an increasingly common phenomenon, it is by no means the standard approach to digitization for libraries, especially for research libraries. Collaboration requires more effort and more time spent on project management, and it can make a project more complex technically, since involvement of other libraries might require some elements of interoperability. Funding is another significant factor in creating partnerships for digitization. Larger libraries are more likely to find funding for both equipment and staffing to meet the matching requirements of a grant. A small institution must often struggle to find resources even when some external funding for a project is possible. Therefore, funding is often a barrier to multitype collaboration.

[5]The Colorado Alliance of Research Libraries had a collective sets acquisition program from 1979 to the early 1990s, and today engages in collective purchasing of electronic books.
[6]Although this directory is intended to provide a comprehensive listing of projects, there is an unfortunate misperception that only ARL members are allowed to submit information.

A. Success Stories: Gathering Momentum

Nonetheless, libraries have been collaborating on digitization initiatives for some time, and there is a growing list of success stories involving groups of libraries planning digitization projects together so that the consortial result is richer and better organized with increased access to all data than a set of independent efforts would have been. In some cases, availability of funding was a key factor. In other cases, the major motivation for collaboration was the knowledge that very closely related collections, together, would represent a more significant digital resource. In still other cases, sharing of expertise, or sharing of the technology infrastructure made a project affordable and moved partners toward the goal of operationalizing digitization, decreasing the dependence on external funding. This model, where digitization efforts are sustained over time without external funding, is still very rare.

In 1997, the Library of Congress and Ameritech established a partnership that would bring the special collections of other libraries into the Library's American Memory Project (http://memory.loc.gov/). For 3 years, ending in 1999, Ameritech funding enabled the Library of Congress to augment its own American Memory digitization project with related collections held in other museums and libraries. Most of the partners were libraries but some museum resources were included. Following the program and guidelines established by the Library, the collections of the partner projects are now accessible via the Library of Congress Web site as well as the awardees' sites. When combining the work of the Library of Congress and the Ameritech awardees, more than 7 million digital objects from the unique collections of the Library and its partners are available to the world. This digital collection is the single largest digital collection of primary resources. With the Library's emphasis on K–12 use of the collections, the Library has created curriculum guides and lesson plans plus guidance for teachers in how to use primary source materials. The American Memory Fellows Program is an intensive continuing education opportunity for teachers, offered since 1997 (http://memory.loc.gov/ammem/ndlpedu/amfp/index.html).

The Library Services and Technology Act (LSTA) of 1996, established through the Museum and Library Services Act 1996, has two major library components, the National Leadership Program and the state-funding component. The latter is administered by the State Library agencies and provides funding from IMLS for local and statewide programs, including collaborative programs. LSTA

> . . . promotes access to learning and information resources of all types of libraries for individuals of all ages. Through the legislation, IMLS provides funds to State Library Agencies using a population-based formula. State Libraries may use the appropriation to support statewide initiatives and services; they may also distribute the funds through competitive

sub-grant competitions or cooperative agreements to public, academic, research, school, and special libraries in their state. LSTA outlines two broad priorities for this funding. The first is for activities using technology for information sharing between libraries and between libraries and other community services. The second is for programs that make library resources more accessible to urban, rural, or low-income residents, and others who have difficulty using library services.

Each state has developed a five-year plan outlining its programs. These programs support the LSTA goals, which are to:

- establish or enhance electronic linkages among or between libraries
- link libraries electronically with educational, social or information services
- help libraries access information through electronic networks
- encourage libraries in different areas and different types of libraries to establish consortia and share resources
- pay costs for libraries to acquire or share computer systems and telecommunications technologies; and
- target library and information services to persons who have difficulty using a library and to underserved urban and rural communities (IMLS, 2001).

The other component of the IMLS program is the National Leadership Grant Program, which supports programs that have a national impact in one of the following areas:

- Education and Training
- Research and Demonstration
- Preservation and Access
- Library/Museum Collaboration

Digitization projects can fall into any of the four programs; however, the largest number are submitted under the Preservation and Access Program. Examples of these projects can be found at the IMLS Web site—"IMLS Support for Digital Projects."[7] Examples of these projects include:

- "Hoagy Carmichael Jazz Collection," a project of Indiana University, which makes accessible digital sound recordings, photos, and printed materials about Carmichael.
- Missouri Botanical Garden Library's database of plant images and associated data, which can be added to by other botanic organizations, along with a model program for connecting images of any type with associated data.
- University of Pittsburgh's project done in cooperation with four Chinese research libraries, to deliver digital copies of articles from Chinese-

[7]IMLS Support for Digital Projects (http://www.imls.gov/closer/cls_po.asp) lists projects that include creation of digital content, as well as creation of Web sites and Web resources that support a variety of library and museum activities.

language academic journals to researchers throughout the United States.

• "The American Missionary Association and the Promise of a Multicultural America: 1839–1954," a project of the Amistad Research Center at Tulane University and the Louisiana State University Digital Library. They collaborated on digitizing materials from the Amistad experience, making those resources available both via the Internet and via CD for the K–12 community.

Another national funding initiative is the National Science Foundation's Digital Library Initiative (http://dli2nsf.gov). NSF has provided millions of dollars for digital library research projects. The NSF-funded projects have explored matters related to the digitization and display of text and media. The agency has funded projects looking at interoperability (a single-search method of finding resources in multiple locations) of digital libraries as well as early projects exploring retrieval of information in the networked environment. In the late 1990s NSF introduced the National Science Mathematics, Engineering and Technology Education (SMETE) Digital Library (or NSDL) (http://www.smete.org/nsdl/projects/index.html),[8] conceived to support excellence in SMETE education. The NSDL will be a comprehensive information system built as a distributed network and will develop and make accessible collections of high-quality resources for instruction at all levels. Multiple services will be developed to support the educational community and effective use of the NSDL resources. More than 40 NSDL awards are given annually to develop resources in the areas of science, math, engineering, and technology for the K–12 community. Through November 2000, the group agreed to the following:

• The creation of an interim governance structure
• The establishment of a set of working groups to examine the issues involved in collaboratively developing the NSDL; and a commitment to produce a document that communicates the vision, goals and plans of the NSDL.

The document, *Pathways To Progress: Vision and Plans for Developing the NSDL, March 20, 2001* (Manduca, McMartin, and Mogk, 2001), establishes the educational goals and principles underlying the development, interim governance structure, and Core Integrated System. Additionally it begins to identify the standards for metadata and options for interoperability.

---

[8]NSF established the program under a program solicitation (SNF 00-44) to establish an educational digital library for science, mathematics, engineering, and technology.

Some of the NSDL projects are oriented around infrastructure to support digital library development, and some are subject specific, such as The National Biology Digital Library (http://www.inquiry.uiuc.edu/partners/nbdl/nbdl.php3 and http://cecssrv1.rnet.missouri.edu/NSDLProject/index.html), a multi-university project with the Missouri Botanical Gardens as a partner, or the Digital Library for Earth System Education (DLESE) (http://www.dlese.org/). Other NSF-funded digital library projects have also involved partnership with several libraries, library science programs, and/or computer science units. One example is the Indiana University project for digital music (http://www.dml.indiana.edu/index.html). A list of the NSF Digital Libraries grants, both phases one and two, can be found at the NSF Web site for the Digital Libraries Initiative (http://www.dli2.nsf.gov/). The Digital Libraries Initiative is funded by many federal agencies in addition to NSF.

Another important collaborative initiative, The Digital Library Federation (DLF) (http://www.diglib.org/dlfhomepage.htm), began in 1996 under the auspices of the Commission on Preservation and Access.[9] A membership organization, the DLF focuses primarily on establishing standards and best practices, and on research and development in leading edge areas of digitization. Although the DLF does not directly produce digital content, it has produced a body of work that reflects the DLF-funded research conducted by the membership organizations.

Both the University of Michigan and Cornell University are DLF members, and with Andrew W. Mellon Foundation funding, they have collaborated to produce a very large and ongoing project called *Making of America* (http://moa.umdl.umich.edu/). The project focuses on materials published from 1850 to 1877. The project has demonstrated a successful model for presenting text documents in digital format that are not directly searchable by the user, but which have been scanned with "dirty" or uncorrected optical character recognition for full text retrieval of textual information. This project demonstrates two aspects of research library collaboration on digitization: it is a research and demonstration project, and it has also provided a dramatic increase in the number of digital primary resources available. The *Making of America* project's Web site currently shows 10,912 volumes and 3,166,450 pages available. Also with Mellon funding, Duke University's Perkins Library, Columbia University's Rare Book and Manuscript Library, and the University of California at Berkeley's Bancroft Library collaborated to create the *Digital Scriptorium* (http://sunsite.berkeley.edu/Scriptorium/), a demonstration project centered

---

[9]The Commission on Preservation and Access merged with the Council on Library Resources, creating the Council on Library and Information Resources. The DLF program is a project of CLIR (http://clir.org/diglib/).

on medieval manuscripts. Two other collections, Union Theological Seminary in New York and the De Bellis Collection in California also contributed material to the 8500 color images now available. With additional National Endowment for the Humanities funding, other digital resources will be added, including collections from the Huntington Library (California), the Ransom Center at the University of Texas, Austin, and the New York Public Library, as well as smaller collections. The demonstration project is evolving into an important resource enabling access to very rare materials, some of which are in little-known collections.

B. Statewide and Regional Library Projects

In addition to the IMLS-funded projects just discussed, there are several statewide academic or largely academic digital library initiatives that include digitization as just one component of the overall plan. Several of the more prominent projects are the California Digital Library (http://www.cdl.org), the Kentucky Virtual Library (http://www.kyvl.org/), VIVA, the Virginia Academic Library consortia (http://www.viva.lib.va.us/viva/collect/image.html), and Galileo (http://neptune.libs.uga.edu/cgi-bin/door/homepage.cgi?_id= 1021320041) supporting all libraries in Georgia. These projects include a range of digital library components, including access to online databases, full text databases, library online catalogs, portals or gateways to Web resources, and digital content from their special collections. Most of these projects are designed to increase access to these resources for the general public and K–12 community.

At a state level there are several important collaborative initiatives designed around digitization of primary resources. One of the earliest was the California Digital Library (CDL) (http://www.cdlib.org/).[10] Another is the Online Archive of California (OAC) (http://www.oac.cdlib.org/). The initial focus of the OAC was building a database of encoded finding aids from the collections of the nine University of California libraries. The CDL now has more than 40 members including the libraries from the University of California System, California State University System libraries, and the California State Library, as well as museums and public libraries. In 1998, the CDL began its first thematic project, the development of the Japanese American Relocation Digital Archive (JARDA).[11] This project, funded by

[10]The CDL is a library of the 10 University of California campuses created in 1997, but it is made up of resources contributed by those campus collections as well as by others.

[11]JARDA provides a gateway to the personal and institutional documentation of the era. Collaborators on the project include California Historical Society, California State Archives, CSU-Fullerton; Japanese American National Museum; UC Berkeley's Bancroft Library; UCLA's Young Research Library Department of Special Collections; the University of the Pacific; and the University of Southern California.

the participating organizations as well as by LSTA funds, inventoried the California collections on Japanese American relocation, created Encoded Archival Description (EAD) finding aids, MARC collection-level records, and marked-up electronic texts using the Text Encoding Initiative standard (TEI). It presents digital images representing 10,000 images and 20,000 oral histories, diaries, letters, drawings and photos about the 11 camps (Ober, 2001). This collection is just the first for CDL—developing virtual thematic collections is part of the CDL strategy. "The ideal digital library leverages collaboration to provide access to high-quality content and also encourages, indeed enables, the creation of new scholarship" (Ober, 2001). The project has provided the CDL with a means of building and managing the technical infrastructure required for digital libraries. JARDA provides an excellent example of how curators and systems librarians worked together not only to develop the appropriate infrastructure to support the virtual collection, but also to provide the end user with one place to locate materials on this topic. Curatorial collaboration across the project participants is a hallmark of the project, reducing duplicate effort and increasing the total amount of unique information available. Theresa Salazar, Bancroft curator of Western Americana, notes that, "Those libraries [without significant technical support] can use the technical resources of the better staffed institutions to get their materials included in this digital archive." She goes on to note that working together helps librarians discover unique holdings in other libraries (Ober, 2001).

The Washington State Library, using LSTA funding, has a 2-year initiative involving the University of Washington and Washington State University libraries along with nine public libraries (http://digitalwa.statelib.wa.gov/). The projects used the DiMeMa, Inc., CONTENTdm software (http://contentdm.com/) for creation of metadata and digital objects. The State Library also sponsored two 3-day training sessions on digitization for Washington historical societies, museums, libraries and state agencies, and developed a set of statewide best practices. All the collections are accessible through the Washington State Library's Web site.

There are also examples of regional digitization initiatives. The North Suburban Library System (Wheeling, Illinois) (http://www.nslsilus.org/) is the coordinator for the "Digital Past" (http://www.digitalpast.org). In this project the member libraries, frequently working with local historical societies, digitized collections that convey the history of their community. Northwestern University Library served in a technical consulting role, providing information on appropriate equipment for scanning, scan standards, etc. Each library did its own scanning and creation of metadata, with the NSLS providing servers for the digital collections and hosting the database that provides access to the collections.

III. Museum Collaboration

The museum community does not have the same tradition of collaboration that the library community does. Common examples of cooperation among museums are the sharing of collections for exhibits, traveling collections, and research. One of the most important museum collaborative efforts can be found in the activities of museum professional associations, which are active and diverse. Museum professionals have joined these organizations, a key collaborative activity, and museums themselves join national and regional collaboratives.[12]

In the past decade, several major museum collaborative initiatives have been undertaken. For instance, in 1997, more than 20 major art museums initiated the AMICO project with the goal of creating a collection of digital works that can be licensed for educational uses.[13] The AMICO Web site describes the resource as including "over 11,000 paintings, over 4000 sculptures, over 9000 drawings, over 11,000 prints, over 23,000 photographs, over 1000 textiles, over 1000 costumes and jewelry, over 4500 works of decorative art, over 500 books and manuscripts." Just prior to the establishment of AMICO, the MESL[14] project was established to explore options for licensing digital museum works. CIMI,[15] an international museum organization, was established in 1990, creating a collaborative environment in which museums work on standards and technology-related research. The Museum Computer Network[16] is a collective effort making contributions in a Web environment.

[12]The American Association of Museums website (www.aam-us.org) is a good place to see the activities of the AAM, and its 24 affiliates, which include separate organizations for many other types of museums including historical societies and botanical gardens. The Association of Art Museum Directors (www.aamd.org) is just one of several examples of professional associations for museum administrators.

[13]The AMICO Web site is http://www.amico.org/. A press release about the initiation of the organization can be found at http://www.amico.org/docs/press/pr.971015.founding.html.

[14]The Museum Educational Site Licensing Project was founded with the support of the Getty Art History Information Program. More information is available at http://www.fmch.ucla.edu/MESL/mesl.htm.

[15]http://www.cimi.org/ is the site describing all the CIMI projects, including development of and advocacy for museum standards in technology arenas.

[16]The Museum Computer Network (www.mcn.edu) is, to quote its Web site, "a nonprofit organization of professionals dedicated to fostering the cultural aims of museums through the use of computer technologies. We serve individuals and institutions wishing to improve their means of developing, managing, and conveying museum information through the use of automation. We support cooperative efforts that enable museums to be more effective at creating and disseminating cultural and scientific knowledge as represented by their collections and related documentation." The MCN has an annual conference.

Whereas libraries have been taking part in extensive interlibrary sharing of their collections, museums (beyond their loans of "educational" collections to schools) do not engage in resource sharing beyond the loaning of materials for temporary exhibits, or research, and occasional provision of collection catalog data. For museums, a public trust responsibility for the proper stewardship of unique collections takes precedence over sharing of the collections. Therefore, museums lack the high-priority purpose for spending staff time and energy in collaborative activities that libraries have. On the other hand, while libraries have been sharing the portion of their collections that are *not* unique, libraries and museums have similar policies on unique items, including the primary resources often targeted for digitization, with great care taken to protect, preserve, and carefully display such collections and items in those collections, with limited resource sharing. Museum inventory information is seldom available to the public, and if a museum has digital objects associated with the inventory process for identification purposes, the displayed image is generally a low-resolution image. Further discussion of the differences in organizational culture and practices between libraries and museums will take place in the section on issues in library/museum collaboration.

Until the availability of digitization, access and use of collections was usually limited to the local facility. With the exception of nationally focused museums such as the Smithsonian, Art Institute of Chicago and the New York Metropolitan Museum of Art, museums have always regarded their collections as being of primary interest to those who live in the geographic vicinity of the facility, or those who are visiting the community. Unlike most libraries, the museum is a key part of a community's economic development or tourism strategy, one of the major draws to a community or region.

The Internet age, however, changed the environment. It gave cultural heritage institutions the opportunity to make their collections accessible from any location in the world, 365 days a year, 24 hours a day. At the same time, the Internet created an increasingly competitive environment. A Denver museum will be competing with a San Francisco museum for both virtual visitors and on-site visitors. On the other hand, cultural heritage institutions with seemingly unique special collections will discover others with similar or complementary holdings. There are new opportunities and challenges in meeting unique missions in a networked age. The greatest gains for the public can be seen through increased access to resources that span the boundaries of the physical collections. One of the key issues for museums is realizing those gains for their visitors while maintaining their individual identities, enhancing their positions in their communities, and building gate-count-based revenue.

One answer is emerging through demonstration or model projects that bring similar collections together virtually through joint efforts to create Web-based exhibits:

- ArtsConnectEd: The Walker Art Museum and the Minneapolis Institute of Arts share online resources and high-end Web displays at ArtsConnectEd (http://www.artsmia.org/aboutace.html). The site focuses on teacher lesson plans and curriculum guides, online art works, and online activities. Virtual tours and 3D displays are examples of the creative leadership on the shared site.
- Odyssey Online: A three-way partnership has supported development of a museum education exhibit called Odyssey Online (http://carlos.emory .edu/ODYSSEY/). This display about Africa is rich and complex, but captivating for kids and teachers alike, and involved the Michael C. Carlos Museum at Emory University, the Memorial Art Gallery at the University of Rochester, and the Dallas Museum of Art.
- Chief Plenty Coups Electronic Field Trip: the Western Heritage Center and the Yellowstone Heritage Partnership developed an electronic field trip. The Web site includes text, graphics, audio, curriculum guides, and suggested lessons on the Yellowstone River Valley region (http:// plentycoups.org/educate/home.html).

IV. Museum/Library Collaboration

In "The Rules of Collaboration," Michael Schrage identified requirements for successful collaboratives. Here are a few that are applicable to museum/ library collaboration:

1. Competence: A collaboration of incompetents, no matter how diligent or well meaning, cannot be successful.
2. A shared, understood goal is required. Collaboration is not described in terms of relationship, but in terms of the objective to be achieved.
3. Mutual respect, tolerance and trust are important; there must be a minimum threshold of mutual respect, tolerance, and truth. Friendship isn't required.
4. Collaborators must focus on one another's strengths.
5. Creation and manipulation of shared space: collaborations rely on shared space, which permit real-time access to that shared space, personnel, and technology.
6. Continuous, but not continual communication—Constant communication isn't required; however, a group must develop a tempo or flow of communication that prevents them from interfering with one another while ensuring that events are proceeding.
7. Formal and informal environments: The formal and informal communication environments expand the ability to solve problems.
8. Clear lines of responsibility, but no restrictive boundaries, may involve no clear division of labor. Individuals may be responsible for

a specific task(s), but they are also free to consult, assist, and solicit ideas from their partners. Asking one another the tough questions is critical to the success of the collaborative.

9. Decisions do not have to be made by consensus. But if the collaborators consistently diverge, the collaboration ultimately dissolves.
10. Physical presence is not necessary. Use of a full range of technology takes place over a full range of technology—phone, fax, and the Internet.
11. Effective use of outsiders. Successful collaborators are constantly on the lookout for people and information that will help them achieve their mission (Schrage, 1995, pp. 88–89).

It is often the case that the availability of funding encourages creativity. The Library of Congress and Ameritech funding served as one example, and currently, IMLS is a major agent of change encouraging a new culture of library—museum collaboration. As described earlier, the Library of Congress American Memory Project has been digitizing collections from the Library's collections. Through the Ameritech funding libraries and museums were able to digitize selections from their collections adding them to the Library of Congress's National Digital Library. The American Memory site provides searching across these collections, as well as access to the individual collections. Examples of museum and library projects available at the American Memory site include projects on the American Indians of the Pacific Northwest, the Everglades, and on the settlement of the Ohio River Valley.[17]

In addition to the contribution of content, the Ameritech project caused the Library of Congress to investigate a wide range of issues related to digital collections prior to initiating this collaborative effort. Each participating institution had to provide metadata describing the digital objects in the collection to the Library. Because participants used a variety of metadata standards, the Library developed crosswalks between different metadata standards. The contribution in standards development and identification of issues for collaborative projects stand as important contributions of the LC/Ameritech program.

Unlike the LC/Ameritech program where museums and historical society collections were included in the initiative, the National Science Foundation initiatives have not directly involved museums. Rather, museums ben-

---

[17]The Pacific Northwest project involved the University of Washington Library, the Eastern Washington State Historical Society, and the Museum of History and Industry, in Seattle. The Everglades project involved the University of Miami Library, Florida Atlantic University, and the Historical Museum of South Florida. The Ohio River Valley project involved the University of Chicago Libraries and the Filson Club Historical Society in Louisville, Kentucky.

efited from these awards as project partners, and NSF-funded research results impact museums and libraries.

Examples of library-hosted projects with a historical society as a partner are Electronic New Jersey (http://www.scc.rutgers.edu/njh/), Historic Pittsburgh (http://digital.library.pitt.edu/pittsburgh/), and Park Forest, Illinois' Planned Community (http://findit.sos.state.il.us/PFS/). Foundations or other local sources funded all three of these projects. However, the greatest impetus to museum/library collaboration has been through the IMLS and its National Leadership Grants supporting museum/library collaboration. Through IMLS funding, a growing number of academic libraries are partnering with museums, historical societies, and other scientific and cultural heritage organizations. The IMLS presented these communities with financial incentives to develop joint projects and to work together to create new approaches to meet the common goals and purposes of creating better and more accessible collections that meet the needs of a knowledge society.[18] Dozens of large and small cultural heritage institutions have partnered with other organizations, including libraries, to bring their resources to a broader audience, and to overcome limits of geography, preservation concerns, exhibition space, and time.

A. The Colorado Digitization Project and Other IMLS Projects

The largest and most complex of the IMLS-funded projects is the Colorado Digitization Project (CDP) (http://coloradodigital.coalliance.org/) (Allen, 2000). The CDP was conceived by a group of Colorado librarians participating in an annual Colorado resource sharing planning retreat. When considering what else should be included in the Colorado digital library, they determined that access to special collections and unique resources representing Colorado's heritage was the key component was still missing. As the heritage of the state and region was represented through a wide range of resources held by a wide range of institutions, it was clear from the beginning that libraries alone could not build this component of the digital library. Colorado's museums, historical societies, archives, and libraries had to do the work together. A 1-year LSTA grant from the Colorado State Library funded the initial development of the collaborative. In addition to identifying existing digital initiatives and developing best practices or standards that could be adopted statewide, the project had as a primary objective building the collaborative.

---

[18]Full information on the IMLS grant opportunities involving collaboration between libraries and museums is available at the IMLS Web site, www.imls.gov. Previous grants are also listed.

The collaborative design is reflected in all aspects of the project governance, management, and funding. The Steering Committee consists of representatives from each type of cultural heritage institution as well as partner organizations; the steering committee also reflects the geographic and size differences among those institutions. The Steering Committee now includes individuals representing the Colorado State Library, the University of Denver, The Denver Museum of Nature and Science (DMNS), the Littleton Historical Museum, the Colorado Alliance of Research Libraries, the Pathfinder and High Plains Library Regional Library Systems, and the Colorado Historical Society. The Alliance provides the CDP with server space to support their Web site and digital archive, as well as access to its telecommunication infrastructure. Since a number of Alliance members are CDP grantees, the CDP mission is reflected in the Alliance strategic plan through emphasis on development and expansion of the Colorado–Wyoming digital library (http://www.coalliance.org/reports/strategicplan00.htm). The Colorado Regional Library Systems have funded some of the CDP training initiatives, as well as grants to nine smaller institutions. The State Library through the Access Colorado Library Information Network (ACLIN) (http://www.aclin.org) is collaborating with CDP by creating *Heritage—The Gateway to Colorado's Digitization Projects*, a union catalog of metadata for the state that is a part of the Colorado Virtual Library. In addition to the Steering Committee the CDP utilizes a task-force structure. Six task forces are responsible for the development of the Web site, union catalog of metadata, metadata, scanning, collection management, and museum work. Membership on these task forces is not limited to CDP project partners, but rather is open to any interested curator, librarian or archivist. Task forces are easily created and when their work is done they go out of business. All task forces have individuals from different cultural heritage institutions and the resulting products not only reflect the needs and interests of these institutions, but also help spread the word about the collaborative. Many of the task force members have made presentations about the CDP, their institutions' involvement in the project, and their projects.

Another area of collaboration is in the infrastructure for image capture. The CDP established five regional scan centers. Either a library or a regional library system hosts each of the scan centers. The host site provides a physical location for the workstation and scanner as well as technical assistance. Each project using the equipment is responsible for their scanning. The CDP has provided the scan centers with a workstation, scanner, and software. The scan centers share experiences using a listserv. In addition to providing Heritage (the catalog) and scan centers, CDP offers a range of digitization training, staff development programs, and project funding.

The CDP demonstrates a collaborative model that provides digitization infrastructure to the state, enabling both small and large cultural-heritage institutions to engage in digitization without needing to invest in training, software, scanning hardware, the database and interoperability solutions, or user interface. All those resources are provided through the Project to participants, who received small incentive grants to launch appropriately scaled projects. Most projects also encouraged collaboration by requiring multiple institutions to work together on shared collection strengths, and all projects emphasized an audience common to all cultural heritage institutions: K–12.

Within the CDP, some of the library–museum partnerships demonstrate that very small institutions can successfully work together, and that large and small institutions of all four types (libraries, museums, archives, and historical societies) can collaborate using a shared statewide infrastructure. In a *First Monday* article (Allen, 2000), Nancy Allen described the dramatic array of partnerships encouraged by CDP mini-grants and the infrastructure for digitization. They include an academic library and a large historical society bringing together aspects of Colorado's only Japanese internment camp, a public library and a local history museum presenting images of clothing worn in each decade from 1860 to 1960, a specialized museum on prisons and the local public library working on historic prison material, a special library and a small museum digitizing photographs documenting the history of mining, and a botanical garden working with relevant societies.

In addition to the CDP, IMLS has funded a number of other museum/library digitization initiatives, including:

- "Connecticut History Online" (http://www.lib.uconn.edu/cho/), a collaborative initiative of the Connecticut Historical Society, Mystic Seaport Museum, and the Thomas J. Dodd Research Center at the University of Connecticut. Together the three organizations established a comprehensive Web-based virtual collection of images documenting the Connecticut community.
- "Images of the Indian Peoples of the Northern Great Plains" (http://www.lib.montana.edu~elainep/imlsabst.html), a project involving the Museum of the Rockies and the Montana State University Libraries creating a database on culture of the Plains Indians.
- "Digital Cultural Heritage Community" (http://images.library.uiuc.edu/projects/dchc). University of Illinois at Urbana Champaign partnered with three local museums and three elementary schools to build a model and test an electronic database of historical images in digital format. Another project involving the University of Illinois at Urbana is the Global

Cultural Memory Project, an expansion of a "proof of concept" project in Champaign, Illinois, with local archive and library partners.

- "Illinois Alive" (http://www.rsa.lib.il.us/~ilalive), a project sponsored by the Alliance Library System involving the 26 member libraries including Knox College, Illinois College, Bradley University, and the University of Illinois working with the Illinois State Historical Library and several county historical societies to create a regional digital library of archival resources relating to Illinois history, 1818–1918.

B. Other Large Collaboratives Involving Museums and Libraries

Several other states have begun statewide collaborative digitization initiatives with all types of cultural heritage institutions, including North Carolina, Missouri, New Mexico, and Minnesota. The North Carolina State Library (http://www.ncecho.org/) and the Missouri State Library (http://www.virtuallymissouri.org/)[19] are furthest along on their initiatives involving all cultural heritage institutions in their states. Each has completed its planning process, and each included all types of cultural heritage institutions. The plans, best practices, and options for collection analysis were all developed through the collaborative work of the cultural heritage communities.

A major project of the Research Libraries Group (RLG) is the Cultural Materials Alliance (CMA). For the CMA, a group of RLG members with a special interest in the availability of digitized cultural materials agreed to define common terms and conditions for content contribution, collective licensing, and service development. The initiative will include a wide range of cultural materials that reflect and document the shared global culture of humankind and are used in research and learning. These materials will come from library special collections, archives, museums, historical societies, and other repositories from RLG member organizations. RLG states,

> One of the defining characteristics of the alliance is that participants have reached agreement on a set of common terms and conditions under which content can be distributed. The service will initially focus on delivering alliance participants' content under these terms and conditions. Later, a set of terms and conditions governing contributions from members not in the alliance may be developed (http://www.rlg.org/culturalres/index.html).

Participants will contribute metadata to a new system developed by RLG. Metadata from a wide range of systems, including locally developed systems, MARC, Visual Resources Association Core, and EAD, can be contributed. These records will be converted to an RLG data model using

[19]The Missouri State Library initiative is funded by an LSTA grant and it is being led by the Missouri Library Network Corporation.

XML (extensible markup language) tools. The RLG's new service will allow users to:

- Focus on information specifically about cultural materials, at both collection and item level
- Easily search across and within multiple collections, revealing contextual links that would not otherwise be discovered
- Locate information that is not currently available on the Web, or is available but widely dispersed, difficult to locate, and not delivered in consistent ways
- Browse large results sets using multimedia microsurrogates for the cultural materials
- License information for use in certain nonacademic applications (http://www.rlg.org/culturalres/index.html)

Initially the Alliance will serve metadata and thumbnail images, with links to the access-level images residing on the content owner's site. A subscription release should be available in 2002.[20]

V. International Library/Museum Digitization and Collaboration

The United Kingdom has been a leader in digital library collaboration. Much of the work there is driven by legislative efforts requiring public organizations to increase access to, manage, and archive their information in digital format. In the United Kingdom, the recognition that libraries and other cultural heritage institutions must work together came from the Warwick II digital preservation workshop in March 1999. The participants identified a number of reasons for establishment of such a coalition:

- Participants needed to collaborate to get the topic of digital preservation on the agenda of decision makers and funding agencies
- With the proliferation of projects, an umbrella organization to help coordinate and monitor the activities was important
- Many of the technical and some of the organizational issues are the same for all organizations
- A coalition could tap additional skills and funding and help address and contribute to the development of national strategies, infrastructure and skills in digital preservation (Beagrie, 2001).

---

[20]http://www.rlg.org/culturalres/index.html is the URL at RLG for this project, and a content preview is available in *RLG News*, Spring 2001, http://www.rlg.org/rlgnews/news52.pdf.

The outcomes of the summit include decisions that the UK agenda would be developed within an international context, and that the coalition would operate on four levels:

- Activities of member institutions would be undertaken individually, but accomplished and coordinated in line with their commitment to the principles of openness and dissemination
- Core activities would be those of interest to all members and supported by resources from the membership
- Collaborative projects would be funded from a variety of sources
- There would be a development of a national digital archiving infrastructure

One of the earliest initiatives in the United Kingdom was the development of the Arts and Humanities Data Service, a program of the Joint Information Systems Committee (JISC) (http://ahds.ac.uk/). The AHDS was designed to respond to and address the problems associated with digital content. AHDS collects, describes, and preserves the electronic resources which result from scholarly research in the humanities and makes the collections readily available to scholars through an online catalog designed to interoperate with other finding aids (Greenstein and Trant, 1996).

Another JISC-supported initiative is the Distributed National Electronic Resource (DNER), a managed environment for accessing quality-assured information resources on the Internet which are available from many sources. These resources include scholarly journals, monographs, textbooks, abstracts, manuscripts, maps, music scores, still images, geospatial images, and other kinds of vector and numeric data, as well as moving picture and sound collections. DNER is:

- Providing a UK focus for the development of practices, policies and strategies for the preservation of digital materials.
- Generating support and collaborative funding from and promoting interworking with appropriate agencies worldwide.
- Contributing to the DNER management team and activities, managing DNER Administration and resources section, and advising DNER programs and staff on digital preservation policy (JISC, 2001).

The Consortium of University Research Libraries (http://www.curl.ac .uk) through the CURL Exemplars for Digital Archives (CEDARS) project, aims to address strategic, methodological, and practical issues (http://www .leeds.ac.uk/cedars/) and will provide guidance for libraries in best practice for digital preservation. The lead institutions include Oxford University, Cambridge University, and University of Leeds, with involvement from other CURL and non-CURL organizations.

A third major U.K. digital library initiative is the UKOLN (UK Office for Library Networking), funded by The Council for Museums, Archives & Libraries, JISC of the Higher and Further Education Funding Councils, as well as by the European Union (http://www.cordis.lu/ist/). UKOLN is a national center for digital information management. It provides services to the library, information and cultural heritage communities. Its goals are to:

• Influence policy and inform practice
• Advance the state of the art and to contribute to knowledge
• Build useful and innovative distributed systems and services
• Promote community building and consensus-making through awareness and events services.

UKOLN has established a wide range of services for the cultural heritage community, including technical standards and online newsletters, as well as mirror sites for many of the major digital library portals.

In 2001 £50 million for digitization from the New Opportunities Fund (http://www.nof.org.uk/)[21] was made available to libraries, museums, and other cultural heritage institutions. The Fund

> . . . will provide a unique model for the creation of innovative on-line learning resources for the potential benefit of every citizen in the UK. The programme brings together a wide range of partnerships representing the community and voluntary sectors, local authorities, libraries and archives, museums, further and higher education and the private sector. Projects, which are designed to support lifelong learning under one of three broad themes: cultural enrichment, citizenship, and reskilling, will transfer text, drawings, photos, maps, film and sound recordings into easily accessible electronic format. Interactive and interpretive materials will enhance a support source items. The adoption of rigorous technical standards will ensure the accessibility and sustainability of the material for future use (NOF-Digitise, 2001).

The project will use UKOLN technical standards.

The National Science Foundation has established a program for international digital library projects (http://www.nsf.gov/home/int/). The NSF funds the U.S. grantee, while the international partner must be funded by an organization in its country. Several national libraries are taking the lead in establishing digital libraries reflecting the cultural heritage of their country. The National Library of Australia is a particularly useful model. They host an important international forum, PADI—Preserving Access to Digital Information, a gateway to digital preservation resources (http://www.nla.gov.au/padi/) (Brandis and Lyall, 2001). The National

---

[21]The New Opportunities fund was established to distribute U.K. lottery receipts in the form of grants to health, education, and environment projects throughout the United Kingdom. One of the specific initiatives is digitization.

Library of Canada has established its role in the digital library environment in a document, "Positioning the National Library of Canada in the Digital Environment: Strategic Directions (National Library of Canada)." It states that the National Library will take a lead role in enabling Canadians to access information in the digital environment in order to support and contribute to the development of a knowledge-based society for Canada and to document, preserve, and promote the Canadian experience published in digital formats. To this end, the National Library will collaborate with libraries and other public institutions, not-for-profit organizations, and the private sector.

The Denmark's Electronic Research Library is a 5-year project (1998–2002) funded by the three Danish Ministries of Culture, Research, and Education with the goal of developing the four key components of a digital library—national infrastructure, library infrastructure, digital resources, and user facilities. The strategic plan notes that digitization is a key component and identifies the key issues that need to be addressed, including copyright and digital archiving. Forty-five research libraries have submitted proposals, with a third of them being in the area of digitization (http://www.deflink.dk/eng/).

Lorcan Dempsey describes the planning framework for a multinational initiative that was undertaken in the late 1990s among the European Economic Community (Dempsey, 2000). This very long-term planning will lead to digitization and preservation collaboration among "memory institutions."

VI. Issues in Museum/Library Collaboration

Collaboration in any environment is challenging, and museum/library collaboration is no different. In the past 5 years, cultural heritage organizations have gained significant experience in interinstitutional collaboration on digitization projects, so we can begin to make some observations about the collaboration, including the issues that arise when libraries, museums, historical societies, and archives work across the boundaries in collaborative digitization projects.

There is a wide range of opportunity for collaboration among libraries and museums. Some projects have both parties playing equal roles, contributing content, staff expertise, technical infrastructure, and resources. However, it is more common to find that the partners contribute different components of the project, building on each type of expertise.

A. Models for Collaboration among Libraries and Museums

The Colorado project asked the projects to include collaboration between different types of cultural heritage organizations. Although initially the Steering Committee believed that both partners would contribute content, some of the projects follow that mode and some do not. The Pikes Peak Library District and the Pikes Peak Hill Climb Club both contributed content, with the library taking responsibility for scanning, creation of metadata, and the Web site. The virtual environment provides the first and maybe only opportunity to bring dispersed collections together. The University of Northern Colorado Michener Library is collaborating with the Greeley City Museum to create a virtual exhibit celebrating the 25th anniversary of James A. Michener's *Centennial*. Each organization had unique resources to contribute to this virtual exhibit. In projects led by school libraries, the libraries brought to their projects not only knowledge required to create metadata and design Web sites, but also expertise in development of lesson plans. For many smaller historical societies and museums the most significant contribution they make is in the knowledge of the collection, the history of the area, and the content. Museum partners bring to these projects knowledge of how to present information within context, an important new approach to Web-based information dissemination.

The Brooklyn Expedition is a project of the Brooklyn Children's Museum, the Brooklyn Public Library, and the Brooklyn Museum of Art. This Web site was designed to increase educational services to the Brooklyn community and develop a model for attracting and training people from diverse backgrounds in information technology, library science, and museum programs (http://www.brooklynexpedition.org). Funded by IMLS, the Museums contributed the content, the Web design, and associated public programming. The Library provided much of the technical infrastructure, links to library collections, and public programming arenas.

The Carnegie Mellon Library project, funded by IMLS, had three partners—the Library, the University Department of Computing, and the Carnegie Mellon Museum. Each partner had very specific roles and responsibilities. The Museum provided the content, a dinosaur, and associated artifacts and resources. The Library was responsible for the metadata standards and creation, while the computing department designed new Web searching capabilities.

B. Organizational Culture

The issue of organizational culture presents some of the more serious obstacles and most important benefits for museums and historical societies wishing to collaborate with libraries and archives. As demonstrated earlier, libraries have a long history of collaboration across different types of libraries. Collaboration among libraries is so extensive that there is now found among librarians a set of positive assumptions about collaboration that flows from an experience-based understanding of the benefits of working with others to

achieve a common goal. Shared costs, shared access systems, shared programs, shared support infrastructure, and shared access to training are examples of well-known benefits. This set of understandings about the benefits of
collaboration is not as common in the museum community. The museum
community with its culture of interinstitutional respect has relatively few
common programs, and even fewer funding opportunities designed to
encourage sharing in the way libraries have done. Further, internally libraries
and museums have developed different cultures in several major areas related
to digitization. The areas of concern include physical security of the collections, protection of the objects' intellectual property rights, protection of
confidentiality, how to appropriately disseminate information on the Web,
and metadata standards.

Graduate library programs and professional training inculcate a set of
values that flow out to the organizations in which librarians work. These
include emphasis on open access to information without restrictions, freedom
of information, and even-handed collection policies designed to place information on all subjects and perspectives in the hands of the public. As a result,
libraries promote finding guides through online catalogs designed to list and
advertise the whereabouts of each item in a library's collections. Through
collection development policies, librarians present information on multiple
perspectives. Librarians generally enable library users to interpret the information as they please, with a minimum of interpretation by the library staff.
Libraries avoid censorship to as great an extent as possible within each community, on principles related to freedom of information and free access to
information. Libraries around the world have adopted standard methods of
describing each item in the collection so the catalogs they present to the
public can interoperate with other library catalogs all based on the same standards, leading to widely available systems of interlibrary lending. These interlibrary loan systems (such as the OCLC Interlibrary Loan system for national
and international lending, or Ohiolink or the Colorado Virtual Library for
statewide lending) allow public access to collections that transcend ownership limits. In many cases, a reader can search many library collections at the
same time, finding out which libraries own copies of a needed item.

In comparison, museums collect primarily unique and monetarily or
intellectually valuable objects, which require significant attention to issues of
security and preservation. The museum finding systems are designed for
museum staff that work with the collections, not the public. In large museums
over 90% of the collections are in secured storage with access limited to the
curatorial staff. Sometimes, these stored collections are not even available to
scholarly visitors. Many small museums and historical societies have not
adopted computerized collection management systems, and while such
systems are based on databases with similar elements, the systems are not

based on national or international standards, and they are not designed to support intermuseum or cross-museum collection searches. These systems are designed to support the registry and collection management/curatorial functions of the museum or historical society. The culture of conservation is far stronger in museums than it is in libraries, even in library special collections. Further, museums have a much stronger tradition of liaison with the K–12 educational community and development of interpretive exhibits prepared by curatorial staff or subject experts. This sort of interpretive material is presented to the public, placing collections into a context of culture, politics, natural history, or other information assembled along with the perspectives of the curator. This tradition of interpretive exhibit is very much counter to the library tradition of unbiased presentation of finding guides that leave interpretation of collections to the user.

There are many implications of these differences in the traditions, systems, and cultures of libraries and museums.

C. Metadata and Interoperability

Agreement on metadata standards is key to increasing access to cultural heritage collections. Yet this is the area that has the greatest potential for conflict. The library community has a strong tradition of cataloging standards, both for the description of materials and for the transmittal and retrieval of data. The archival community has standards related to preservation and conservation of resources, but only recently codified the finding aid structure into a standard, The Encoded Archical Description (EAD) (http://www.loc.gov/ead/).[22] Standards within the museum community, where they exist, tend to be along discipline lines; for example, the art museum community has adopted specific standards for the description of art objects, yet that approach may be very different from the description used by a history museum or a zoological museum. Additionally within museums and historical societies there are frequently separate approaches for the three types of materials—collections (artifacts, works of art, etc.), archives, and libraries—each with its own standards and until recently its own automated systems. Therefore, it is a challenge to determine standards that will support collaborative initiatives and interoperability between and among the different systems in use.

Many collaborative digitization projects are centered on a joint Web site that contains Web-based exhibits featuring digital versions of text, photos,

[22]Encoded Archival Description (EAD) is a Standardized General Mark-up Language (SGML) Document type definition that provides the protocol for conveying information found in the traditional archival collection finding aids. A description can be found at the Library of Congress EAD site.

objects, music, or video. Sometimes "exhibits" may contain a set of digital objects with little or no descriptive information to place the objects in context. This approach can be confusing for the viewer, since the presence of an image caption alone is usually insufficient to constitute a real exhibit, such as the public expects to see in a museum. When cultural heritage institutions create Web-mounted images, they also need to create descriptions of the images. Those descriptions can and often are used in two ways. One way is as the contextual description found in an online exhibit, where the viewer moves from one image to another, progressing through a collection presented in some logical sequence, with narrative linking the images and providing an educational experience. The second approach is to offer a database of metadata, which will provide detailed access to and information about the individual digital objects.

Libraries have been using the MARC standard, linked to the *Anglo-American Cataloging Rules*, 2nd edition, to create standard cataloging entries for their online catalogs. Since the mid-1990s the digital library community has developed new, less complex standards for the description of electronic resources, including digital objects; the best known of these is Dublin Core (http://dublincore.org/index.shtml). The developers of the Dublin Core include individuals from the library community, computer scientists, publishers, and scholars. Because of this broad-based community development, Dublin Core is being adopted by many organizations including the Consortia for the Computer Interchange of Museum Information (CIMI), which has developed a specific Dublin Core extension for the museum community. Many states, including North Carolina, Minnesota, and Colorado, have developed their own Dublin Core definitions. Unlike the MARC or Dublin Core record describing the item or the collection, the Encoded Archival Description reflects the hierarchical relationships within collections shown in most archival finding aids. A third standard for the description of digital text resources is the Text Encoding Initiative (TEI) (http://www.tei-c.org/), an SGML document type definition for encoding both the content of a document and creation of a header that carries the descriptive information. Organizations describing digital government documents use the Government Information Locator Standard (GILS). When different types of institutions collaborate on digitization, it quickly becomes clear that a variety of metadata standards are used. Add to this the variety of controlled vocabularies and different approaches to presentation of information, and the result is a complex, potentially controversial environment. A good overview of this environment is described by Murtha Baca (Baca, 1998).

Many people, including special collections librarians, are facing this field of complex metadata standards with hopes that the World Wide Web will offer the solution. However, while a searcher may find a Web site containing an online exhibit by using a standard Web search engine (especially if care is taken to include descriptive language in the HTML coding), different Web search engines work differently, and results vary widely. The Web site may be in the top 10 or 20 retrievals shown by one search engine, and may be buried in the hundredth set of another. Further, databases that are part of Web sites are not searchable by Web browsers. Therefore, a purely Web-engine-based approach to retrieval is not reliable and is often not at all effective.

In order for collaborative digitization projects to realize the goals of increased access to the collection, exposure of new users to their resources, and use in the K–12 community, users must be able to retrieve descriptive information about the digital objects. Some projects address this by creating a single database for the project, accessible from the Web sites of the participating projects. In these cases all project participants must adhere to the same standards and generally use the same data creation system. Probably the largest of these initiatives is the California Digital Library's Online Archive of California. College and university libraries' archives, the State Library, and major museums all create EAD finding aids. The Carnegie Mellon initiative and the University of Illinois collaborative project mentioned earlier have built systems that support data entry into a single institutional retrieval system. A single system, which may be desirable for many reasons, is generally not desirable for larger collaborative projects, as it requires staff of at least one of the collaborating institutions to learn new systems, may require purchase of additional software, and in some instances can require keying into two systems.

The long-standing vision of the networked community is the creation of distributed networked systems, in which both data and content are resident on a variety of networks, and with interoperability between the networks. The National Science Foundation and others are funding significant work to explore new approaches to metadata interoperability. At this point in time, the principal way to achieve interoperability is to make metadata available through a database that is supported by Z39.50, the international protocol supporting intersite search and retrieval. Although many library systems support Z39.50, applying that standard becomes more complex when collaborators include organizations creating Dublin Core records and EAD finding aids, and institutions using a locally developed system or a nonlibrary system. Only a few commercial systems support Dublin Core or EAD and even fewer have Z39.50 functionality along with these new protocols. Some of the problems associated with using different systems can be overcome with the use of crosswalks, which map one standard to another, allowing loading of records created on one system into another system. The Library of Congress has developed many of these crosswalks, and information on the cross-

walks is available at the Library's Web site (http://www.loc.gov/marc/
marc2dc.html and http://lcweb.loc.gov/ead/ag/agappb.html). This approach
still requires software development to implement the crosswalks.

On the horizon is the Open Archives Initiative (OAI) (http://www
.openarchives.org/index.html), which offers a new solution to interoperability. The OAI has defined a means of coding metadata as OAI compliant. The
protocol requires that the data be in Dublin Core structure and XML (http://
www.w3.org/XML/). OAI Harvesters will target OAI compliant systems
collecting the metadata and placing it in an OAI Repository. Institutions
may designate themselves as an OAI Harvester and/or Repository. The
Initiative has a number of test projects and Mellon funding (Waters, 2001;
Lynch, 2001) for seven institutions (Research Libraries Group, University of
Michigan, University of Illinois at Urbana-Champaign, Emory University,
the Woodrow Wilson International Center for Scholars, University of
Virginia, and the Southeastern Library Network) to explore special problems
encountered in harvesting metadata for archives and special collection,
creating portal services based on metadata related to specific topics, and
designing portal services based on metadata. The advantage of OAI is that
it is a relatively low-cost approach to making a site OAI compliant. The
participating institution doesn't have to purchase additional software as is
necessary for Z39.50 compliance. The contributing site's metadata is har-
vested, rather than the institution having to "send" data somewhere. At this
time there is no commercial software that supports OAI; however, many of
the pioneers in the OAI community are making OAI tools available as an
open source. Currently the metadata records only support Dublin Core,
leaving non-DC museum and library automated systems out of the harvesting
loop.

While the cultural heritage community awaits development of the new
technological solutions to interoperability, there are a few interesting
approaches for cultural heritage institutions that provide interim solutions.
In 1998 when the Colorado Digitization Project first began, there were 15
Colorado projects underway. Eight of these projects were based in libraries
and the others were museums or historical societies. A myriad of access
approaches were in place, including Web accessible locally developed databases, collection-level MARC records linked to HTML finding aids, MARC-
based library databases, and exhibits with no metadata for the digital objects.
In exploring the options it was quickly apparent that one large system that
everyone would use was not practical. It would have been nearly impossible
to convert everyone to one system, as the locally selected systems supported
very specialized needs for their institution. Further, the CDP did not have
funding to support such a massive conversion. The CDP considered but discarded use of a Web search engine to solve interoperability problems because

of the previously noted problems with Web retrieval. To meet the primary objective of increased access the CDP decided to create a union catalog of metadata, a catalog that would take records from a variety of systems (library local systems, museum local systems, Microsoft Access-type databases, etc.). A task force compared the different standards or protocols available at the time to determine if there was one that had the greatest overlap in descriptive elements. The task force found that Dublin Core offered the best basis for developing a common set of descriptive elements for a database. The system had to accept records through online input or batchloading, and it had to be Z39.50 compliant so that it could be integrated with the library catalogs accessible through the Colorado Virtual Library. CDP also wanted the capability to design a distinctive Web interface. OCLC SiteSearch (http://www.oclc.org/oclc/menu/site.htm)[23] software was selected, being the only system at the time that supported Dublin Core, offered batchload and online input and was Z39.50 compliant. It was necessary to build a custom data entry system, as the Record Builder functionality of SiteSearch wasn't robust enough to support the complex initiative. One of the CDP partners, the Colorado Alliance of Research Libraries, built the data entry system and developed crosswalks to convert records to the Dublin Core format. Today, *Heritage—Gateway to Colorado's Digitization Projects* can load records from MARC-based library systems, Access-type databases, and museum systems. Web-mounted tools support use of the online metadata system including a list of Colorado subject and geographic terms, and a list of Colorado authors. Links are provided to the CDP standards as well as controlled vocabularies. Although not appropriate to all collaboratives, this approach provided an interim solution that increases access to the digital collections the CDP partners were creating. The CDP is exploring requirements for OAI compliance.

A different interim approach is being taken by Missouri and North Carolina. These statewide initiatives also include the full range of cultural heritage institution types. Both projects are building databases of collections. North Carolina is surveying each cultural heritage institution in the state, identifying collections as well as their status on preservation and organization. These collections are being entered into a database hosted through the state library project North Carolina ECHO—Exploring Cultural Heritage

---

[23]OCLC has announced in a letter to OCLC SiteSearch Users, September 24, 2001, from Frank Hermes, Vice President, OCLC, that as of December 2001 they will discontinue development of the SiteSearch software. Support for SiteSearch will continue through December 2003. OCLC will make the full Java code available on an open-source basis in 2002. The code will be available to anyone for noncommercial purposes and subject to royalties for commercial "resellers."

Online. Missouri is taking a similar approach, and rather than surveying each institution, they are providing an online template for institutions to enter their collections. This approach works well where the library or museum has organized resources into collections. Missouri is also investigating a union catalog of metadata similar to the CDP model for increased access to the collections.

There is great variance in the descriptive standards used by libraries and museums; we find similar diversity in the standards used for subject access to collections. Art museums may use the Getty *Art and Architecture Thesaurus* and libraries will use the *Library of Congress Subject Heading List*, while botanical museums will use taxonomies that reflect the specimens in their collection. Because of the nature of many collections, the subject terminology must be specialized to reflect the depth of the collections. Unless a specific theme or subject is selected for the collaborative initiative, multiple subject lists, thesauri, and taxonomies will be used. Local historical societies frequently find it necessary to create their own subject term list reflecting the unique heritage of the community. The integration of the different subject lists/thesauri is an area that requires research.

The final metadata issue faced by collaborative projects is display of descriptive and administrative information. More specifically, collaboratives must answer questions about display of provenance, donor, cost, and location information. While agreement can be usually reached regarding location, cost, and ownership, there can be some serious differences of opinion relating to donor information. Some organizations want to promote the donation, so donor information is included in the record, while others believe this information should be limited to staff. Closely related to administrative metadata display is the question of how the image is displayed. Some projects have invested significant time and money into development of an interface, whereas a Z39.50 approach removes the metadata and linked image from that interface, using the interface of the requesting site. Each collaborative must work through these issues.

D. Scanning

Museums and historical societies are beginning to use computer-based collections inventory software products supporting linking of a thumbnail image of an object to the database entry about that item. As a result many museums are photographing and digitizing items in their collections or using digital cameras to create digital versions of the items in the collections. These digital versions will allow rapid identification of the item by staff from across the organization while also minimizing the physical handling of the materials. Inventory systems are not designed for public use, and some of the inventory-based digitization projects are being done with very low-resolution images intended only to fulfill the immediate purpose of allowing staff or qualified researchers to identify the item being described. Only recently are the vendors making available Web-based access to the museum catalog, which can provide Web access by the general public.

However, museum Web-based exhibits have many other audiences. These include school children and their teachers, hobbyists and more-than-casual experts, scholars interested in serious research, and the business community that might be interested in using an image of an object in a publication or on a mug. Children now expect the Web exhibit to do things that a museum might not anticipate, such as zoom, turn an image, give a virtual tour, or provide other image manipulation tools. With a low-quality image, zooming or enlarging the picture results in a poor-quality product, as it pixilates into an unfortunate blur, frustrating the 5th-grader and the scholar alike. It is a challenge for a library or a museum to plan ahead for an unknown future filled with opportunities to repurpose work. In this case, best practice such as that documented by the California Digital Library recommends that an institution capture images at the highest practical resolution, making repurposing possible, and creating flexibility for audiences not currently anticipated. It is expensive to digitize an artifact, text, or photo; it is even more expensive to photograph an object and then capture that photo. The general rule is to go through that expensive process once at a high enough quality so that the work will not have to be redone in the future when a now-unknown new purpose is demanded. Just as the museum can pull images from the collections management system originally designed for staff use and put those same images onto a Web site designed for teachers and learners, libraries can pull images created for a special collections exhibit and use them to generate high-quality photo services for scholars of the future, limiting use of fragile original documents and supporting a preservation plan.

Museums and libraries often have different perspectives on the risks associated with use and presentation of higher quality images. A library is used to telling each online catalog user exactly where in the building the user should go to find the item needed. The call number is on the book spine, and the map of the library is on the Web site, showing what floor of the stacks to visit. Even if a virtual document is available in an online library exhibit or linked to a catalog entry, a user can request access to the original. Promoting location information for collections is absolutely the last thing most museums would dream of doing. Museum collections are secured and usually not available for public access. Location information represents a tremendous security risk. These differences can complicate the effort by a museum and a library to create standard metadata for digital collections that create a joint exhibit or catalog. The metadata for a library-created entry contains location information, which must be suppressed in the case of a museum-created entry.

Another major issue for museums is unauthorized use of their materials. There is significant concern on the part of museums that if they put the image of an item in their collection on the Web site, the image will be used without their permission or without a royalty fee. Although both libraries and museums are generally sensitive to the risks of having Web users download images, museums often depend on the ownership of their collections to generate revenue, whereas libraries usually do not. In addition to the revenue-based concerns, museums may decide not to make images of objects available to the public for other reasons, including ownership, rights, or confidentiality concerns. Therefore, libraries tend to be more willing to use higher quality images in virtual exhibits than are museums. Library/museum partnerships will need to determine how to address the very serious concern of protection of intellectual property. Some projects are using watermarking, while others are displaying very low-resolution images not adequate for commercial use. It is important for the museum to feel comfortable that their intellectual property isn't being modified or stolen. Thumbnail displays derived from much higher quality access and/or master images usually do not pose a threat to either type of institution, since a business application of a thumbnail image is not practical. Even a t-shirt could not reasonably be made from a downloaded thumbnail; the image quality would not support enlargement. But a cultural heritage organization that creates higher quality master images can show the public the thumbnail and can offer scholarly users the high quality images after moving the viewer through a rights protection process, leaving open the option of repurposing the images for new audiences.

E. Rights and Other Legal Issues

Large museums generally have formal processes of obtaining rights to exhibit donated collections or loaned objects and collections. However, smaller museums and historical societies may not have been paying much attention to deeds of gift, or terms of deeds. Libraries are rapidly learning about the ever-evolving copyright environment, but smaller libraries may be in the same position as smaller museums in regard to deeds of gift, and may be confused by the complications related to the issue of when the library has the right to use a work in an online exhibit.

The entire area of fair use by cultural heritage institutions with an educational mission is very complex. An overview prepared by Jean Heilig (Colorado Digitization Project, 1999) summarizes the questions any cultural heritage institution should ask when moving into the online environment. Determining when something is appropriate for digital publishing as part of a catalog of digital objects or an online exhibit is not an easy matter. Determining ownership is a first step; then the library or museum must determine whether the item was donated for a particular purpose, and if that purpose included all forms of display. For example, the photographer often retains rights to a photo even if the print of the photo resides in a library or museum collection. For published works, there are guidelines indicating when the publication is in the public domain, when no copyright applies (http://www.unc.edu/~unclng/public-d.htm). For published works generated by the U.S. government or via contract with public funds, there is usually no copyright restriction. For unpublished works, there are other issues. For instance, a digital reproduction created by a library is not the same work as the original. The deed of gift may not enable the library to create derivative works for distribution, even for educational purposes, while another deed may pass all rights along to the library along with the collection, freeing the library to create and distribute derivative works for any purpose. A great many resources are available on Web sites because case law and legislative action are both changing the intellectual property and copyright environment monthly. A few of these resources are listed at http://coloradodigital.coalliance.org/legal.html. One work that is helpful for museums is *A Museum Guide to Copyright and Trademark* (Steiner, ed., 1999).

Museums and libraries may also be concerned about the impact of Web-distributed digital collections on in-person visitation. For museums that derive a portion of their funding from gate receipts this is a major concern. As with the security issue and the intellectual property issues noted earlier, the impact on revenue must be considered. To date there is little research on the impact of Web-mounted digital images on museum/library visitation. Dr. Ross Loomis, Department of Psychology, Colorado State University, is currently undertaking research on this specific issue. The outcomes of his research will provide the kind of information library and museum managers need to decide to participate in wide-scale digital distribution of their collections.

In the library community, it is common to license digital resources and to authenticate access to those resources by some technology-based device such as IP address limiting or proxy servers. For unpublished collections, or digitized collections based on original works held by individual libraries (and where rights issues have been resolved), individual libraries have not adopted the model of licensing. There are some exceptions for digital products of interest to many libraries, such as the RLG project. In the museum community, the collaborative AMICO project is similarly centered on the idea that works can be licensed for educational use, and AMICO offers a range of subscription options including consortial pricing. Some museums have partnered with Corbis (http://www.corbis.com), a corporate digital image company with a Web site designed to make money from any use, educational or not. Corbis has 2.1 million online images, some of which are of fine art, and sells them for popular use in e-cards, screensavers, photographic prints and framing, publishing, calendars, etc., at "shopping cart" prices.

F. Digital Archiving

When digitizing resources, an institution should build preservation activities into the process of handling the material for capture. Any digitization project needs to consider the future, addressing questions about how the images will be made available to future Web site visitors and researchers. A guidebook to many of these issues has been published by the Northeast Document Conservation Center (Sitts, 2000).

But once again, there are no easy answers to those looking for solutions allowing permanent access to digitized cultural heritage resources. A list of Web-based discussions and reports on the evolving international opinion and research on preservation of digital resources can be found at the Berkeley Sunsite Web site (http://sunsite.berkeley.edu/Preservation/). Of particular note is Howard Besser's Web site called "Information Longevity" where Dr. Besser cites a number of international conference reports and white papers on the issue (http://sunsite.berkeley.edu/Longevity/). The Harvard University Library has published their digital repository services guide, designed to present how Harvard University units can use the HUL Digital Repository Service (DRS). It highlights the types of digital materials accepted for deposit, the services of the DRS, and the rights and responsibilities of object owners within a single university, for university records in digital form, as well as long-term procedures for preservation and access.

At this time, digital versions of text, maps, or photographic material are not viewed as an appropriate format for permanent preservation, so discard of the original is not an option widely viewed as feasible. The digital versions *are* an important component of an overall preservation plan, since they may dramatically reduce handling and can improve the preservation environment for the original work. Microfilm for paper-based resources and cold storage for photographic resources are still considered superior methods for long-term preservation, and while digital capture is the only sensible option for audio and video formats, there are serious questions about the best method of moving digital formats into the future.

Digitization is rejected as a preservation medium for a variety of reasons. First, the digital object must be "recorded" on some sort of medium, such as compact disk, tape, or DVD, and the life expectancy of the CD or DVD optical storage media (generally regarded as our "best bet") is still a target of research and by industry groups or others, such as the National Media Lab

(Gilbert, 1998). It should be noted that DVD is not recommended for even a temporary storage format, because that format is not yet standardized. In addition to the question of media, there is the even more vexing issue of the software needed to retrieve images stored on optical media. Both the computer operating system and the specific image viewing software required to retrieve the data must be kept current. Both change with product upgrades and usually, the software vendors fail to support more than two or three versions prior to the current release.

Therefore, a program of quality control for the stored images, as well as a regularized migration strategy, is required to upgrade software needed to access stored images and other digital file formats, and careful attention to the permanence of the storage medium itself must be part of any plan. We want to avoid the problems that we have experienced with word processing files that are not accessible either because the new computer does not have a 5.5-inch drive, or because we no longer have the software to retrieve the data on the floppy.

Some research has also been done to investigate the feasibility of emulation of older software rather than migration to newer forms (Holdsworth and Wheatley, 2001; Holdsworth, 2001; Wheatley, 2001; Rothenberg, 1999, 2000; University of Michigan, School of Information, 2001). While most digitization projects struggle with the entire issue of digital object preservation, migration seems to be emerging as the best practice, although it can be expensive and must be built into ongoing operations (RLG, 1996).

There is currently some discussion about the need for collaborative solutions to this issue on a regional or national basis. OCLC is exploring a program of archival activities for digital federal publications (Http://www .oclc.org/oclc/archive.htm), and RLG is exploring common solutions for all its members (http://www.rlg.org/longterm/). OCLC and RLG are collaborating on a white paper about the need for trusted repositories as a key strategy of a national digital object preservation program (RLG, 2001). As previously mentioned, other national libraries, such as that of Australia, are addressing this topic as well. This issue needs to be faced by all cultural heritage institutions, and while the library community is engaged in discussion of the options, the museums involved in digitization projects must be at the tables where solutions are found.

VII. Funding

Although collaborative grant applications are often well received by field reviewers and panelists, and are the norm for large foundations such as Mellon, there are times when collaborators may have doubts about the risks associated with multi-institutional projects. Because most funding is highly competitive, some institutions feel that participating in a group project puts the individual institution's chances for funding from the same agency at risk. Further, a close analysis of the cost/benefit ratio of each grant application might yield concern about the flow of funding to each participant.

The major federal sources of funding for digitization and digital library development by cultural heritage institutions include the National Endowment for the Humanities, the Institute for Museum and Library Services, the National Science Foundation, and to some extent, the National Endowment for the Arts. The Department of Education has funded programs to create online content for schools, and in many states, Library Services and Technology Act funds (through IMLS) are used for digitization programs.

Each of these agencies has an extensive Web site with detailed information about the funding programs available, application information, and information about previous awards. While the effort involved in preparing a grant application is substantial, the rewards can be great, since some of these agencies have maximum awards of $500,000 and up for large, multi-year projects.

In addition, there are many private foundations that support technology-based projects including digitization. Some limit awards to a state or region, while some have national impact. Generally, foundation grants are smaller, but the application process may be considerably simpler than it is with one of the state or federal funding sources.

VIII. Conclusion: Together, We Bring Benefit

Despite the need to work through all these issues—metadata and interoperability, scanning and presentation of images, security, rights, and archiving—museums and libraries have a great deal in common as cultural heritage organizations. Although there is still not a single term or phrase that applies to all four types of institutions, the commonality of purpose has led the phrase "memory institutions" to be used in the European Community. This commonality of purpose is a great uniting force for these institution types. Libraries, archives, historical societies, and museums all serve the public good through collections and programs celebrating their communities' scientific, creative, and cultural heritage, and all inform visitors about the richness of the past and the potential of the future. Most of these institutions place emphasis on educational programs, taking special care to reach out to the educational community.

Museums have a strong tradition of programs designed for K–12 students and teachers, but public libraries also have strong programming for

K–12, often in partnership with school libraries. Academic libraries receiving public funds generally have open access policies and may also support K–12 outreach activities, often benefiting from participation in state funding programs for libraries and library resources. Further, the K–12 user community is not the only type of audience that libraries, museums, archives, and historical societies have in common. The Colorado Digitization Project engaged in a planning process that resulted in a document analyzing the general categories of users important to CDP partners (http://coloradodigital.coalliance.org/users.html). Casual users, scholars, hobbyists, and the business community are also categories of visitors common to all cultural heritage organizations.

In addition to these programs there are other tangible benefits to collaboration:

- Increased access to collections: through collaboration and digitization, institutions can bring new users to their collections. Users or visitors who are familiar with one partner but not with another will become part of the user base of both institutions.
- Economies of scale: Many collaboratives realize economies of scale. The buying clubs that have developed among libraries allow each library to reduce its cost. The same can exist for digitization projects. The Louisiana State University Digital Library has established a digitization laboratory with a range of equipment and staff expertise. Libraries and museums may contract with the Digital Library for the conversion of their materials, eliminating the cost associated with equipment selection and purchase; addition of technical staff; etc. In Colorado, the CDP's five regional scan centers are available to all the projects at no cost. The WRLC, a Washington, DC-area library consortium, was awarded an IMLS grant to establish digitization infrastructures for the group.
- Resource sharing: As noted earlier, many collaboratives will realize the benefit of sharing resources, particularly people resources. Collaboratives can capitalize on the expertise of their partners in both subject and technical knowledge.
- Training: For many years consortia/collaboratives have played an important role in meeting the continuing education needs of their members. Digitization collaboratives can develop training programs and training materials that can be used by all participants.
- Learning new approaches: One of the most important roles of these museum/library collaboratives is exposing staff to new solutions to problems. For example, many libraries are struggling with how to provide online introductory information on their special collections, reducing the number of questions from the casual user. The museum exhibit offers an

excellent model for how to provide the introductory information. Similarly museum staff will have to look for new options for meeting the virtual scholar's research needs. The exhibit is insufficient for that clientele. The library database approach, with metadata on the individual images, may provide a solution that supports the distant scholar.

A collaboration of cultural heritage institutions can expand on the impact each type of institution brings to society. In the words of Lorcan Dempsey, who was at UKOLN at the time he wrote the research framework for the collaborative European effort,

> Archives, libraries and museums are memory institutions: they organize the European cultural and intellectual record. Their collections contain the memory of peoples, communities, institutions and individuals, the scientific and cultural heritage, and the products throughout time of our imagination, craft and learning. They join us to our ancestors and are our legacy to future generations. They are used by the child, the scholar, and the citizen, by the business-person, the tourist and the learner. These in turn are creating the heritage of the future. Memory institutions contribute directly and indirectly to prosperity through support for learning, commerce, tourism, and personal fulfillment. They are an important part of the civic fabric, woven into people's working and imaginative lives and into the public identity of communities, cities and nations. They are social assembly places, physical knowledge exchanges, whose use and civic presence acknowledge their social significance, and the public value accorded to them. They form a widely dispersed physical network of hospitable places, open to all. They will continue to fulfill these roles, as people wish to enjoy the physical experiences they and the use of their collections offer (Dempsey, 2000).

With such a powerful collective mission, collaboration among cultural heritage institutions, as they work to meet the future through digitization of their primary resource collections, can only yield great results.

References

Allen, Nancy (2000). Collaboration through the Colorado Digitization Project. *First Monday* 5.

Baca, Murtha (1998). Introduction to metadata: Pathways to digital information. *Getty Research Institute*, http://www.getty.edu/research/institute/standards/intrometadata/index.html.

Beagrie, Neil (2001). Towards a digital preservation coalition in the U.K. *Ariadne*, Issue 27, http://www.ariadne.ac.uk/issue27/digital-preservation/intro.html, March 23.

Brandis, Leanne, and Lyall, Jan (2001). PADI: Preserving access to Australian information and cultural heritage in digital form. *National Library of Australia*, http://www.nla.gov.au/nla/staffpaper/lyall3.html.

California Digital Library (2001). *CDL Digital Object Standards*. http://www.cdlib.org/about/publications/.

Colorado Digitization Project (1999). *Legal Issues to Consider when Digitizing Collections*. http://coloradodigital.coalliance.org/legalissues.html.

Dempsey, Lorcan (2000). Scientific, industrial, and cultural heritage: A shared approach. *Ariadne*, Issue 22, http://www.ariadne.ac.uk/issue22/dempsey/.

Gilbert, Michael (1998). Digital media life expectancy and care. *University of Massachusetts Amherst*, http://www.oit.umass.edu/publications/at_oit/Archive/fall98/media.html.

Greenstein, Dan, and Trant, Jennifer (1996). AHDS: Arts and Humanities Data Service. *Ariadne*, Issue 4, http://www.ariadne.ac.uk/issue4/ahds/.

Harvard University Library (2001). *DRS (Digital Repository Service) Policy Guide*. http://hul .harvard.edu/ois/systems/drs/policyguide.html.

Holdsworth, David (2001). C-ing ahead for digital longevity. *CAMiLEON Project, University of Leeds*, http://129.11.152.25/CAMiLEON/dh/cingahd.html.

Holdsworth, David, and Wheatley, Paul (2001). Emulation, preservation, and abstraction. *CAMiLEON Project, University of Leeds*, http://129.11.152.25/CAMiLEON/dh/ep5.html.

Institute of Museum and Library Services (IMLS) (2001). *Grants to State Library Agencies*, http://www.imls.gov/grants/library/lib_gsla.asp.

Joint Information Systems Committee (JISC) (2001). *Neil Beagrie*, http://www.jisc.ac.uk/dner/contacts/nb/#about.

Lynch, Clifford A. (2001). Metadata harvesting and the Open Archives Initiative. *Associaton of Research Libraries (ARL)*, http://www.arl.org/newsltr/217/mhp.html.

Manduca, Cathryn A., McMartin, Flora P., and Mogk, David W., eds. (2001). *Pathways to Progress: Vision and Plans for Developing the NSDL*, http://www.smete.org/nsdl/workgroups/coordcomm/Whitepaper.pdf, March 20.

National Library of Canada (2001). *Positioning the National Library of Canada in the Digital Environment: Strategic Directions*, http://www.nlc-bnc.ca/10/8/a8-1002-e.html.

NOF-Digitise (2001). *New Opportunities Fund nof-digitise.org homepage*, http://www.nof.org.uk/tempdigit/index.htm.

Ober, John (2001). The digital library triumvirate: Content, collaboration and technology. *Syllabus Magazine*, May.

Research Libraries Group (RLG) (1996). *Preserving Digital Information: Report of the Task Force on Archiving of Digital Information commissioned by the Commission on Preservation and Access and the Research Libraries Group*, http://www.rlg.org/ArchTF/.

Research Libraries Group (RLG) (2001). *Attributes of a Trusted Digital Repository: Meeting the Needs of Research Resources*, http://www.rlg.org/longterm/attributes01.pdf.

Rothenberg, Jeff (1999). Avoiding technological quicksand: Finding a viable technical foundation for digital preservation. *CLIR Report* 77, January.

Rothenberg, Jeff (2000). An experiment in using emulation to preserve digital publications. *Networked European Deposit Library (Nedlib)*, http://www.kb.nl/coop/nedlib/results/NEDLIBemulation.pdf.

Schrage, Michael (1995). The rules of collaboration. *Forbes ASAP Supplement*, June 5, pp. 88–89.

Sitts, Maxine, ed. (2000). Handbook for digital projects: A management tool for preservation and access. *Northeast Document Conservation Center (NEDCC)*, http://www.nedcc.org/digital/dighome.htm.

Steiner, Christine, ed. (1999). *A Museum Guide to Copyright and Trademark*. American Association of Museums, Washington, DC.

UKOLN (2001). *UKOLN home page*, http://www.ukoln.ac.uk/.

University of Michigan, School of Information (2001). *CAMiLEON Creating Creative Archiving at Michigan and Leeds: Emulating the Old on the New*, http://www.si.umich.edu/CAMILEON/.

Waters, Donald J. (2001). The metadata harvesting Initiative of the Mellon Foundation. *Association of Research Libraries*, http://www.arl.org/newsltr/217/waters.html.

Wheatley, Paul (2001). Migration—a CAMiLEON discussion paper. *CAMiLEON Project, University of Leeds*, http://www.personal.leeds.ac.uk/~issprw/camileon/migration.htm.

Swedish Libraries 2001: An Increased Role in the Education Society While Adjusting to Harder Economics and Technology

Mats G. Lindquist
Göteborg University Library, Economics Library
40530 Göteborg, Sweden

Libraries in Sweden, both public and academic, are facing the same economic hardships as all public sector activities. In this respect the situation in Sweden is similar to that in many other countries.

Another, not country-specific, phenomenon is that an increasing number of citizens are engaged in studies of one kind or another; "lifelong learning" is a reality. This, naturally, has an impact on the demand for library services.

The technological developments in telecommunications (Internet) and electronic material (multimedia, e-journals, e-books, and new genres of material) have been adopted and applied by all kinds of libraries and are beginning fundamentally to change the nature of library operations.

Economic and technological pressure has led to organizational changes: for public libraries it has meant centralization and concentration (e.g., fewer branch libraries); for university libraries there is a tendency toward decentralization of the traditional library services, which gives more power to the individual faculties of the university, but there is also a trend toward centralized management of electronic material. A second organizational response is integration and cooperation between the different library sectors: library users are no longer neatly clustered in the "public" or the "academic" sphere, so both material flows and service offerings must adjust to this reality.

This paper was presented at the Third Nordic–Baltic Library Meeting, October 25–26, 2001, Tallinn, Estonia. Dr. Lindguist is a board member of the Swedish Library Association.

I. University and Academic Libraries

The number of institutions for higher education (university colleges) has increased significantly during past decades, and three of them have been given university status. Currently Sweden has 11 universities and four specialized institutions with university status (Chalmers University of Technology, the Royal Institute of Technology, Karolinska Institutet, and Stockholm School of Economics). The number of university colleges and other academic institutions is 18, making a total of 33 academic libraries. (In the category "research libraries" Sweden also has 33 government-funded special libraries, and the Royal Library.)

The number of courses offered, and the number of students have also been rising, which has resulted in increased demand for library services.

Swedish academic libraries are, by legislation, open to the public, and not, as in some countries, exclusively available to the members of the academic community. Academic libraries therefore experience their share of the general increase in demand for library services. The share of "public" usage of an academic library is typically on the order of 20–30% of total usage.

The situation for the libraries is different for, on the one hand, the older (and larger) university libraries, and, on the other hand, the relatively new libraries at the university colleges. The latter have been in a building-up phase, so the financial situation has been better. (Although recently these libraries have also faced cost cuts.) But even so the collections at the university colleges are far from comprehensive, especially regarding older material. Public libraries have been used to supplement the holdings, often by ILL requests. The Council for Cultural Affairs estimates that one-third of the ILL traffic to public libraries comes from students of one kind or another. But mostly it has been the older university libraries which have provided the ILL material. To ameliorate the effects of the imbalance in collections, and the resulting ILL load, the government, through BIBSAM, the department for national cooperation and development at the Royal Library, has financed a compensation scheme for net-lenders. The annual budget for this scheme is SEK (Swedish kronor) 10 million.

Local circulation is still growing in volume. Local loans (the national total) increased by 23% between 1998 and 2000, and the trend seems likely to continue.

The main factor affecting academic libraries is technology. The digital revolution is well in progress (see more in section III) and all libraries are involved as participants, as beneficiaries, or in some respects as victims.

Whereas previous waves of technology (library automation systems and information retrieval in databases) meant rationalization of work and often led to additional funding, the present wave of technology means an increase in work which must be accommodated in existing budgets. The exception is digitization projects, which mostly are done with extra funding.

II. Public Libraries

For public libraries a couple of factors, one demographic and one economic, are significant for the current situation. The population is decreasing in many communities, so the tax-paying base has become smaller, and in many places library branches have been closed. The volume of acquisitions has gone down as a consequence of the reduction of funding.

A survey by the National Council for Cultural Affairs showed that during the period 1988–1999 the number of closed branch libraries was 376. (This is the total for all 289 communities.) In 85% of these cases the reason was cost savings. Decreases in population are also a contributing factor in many cases, especially sparsely populated areas.

The total number of public libraries in Sweden's 289 municipalities was 1472 (counting both main libraries and branches) in 1999. This is 267 less than in 1989, so the decline in number was 15% during that period.

For the same period there has also been a decline in total holdings of 3.5% to 47,527,000. However, the holdings of AV material have increased from 2 million to 2.8 million. The number of subscriptions to newspapers and journals has gone down from 153,000 to 117,000 (a decrease of 24%).

In spite of the decline in holdings, circulation figures are up: the total number of loans (1998) is about 82 million, of which 11% are AV material. This is an increase in the total of 12% from the 1989 figure. The proportion of nonfiction in circulation has increased and is now about the same as fiction (30%); the remaining 40% is children's material.

The increase in use is primarily due to the fact that more people are engaged in some kind of studying. Students from all levels use the public libraries either because of a lack of an adequate school library, or as a complement to the school or university college library. The Adult Education Initiative (in Swedish, Kunskapslyftet) is the largest adult education investment initiative ever undertaken in Sweden. All municipalities in Sweden are taking part in the project, which began on 1 July 1997 and is set to continue up to and including 2002. Its aim is to raise educational levels and to reduce unemployment.

The Initiative is relying very much on the public libraries for supporting its activities, but the libraries have not (with few exceptions) been given funding to meet the increase in demand. The consequence has been that other library activities, for example, services to children and to the elderly, have been reduced.

In both primary and secondary schools new educational methods are being introduced. Problem-based learning and other methods with more active student participation lead to an increased use of the public libraries. In general, the school libraries do not have sufficient resources to meet this demand. Only 16% of the primary schools (up to the 9th grade) have a library that is staffed more than 1 hour per day. The National Agency for Education has been given a special task by the government to strengthen the role of school libraries in the educational process.

In attempting to make the local government administration more cost-effective, during the past decade local governments have to an increasing degree changed the organization so that libraries are put together with other, mostly larger, activities. The result has been that library issues have received less attention from the political decision makers with increased difficulties with funding as a consequence.

State initiatives for the development of public libraries are in the form of grants to public libraries; these are managed by the National Council for Cultural Affairs and are for the purpose of

- increasing the public libraries' possibilities of reaching new groups,
- developing new methods and forms of activity,
- maintaining an even standard.

The Web pages (2001) of the Council contain the following summary of the subsidies:

> The subsidies to regional public library activities (subsidy units) for 2001 amount to SEK 36.6 million, of these SEK 2.8 million is earmarked for developing regional library services and may be applied for by county libraries. The same amount, SEK 2.8 million, is allocated to developing local public library activities. The following areas are given priority: new information technology, promotion of reading and outreach activity and establishment of workplace libraries. The grants are allocated on a continuous basis during the year.
>
> Government subsidies for purchasing literature for public and school libraries may be applied for by municipalities. The intention of the grant is to increase the availability of literature for children and young people at public and school libraries. It is also meant to stimulate children's and young people's interest in reading books. The grant should be used for purchasing literature for children and young people. The grant totals SEK 25 million.
>
> Government grants for activities that promote reading, mainly for children and young people, may be applied for by schools, libraries, booksellers, societies and other associations. The appropriation is SEK 5 million. From 1999 there is an appropriation of SEK 500,000 for grants to municipal libraries for subscriptions to cultural periodicals.

III. The Digital Revolution

Perhaps the most visible change at the academic libraries is the increase in the number of electronic journals that are available. Almost all academic libraries offer the same packages, due to national consortium buying, so they all provide access to as many as 4500 titles. In some cases these are supplemented by individual electronic titles or smaller packages.

The growth has happened during the last few years: In 1998 the national total of electronic journal subscriptions at academic libraries was 44,000, in 1999 it was 90,000, and in 2000 it was 128,000. The number is still going up.

The effect of this increase in e-journals has been that a "critical mass" of material has been reached which is a prerequisite for stimulating use. And usage statistics are, indeed, high. With increased use we can also see a change in attitude toward preferring electronic access instead of print.

Electronic books have only recently been introduced. Göteborg University library has pioneered this extension of electronic offerings by buying (access) to more than 500 titles from NetLibrary, which also contains some 4000 freely accessible works (with no copyright). A consortium is in the process of being formed for further purchases. The service is still too new to draw conclusions for future developments. There are still many issues unresolved, and the future role for libraries regarding e-books is not entirely clear (Lynch, 2001).

The acquisition of (access to) e-journals has mostly been done in consortia, the largest being on the national level (e.g., Springer, Academic Press, and Elsevier). In spite of the fact that the consortium consisted of practically all academic libraries in Sweden it was not possible to obtain price discounts; the commercial publishers could not be made to bend from their position "the same money as before with a little increase." So the cost for the libraries has been based on what they have bought in the past. The positive side of this deal is that all participating libraries get access to the combined holdings of the consortium (in the Elsevier case some 1100 titles).

The national consortium deals for e-journals have been bargains for the libraries at the university colleges which had very few subscriptions, and consequently gained access to a large number of titles for very little money. For the large university libraries the effect has been that they are locked at a very high spending level which is increasing at five times the inflation rate. Obviously this situation is not stable when funds for acquisitions are not increasing.

Commercial publishers are still avoiding meeting their real consumers ("end users") in a market situation; for them a more profitable strategy is to collect money via libraries. Examples of point purchases directly by users are probably growing, but as long as the "pay-per-view or item" model is not widely applied the bulk of the traffic will go via libraries.

The uncertainty regarding long-term economics has contributed to continued renewal of print subscriptions (in addition to the electronic). Some university libraries have a policy of cancelling print subscriptions for e-titles, but many do this very selectively. In 2000 the national total for print subscriptions was 150,000, which actually is an increase from the year before (135,000).

To an increasing extent materials produced at universities, such as dissertations and reports, are being distributed as Web resources, mostly on the library's pages. Concerns over copyright issues have made the transition to electronic full texts slower than technology permits. The experience at Lund University Library, however, shows that it can be relatively easy to secure permission to reissue previously printed articles as part of the dissertations database (for dissertations that contain such material). Some researchers are still hesitant to "go electronic only" since they are worried about the merit of electronic publications.

Digitization of historical material is another activity that is becoming a part of the digital library. A number of projects are in progress, or have been completed, at the Royal Library and at academic libraries. A couple of examples will illustrate this. At Göteborg University library the subject for digitization are the archives of the Swedish East India Company (in operation 1731–1813) (http://www.ub.gu.se/samlingar/handskrift/ostindie/) and at Lund University Library there is a project for digitizing medieval manuscripts (http://www.lub.lu.se/ub/handskrift/index.html).

For public libraries it is also true that the "virtual library" is a reality: many of the service offerings of the library can be delivered on the Web, such as identifying interesting works, ordering items, and renewing loans. A case in point is the Stockholm Public Library, which has about 18,000 visits to its Web site per week, which is about the same as the number of physical visits.

Several public libraries (e.g., Nacka and Stockholm) have started a service to circulate electronic books.

And perhaps most important: public libraries are providing Internet access to groups that otherwise would not have that possibility.

IV. Cooperation and Integration of Library Sectors

In the Library Law (of 1997) the government gave all libraries in Sweden the task of being the backbone for a national infrastructure for information and knowledge, and for making our cultural heritage available. All libraries must make their collections available free of charge to any and all categories of users. Furthermore it is stated that "county libraries, loan centers, academic and government funded research libraries shall cooperate with public and school libraries to give patrons a high quality library service."

The present library scene in Sweden gives several examples of cooperation and coordination between different library sectors, and these all contribute to bringing the different library sectors closer to each other.

Just recently we saw the origin of a common professional organization for libraries and librarians: the Swedish Library Association (Svensk biblioteksförening) is a merger of the professional society for university and research librarians (SBS) and the association for public libraries and librarians (SAB).

The education of librarians is no longer oriented toward specific library sectors; all educational programs (at Borås, Lund, Umeå, and Uppsala) give a broad academic education leading to a M.Sc. degree. Graduates are prepared for work in all library sectors, as well as other types of information work.

Integration of school libraries with public libraries is common and the phenomenon is increasing. Unfortunately the motive has often been to save costs, so the potential for cross-fertilization has not been fulfilled.

In some places the libraries of university colleges are merged with the public library, for example on Gotland and in Härnösand. In Karlstad and Norrtalje there are also cooperative programs between academic and public libraries. On the regional level there are a number of cooperative projects to make pooled resources available on the Web (for example Kunskapsporten [The Knowledge Gate] in Scania, and Kunskapsnät [Knowledge Network] in Sörmland).

On the national level probably the most important project is the joining of the two national union catalogs into a common search interface. It is LIBRIS, the union catalog for research libraries, and BURK, the union catalog for public libraries, which will be made available for simultaneous searching. The service opened in September 2001 at www.bibliotek.se.

Another cross-sectorial activity which deserves mention is the ALM Group (in Swedish ABM), an informal forum for joint consultation between archives, libraries, and museums.

It was initiated by BIBSAM in 1991 with the aim of identifying and promoting cooperation between institutions in the three sectors covered by the Group. The main focus was, and is, on simplifying cross-sectoral information provision, on the basis of the new and expanded possibilities offered by modern information technology.

One of the most important projects resulting from the Group's work deals with the creation of a common national authority file for corporate names, topographic names, and names of persons. However, it is important to point out that the Group itself neither funds nor administers any projects. Its role is in the conception, delivery, and supervision of projects." (From BIBSAM's Web site.)

Furthermore there is a project in progress on "Image Databases and Digitisation—Platform for ALM Collaboration." This is a joint project between the Royal Library, Nationalmuseum, the National Heritage Board, and the National Archives of Sweden. An English version of the Web pages is announced to be available at http://www.kb.se/ABM_plattform/Default_Projektet.htm.

With a continuous convergence in the form and technology for library, archive, and museum materials, initiatives such as these will become even more important in the future.

References

BIBSAM (2001). ALM consultation, http://www.kb.se/bibsam/english/alm/first.htm (accessed August 3).

Ericsson, Acke (1995). Ett bildat folk—de högskolestuderande och folkbiblioteken. The Swedish National Council for Cultural Affairs, Report 1995:1.

Lynch, Clifford (2001). The battle to define the future of the book in the digital world. *First Monday* 6, June, http://firstmonday.org/issues/issue6_6/lynch/index.html.

Statens kulturräd: Kulturstatistik, http://www.kur.se (accessed August 3, 2001).

Links

The Adult Education Initiative, http://www.kunskapslyftet.gov.se/english/index.htm.

BIBSAM—the Royal Library's Department for National Co-ordination and Development, http://www.kb.se/bibsam/english/first.htm.

Göteborg University Library, Project for digitizing the archives of the Swedish East India Company, http://www.ub.gu.se/samlingar/handskrift/ostindie/.

Guidelines for interlibrary lending (ILL) and document delivery in Sweden, http://www.kb.se/bibsam/english/ill/guidelines.htm.

Image Databases and Digitisation—platform for ALM Collaboration (cooperative project), http://www.kb.se/ABM_plattform/Default_Projektet.htm.

Kunskapsnat Sörmland, http://lib.oxelosund.net/libsok/.

Kunskapsporten, Skäne, http://www.lub.lu.se/kunskapsporten/.

Lund University Library, project for digitizing medieval manuscripts, http://www.lub.lu.se/ub/handskrift/index.html.

The National Agency for Education, http://www.skolverket.se/english/index.shtml.

Nilsson, Kjell: Co-ordination of license agreements in Sweden http://www.kb.se/bibsam/dbupphdl/arkiv/pp/budapest.htm.

The Swedish National Council for Cultural Affairs (Statens kulturräd), http://www.kur.se/.

The Humanities Computing Center and Library Collaboration in New Scholarly Communication Processes

Jennifer Vinopal
Bobst Library
New York University
New York, New York 10012

I. The Digital Revolution and the Library

A. Questioning Libraries and the Academy

It is commonplace now to say that the digital revolution is changing the nature of librarianship and the role of the library in higher education, and thus creating new challenges for librarians. Even a partial list of recent concerns is daunting: new pricing schemes for electronic content, asynchronous and synchronous distance services, the growing use of metadata, the rising cost of serials, the transition from "just-in-case" to "just-in-time" (and even "just-for-you") collecting, the effect of licensing restrictions on traditional library services, etc.

While recognizing the challenges posed by our increasing creation, collection, and use of digital resources and the evolving role of the library in the academy, most experts reassure us that libraries retain their time-honored mission as collectors and guardians of the information scholars need to do their work. "What scholars want from librarians of the future is not so different from what they have wanted all along—the full range of resources they need to do their work" (American Council of Learned Societies/Council on Library and Information Resources, 1999). "Libraries are and will remain central to the management of scholarly communication for the foreseeable future" (Okerson, 1992). According to the results of a 1998–99 international survey on the role of the academic library in the year 2005, "The primary goal of the library will remain the responsibility for building of collections suitable for its parent institution" (Feret and Marcinek, 1999).

Yet how can this reassurance be reconciled with what we see, statistically, as grave challenges to the centrality of the library's basic services to its academic community: declining gate counts, declining circulation figures, decreasing use of print resources (including stacks collections and print reserves), plus the significant drop nationwide in reference statistics? Plus, when we do communicate with our users, we perceive that their expectations of library services have changed dramatically. However, how to respond is unclear because "we do not really know what university and college administrators and faculty want or expect the library to contribute to the institution's mission" (Troll, 2001).

In other arenas, the importance of the library to the mission of the academy is also being called into question, and librarians and their allies have been put on the defensive. A lecture by Nancy Kranich, Past-President of the American Library Association, was called "Why Do We Still Need Libraries?" The title of a position paper of the Association of College and Research Libraries (ACRL) asks "Do We Need Academic Libraries?" The report takes its title from a question asked in 1999 to library directors at member institutions of the Middle States Commission on Higher Education. The query was prompted by the controversial issue facing the commission of the accreditation of transregional and virtual institutions (Hardesty, 2000). As one can imagine, the ACRL report went on to answer with a firm "yes." As the possibilities of digital technology continue to push the boundaries of our definition of the academy, no part of the academy, no matter how intrinsically valuable we think it, will remain unquestioned.

At the same time, similar challenges to the academy are posed by technophiles and Luddites alike. David F. Noble cautions against "technological fetishism" in the "current mania for distance education" and warns of "the commodification of higher education" (Noble, 1999). On the other hand, John Unsworth, in responding to Sven Birkerts's *The Gutenberg Elegies*, writes about resistance to change and the "electronification of scholarly communication" in the academy, saying "the defenders of traditional academic practices find themselves in strange collusion with both the traditional and the emergent enemies of intellectualism" (Unsworth, 1996). These trends of commodification and anti-intellectualism in the academy hit the humanities particularly hard, as the humanities, more than the sciences and social sciences, are subject to criticism for their irrelevance to "real life."

To think critically about the state of libraries and the academy in the electronic age, it is important to first distinguish the content we supply (knowledge, services, etc.) from how we access or deliver them. And, while it would be naïve to believe that the latter will not in some way affect the former (and vice versa), they should still not be confused or taken one for the other. Doing so often results in overinvesting the medium with a significance that rightfully belongs on the side of the content. The subsequent fetishizing or demonizing of the medium itself inhibits a clear analysis of the content's value. We first need to consider whether, regardless of new methods of delivery, we still believe in the value of the content (knowledge) we provide. Only then can we ask: What is the best way to provide students with what we consider a worthy education?

B. Librarianship: A Job and a Profession

So, too, in the library there is an essential difference between the core mission and goals of our profession (our "content") and the daily jobs we do as librarians in order to deliver the value of our mission to our users. This distinction may seem too obvious to dwell on. However, at work and in the library literature, one often sees a conflation of the two. Librarianship as a profession (like many others) embodies a core set of beliefs or values. The ALA's draft statement on core values lists

> connection of people to ideas; assurance of free and open access to recorded knowledge, information, and creative works; commitment to literacy and learning; respect for the individuality and the diversity of all people; freedom for all people to form, to hold, and to express their own beliefs; preservation of the human record; excellence in professional service to our communities; formation of partnerships to advance these values (ALA Core Values Task Force, 2000).

On the other hand, librarianship as a job is made up of tasks, projects, and services that are physical, time-based manifestations of these core values. Understanding this distinction means not allowing ourselves to be trapped into thinking that, for example, user education equals in-house bibliographic instruction, collection development equals merely buying and storing books and journals, knowledge management equals maintaining the card catalog, and reference assistance is acquired by visiting a reference room and talking to a librarian who sits behind a desk. In these four examples, I purposely chose an obviously outdated equation to make my point. Yet, one can certainly find contemporary examples that fit the equation. The resistance in some quarters to radically rethinking the traditional reference model comes to mind.

Seeing the usefulness of our basic services called into question, some have expressed a desire to secure our jobs in the future by discovering how to better implement those services (through, for example, a better or different use of digital information technologies). However, while it may provide some impetus to understand and adapt usefully to changes in our user community, this rather reactive approach seems to me to be more a symptom of our comfort with the status quo than a real compulsion to understand the evolving relationship between the library and the academy in the first place. If we are concerned about our usefulness to and future role in the academy (and the future of the academy itself), and we believe our core values remain legitimate, our goal should be to discover how to apply those values in ways useful to our users. This we can only do by examining and understanding the changes affecting the academy and our user community's functioning within it.

The role of the librarian has traditionally been limited to assistance with the research process: collecting, organizing, and preserving research materials, providing reference services, teaching bibliographic instruction classes, etc. There is currently widespread interest in reexamining the instructional side of the librarian–faculty relationship (the collaboration of librarians with faculty to improve the information literacy skills of students, supporting the use of classroom technology, and so on) but little parallel investigation of potential librarian roles in the other half of faculty's academic activity: scholarly communication.

In this article, I examine one segment of the academic library's user community—humanists—and one aspect of their intellectual activity within the academy—the scholarly communication process—in order to discover if and how the library can better support this group. (In this study, the term "humanities" will be used in a broad and purposely imprecise sense, to mean the arts, humanities and related disciplines.) I focus specifically on the new challenges and opportunities presented to humanists by digital technology, and provide an overview of the issues involved in establishing a Humanities Computing Center in order to support humanists' needs in this area. Finally, I suggest that, to take on potential new roles in facilitating the humanities scholarly communication process, librarians need to develop new competencies and skills, and the library organization as a whole needs to consider some fundamental changes to adequately support these new responsibilities.

II. The Evolution of Scholarly Communication in the Humanities

A. How Humanities Scholarly Research and Communication Processes Are Changing in an IT Environment

New types and increased availability of information technology resources are having an enormous impact on scholarly research and communication processes. Some of these changes, particularly in the areas of access and budgets, are readily visible and familiar to those working in libraries. A few examples suffice: quick, easy access to catalogs and databases; at colleges and universities with the financial means, the availability to the scholar of "free" digitized primary source materials (be they licensed or locally created); ease of scholarly communication at all levels, from e-mail to Web publishing; wider and faster access to materials through interlibrary loan. Of course, the cost of this digital world (often hidden from the user) belies the "free for all" appearance of library resources: it will cost more money, not less, to publish (and thus will cost more to acquire these materials); money must be made available for the equipment and technical support to enable scholarship; costs of content and delivery mechanisms are prohibitive for many libraries; preservation and archiving add greatly to overhead; etc.

Less obvious to librarians but equally fundamental to the evolution in scholarly communication are the changes in work patterns due to the adoption of information technology. Although the humanities still lag behind the sciences and social sciences in integrating computing into the research process, now, because of the increasing availability of relatively easy-to-use and affordable tools, humanists are becoming more reliant on and comfortable with many different types and applications of this technology. As they see the potential for exploitation in a given context (for example, the growing use of classroom technology for everyday teaching needs), humanities scholars are beginning to understand how this technology can be used to solve their own research problems. And, as more scholars avail themselves of electronic tools to exchange ideas (e-mail and, in particular, scholarly electronic discussion forums such as listservs), they are more likely to come in contact with, be influenced by, and even work more closely with scholars in other disciplines. Humanists' work is becoming more collaborative (or, in some cases, even team-based), and this work has a tendency to be more interdisciplinary. At the same time, scholars are gaining an understanding of methodologies that are different from the ones applied in their own fields, and fields of study are adapting to this cross-fertilization of methods. These changes can be seen in, among other things, curriculum modifications in programs and departments, increased joint faculty appointments, and the growth of interdisciplinary studies in humanities publishing. Although these changes are not entirely due to the digital revolution, the increased availability of IT on campus has helped open the doors to sharing and overlapping among the disciplines.

Many also claim that working with computers in itself has a fundamental impact on the way humanists think about and organize their research. Computers "make explicit what in the past has been done intuitively; the preparation of data in a logical, formalized manner is an intellectually informative task and can reveal types of evidence and questions that would not otherwise have emerged" (Pavliscak *et al.*, 1997). In 1996, John Unsworth suggested that the object of study itself might change due to the new types of research possible using computers.

> [W]e can expect to see increasing interest in editing (including the theory of editing), in bibliographic and textual scholarship, in history, and in linguistic analysis, since these are areas in which the new technology opens up the possibility of re-creating the basic resources of all our activities and providing us with revolutionary tools for working with those

resources. . . . [E]ven at its more formal, more filtered levels, electronic scholarly communication still retains the quality of making present that which was hitherto remote, difficult to access, and generally impossible to recontextualize (Unsworth, 1996).

Technology not only permits new ways of communicating and discovering, it makes possible new forms of presentation. The library literature on
the relationship between scholars and technology focuses almost exclusively
on the *use* of electronic research resources and rarely acknowledges the question of humanists as *creators* of digital material. But while the academy's
emphasis is still primarily on the print monograph in the humanities, more
and more academic publications are documenting an increasing interest in
the idea of humanists as producers of digital materials or "e-projects." These
new genres of communication and publishing look remarkably different from
their print counterparts.

B. What Might New Scholarly Communication in the Humanities Look Like?

Scholarly communication must not be confused with scholarly publishing,
the latter being only a part of the former. Christine Borgman defines scholarly communication as "the study of how scholars in any field . . . use and disseminate information through formal and informal channels. [It] includes the
growth of scholarly information, the relationships among research areas
and disciplines, the information needs and uses of individual user groups, and
the relationships among formal and informal methods of communication"
(Borgman, 2000, p. 414). In an IT environment, the more traditionally
hidden (or nonpublishing) aspects of scholarly communication—personal
communications, for instance—could potentially be integrated more easily
into new forms of scholarly publishing.

Stanley Chodorow offers one view of the future:

> While the traditional system of communication included private and public discourse . . .
> the electronic environment unites and mixes these types and stages of communication. The
> use of the Web can put a private communication into the public domain. The publication
> of research results on the Web can be the basis for a set of comments and links to other
> results created by the participants in the research field. An electronic record of scholarship
> could grow organically as scholars make contributions to a database or to a series of linked
> databases that evolve as the collective work progresses" (Chodorow, 2000, pp. 90–91).

Robert Darnton's now famous model of what he calls the e-monograph
combines a similar collection of heterogeneous yet related elements, both
public and private:

> I think it possible to structure it in layers arranged like a pyramid. The top layer could be
> a concise account of the subject, available perhaps in paperback. The next layer could

contain expanded versions of different aspects of the argument, not arranged sequentially as in a narrative, but rather as self-contained units that feed into the topmost story. The third layer could be composed of documentation, possibly of different kinds, each set off by interpretative essays. A fourth layer might be theoretical or historiographical, with selections from previous scholarship and discussions of them. A fifth layer could be pedagogic, consisting of suggestions for classroom discussion and a model syllabus. And a sixth layer could contain readers' reports, exchanges between the author and the editor, and letters from readers, who could provide a growing corpus of commentary as the book made its way through different groups of readers (Darnton, 1999).

It is interesting to note that Darnton's model also capitalizes on the interdependence of research and teaching and is an example of how these two scholarly activities are, according to some, becoming less and less distinct in a digital environment.

Clifford Lynch identifies other new genres of scholarly communication not addressed by Chodorow and Darnton: network-based distributed seminars; collaborative research environments (or "collaboratories") that also document the research and knowledge creation process in order for them to be stored, reviewed, replayed, and annotated; instructional media systems; and Web sites as monographs and encyclopedias (Lynch, 1999).

Some scholarly publishing ventures are currently realizing visions such as Chodorow and Darnton suggest above, most notably the ACLS and Andrew W. Mellon Foundation's History E-Book Project (http://www.historyebook.org/) and Gutenberg-e (http://www.theaha.org/prizes/gutenberg/), a joint venture of the Mellon Foundation, the American Historical Association, and Columbia University Press. In their effort to encourage experimentation with technology use in the humanities, both projects have as one of their goals the exploration of new methods and models for presenting scholarly knowledge in electronic form. They intend to look at issues such as alternative publishing models, the possible size and scope of such a publication, peer review, editing and production, types of content (e.g., inclusion of primary as well as secondary source materials), and the use and value of new forms of scholarship to the field.

C. Disincentives to the Adoption of Digital Technology in the Humanities

Although these well-funded projects offer potential models for future electronic publishing, and despite the growing exploitation in the humanities of ever more available technology, we mustn't underestimate the disincentives in the academy to the widespread adoption of digital technology in the humanities. The problems outlined in this section are particularly acute in those fields, which, unlike the sciences and more quantitative social sciences, don't have an extensive tradition of computer use in research and scholarly communication. One result of this disparity of IT use is that the institutional expectations of and commitment to supporting humanists' computing needs is much lower.

The authors of the 1997 ACLS report entitled "Information Technology in Humanities Scholarship" are careful in their discussion not to "give the impression that computer-based research in the humanities is thriving" (Pavliscak *et al.*, 1997). In summarizing a 1998 U.K. study by the Arts and Humanities Data Service (AHDS) investigating "mechanisms for encouraging greater scholarly exploitation of information technologies and digital resources within the arts and humanities," Greenstein and Porter list in descending order of usage the digital information objects arts and humanities scholars are using. The first four are discovery and research resources: reference, secondary, and primary resources, and mixed media materials. In fifth place are "IT applications as a means of creating new kinds of information objects and artifacts (e.g. historical or archaeological simulations, digital art or performance pieces, etc.)" (Greenstein and Porter, 1998, pp. 147, 151).

Disincentives to the adoption of digital technology in the humanities come in a variety of forms and from a wide range of sources, and the academic literature on the question has identified impediments as well as possible solutions. Academic institutions themselves take the brunt of the blame here, as they are in the ultimate position to facilitate or inhibit change within the academy. Without the encouragement and support of the institutions on which academics depend for their living, scholars are unlikely to risk exploring new methods of scholarly communication.

Where will the resources come from? Humanists need equipment, technical support, training, and time to learn and create. Access to computing and communications resources is less automatic for humanists than for computer scientists (American Council of Learned Societies, 1998), and this problem is even more acute for humanists at smaller institutions without the financial means of larger research universities. Typical project funding tends to be too short-term for the type of learning and work needed to create a digital project, and humanists, because of the nature of their research subjects, tend to be less able to leverage a commercial base than their science counterparts (American Council of Learned Societies, 1998). And whereas first-wave adopters of technology are usually self-taught experimenters, second-wave users will most certainly need even more encouragement, training, time, and ongoing support and services to make this transition.

The assessment and reward structure in the academy (tenure, promotion, raises, grants, awards) also discourages innovation. Uncertainty about peer review or other indicators of quality of the digital scholarly object creates a credibility problem for the scholar whose work relies heavily on information technology. How does a tenure committee, often composed of faculty unfamiliar with new technologies, assess the value of an electronic scholarly work created without a traditional peer-review process? A 1992 Mellon report recognized that "[a]ny new system will have to satisfy scholarly and institutional leaders that it is adequately peer reviewed and reliable before new types of publications can be rewarded. Until assurances of such rewards are in place, faculty will be reluctant to put their best work in new forms" (Okerson, 1992). Randy Bass is an unusual example in the humanities for having received tenure at Georgetown with a résumé based in large part on work with new media technologies. In his 1999 plenary address to the American Association for Higher Education Forum on Faculty Roles and Rewards, he acknowledged that models for the successful negotiation of tenure based on electronic publishing are extremely rare. He introduced himself to the audience simply by stating "my primary qualification for addressing you today is that I'm still employed" (Bass, 1999).

Among others, the ACLS has also recognized that the lack of reward structure for innovation in the humanities has an added impact on new methods of scholarly investigation: "cross-disciplinary work is viewed with skepticism by many in academia, who fear that such work will not be rewarded comparably to intradisciplinary work, and that work involving development and implementation of systems may be stunted because of insufficient support for specialized implementation staff, documentation, evaluation, and other essential complements to the core intellectual work" (American Council of Learned Societies, 1998). Also, the creation of scholarly resources using digital technology, particularly in the absence of good publishing models, will require substantially more time than the average project destined for print publication and, in some cases, there may be no measurable outcome from such experimentation (Duffy and Owen, 1998, p. 184).

Thus, the status quo is remarkably attractive to humanists, especially untenured faculty. And ironically, younger academics who, more and more, are closer to or part of the generation weaned on information technology are the ones for whom this type of experimentation is most discouraged. Willard McCarty observed that "advances, such as the great Dartmouth Dante Database, have been made by senior academics, who can afford to take the risks incurred by investing significant time in such a new way of working. Their achievements are most admirable, but since they tend not to need anyone's permission, the basic institutional commitment tends not to be made" (McCarty, 1998).

Scholarly societies have a part to play in encouraging scholars and academic institutions to favorably view research using and creating electronic resources. The MLA, for instance, has sessions at its annual conference on humanities computing and has issued guidelines regarding faculty work and digital resources: *Guidelines for Evaluating Work with Digital Media in the Modern Languages* (Modern Language Association: Committee on Information Technology, 2001a); *Guidelines for Institutional Support of and Access to IT for Faculty Members and Students* (Modern Language Association: Committee on Information Technology, 2001b); and *Revision Plan for the Guidelines for Scholarly Editions of the Committee on Scholarly Editions* (Modern Language Association: Committee on Scholarly Editions, 2001). These types of statements by scholarly societies, in conjunction with a commitment to address the problem of peer review and quality assurance (like that attempted with the History E-Book project and Gutenberg-e, discussed earlier) may yet have an effect on the reward structure in the academy.

Additionally, in order for computing in the humanities to flourish, scholars also need more information about standards and best practices, and examples of successful projects in their research areas. They need to become familiar with the world of digital resources in their subject area, to consult with colleagues and with other computing experts to plan and carry out their ideas, and to learn from others' mistakes. And, if they want their digital research resources to have a longevity and usefulness outside of their own immediate needs, they have to be able to design resources that can potentially interact with other like projects, which means an additional emphasis on cooperation and conformity with other projects out there in the world. Although there are already good national and international mechanisms for sharing information on digital projects—such as the Digital Library Federation (DLF) and the National Initiative for a Networked Cultural Heritage (NINCH)—academic institutions still need to provide the infrastructure and support to facilitate this sharing of information.

D. Some Solutions

Sarah Porter creates a four-tiered model of support that arts and humanities scholars require before they can effectively exploit digital technology in their research and scholarly communication: information (about resources, their creation and use, etc.), training, high-quality data resources, and a reward structure offering professional incentives to use or create digital resources in research and teaching (Porter, 1998, pp. 193–194).

Some academic institutions are addressing these needs by incorporating humanities computing into their curricula. An increasing number of schools are modifying or creating positions within "traditional" humanities departments that incorporate humanities computing into the job descriptions. Other institutions (particularly in the United Kingdom) are addressing these needs by making humanities computing a discipline in its own right as part of the humanities curriculum at the college and graduate level. Willard

McCarty makes the case that humanities computing—what he calls the *yenta* among disciplines—should become part of the academy because of its fundamental interdisciplinarity and what, methodologically and even philosophically, it can offer the other disciplines.

> The fundamental pragmatic reason for locating humanities computing within the institution as an interdisciplinary scholarly activity in its own right is rooted in the fact that from the computational perspective of data and explicit procedures, the arts and humanities overlap methodologically to a very high degree. Humanities computing reveals a substantial common ground of technique from which to address research and teaching problems across the disciplines. . . . Humanities computing is by nature in everyone else's business, and thus a communal instrument for the probing and strengthening of community (McCarty, 1998).

As a program of study, humanities computing can address all four needs mentioned by Porter: information (about resources, their creation and use, etc.), training, high-quality data resources, and reward structure. The curriculum provides the information and training, and outcomes of such study would be the creation of high-quality resources. That the field of humanities computing is, in some quarters, being recognized as such and included in some universities as an academic discipline is a step along the road toward an improved reward structure for this type of scholarly activity.

III. New Roles for Librarians in the Humanities Scholarly Communication Process

A. The Humanities Computing Center

Humanities computing is, by its very nature, a collaborative activity. Practically, no matter how well trained, funded, and connected a scholar is, she will need the help of others, both on campus and off, to realize her project. In order to create a welcoming environment for humanities computing activities, the institution needs to make ongoing and perhaps dedicated services available to humanities scholars, and to encourage the collaboration necessary for these types of projects. As they are already in the business of providing information services, two natural partners for such collaboration include campus computing units and libraries. Other potential partners include the scholar's own department or others in the institution, computer scientists, software developers, other ongoing scholarly projects, university presses, and national agencies.

How can university units whose mission it is to promote and support the use of IT on campus work to address some of the disincentives to the development of humanities computing outlined earlier? Is it appropriate for the library to take on a collaborative role in the humanities scholarly communication process? There is precedent for librarians working with faculty in the area of scholarly communication. Librarians helped to create the SPARC initiative, "a worldwide alliance of research institutions, libraries and organizations that encourages competition in the scholarly communications market" (SPARC, 2001). Librarians have been instrumental in this effort to counter the trend of ever-higher journal pricing and the SPARC effort has thus been able to provide scholars with alternative, high-quality scholarly publishing venues.

James Neal, Columbia University Vice President for Information Services and University Librarian, encourages entrepreneurship and innovation in the academic library, which he sees as

> both a historical archive and a learning and research collaboratory. . . . Academic libraries will become centers for research and development in the application of technology to information creation and use. They will become aggregators and publishers, and not just consumers of scholarly information. They will function as campus hubs for working with faculty on the integration of technology and electronic resources into teaching and research.

And he adds: "The framework for academic library participation in the learning and scholarly communication processes must be rethought, and new structures for promoting library partnerships with faculty are essential" (Neal, 2001, pp. 1–2, 7).

As noted in Section I, the role of the librarian has traditionally been limited to assistance with the research process—collecting, organizing, and preserving research materials, and providing reference services. In order to take on the new entrepreneurial and collaborative responsibilities imagined by Neal, librarians will have to learn to think of themselves as true partners and even, in some cases, as agents of change in the scholarly communication process (the SPARC initiative being a good example). This will be a difficult mindset to adopt for a profession that has tended to perceive its role as properly reactive to the needs of the users it serves. And it will take strong leadership to create an environment in which current roles and services can be thoroughly questioned and new ways for the library to carry out its mission can be imagined, tested, and implemented.

Libraries are, in fact, particularly well suited to partner with humanists interested in incorporating information technology into their scholarly communication activities. Of Porter's four areas of support needed to encourage arts and humanities computing—information, training, high-quality data resources, and a reward structure—libraries can and do contribute directly to the first three already. Our core values as librarians—connection of people to ideas, free access to information and knowledge, a commitment to learning—apply here even as the research and publishing environment we work in evolves. In order for librarians to take on new roles as collaborators and even agents of change, we need to better understand what we can bring to collaborative work in humanities computing and how to prepare ourselves for this work.

Humanities computing can occur in many places and in many ways: on the scholar's office or home computer, in a departmental lab, via e-mail, using commercial or home-grown resources or a combination of both, or on or off a network. It can involve using previously existing resources, repurposing other digital materials, digitizing analog resources, or creating entirely new research materials. But how can a scholar imagining a potential project find the breadth of information and tools needed to plan and realize a viable, functioning, and durable digital resource? On more and more campuses, university support for humanities computing is manifested in the creation of a Humanities Computing Center (HCC), where "scholars use computing tools in the pursuit of their research (e.g., text analysis), and in creating new scholarly and artistic works (musical compositions, thesauri, scholarly editions, etc.)" (Jerome McDonough, personal communication, July 2001). The HCC consolidates many disparate resources and services, providing equipment, materials, staff expertise, and knowledge in one location. They can provide a solution to the "treasure hunt" many scholars experience when seeking information and support for their IT needs.

HCCs vary considerably in their mission and goals, the equipment and services offered, location on campus, the ability of staff to support faculty projects, the number of projects that can be handled at a time, the involvement of the staff in national or international initiatives, and so on. Differences are dependent on such factors as budget, staffing, equipment, the facility's mandate, reporting lines, ongoing university or division-wide administrative support, and even intangibles such as how the facility has evolved over time because of use, which subset of the potential user community actually avails itself of the facility, or the types of projects being done. However, all HCCs function within a network of preexisting campus IT and information services, and most benefit greatly from collaboration with these units.

To supplement the scant professional literature on the question of potential roles for librarians in an HCC, I spoke to six professionals in the area of scholarly computing to determine what practitioners in the field thought about the ways librarians are working to facilitate scholarly communication in the electronic environment. Though my goal in this article is to focus on the humanities, a broader approach to information gathering on this topic is beneficial in order to put ideas about computing and scholarly communication in other disciplines at the disposal of those interested in supporting and encouraging computer use in the humanities. I therefore did not limit my interviews solely to people involved in humanities computing. The last part of this article makes extensive use of ideas and quotes from my conversations with Sayeed Choudhury (Hodson Director, Digital Knowledge Center, Sheridan Libraries, Johns Hopkins University); Jim Duncan (Coordinator, Information Commons & Electronic Services, Hardin Library for the Health Sciences, The University of Iowa); Carol Hughes (Director, Collections Management, Questia Media, Inc., formerly Interim Director, Information and Research Services, The University of Iowa); Ron Jantz (Data Librarian, Alexander Library, Rutgers University); Jerome McDonough (Digital Library Development Team Leader, Elmer Holmes Bobst Library, New York University); and Daniel Pitti (Project Director, Institute for Advanced Technology in the Humanities, Alderman Library, University of Virginia).

B. What Librarians Bring to the Table

There was a high level of agreement among the interviewees and the pertinent articles regarding the core areas of librarians' knowledge that are most useful in partnering on scholarly computing projects. Although librarians are not necessarily unique in possessing many of these skills, their education and training emphasize and inculcate these qualities as the very foundation of the profession. They fall into four general categories that represent knowledge of and concern with people, materials, access, and the wider scholarly perspective.

Librarians have a public service training and perspective and tend to have good communication skills. Their training and experience in the reference interview allow them to tease out details about the researcher's needs, and their understanding of user behaviors—how users search, access and use resources—enables librarians to select and use print or electronic materials appropriately in response to users' research needs. They are also familiar with pedagogical methods and have experience teaching.

Librarians also have a good understanding of the relationship of print to electronic resources and the unique advantages and disadvantages of each. They apply their knowledge of preservation and archiving to both the print and, increasingly, the electronic world. In addition, librarians have a great concern for questions of access: indexing, searchability, knowledge organization and representation, and the selection of materials, regardless of format, that are appropriate for the library's user community.

Our considerable experience in both the information and scholarly worlds is a valuable combination for the academic community we serve. We have an understanding of current library operations and the general library landscape, we take the long view on information creation, organization, and storage, and we are deeply concerned with and knowledgeable about issues of copyright, intellectual property, and fair use. In addition, as specialists ourselves in the scholarly disciplines in which we work, we can combine our understanding of the research methods and scholarly communication processes within a field of study with our knowledge of the world of research materials and processes, and, in particular, the digital projects and developments in that discipline.

Despite the wealth of knowledge and experience the library has to offer, in a digital world it is no longer reasonable to expect that the library will be able by itself to support all of the research needs of the institution. We are becoming more and more open to and dependent upon intrauniversity partnering with other units to accomplish new initiatives. Lippincott has observed that the increasingly networked information environment has had an effect on the relationships between librarians and information technologists, with a "move towards shared responsibility in conceptualization of projects, authority, [and] allocation of resources" (Lippincott, 1996). The usefulness of collaboration between libraries and campus computing units is so evident that many campuses are increasing collaboration across the board or, in some cases, even merging the units. Such reorganization may take at least three forms: administrative realignment of reporting and budgetary lines, collaborative realignment to provide greater working-level linkages, or blending realignment of the two units into a single, cohesive information services division (Dougherty and McClure, 1997).

C. What Do Collaborating Parties Stand to Gain?

Collaboration brings both difficulties and rewards of its own. Kate Nevins, in an article entitled "Partnerships and Competition," outlines some of the difficulties encountered when libraries partner with nonlibrary organizations. She says we're not accustomed to it; we don't all necessarily share common goals, values and culture; we can't assume that our partners don't compete with libraries or (if there are several partners) with each other; and we don't have the established infrastructure for working with nonlibrary partners (Nevins, 1997). Tensions often exist among campus partners with different cultures, for example, charging for services, different academic credentials of staff, different salary structures, differences in stature and status in the academic community, or the question of who will manage the information resources (Woodsworth, 1998, p. 30). There are also "different attitudes towards change, different levels of technological expertise, lack of understanding of the skills of other participants, [a] desire to control one's own resources, [and] the budget process" (Lippincott, 1996).

Benefits include the two units working together to stave off declining levels of support, develop user-oriented services, sustain growth and develop information and network services, get and share resources, negotiate with vendors (minimize cost and maximize access), coordinate the management of various units responsible for the information technologies on campus, find space on campus for workstations, and measure effectiveness of computing and information services (Woodsworth, 1998, p. 29). Other incentives include shared resources, expertise, ideas, and synergies, making new connections, and the creation of a critical mass (of people, expertise, resources, etc.), allowing libraries to do in partnership what they couldn't do alone (Nevins, 1997).

Two or more organizations or divisions pooling resources will, given a healthy and cooperative partnership, accomplish more than any one individually. Whether the HCC is a stand-alone unit on campus or a collaborative creation of preexisting units, in order to provide a high level of support to projects and grow with changes in technology, standards, and user need, it will by necessity be a place dependent on collaborative relationships within and outside of the institution. There are also significant implications for funding. For example, outside funding, often hard to come by for humanities projects, may be easier to attract when projects are realized collaboratively. Mary Shaw, of Carnegie Mellon University, observed that "there is a scale of funding in technology that, if we thought carefully and creatively, might admit an incremental funding for collaborative projects that could leverage the technology developments. Assuming genuine collaborations rather than shotgun weddings, this could provide a quite respectable level of funding for the humanities partner as an add-on to a large project" (American Council of Learned Societies, 1998). Here Shaw is talking specifically about humanities partnering with larger, better-funded computer science projects, but the same argument can be applied to partnerships among humanities projects: smaller projects joining other larger, well-established, and better-funded projects can leverage off of the experience and reputation of the larger partner. Such collaborations, often involving partners from outside the academic institution, need to be forged, negotiated, and realized with the assistance of local expertise. The Humanities Computing Center could be the ideal locus for such planning.

All interviewees agreed that on-campus collaboration is a fundamental way of accomplishing a digital project. Common on-campus partners in such a center are campus computing, libraries, and interested faculty (who may, for example, sit on a center's planning or advising committee). Other units that may have an ongoing or occasional affiliation include TV and media services, other computing centers, and interested departments or individuals. Each campus unit has its own area of expertise that it can bring to bear on a digital project, and the needs of each project will, of course, determine the nature of the collaboration formed to accomplish it. Jerome McDonough says: "The range of projects supported by HCCs is too extensive to make blanket pronouncements. The type of support required by one project might best be supplied by librarians; on another project, you may need significant technology support that would be better supplied by members of an IT staff." While there will be some commonalities among most projects, in this model, where partners and processes change depending on the needs of the individual project, the partnering relationship remains a work in progress. To be successful, this requires a great deal of flexibility within the administrative structure of the facility and a high level of communication among partners in the facility and on the project itself.

The scholarly materials themselves may provide the impetus to partner in nontraditional ways. Libraries are filled with the stuff that scholarly research is made of. Important archival source materials, frequently only available for in-library consultation, may be made available for digitization and thus integration into a scholar's digital project if it is a collaborative project between the library and the faculty member. The library benefits, too, as it can leverage its special collections in order to be included in interesting and potentially well-funded and high-profile digitization projects seeking to use those materials. And, with the right planning and care, the library's research collections could be enhanced by incorporating the digital content produced by its partners. Greenstein says: "That content has enormous educational and cultural value, but only if it is assembled into professionally managed collections, maintained over time, and made meaningfully accessible to other end users through online portal and other services." Additionally, some user communities "may be in a position to supply tools to a digital library service environment that can enhance that environment's functionality." As libraries invest more and more in digital library collections and services, "there will be significant pressure to measure performance and value of investment in terms of use. By engaging with user communities more effectively, libraries can inform investment decisions by anticipating their potential benefits (and beneficiaries, where some financial return on investment is sought)" (Greenstein, 2000, pp. 296–297).

D. Collaboration Changes Processes and Products

In discussing the location of the Institute for Advanced Technology in the Humanities (IATH) in the library, Daniel Pitti said that, despite the fact that it doesn't report administratively to the library, ". . . putting all of these people near one another fostered a great deal of collaboration and mutual support between them, especially as they began to build up and share expertise. Even though the models were different [between the units], there were certainly a lot of the same computer skills and understanding that were shared." Pitti goes on to describe the collaboration itself as an evolving thing that needs to be negotiated carefully by the parties involved. "We suddenly find that we really have to get much closer and work much more closely with one another, but that this is a completely new thing and we don't really know how to do it because we've never had to work quite this intimately with one another. So we're beginning to negotiate how to do that and to work out the politics of it on one hand, but also to work out what the standards requirements and systems requirements are on the other. But in the process of the negotiation, some functions that might have been done by one of those communities may in fact be taken over by others. The activities and functions could move between those groups as we work out over time exactly who's going to contribute what and how."

As the nature of collaboration changes—as skill sets grow and responsibilities shift—the nature of what is being collaborated on and its outcomes also change. For example, some libraries and HCCs are beginning to work with faculty and/or university presses to publish and archive the digital projects that have been produced on campus. In some cases, it is libraries that are becoming the "publishers" of homegrown digital projects, with librarians selecting locally created materials appropriate for their collections and the library providing access to that material like any other in its collection. Clifford Lynch warns that "[l]ibraries will need to take a much broader view of how they define the potential universe of materials that are candidates for acquisition and incorporation in their collections." And he adds that "[i]dentifying materials for potential acquisition will require a close, continuing and open-minded dialog and collaboration with working scholars" (Lynch, 1999). Some university presses are also starting to venture into digital publishing. In addition to the academic presses involved in the History E-Book and Gutenberg-e publishing projects, the University of Virginia in October 2001 announced that it will create the first electronic imprint devoted exclusively to publishing original, peer-reviewed digital scholarship in the humanities (not simply electronic versions of print books).

Whatever the model for "publication" followed, these digital projects are, more and more, being brought into the peer-review process of library selection and university press publication, and that means new exigencies regarding a whole range of issues that wouldn't necessarily be important were the project designed as a "one-off" resource. Projects primarily intended to satisfy the individual needs of one scholar alone might tend to be quirky in design, treatment, scope, etc. For projects seeking a broader audience and greater longevity, other design issues need to be addressed: adherence to standards; choice of data formats; archival issues; stabilization of data; scope of project; commitment to a coherent overall design, fit, and perhaps even inter-operability, with the rest of the projects in the field (what David Seaman calls creating projects that "play well with others"); etc. These considerations certainly apply for projects destined to become part of the library collection and maintained "in perpetuity," and project managers will need to collaborate with library staff who have expertise in these areas in order to create data that can be maintained and migrated over time. In addition, the funding implications of such decisions are great. Grant-funding agencies are looking for these issues to be addressed in grant applications to ensure that their money is properly spent on well-designed, stable data that will last.

E. Partnering Relationships

As mentioned earlier, tensions that inhibit healthy partnerships between libraries and campus computing include their different cultures, different academic credentials and salary structures, differences in stature and status in the academic community, different levels of technological expertise, and a lack of understanding of the skills of other participants. However, librarians' training itself can help bridge some of these gaps. As information professionals, librarians' strength lies in what Biddiscombe calls the intermediary problem-solving role, as they "understand how the technology can be used to further the learning experience." He goes on to say, "It is here also that the very qualities demanded of information professionals in the context of the academic community are no less needed in the relationships between the differently qualified professionals in a hybrid team. The open problem-solving approach is equally necessary for effective teamwork in the learning support environment" (Biddiscombe, 2000, p. 78). Over time, team members sharing goals, skills, knowledge, and experiences will make them less dissimiliar and should ease those tensions. In fact, Lippincott recognizes that the traditional division of complementary skills into "content" for librarians and "conduit" for computing professionals is becoming blurred (Lippincott, 1996).

It is undeniable that this blurring of traditional roles and the mutual respect necessary for teamwork in an IT environment cannot be achieved without good communication and an openness to understanding the professional goals and expertise of other partners. However, to be (and to be perceived as) real assets to a team working on digital projects, librarians need to have a better set of computing skills than would otherwise be necessary working in a more traditional—though networked—library setting. Jim Duncan suggests:

One way that the librarians can get credence is for them to get as much expertise as possible in the kinds of technologies that the computing people are already knowledgeable about. I'm not suggesting that librarians become programmers. But it seems to me that one reason that we [at the Information Commons] have been able to play nicely with others in the field here on campus is because we've really proven that we've got technical chops and we've been able to produce some things that are significant and we've earned their respect. . . . And so they naturally think of us as partners now instead of those librarians who are kind of stuck in the mud and focused on text.

(The question of how librarians can improve their technical skills will be the focus of Section IV of this chapter.)

Interviewees had a range of reactions to the question: What is the nature of the relationship between the HCC staff and the scholars they are partnering with in order to accomplish these projects? How the relationships are imagined, formed, and function depends on many things, such as the nature of the facility, the services it provides, and its stated and actual mission. Carol Hughes suggests, "It's not a peer-to-peer collaboration." Staff need to realize that ". . . this is [the scholar's] career, not yours. This is their tenure, this is their class, they're the ones that are really on the line. But in the other sense, it is very much the same kind of collaboration that you got when you approached faculty and talked them into letting you come into their class and do a BI. You tell them what the skills are and what you can add to their curriculum. And so you keep in mind: 'What is it they're trying to teach? What is their main message?'"

For Daniel Pitti, how this relationship is defined depends on the mission of the organization. "The way we [at IATH] like to look at the Institute is that it is collaborative in nature. While it's driven by a particular faculty member's research interest, the intellectual work with respect to designing the system within which they're going to do their research is really done in collaboration with the institute staff and they're functioning as peers with the faculty member. We don't consider ourselves a service bureau as such, but as collaborators."

The scholars using the facility will also bring their own expectations to the partnership, based, in part, on their knowledge about and relationship to the facility itself and its staff. Jim Duncan explains that when planning such a facility, "You need to have faculty involved. It was critical for the success of the [Information] Arcade—the original concept—to have members of various faculty departments involved in casting that vision for what kind of facility would best serve them and I think what that also does is gets you immediate usage from those same faculty. If they feel like they've had what they want translated into reality they will come and use those facilities then." Working together as a team to realize a shared vision can thus promote a feeling of true partnership rather than a client/server relationship.

F. The Location of the Humanities Computing Center

Where on campus should these Humanities Computing Centers be located? While some might consider the library the most logical place for such a facility there is no consensus that this is the best solution. It can be argued that an administrative affiliation of such a center with the library is crucial because of the library's content and its longstanding commitment to pedagogy and research. However, one can also make the case that involvement in this type of scholarly activity has never been and should probably not be the domain of the library. Willard McCarty says:

> Historically at least libraries have not gone beyond the provision of resources, 'electronic books' if you will, to the application of them in the pursuit of knowledge; such is not the role of the library and never has been. . . . I suspect that nearly every library now has an "e-text" or multimedia centre, but as far as the question of this Seminar is concerned, that fact only marks the distinction between humanities computing and the resources with which to do it. I conclude that the library is in general not our natural home (McCarty, 1999).

According to some interviewees, having the HCC only loosely affiliated administratively with the library is a real benefit to the good functioning of the facility itself. According to Daniel Pitti, for such a facility to flourish in a library depends on how well the library's mission, as it is interpreted and carried out by the administration, tolerates a research and development work model and rhythm that differs substantially from the traditional library service model. He suggests that putting it administratively within a library will require not just new librarians but new University Librarians: "IATH, while it resides inside of Alderman Library, is not administratively part of it. We answer directly to the Vice President for Research. And it crosses the University's schools. . . . I think that physically [Humanities Computing Centers] do belong in libraries. Administratively, I'm not quite sure. I would say they do but only if the library culture can be expanded where they can exist within a hospitable environment. But I think it requires a certain amount of shift and accommodation away from traditional assumptions and models that are mass-production oriented and intolerant of research and failure." He compares IATH to the Electronic Text Center at the University of Virginia: "It administratively is within the library and it has much more of a traditional library service model. People come in and then there are people there who help them out and provide a service as such. And the Institute very clearly defines itself as being something different than that. So we have really two entirely different models."

Like IATH, the Scholarly Communication Center at Rutgers is located within a library but reports to the Director of New Brunswick Libraries. The staff at the SCC is given a good deal of latitude in choosing projects and how they accomplish them. Ron Jantz explains, "The Scholarly Communication Center is not involved in any of the real operational issues of either the library or campus computing and to me that is a very significant distinction. What that allows us to do is have quite a bit of freedom in launching new projects, in launching research or technology that might be useful to these digital projects. . . . I believe the end result of this approach is severalfold: new technologies being made available to librarians and the library and new information sources that would not likely have been made available to R.U. and the public." And, echoing Pitti's concern for the time frame and experimentation necessary to realize digital projects, Jantz says, "I think it is very difficult to stimulate innovation when you are in an organization that puts a lot of pressure on dealing with the near-term, immediate problems."

McDonough says: "I don't think it's that important for humanities computing centers to be in or affiliated with libraries. . . . Certainly scholars may draw upon library resources in the course of these efforts, but that doesn't lead to any requirement that HCCs and libraries be bound at the hip. That being said, where HCCs exist on campuses separate from the campus library, it would be a very good idea for librarians to stay in regular contact with those centers to ensure that the materials they provide, both print and digital, are supporting scholars' work within the HCCs. And certainly the public service training and perspective that reference librarians employ in their work transfer well into providing support within a different context such as an HCC. So, while there's no strong reason for HCCs to be in or affiliated with libraries, there's also no strong reason why they shouldn't, and for some campuses, placing HCCs within the library may have benefits such as making noncirculating materials available to scholars within the HCC."

It is obvious at this point that, despite all of the advantages to librarian involvement in digital project creation and in staffing an HCC, the question of the library's ability to be a substantial and ongoing participant in the HCC is murky. Concerns raised earlier about the nature of library administration, its ability to support new work models and time scales for accomplishing projects in the digital realm, and the potential hindrances of restrictive reporting structures, in addition to practical considerations such as librarian release time and the acquisition of new skills, make one wonder about the practicality of really involving librarians in these endeavors.

The issue of library subject specialist participation in a new computing facility came up during the planning process for the University of Michigan's Knowledge Navigation Center in the early 1990s. The question was:

> While the traditional role of library subject specialists as partners in the scholarly process was one role the planning group pointed to time and again as reassurance that a new service unit had an obvious place in the library, it was also the source of one of the greatest challenges. How would such expertise be incorporated in any proposed facility? . . . Lurking in

the background was the obvious question: Would subject specialists be expected to 'put in time' or staff the facility? (MacAdam, 1998, p. 93).

It is not easy for libraries to give over the time and expertise of their staff to new computing endeavors. The Information Arcade is a collaborative effort of the University of Iowa Libraries, the Office of Information Technology, and the academic faculty and is designed to support the use of electronic resources in research, teaching, and independent learning. Libraries deal with content, supporting its selection, installation, use, and also the technical support for equipment located in the Arcade. The OIT manages the hardware and develops multimedia and instructional software (Lowry, 1994). However, the Information Arcade was staffed only with graduate students, and Carol Hughes says the Arcade seemed like ". . . a student-run auxiliary [to the library]. They were separate. If you staff it this way, and you don't have librarians in the facility who are also really integrated into the rest of the library, it becomes this other appendage. . . . So I think it needs to be librarians [staffing such a facility] and it needs to be librarians who are really plugged into the rest of the crowd, and make sure it's not a little fiefdom on the side."

The Digital Knowledge Center at Johns Hopkins partners with the library on projects requiring the special knowledge and expertise of librarians, but the DKC has its own staff to accomplish projects. Sayeed Choudhury explains that in staffing a center, "You need to hire someone who can do *this* job, to manage the types of attributes or characteristics or skills that you're looking for. Don't worry about what the degree is. . . . If you can find a librarian who can do the things you need to do, great, if you can find somebody else, fine. It doesn't really matter at this point. There's a lot of fluidity in terms of people's skill sets and what they can do. . . . I do think that there are plenty of people in the library community who could fit into some of the things we're trying to do. But there are also people who have more non-traditional backgrounds who might be able to fit in. . . . I think the real strength here is bringing in the computer science expertise when it's relevant and when it makes sense and having that rounded out or, if you will, maybe even driven in some cases by the other sorts of skills."

How will librarians participate in the activities of an HCC? As consultants? As staff? Will they be "borrowed" from a campus library or hired outright as employees of the HCC? If staff lines are shared between library and HCC, how will libraries alter work assignments to provide them that release time? How libraries and librarians might be involved in an HCC will depend on whether or not the library is willing and able to redefine how it accomplishes its mission vis-à-vis the academic world. Whatever the model for librarian participation (be it as full-time staff, consultants, through shared staff lines, etc.), what knowledge and skills will librarians need to acquire in order to be conversant with the issues and technology relevant to humanities computing?

IV. Professional Development Issues for Librarians

A. Personality, Knowledge, and Skills

Although it is easy to create a wish list of recommended skills for librarians (or others) wishing to become involved in digital library or scholarly computing work, experts are careful to distinguish between three different types of qualities potential staff might possess: specific computing skills, a broader knowledge of issues and technology in the field, and particular behavioral or personality traits. As the traditional library and the digital library become less and less distinguishable from each other, the emphasis in library want ads is on the latter qualities rather than the former. Kimberley Robles Smith and Beverly P. Lynch compared library job advertisements appearing in *College & Research Libraries News* for the month of March in 1983, 1988, 1993, and 1998. They concluded that recently "there was no tendency . . . to list numerous computer skills across the board. The most consistent computer related skills were broad and general. . . . The requirement of behavioral traits also increased with time in these jobs. The earliest data emphasize skills, not behaviors . . ." (Robles Smith and Lynch, 1999, p. 269).

Their findings support Roy Tennant's suggestion that in hiring staff to work in a digital library environment, it is best to emphasize personality traits over skills. As change is the only constant, "it may be more productive to choose staff who can evolve as the needs of the organization change." Tennant suggests qualities to look for include a capacity to learn constantly and quickly, flexibility, skepticism, a propensity to take risks, a public service perspective, the ability to work with others, skill at enabling and fostering change, and the capacity and desire to work independently. And he states that "[a]nyone who exhibits [these traits] will be able to pick up whatever skill or experience is deemed necessary" (Tennant, 1998, p. 102).

Jim Duncan concurs and explains that when hiring staff for the Information Commons, "[w]hat I look for as a common thread is not that they already know the tools but that they have a sense of pedagogy, of scholarly communication processes, teaching, learning, user services . . . those are the kinds of things I can't teach them because that's just exhaustive and some people just will never pick that up. But if they've already got those skills we can teach them the tools. We can expose them to the variety of technologies and media and then they start to apply those deeper lessons they've learned through their academic careers and they see the connection with the tools and then they start coming up with some very interesting ideas."

Most interviewees and the relevant literature also emphasize the importance of having a familiarity with some of the broad knowledge areas pertinent to digital project work. These areas include a familiarity with intellectual property law, issues in electronic publishing, graphic and instructional design, the various media types (how they interact and can be delivered to the user), usability, cataloging and metadata, information retrieval, appropriate data and metadata standards for digital materials, and project management (including managing quality assurance).

As for specific skills, Tennant suggests staff have experience in imaging technologies, optical character recognition, indexing and database technology, programming, and Web technology. Other recommended basic computing skills include basic programming, basic markup languages, the basics of database design, and experience with digitization and multimedia technologies. Most often, however, these basic skills were considered important not in and of themselves, but because the specific information gleaned is generalizable to other situations. For example, though you may have no intention of ever becoming a programmer, taking a basic programming course to learn a structured programming language enables you to understand what computers can and cannot do, to know how much work is involved in making them do a particular task, and to communicate to a programmer the needs of the project at hand.

In addition, it is important to know about developments in scholarly communication and to keep up with what's happening in business, industry, and entertainment. Duncan suggests going to conferences not usually attended by librarians, such as Comdex, the Apple Worldwide Developers Conference, and Web publishing conferences. "I think it's valuable to see what's happening out in the industry and in entertainment, in business, and then take those lessons and bring them back to the library and figure out how we can run our own kinds of services, create our own kinds of materials, using those same kinds of tools and techniques." Choudhury recommends joining organizations such as the Association for Computing Machinery's special interest group on Computer–Human Interaction, which offers listservs, publications, and conferences.

The curricula of humanities computing programs provide an excellent idea of the nature and combination of skills and knowledge necessary for work in the field. Like the distinction among skills, knowledge, and personality traits discussed earlier, programs differ in the way they balance these factors. While some place heavier emphasis on the acquisition of technical skills, others take a more theoretical approach. For example, the University of Alberta's M.A. in Humanities Computing offers courses such as project design and management, computers and culture, knowledge management and analysis, computer tools for humanities teaching and learning, and multimedia for the humanities (University of Alberta, 2001). The Centre for Computing in the Humanities, King's College London, offers a B.A. minor and postgraduate classes in humanities computing. Course offerings include digital imaging, issues in electronic publishing, introduction to relational databases, and text analysis. And, the University of Virginia's new master's degree in Digital Humanities will provide hands-on computing experience and an historical background in computing, and it will cover cultural, theoretical, and even philosophical issues in humanities computing. In addition to courses such as information technology design and client-based approaches to developing software for the humanities, the program will also cover topics such as the critical issues and theoretical concerns that emerge from the intersection of humanities research and teaching with the tools and concepts of computational approaches to analysis and interpretation, and knowledge representation, whose topics include logic, philosophy of language, visual representation, bibliographic methods, information design, visual and textual models of epistemology, esthetics, and metaphysics of form.

Daniel Pitti suggests that this new program of study may also provide a model for librarian professional development in the area of humanities computing. "In some ways that's really a difficult and problematic thing at the moment. I think that Virginia is somewhat unique here in attempting to pioneer education in this area." He added that the new master's program "becomes sort of the prototype of a new form of education, a new discipline in some respects, and one which is influenced by, but also will probably influence, library education."

As discussed earlier in this article, it is commonly agreed that the knowledge and skills acquired in library education and training are desirable in an HCC. However, does it logically follow then that this is a natural activity for libraries to involve themselves in? Or, to go one step further, that library schools should be actively contributing to the formation of people prepared to work in teams to collaborate on discipline-specific computing projects? I have already said that how the first question is answered depends on whether or not the library and university administration see the goals of such a center as consistent with the mission of the library. How library schools respond to the second question depends on many things, not the least of which is the need to maintain enrollment figures in order to remain solvent. Simon Tanner observes that "[p]eople with the requisite mix of project experience and technical ability are in short supply for staffing digitisation projects at present . . ." and says that training "will reap immediate benefits in terms of increased productivity and raised confidence." However, he sees shortcomings in current library school education and notes that "the management roles that librarians now fill are not covered in sufficient depth by our formal education process, for instance, project management and fundraising" (Tanner, 2001, p. 335).

Over the past decade, as many library schools sought to revitalize their curricula and prepare information professionals for an IT-rich future, there have been intense debates over the curricula of these programs, their names (to use or not to use the "L" word), and even the question of whether or not to maintain ALA accreditation. Some, like the University of Michigan's School of Information (which offers specializations in areas such as Human–Computer Interaction and Archives and Records Management), decided to drop the phrase "library and information science" from their names and broaden their scope to include computer science, the humanities, and social sciences. Others, like the University of California at Berkeley, opted to forgo ALA accreditation entirely to focus on information management issues.

Daniel Pitti, referring to these changes in library schools, says, "In some ways I think some of those that are being most successful at redefining themselves and attracting students are those that are expanding their mission and taking on more things that have to do with the kinds of research that go on here [at IATH]—looking at the kinds of technology that are involved and beginning to develop courses around it." He offers as examples the University of Michigan, and the University of Washington's Information School. "I think those are the library schools that in fact are securing their future by doing this and recognizing that there is a clear trend within the humanities research community towards digitization and in order to continue that trend you have to have people that are trained and know how to work with the technology."

B. Training Issues

Assuming the library is to be affiliated in some way with the Humanities Computing Center, it is important to provide instruction or training for librarians appropriate for the extent of their involvement with the facility. (Of course, other staff also need to be trained, but as the focus in this section is specifically on librarians' professional development needs, nonlibrarian staff needs will not be directly addressed here). In order to properly integrate the HCC into existing services, it is likely that changes will need to be made to existing library procedures and policies in order to accommodate the new service. Thus, even those librarians not directly involved in staffing the facility or collaborating on humanities computing projects will need to be trained, to a greater or lesser extent. Training issues to consider include knowing what services the facility provides in order to properly refer potential clients (for example, from the reference desk), how to talk about the facility during faculty liaison activities, and collection development issues around content used or created in the HCC. Before this happens, however, the environment needs to be such that people feel comfortable with or, at the very least, receptive to this new service and to the changes it will mean for their daily jobs.

How does one overcome the natural resistance often encountered when introducing new services and encourage librarians to become knowledgeable, energized, and involved? In order to "buy into" and support a suite of new services or, as in the case at hand, a new affiliated facility that will undoubtably affect current library operations to a certain extent, staff first need to understand the reasoning behind the new endeavor. Information should be provided that answers basic questions: "Whom will it serve?" "How is it different from what we already do?" "Why is the library involved?" and "How will my job be affected?" Other potential questions include "If I want to be involved in project development, how can I find the time in my week to do so?" and "Will I be able to use the facility for my own work?"

When seeking to include librarians as partners in project development in the HCC (no matter what level of partnering you are hoping for) you need to target the right librarians for outreach and training and, if you sense reluctance, identify where it originates. Jim Duncan asks, "How do we identify projects that are in content areas that are of interest to particular librarians and then how do we get them comfortable with the technology? Oftentimes we can get them over the hurdle of this concept of changing their role easier if we can get them the training on the tools. I think a lot of the trepidation comes into play with 'I don't know how to use this software package. It's very difficult for me to learn this kind of thing on my own.' And so in bringing them into a team surrounding where it's real supportive, getting them the training hands-on that they need, giving them a lot of flexible time to explore and get comfortable with that, then they start to buy in to it much more readily."

Far from being irrational fears, a librarian's anxiety about technology might very well be motivated by entirely reasonable considerations. Library professionals are justifiably concerned about maintaining a mastery (and also the appearance of mastery) in their field when working with teaching faculty and other scholars. You need to be very supportive of tentative librarians, says Carol Hughes: "When you get with a group of people who are uncomfortable or don't feel they have the support and the technical expertise, they are concerned that they come off in an absolutely professional manner with the faculty when they're face to face. They have to feel very comfortable in their own skill set. . . . You have to be really careful that they feel supported, so they don't feel overwhelmed and they don't feel stupid in front of the faculty."

One particular motivation for librarians to learn new skills is if there is prestige to be gained through the activity. Carol Hughes relates how Iowa's Information Arcade and the Teaching With Innovative Style and Technology (TWIST) program developed a robust and well-attended training series. "The motivation for librarians to enroll in these classes derives in large part from the esteem in which TWIST [librarian–faculty] partnerships are held. The opportunity to work more closely with faculty from a new base of expertise that is so 'in demand' by the faculty is seductive" (Hughes, 1998, pp. 31–32).

However, any new service offered can be perceived as simply another addition to an already busy job, and this disincentive to become involved can have a cumulative effect if it causes feelings of resentment and has an impact on outreach and, eventually, service. Good time management skills can only go so far toward solving the problem of having too much work and not enough time. At some point, the situation needs to be acknowledged and addressed administratively. Duncan says, "What I've tried to do is figure out ways to help them find the flex time to be able to contribute on such projects. I've even battled on that kind of thing myself where I've said, 'OK, if I'm going to do this then I need to release this responsibility' and I get approval from my supervisors to do that and we get it reassigned to somebody. Because we can't always be going at this 120% rate—otherwise our end product will not be up to snuff. There are going to be things that get lost in the cracks. Sometimes there need to be hard decisions made about what we're willing to sacrifice here for the next 3 months. It may be that we cut back on a particular service and in exchange we're going to do this really innovative thing." How a library administration responds to this question is a measure of the library's true commitment to the endeavor. The success of such partnerships is dependent on the library's answer.

C. What Types of Learning Opportunities Can We Offer?

Let us assume an encouraging environment with sufficient time and job flexibility for designated or self-selected librarians to undertake new professional commitments such as becoming affiliated in some fashion with a Humanities Computing Center. How and where should they learn, and who should teach them the new skills they will need? In addition to becoming involved in the organizations and conferences mentioned above, there are myriad workshops, seminars, and so forth on issues pertinent to work in humanities computing (to give just two excellent examples, the University of Virginia's Rare Book School's courses and the Northeast Document Conservation Center's School for Scanning). A subscription to the Humanist listserv alone will provide you with information about more workshops in the United States and abroad than one person could ever attend (Office for Humanities Communication [U.K.], 2001). In addition, for information professionals willing to take time off for postgraduate work, the University of Virginia is considering creating a postgraduate program in Humanities Computing that would offer individuals practical, full-time experience. Pitti explains: "One of the things we are toying with [at IATH] is the idea of putting together a 2-year postgraduate [which could be post-doctorate or post-masters] fellowship or residency where you bring in young graduates for a 2-year period to work within the Institute where they would learn more about the technology and working collaboratively with faculty members and the like. That would be one way of helping to educate and create the kind of people that employers seem to want."

However, a library committed to building a partnership with other campus units to create a collaboratively run HCC will also want to present learning opportunities closer to home in order to communicate to staff that it takes its commitment seriously and expects involved staff to be able to participate fully in the Center's activities. These opportunities can be organized by the library itself, or better yet, through the new facility. In creating the Knowledge Navigation Center at the University of Michigan, planners asked themselves, "How will library staff take on the roles required of them in the present and future academic library? Although envisioned as a public service unit, the planning group felt from the outset that, of all the purposes a new facility might serve, none was so critical as providing staff with a place to learn and experiment with new technology" (MacAdam, 1998, p. 96). Moreover, encouraging librarians to see the Center as a place to experiment and accomplish *their own* projects will automatically increase librarian comfort, interest, and involvement with the facility and ensure that it isn't viewed (suspiciously) as a unit disconnected from (and perhaps also drawing crucial resources away from) the rest of the library.

All sources consulted were skeptical or outright opposed to "just-in-case" teaching. One problem with such a method is that no one is ever quite satisfied with the result. Sayeed Choudhury says, "I think that you do want to be careful about audience, in terms of who this [training] is actually intended for. Everybody wants professional development at some level or another. And we have had cases locally where we have a professional development opportunity and because it's such a wide audience and a diverse group, some people leave saying 'I knew all that' and others end up saying 'boy I'm really overwhelmed, that was too much.' So the more specifically you can target the classes the more impact you might have."

Who trains is also an important question. When hiring trainers to come to the facility and train staff, Jerome McDonough says to exercise caution. "I guess my only real recommendation or caveat about [outsourcing] in-house training [rather than sending staff away to be trained] is that its biggest advantage is that it allows the training to be customized to your staff's needs. Take advantage of that, or it's probably not worth the money. Make sure that you're dealing with trainers who are willing to do some reasonably substantial work with you to elicit what the real training needs are and customize their training to your environment. Many training companies say they do that; within my experience, few do it well." If, instead, you opt to have Center staff do the training, Ron Jantz and Jim Duncan both acknowledge the strain it puts on limited staff resources, and this is all the more critical in facilities that are understaffed. In addition, the results of such training are questionable. The 1997 SPEC Kit on Electronic Scholarly Publishing acknowledges what most interviewees also felt, that "classroom training has drawbacks: most users will not retain much of what they learn unless they have to use it immediately, and training them in a specific tool may have limited value" (Soete, 1997, p. 14).

Duncan summarizes the drawbacks in organizing a staff-taught professional development program and suggests an alternative: "Well, there are two negatives: one is that it's going to consume a great deal of your time or whoever else is involved in planning and designing that training; second, there's the same kind of danger where the librarians who would be attending that training would get that hands-on experience but then would go back to their offices and their desks and they wouldn't ever follow through with actually implementing. Though from my perspective, if you identify projects—real-world opportunities—for them to use that training then you do it hand-in-hand, you get them the training they need and then they actually practice that through real-world projects."

Indeed, it was agreed that the best way to maximize the use of staff time, target an audience, teach specifically to their needs, and choose an appropriate learning model is by focusing on the moment of need linked to real-world projects. Hughes agrees that it is best "to have people who have this as a big chunk of their job so they have a reason to spend half a day every week doing it." Just as some libraries provide new employees with a partner or mentor to get them acquainted with the new work environment, libraries and HCCs can capitalize on in-house expertise by partnering employees working on projects in order to facilitate the transfer of immediately applicable knowledge within the organization. In this "Next to Nellie" approach, where an employee learns a new skill by sitting next to their more knowledgeable colleague (the hypothetical "Nellie") (Paterson, 1999), care should also be given to training the trainer to teach well, so the partnering relationship is a fruitful, not discouraging, one.

With all the discussion about online education, and given the focus in an HCC on the network as a distribution method, it would seem appropriate to consider online learning, either through tutorials or an online class, in this discussion. The Metropolitan New York Library Council (METRO) organized a series of focus groups to discuss professional development needs in New York area libraries. According to the summary of these focus groups, participants identified the benefits of online learning as "the ability to do work at one's own pace, individualized attention, and the ability to complete the training without leaving one's workplace." The disadvantages were "the need for self-discipline of online learners" (Metropolitan New York Library Council [METRO], 2001, p. 4). On the other hand, the METRO group said that the benefits of classroom learning are "being away from the regular office environment and the spontaneity of the classroom. The ability to get away from the office provides participants with a break, allows them to network with others they don't know, and makes a clear statement that the course is part of the individual's job. In addition, interruptions are almost nonexistent" (Metropolitan New York Library Council [METRO], 2001, p. 4). Also, just as staff time may be taxed by in-house training, developing online tutorials or running an online class can also become extremely time-consuming. Hughes says that at Iowa they tried online tutorials, but determined that "[u]ntil we gain more experience with how faculty and staff use the tutorials it seems that personal instruction and ongoing 'facework' are required to support individual learning of new technologies" (Hughes, 1998, p. 32).

Of course, other local expertise should not be overlooked. Libraries or HCCs can also turn for help organizing professional development opportunities to other on-campus individuals, programs, or units with computing expertise and units or organizations within or outside of the institution that might assist with developing staff learning opportunities. Staff from other campus computing facilities could be asked to do training, run a series of workshops, or share their expertise through consultation on certain projects. Campus units such as New York University's Center for Teaching Excellence, whose goal is to organize development efforts throughout the University, could offer ideas, consultation, and play the role of matchmaker among potential institutional partners.

Regional library organizations can also be a good source of support in this area. The METRO focus group identified how an organization such as METRO can help individual libraries carry out training. They suggested that METRO provide training, assistance, or guidance for members who conduct or want to establish their own professional development programs, and that METRO could also act as a clearinghouse about the professional development activities taking place in METRO's member organizations, so that other members could participate (Metropolitan New York Library Council [METRO], 2001, p. 3).

D. Conclusion

This article was intended to be a broad overview of the issues concerning the creation of a Humanities Computing Center to support new IT-based methods of scholarly communication in the humanities, and the challenges posed to libraries by the creation of such centers. Throughout the article I raise many questions and provide few answers. The core dilemma underlying this discussion is: Should this type of endeavor be part of the library's mission? While this question can be investigated and debated at ground level, ultimately, of course, the answer must come from our leaders, who are in a position to interpret and change policy and to create institutional mandates. The best grassroots efforts to establish and maintain an HCC cannot be sustained without a substantial and ongoing commitment from the host or collaborating unit(s) and the university administration.

Answering "yes" will not be easy for libraries. If it is to be truly involved in supporting new forms of humanities scholarly communication, the library will need to move beyond the traditional distinction between the library as provider of information (us) and academics as creators of knowledge (them) and involve itself in efforts (both on campus and off) to partner with scholars and other information professionals to focus on activities that have not traditionally been part of the academic library's concerns. If the answer is "yes," library and university administrative support for these initiatives will have to come in many forms, including the creation of an appropriate reward structure for such work; recognition and encouragement of cross-disciplinary scholarship; flexibility in job assignments; organizational restructuring; budget; a commitment to lifelong learning of faculty and staff; and a recognition that the pace of work, its time lines, and its outcomes will be quite different from traditional research. In addition, to ensure that these initiatives are fully a part of the institution, library and university administrations will need to make clear to the entire organization that they are essential to the mission of the organization and to clearly articulate how and why, based on a commonly held understanding of that mission.

So many of the issues related to library support for humanities computing raised in this article remain to be studied at length. What is the impact of humanities computing and the HCC on "traditional" library activities (such as collection development, cataloging, and faculty liaison)? How are librarians actually working in and with HCCs (sharing staff lines? Part-time affiliation? Leaving the library world altogether?)? What types of reward structures have been developed for librarians affiliated with HCCs? How are faculty research and teaching activities being affected by developments in humanities computing? Examining these issues will shine more light on the humanities computing challenge facing academic libraries today.

References

ALA Core Values Task Force (2000). *Librarianship and Information Service: A Statement on Core Values* (5th draft). American Library Association, Chicago, http://www.ala.org/congress/corevalues/draft5.html.

American Council of Learned Societies (1998). *Computing and the Humanities: Summary of a Roundtable Meeting* (Occasional Paper #41). American Council of Learned Societies, http://acls.org/op41-toc.htm.

American Council of Learned Societies/Council on Library and Information Resources (1999). *Scholarship, Instruction, and Libraries at the Turn of the Century. Results from Five Task Forces Appointed by the American Council of Learned Societies and the Council on Library and Information Resources.* Council on Library and Information Resources, Washington, DC, http://www.clir.org/pubs/reports/pub78/contents.html, http://www.clir.org/pubs/reports/pub78/pub78.pdf.

Bass, R. (1999, January 22). Discipline and publish: Faculty work, technology, and accountability. Paper presented at the AAHE Forum on Faculty Roles and Rewards, San Diego, CA, http://www.georgetown.edu/bassr/disc&pub.html.

Biddiscombe, R. (2000). The changing role of the information professional in support of learning and research. *Advances in Librarianship* **23**, 63–92.

Borgman, C. L. (2000). Digital libraries and the continuum of scholarly communication. *Journal of Documentation* **56**(4), 412–430.

Chodorow, S. (2000). Scholarship and scholarly communication in the electronic age. *Educause Review*, 86–92, http://www.educause.edu/pub/er/erm00/pp086093.pdf.

Darnton, R. (1999). The new age of the book. *The New York Review of Books* **46**(5), 5+, http://www.nybooks.com/articles/546.

Dougherty, R. M., and McClure, L. (1997). Repositioning campus information units for the era of digital libraries. In: *Restructuring Academic Libraries: Organizational Development in the Wake of Technological Change* (C. A. Schwartz, ed.), Vol. 49. ACRL, http://www.ala.org/acrl/pil/pil49.html.

Duffy, C., and Owen, C. (1998). The view from the performing arts. *The New Review of Academic Librarianship* **4**, 182–184.

Feret, B., and Marcinek, M. (1999). The future of the academic library and the academic librarian—A Delphi study. Paper presented at The Future of Libraries in Human Communication, Technical University of Crete, Chania, Greece, http://educate.lib.chalmers.se/IATUL/proceedcontents/chanpap/feret.html.

Greenstein, D. (2000). Digital libraries and their challenges. *Library Trends* **49**(2), 290–303.

Greenstein, D., and Porter, S. (1998). Scholars' information needs in a digital age: Executive summary. *The New Review of Academic Librarianship* **4**, 147–156.

Hardesty, L. (2000). *Do We Need Academic Libraries? A Position Paper of the Association of College and Research Libraries (ACRL)* (Position Paper). Association of College and Research Libraries, http://www.ala.org/acrl/academiclib.html.

Hughes, C. A. (1998). "Facework": A new role for the next generation of library-based information technology centers. *Library Hi Tech* **16**(3–4), 27–35.

Lippincott, J. (1996). Collaboration: Partnerships between librarians and information technologists. Paper presented at the Networked Information in an International Context

Conference, Heathrow, U.K., 9–10 February, http://www.ukoln.ac.uk/services/papers/bl/rdr6250/lippincott.html.

Lowry, A. K. (1994). The Information Arcade at the University of Iowa. *CAUSE/EFFECT* **17**(3), http://www.educause.edu/ir/library/text/cem9438.txt.

Lynch, C. A. (1999). On the threshold of discontinuity: The new scholarly genres and the role of the research library. Paper presented at the ACRL National Conference, Detroit, MI, April 9, http://www.ala.org/acrl/clynch.html.

MacAdam, B. (1998). Creating knowledge facilities for knowledge work in the academic library. *Library Hi Tech* **16**(1), 91–99.

McCarty, W. (1998). *What is Humanities Computing? Toward a Definition of the Field* [Web page]. McCarty, Willard, http://ilex.cc.kcl.ac.uk/wlm/essays/what/what_is.html.

McCarty, W. (1999). Humanities computing as interdiscipline. Paper presented at "Is Humanities Computing an Academic Discipline?" An Interdisciplinary Seminar, University of Virginia, Charlottesville, http://jefferson.village.virginia.edu/hcs/mccarty.html.

Metropolitan New York Library Council (METRO) (2001). *METRO Professional Development Focus Group Analysis*. Metropolitan New York Library Council (METRO), New York.

Modern Language Association: Committee on Information Technology (2001a). *Guidelines for Evaluating Work with Digital Media in the Modern Languages* (Committee Report). Modern Language Association, http://www.mla.org/.

Modern Language Association: Committee on Information Technology (2001b). *Guidelines for Institutional Support of and Access to IT for Faculty Members and Students* (Committee Report). Modern Language Association, http://www.mla.org/.

Modern Language Association: Committee on Scholarly Editions (2001). *Revision Plan for the Guidelines for Scholarly Editions of the Committee on Scholarly Editions* (Committee Report). Modern Language Association, http://www.mla.org/.

Neal, J. G. (2001). The entrepreneurial imperative: Advancing from incremental to radical change in the academic library. *Portal* **1**(1), 1–13, http://muse.jhu.edu/demo/pla/1.1neal.html.

Nevins, K. (1997). Partnerships and competition. Paper presented at the ACRL 8th National Conference: Choosing Our Futures, Nashville, Tennessee, 11–14 April, http://www.ala.org/acrl/invited/nevins.html.

Noble, D. F. (1999). *Digital Diploma Mills, Part IV: Rehearsal for the Revolution* [Web page]. http://communication.ucsd.edu/dl/ddm4.html.

Office for Humanities Communication (U.K.) (2001). *Humanist Discussion Group* [electronic seminar], http://www.princeton.edu/~mccarty/humanist/.

Okerson, A. (1992). *University Libraries and Scholarly Communication: Synopsis* (Study). Published by the Association of Research Libraries for the Andrew W. Mellon Foundation, http://etext.lib.virginia.edu/subjects/mellon/synopsis.html.

Paterson, A. (1999). Ahead of the game: Developing academic library staff for the 21st century. Paper presented at The Future of Libraries in Human Communication, Technical University of Crete, Chania, Greece, http://educate.lib.chalmers.se/IATUL/proceedcontents/chanpap/paterson.html.

Pavliscak, P., Ross, S., and Henry, C. (1997). *Information Technology in Humanities Scholarship: Achievements, Prospects, and Challenges—The United States Focus* (Occasional Paper #37). American Council of Learned Societies, http://acls.org/op37.htm.

Porter, S. (1998). Into the future: Scholarly needs, current provision, and future directions. *The New Review of Academic Librarianship* **4**, 190–214.

Robles Smith, K., and Lynch, B. P. (1999). The changing nature of work in academic libraries. Paper presented at Racing Toward Tomorrow: Proceedings of the 9th National Conference of the ACRL, 8–11 April, 1999.

Soete, G. (1997). Transforming libraries: Issues and innovations in electronic scholarly publication. *SPEC Kit* **233**, 1–39.

SPARC. (2001). *The Scholarly Publishing and Academic Resources Coalition (SPARC)*, [Web site]. SPARC, http://www.arl.org/sparc/home/.

Tanner, S. (2001). Librarians in the digital age. *Program* **35**(4), 327–337.

Tennant, R. (1998). The most important management decision: Hiring staff for the new millennium. *Library Journal* **123**(3), 102.

Troll, D. A. (2001). *How and Why are Libraries Changing? [Draft]* (White Paper). Digital Library Federation, http://www.clir.org/diglib/use/whitepaperpv.htm.

University of Alberta. (2001). *M.A. in Humanities Computing at the University of Alberta*, http://huco.ualberta.ca/.

Unsworth, J. (1996). Electronic scholarship or, scholarly publishing and the public. In: *The Literary Text in the Digital Age* (R. J. Finneran, ed.), University of Michigan Press, Ann Arbor, http://www.iath.virginia.edu/~jmu2m/mla-94.html.

Woodsworth, A. (1998). Computing centers and libraries as cohorts: Exploiting mutual strengths. In: *Computing, Electronic Publishing and Information Technology: Their Impact on Academic Libraries* (R. Downes, ed.), pp. 21–34. Haworth Press, New York.

International MARC: Past, Present, and Future

Sally H. McCallum
Library of Congress
Washington, DC 20540

I. Introduction

MARC is exceptional. It is used by thousands of library staff and patrons to catalog and find resources, it is a major ingredient of large international networks and internationally distributed systems, and it is discussed by librarians from Vietnam to Argentina to the United Kingdom as they wrestle with automation possibilities for their libraries. Where did it come from, what is it, how did it spread, and where is it going are the points to be addressed in this review. While the MARC family of formats is discussed, the emphasis, especially in the later developments, is on MARC 21, which is used worldwide.

II. How MARC Started

A. Focus on Standards

MARC is the acronym for MAchine Readable Cataloging coined in the late 1960s for a data format that was being designed to carry bibliographic data. Libraries have a very long history and heritage. There is evidence of repositories of written clay tablets in very early eras in the Near East and the library of Alexandria dates from around the 4th century B.C. There are well-documented libraries from the Middle Ages in Europe, parts of which still exist today. Document repositories also developed very early in Asia and other areas. However, private library collections grew (in number and in size) and publicly accessible libraries developed after the invention of movable type, which enabled the flowering of printing presses and mass-produced reading material. With the proliferation of collections came more pressing needs to organize the material, so books could be found in large libraries. Thus

ADVANCES IN LIBRARIANSHIP, VOL. 26
This article is a U.S. government work in the public domain.
0065-2830/02 $89.95

bibliographic control ideas, collection classification schemes, and ultimately cataloging principles developed and became increasingly important in the 19th and 20th centuries.

By the 1950s, library activities had certain similarities worldwide: organizing the collections of material by classifying into subject categories, providing catalogs of bibliographic descriptions of items in the collections for patrons to use to find relevant material, and then charging out the resources to the patrons. Librarians had developed their services to include interlibrary loan, which was facilitated by union catalogs. Fortunately standardization had been an early focus of these activities to enable sharing of schemes for classification and subject lists, and for interfiling and sharing of bibliographic descriptions.

Therefore, when computer technology started spreading into the business community in the 1950s, some librarians were immediately interested in its possible application to the labor intensive and complex library processes. In the United States, several studies were carried out (King *et al.*, 1963; Licklider, 1965) and investigations were also undertaken in other countries. While all library processes were under consideration, one of these studies, by Lawrence Buckland, funded by the Council on Library Resources, focused especially on bibliographic data since it is an essential element of most library processes (Buckland, 1965). The degree of standardization of bibliographic data in the United States made this part of the library application particularly amenable to computer processing.

B. MARC Development

The Buckland study considered the possibilities of the machine-readable bibliographic record—the data on library cards—and in particular of Library of Congress records. The Library maintained a special set of printed cards dating back to 1898 representing all cataloging since that date by the Library for its large and broad collection. This card set was used to support the Library's card distribution service, which had begun in 1901. A community-wide group, with representatives from universities, research agencies, government agencies, and private industry, considered the Buckland report, and, after two meetings in 1965, the following recommendations emerged. The Library of Congress should produce machine-readable records to help libraries that were developing automated systems; these records should include all the information on the Library's printed card plus additional information that might be useful to take advantage of computer technology; and the Library of Congress should take a leadership role, with involvement of the broader community, and take the results to broader standardization.

For this initiative, the Library of Congress hired a computer specialist, Henriette Avram, to head the project, and her initial team included Library of Congress staff with strong cataloging expertise, Lucia Rather, and with strong reference experience, Ruth Freitag. The official MARC Pilot began in January 1966 with an enlarged Library team and a group of 21 participating libraries, chosen from 40 volunteers to be representative of different types of libraries. The broad-based participation in the development of the format was an important ingredient to its ultimate acceptance and success and an important role was played by the Council on Library Resources in providing funding that enabled this participation.

The MARC Pilot continued from January 1966 through June 1968. During that time a draft format (called MARC I) was developed, software to create and use machine-readable records was written, and experimentation took place at the Library of Congress and the Pilot sites. As part of the Pilot, an extended character set targeted at library needs had also been developed. At the conclusion of the Pilot, based on the experience with MARC I in the Pilot, the "MARC II" format,[1] the first edition of the MARC 21 format used today, was finalized and published (Avram *et al.*, 1968). The Library of Congress was ready to implement a general MARC record distribution service, which debuted in March 1969.

C. International Interest from the Beginning

Especially significant for this discussion is the international interest in the Library of Congress MARC project that started even before MARC II was in its final form. Staff from the British National Bibliography participated in a review of the MARC I format in preparation for a MARC pilot project in the United Kingdom, and thus influenced the design of MARC II. Henriette Avram has written that "the interest expressed by the British . . . and many visits from foreign librarians directed thinking toward a standard communications format suitable for interchanging bibliographic data not from one organization (LC) to many, but among organizations, perhaps crossing national boundaries" (Avram, 1975, pp. 6–7). While the MARC Pilot took

---

[1]The name MARC II later became simply MARC. However, in the 1970s the format was frequently called LCMARC because of its association with records distributed by the Library of Congress. In the 1980s it was renamed USMARC in line with national format names used in other countries at that time and to more clearly identify it. Finally when USMARC was harmonized with CAN/MARC in the late 1990s, the name was changed to MARC 21. By then its increasing global use had made the USMARC name obsolete. Since all these names refer to the same format, in this paper the latest name, MARC 21, will generally be used for simplicity.

on the modest initial goal of providing a vehicle for the dissemination of Library of Congress data, as had been the tradition for over 65 years in the card service, the participants quickly saw the potential for generalized interchange of the new machine-readable record.

III. MARC Format Components

A. MARC Design

The MARC format has three components which have been called, in the MARC literature, *structure*, *content designation*, and *content*. These components generally correspond to the following concepts in current terminology, respectively: *syntax*, *markup* or *tagging*, and *metadata*.

The *structure* or *syntax* refers to the general shape of a record. For MARC, the structure follows an international standard, ISO 2709 (International Organization for Standardization, 1973). The ISO standard specifies a simple "introduction–table of contents–data" configuration for a record. The "introduction," or MARC 21 Leader, is the first 24 bytes of a record, several of which are critical to reading the record. The "table of contents" is the MARC 21 Directory, which identifies and provides addresses for the data content fields; the standard specifies rules for its construction. The standard also defines two types of data fields, variable control and variable data fields. Although ISO 2709 allows some structure options (e.g., the length of components of the directory entries or the length of subfield tags), the international family of similar MARC formats have all used the same options, making the structure the part of these formats that is truly international. The structure is very well suited for bibliographic data as it allows variable-length fields for holding the record content. A field need only be as long as the data it contains. This was very unusual in the 1960s when fixed-length data fields were commonly used.

The *content designation* or *markup* for MARC is the component of the record that identifies the data content or metadata. MARC uses numeric tags to identify subsets of data elements called fields, and subfield codes (primarily) or character positions to identify subelements of fields. These are defined for a MARC format by its designers, but they are set for that format once formulated. For example, MARC 21 has a well-defined set of tags that are used to identify data in all MARC 21 records. The tags are defined in the documentation for MARC 21 standards, such as the *MARC 21 Format for Bibliographic Data* (Library of Congress, 1999).

The *data content* or *metadata* of a MARC record is formulated according to cataloging rules, authority lists, code lists, etc., that are defined outside the format, generally. (Actually some coded values are embedded in the format documentation and are changed through the format change process, but most codes and all other data rules are external to the format.)

In the following sample MARC 21 record the highlighted parts are, respectively, the Leader (first 24 positions), a Directory entry (referencing field 260, imprint), a variable control field (field 005, last change date and time), and a variable data field (field 260, imprint data field). The example illustrates the difference between the variable control and variable data fields. The control fields contain only data and any subelements of the data must be positionally defined, whereas the data fields each have two introductory positions, called "indicators," and two-character subfield codes (e.g., $a in the example) introducing each of the subelements in the field. (In this example the following graphic substitutions for the space and nongraphic control characters have been made: # = space, $ = subfield marker, @ = end of field mark, and % = end of record mark.)

```
00786cam##2200217#i#4500001000700000003000400007005001
7000110080041000280200015000690400018000840500019001021
000024001212450065001452600046002103000020002565000162
0027650400280043865000500046665000270051671000250054 3
@828897@DLC@19941019181203.6@760122s1975####
dcu#######b###f000#0#eng##@##$a0844401765@
##$aDLC$cDLC$dDLC@00$aZ699.4.M2$bA84@1#$aAvram,#Henrie
tte#D.@10$aMARC,#its#history#and#implications#/$cby#He
nriette#D.#Avram.@##$aWashington#:$bLibrary#of#Con
gress,$c1975.@##$a49#p.#;$c23#cm.@##$a"Based#on#an#
article#entitled#'Machine-readable#cataloging#(MARC)
#program,'#which#appears#in#the#Encyclopedia#of#lib
rary#and#information#science,#volume#17."@##$aBiblio
graphy:#p.#37-49.@#0$aMachine-readable#bibliographic#
data$xHistory.@#0$aMARC#formats$xHistory.@2#$a
Library#of#Congress.@%
```

B. International Standardization

An important recommendation from the 1965 conferences that kicked off the MARC Pilot project was for the Library of Congress to see the work through to standardization, where possible. The record structure was relatively easy to standardize. It became a United States standard in 1971 (American National Standards Institute, 1971) and was also processed as a British standard. By 1973 international approval had been reached and it became the international standard noted above, ISO 2709 (International Organization for

Standardization, 1973). International standardization of the field and subfield tags was more problematic, however.

IV. Proliferation of MARC Formats Internationally

A. Multiple MARCs

The MARC Pilot project in the United States stimulated automation and especially format development projects in other countries over the following decade. These projects were usually based in countries, under programs for establishing national formats, but were sometimes built around language groups, such as a French language format project, or in international organizations. Although MARC 21 had been designed to carry data formulated according to various cataloging rules, it could not satisfy requirements emerging from all of the various national projects, especially since the uses of the format were still being defined. There were various obstacles that led to significant differences in data models for bibliographic records, including different functional requirements of different institutions, diverse cataloging codes, lack of agreement on the organization of data in the record, and even lack of agreement on the function of some of the data tagging (Avram, 1975, p. 23). The flexibility of ISO 2709 with respect to tagging allowed these national or agency projects to adopt the common MARC structure but establish their own sets of data tags as needed according to the data models they adopted.

Therefore a number of similar but different MARC formats were designed and implemented around the world, primarily on a national basis. These included AusMARC from Australia, CAN/MARC in Canada, UKMARC from the British National Bibliography MARC project, MONOCLE and then InterMARC from French projects, SWEMARC from Sweden, and FINMARC from Finland, to name a few. Some of these formats were very similar to MARC 21; for example NorMARC adopted MARC 21 and added a few local codes and data elements where needed. All of these formats used ISO 2709 for their structure, choosing the same options within that standard that MARC 21 had used, but they often defined different tags for the data fields and parsed the data into subfields differently.

Germany was one of the few countries that did not use the ISO 2709 structure standard for its Maschinelles Austauchformat für Bibliotheken (MAB) format, preferring instead a German standard. ISO 2709 restricts the Leader section of a record to 24 bytes, with most coded data contained in the more flexible variable fields, but the German approach was to move all coded data into the Leader (similar to the structure of MARC I) and to use a special extensible Leader scheme.

Some of the questions and issues that either united or divided developers of the emerging MARC formats and created this diversity were the following.

B. Field and Subfield Diversity

What is the function of the data tagging? Subfield codes parse primary data elements, with the tendency being to create a subfield for each identifiable piece of data—thus leading to large numbers of subfields. Another approach is to focus subfielding on retrieval needs—identify data separately only if it is needed for retrieval or special processing. When the International Standard Bibliographic Description (ISBD) was established, subfielding also started to be used as a substitute for punctuation in some formats.

What bibliographic functions should the format support? Some agencies needed printing of cards or book catalogs; others were looking forward to online retrieval. If filing was to be supported were special fields or additional content designators needed to accommodate national filing rules? These different functions influenced the data elements that a format needed to specifically identify, and hence the field and subfield structures.

With what library functions should the record assist? To support acquisitions and circulation, for example, local and copy-specific data were needed, but inclusion of local data impacts the sharing of records. Is the record mainly for communication, which implies that acquisition, circulation, etc., data should be defined locally outside the MARC record and not communicated? These considerations affected the fields that were to be defined in a MARC record.

What data content as defined by cataloging rules need to be supported? MARC 21, for example, attempted to support data content broadly, but the cataloging rules that guided its development were primarily the ones used over the past century in United States libraries. There were also other well-established rules, such as those used in Germany and those from France, that point to different approaches, for example, to heading structures. The types of notes specified in cataloging rules influence the specific note fields in the format. Therefore the rules could have an impact on the fields and subfields a format developer needed to define. The ISBD, on which development also started in the late 1960s, fortunately provided a data content core that would eventually be the same across cataloging codes.

What subject heading systems and classification systems need to be accommodated? The thesauri used by an agency could impact the structure of subject heading fields, and the type and purpose of the classification used might have specific format requirements.

C. Record Content Organization Diversity

How should data be organized in the record? How much intelligence should a tag carry? Should the basic title page data (the ISBD data) be kept together or should the title, for example, go into a title tag cluster. Should standard numbers go into a number block or be tagged with the notes with which they are eventually displayed to users? Librarians and computer specialists considered several approaches to the organization of the data, which in turn affected the tags assigned in a format.

What data should go at the field level, subfield level, indicator level? The fields are directly accessed from the Directory in the MARC record, whereas subfields are found by scanning fields. The planned uses of a piece of data by the developers of a MARC format might influence the desirable level, thus affecting the field and subfield structure in the format. For example, if a data element needed to be accessed often, then it might be specified at the field level, so it would be directly accessible from the Directory, rather than the subfield level.

D. Record Model Diversity

How dependent or independent should records be? One school of thought says that the communications record should not be dependent on other records to be used or displayed; another breaks the records into logical hierarchies with one record per level that generally cannot be used without the information from the others in the hierarchy. These different approaches significantly affect record content and the mechanisms for sharing records.

How should record linking be accomplished? Linking by record numbers is possible if there is certainty that the numbers are universal for the data exchange environment, which can best be ensured in a closed environment. Because national systems as visualized in the 1970s could logically be closed, different record linking techniques were employed.

How should subrecords be handled? Even with independent records, there are different approaches to handling descriptions of works contained within another work, such as articles in journals, cuts on recordings, items bound together, and multivolume works. In the original version of ISO 2709, a subrecord technique was described, but other simpler techniques were also used by some developers. Choices here greatly affect sharing of records as an unknown technique could make the record unintelligible with respect to the information in the subrecord.

E. Interchange Models

All these different views of data and divergence of the tagging in the different MARC formats resulted partially from the technical environment of the late 1960s and early 1970s. In the computer and communications area, file transfer was carried out via magnetic tape, not online. Long-distance computer-to-terminal telecommunications were being developed, as is illustrated by their use in the OCLC project in the early 1970s, but there was an expectation that file transfer would occur, especially large files of bibliographic records, on tape medium. The Library of Congress had a periodic distribution of records on tape and OCLC supplied its early customers with tapes containing their records if they subscribed to that service (in addition to printed cards). Thus with environments separated by offline and batch transfer, national differences in formats and records did not generate very much attention.

At the same time, international interchange of records was seen by some as a goal, since, for example, the Library of Congress began programmatic use of foreign national bibliography records in its shared cataloging operations in the 1960s. The international data exchange model that emerged was one in which each country or group would formulate their own MARC format using the standard structure, ISO 2709, but with their own specially adapted tagging. Then upon exchange, an agency in each country would take responsibility for translating the data into the local MARC format for dissemination or use by the libraries in the receiving country. It was soon recognized that this could result in a jungle of translation programs, one for each of the national MARC formats, so efforts to develop umbrella formats were undertaken. The exchange record model was revised so that for international transfer the appointed agency in each country would translate its own records into and translate received records out of the umbrella format in international transfer. Under this model each country would need only two conversion programs.

There were two major efforts for developing umbrella formats which resulted in the IFLA *UNIMARC Format* (International Federation of Library Associations and Institutions, 1977) in 1977 and UNESCO *Common Communications Format* (CCF) (UNESCO, 1984) in 1984. (Actually the CCF was sometimes viewed as an umbrella format between UNIMARC itself and the *UNISIST Reference Manual*, but the Reference Manual was dropped in favor of the CCF eventually.) Both of these formats presented difficulties when used as switching formats because of the loss of data always involved in data transformations, especially when the formats have different data models and different levels of specificity in tagging. In addition, if the conversion programs attempted to capture all of the data in the source formats, the programs themselves were very complex and required change each time either format changed. Since the initial exchanges were for shared cataloging where avoidance of loss in data transfer was highly desirable, the umbrella format model was not successfully implemented.

V. Convergence on MARC 21

The 1970s and 1980s were a period of robust implementation of systems—implementation of automated systems in individual libraries and development of large multiuser shared cataloging systems—both based on standard MARC records. This had a large impact on the standardization of bibliographic records, especially in the United States, and eventually for global standards for MARC.

A. Development of Vendor Systems

Local library system development has been multidimensional. In the early 1970s many large libraries began their own local system development projects. At the same time, computer system vendors, some of whom had provided automated components to libraries even before MARC, began to develop or expand to provide systems for circulation, for loading, searching, and viewing records (online catalogs), for creating and exporting records, and for many other library functions. Throughout the 1980s and 1990s these vendor companies grew, eventually offering integrated multifunction online systems scalable for large and small libraries. Libraries that initially developed their own systems moved to system procurement rather than development as their first systems aged. Vendor systems emerged in many countries, with systems designed around the format of the vendor's location. (Although MARC is a communications format, the parsing and markup of the data internal to a vendor system is usually closely related to a communications format, even though the communications record structure may not be retained. This facilitates record creation and analysis, the format tagging having become a special language for librarians, and makes import and export of records easier.)

As vendors began to saturate the home markets they started looking for external markets, becoming international companies. The different formats in each country hampered this internationalization, and vendors have often responded by limiting format offerings, with MARC 21 being the most prevalent format supported. This convergence on MARC 21 occurred partially because a number of the system vendors originated in a country that used MARC 21 as the national format, or, if the vendor came from another country, it wanted to introduce the system into a MARC 21 market, such as the United States market. The large numbers of libraries, strong standards orientation, common language, and the availability of Library of Congress cataloging in MARC 21 since 1969 made the United States an especially fertile vendor market and country for vendor development.

B. Global Record Sharing

The implementation of shared cataloging systems, largely based on standard MARC records, was another major influence on MARC standardization. In the United States there was, even before MARC, a strong tradition of sharing cataloging. The United States had been highly standardized bibliographically for many years, because of a number of programs such as the collaborative development of cataloging rules, the cost-effective cataloging card services offered by the Library of Congress since 1901, and stability and continuous maintenance of major subject-oriented schemes: Library of Congress Subject Headings (LCSH), Library of Congress Classification (LCC), and the Dewey Decimal Classification (DDC). So the development in the United States of shared cataloging systems that were dependent on a standard record for their success is not surprising.

Following the lead of the founding of OCLC (originally called the Ohio College Library Center but now named the Online Computer Library Center) immediately on the completion of the MARC Pilot project, a number of shared cataloging systems were developed over the next 20 years. These "bibliographic utilities," as they are sometimes called, built large union catalogs through their participants' cataloging activities and through import of records such as those distributed by the Library of Congress. They provided many services such as online copy cataloging, printed catalog cards, computer catalog record files, and interlibrary loan support. Examples of these utilities are OCLC and the Research Libraries Group (RLG) in the United States, AutoGraphics Canada in Canada, PICA in the Netherlands, systems developed by the national bibliography agencies in various countries, and smaller consortia of libraries in many countries.

These network systems initially flourished in national settings, separated by the less robust communications systems of the 1970s and the need to use tape for the batch transfer of files of records. But each used a common format and, as they grew, use of that common format was important to the successful sharing of records. Thus the shared cataloging systems were important to establishment of universal use of MARC formats. Because of the size and outreach of OCLC and RLG, which are both based on MARC 21, the numbers of MARC 21 records became very large, enhancing that format's usefulness for the economies of copy cataloging. As these networks or bibliographic utilities expanded their services worldwide in the 1990s, they developed conversion tools to allow them to load or export non-MARC 21 records, but such conversions were not without loss since the internal parsing of data and input forms were designed around MARC 21.

C. Communications and Computers in the 1980s

There were significant developments in the 1980s that had a great impact on data sharing in libraries, and thus on MARC. All through the decade the communications networks steadily improved, making system-to-system communication more viable for library technical processing and users alike. Finally in the late 1980s the Internet became widespread and online communications took a leap forward. The simultaneous widespread deployment of personal computers that rapidly replaced "dumb" terminals also opened up more real-time communications possibilities.

Various protocols developed to handle the more immediate communications, such as FTP (File Transfer Protocol) and e-mail's SMTP (Simple Mail Transfer Protocol) for e-mail. In the library domain a search and retrieval protocol, somewhat obscurely named "Z39.50," provided the possibility of peer system searching (American National Standards Institute, 1995; International Organization for Standardization, 1998). The records returned in response to a search required agreement with respect to format if they were to be usable by the receiving system. Many implementations settled on a simple display-oriented format called the Simple Unstructured Text Record Syntax (SUTRS) and on MARC 21 as the two most frequently implemented record formats. SUTRS was useful for responses to reference searches but MARC 21 proved to be useful for both reference and for technical processing, since the records retrieved could be screened in the same manner as local catalog records and incorporated immediately into a database to support cataloging.

Thus 1970s batch communications among a few organizations, with complex conversion of data to special formats, was no longer viable. Rapid real-time interchange of MARC records was needed, so MARC format options tended toward the one most compatible to the sending database, the widely used MARC 21.

D. Summary of Factors Favoring MARC 21 Use

1. Communications and Record Sharing

Thus by the mid-1990s, several factors had intensified interest in global format harmonization—a single format used by all—over the previous communications model of national formats with umbrella formats for interchange outside a country. The data and data model factors described in Sections IV.B, C, and D took a back seat to the immediacy of communications and the economies of record sharing.

Many have turned to MARC 21 partly because of the enormous numbers of records natively available in that format. The largest of the bibliographic utilities worldwide, OCLC, uses a MARC 21-based native format, which means that MARC 21 is the record export format with least data loss for that system. In addition, over the past decade, shared cataloging programs began to cross national boundaries and libraries began to achieve a higher level of agreement on cataloging conventions. Project viability required format agreement to ensure interoperability, since format conversion is costly and results in loss of data.

Also, when system vendors sell globally, customizing of formats is expensive. MARC 21 has been the predominant format native to vendor systems, so the extra expense has been passed on to the libraries requesting different formats.

2. Format Maintenance and Participation

Another factor in the adoption of MARC 21 is the commitment for the maintenance of the format that existed since its initiation: the Library of Congress has had several staff tasked with that responsibility. Decisionmaking on format changes, although initially narrowly collaborative among the early implementors, was broadened in the 1970s to include meetings attended by representatives of the American library associations. With the advent of e-mail and listservs in the 1980s, it was expanded to solicit worldwide comments on change proposals. Today with the Web, all change proposals are posted on the MARC 21 Web site and international review is requested. In addition, the United States and Canada continue to hold actual change review meetings where intense discussion among implementors and users takes place.

Consistently applied maintenance and broad participation are two factors that make the MARC 21 format attractive for adoption. Maintaining a format is costly and some national formats could not be regularly maintained after the initial development. This meant that those formats fell behind as library resources that required MARC records took on new forms—compact discs, computer files, digital images, etc. Libraries have had to evaluate the tradeoffs between duplicative investment in format development or participation and dependence on the MARC 21 maintenance process.

E. Adoptions and Harmonizations

A number of countries have adopted MARC 21 or changed to it from national formats over the past decade; for example, Poland and Switzerland adopted

MARC 21, and Australia changed to it from AUSMARC and Sweden from SWEMARC. In the case of South Africa, which had used a UNIMARC-like format for almost two decades, a careful cost–benefit study recommended a shift to MARC 21 in order to be able to take advantage of MARC 21-based records and systems and to be able to join international cooperative cataloging programs. Since the change, there has been a geat deal of activity in individual library automation in that country, with a large number of new automated systems installed. Libraries are now able to participate in international programs and have even become contributors to the international name authority cooperative program headquartered at the Library of Congress.

1. Harmonization with CAN/MARC

Canada and the United States have shared format development expertise for many years, but, as with MARC diversity found elsewhere, the CAN/MARC format and USMARC format differed in a number of details. In 1996 a harmonization effort was undertaken by the National Library of Canada and the Library of Congress, the maintenance agencies for those formats, to completely synchronize them. Since the formats were close already, the National Library of Canada and the Library of Congress were able to work out a series of relatively minor changes that brought the formats together. The current name for the format, MARC 21, was the result of that harmonization, since both of the former national names had to be abandoned for one without national connections.

2. United Kingdom Adoption

In 2001, the British Library, which maintains the UKMARC format, announced that it was going to cease maintenance of that format and adopt MARC 21. This was decided after several consultations with UKMARC users. Some of the advantages of MARC 21, as stated in the report after the last consultation, were "ability to download and derive bibliographic records from a wider range of sources," "more highly evolved family of formats, with superior coverage of non-book media and separate formats for bibliographic and authority data," "better documented and more effectively maintained and supported than UKMARC," and "more effective route to the eventual adoption in the future of non-MARC metadata standards" (British Library, 2001).

This is a major change for the United Kingdom since UKMARC was established shortly after MARC II was completed; however, some segments of the United Kingdom library community had already started to use MARC

21. The British Library was very careful in taking this step since the differences between UKMARC and MARC 21 were greater than the differences in the Canada and United States harmonization project.

For each adoption of MARC 21 by various countries, many issues have to be considered. Are there data elements important to national practices missing? What assistance can the MARC 21 maintenance agencies and other users give in planning migration strategies? How does the country want to organize its input to the maintenance process?

3. Europe's Dilemma

A common format has been a reality for the United States for many years, but it has not been as easy to achieve in other areas of the world. In Europe, over the years three types of MARC formats have predominated: those that basically follow MARC 21, those relating to UKMARC (which itself had a number of characteristics in common with MARC 21), and those based on UNIMARC. But because of language differences, cataloging tradition differences, and national format-based systems and infrastructure commitments, it has been difficult to achieve format unity across Europe, even though librarians fully understand the advantages of doing so. The emergence of the European Union (EU) has been valuable in providing funding for multi-country cooperation and has resulted in general agreement that MARC 21 and UNIMARC would be the two general formats to be used in EU projects. Unfortunately the differences between the data models for those two formats mean loss-prone conversion. To assist interoperability, the EU sponsored development of a valuable utility, USEMARCON (USEMARCON, 1998) that has made it more feasible to develop conversions, even though some information may be lost.

4. Developing Countries

In developing countries around the world a version of the UNESCO format, CCF, has been widely used, partly because it comes as the default on a library software package that UNESCO has distributed free for many years. Although this format does not make its users compatible with the MARC users in the developed world, the free UNESCO bibliographic record construction and online public catalog system has been critical to the development of automated access to information in many places. Today, however, some developing countries are beginning to acquire MARC-based systems in their larger libraries. To avoid creation of a split in resource discovery and sharing, UNESCO will have ready a MARC-compatible version of the system in 2002.

An area that is fast developing its library automation potential is Latin America, including Mexico. These countries are adopting MARC 21, purchasing library systems, and joining bibliographic utilities such as OCLC, in addition to developing their own networks and data sharing programs. They also leverage the UNESCO system for smaller libraries.

F. Versions and Translations

The MARC 21 documentation is made available in several versions. The full format which specifies all the data elements with lengthy content descriptions is a printed looseleaf. The MARC 21 Concise, which contains all data elements but with brief descriptions, is available on the Web and in print. The MARC 21 Lite specifies a subset of the format data elements but is fully compatible with the fuller format versions. It is only available on the Web. These Web versions of MARC 21 have been especially valuable for users both inside the United States and globally.

International interest in MARC 21 has led to development of a number of translations of the format, especially of the concise version. Canada maintains a translation in French of the full format and Spain maintains one in Spanish, but there are also translations into various other languages, including most recently Vietnamese.

The Library of Congress Web site for the format includes the documentation and codes lists used, system lists, format change proposals, and many other resources that assist in use of the format (Library of Congress, 2002). In early 2002, the Web site was made available in Spanish, with links to Spanish-language materials where possible and to the English where Spanish is not available.

VI. New Developments

Looking to the future, many interesting developments are taking place today in the bibliographic and computing environments that will eventually affect all three components of the MARC format: structure, content designation, and content. The following sections explore some of these possibilities.

A. Structure or Syntax

With the advent of the Web in the early 1990s, computer specialists became much more interested in universal data markup standards that have the flexibility to be read, understood, and displayed by any computer system in real time. Initially this took the form of markup for display, epitomized by HTML

(HyperText Markup Language). Data elements were not identified for what they were (personal name, scale note, Dewey classification number), as they are in MARC, but for how they were to be displayed (heading, paragraph, etc.). At the same time various other tagging schemes were being developed that identified parts of an information object in order to facilitate printing or display, such as section or chapter, but again generally did not identify the type of content of the element. Both HTML and the other markups follow a markup structure that was designed for electronic resources, SGML (Standard Generalized Markup Language) (ISO 8879) (International Organization for Standardization, 1986).

SGML is a structure with rules for tagging data. It is comparable to ISO 2709 that defines the MARC record structure. An implementation of the SGML structure, a data format in MARC terminology, is called a Document Type Definition (DTD). It is rigorously defined so that an organization receiving an SGML document with a set of tags specified by a DTD can go to the DTD to validate the tagging and interpret it for display. Construction of the SGML DTD can be very complex, so in the mid-1990s a second markup technique was developed under an adjusted SGML umbrella, called Extensible Markup Language or XML. XML has slightly simpler behavior rules than the original SGML required. With XML a new way to provide the "key" to the markup was developed called a "schema" rather than a DTD, and it became valid to use XML without a schema by simply making it "well-formed."

While these structures are still under development and adoption, another technique for markup, called RDF (Resource Description Framework) is also being explored. RDF makes it possible to mix XML data elements from different schemas in one "package," a flexibility that could prove useful to libraries as they interact with the broader cultural community.

Given the rapid development of improved markup structures for the Internet/Web environment it is not clear yet how MARC will be affected. The structure of the MARC record was innovative and forward looking—and carefully adapted to the characteristics of bibliographic data—but it was not adopted outside the library community and is not a suitable markup for full documents, such as books. MARC was optimized for records composed of many shorter variable-length data elements to which random access is required, whereas SGML and XML initially targeted full-text markup and focused on sequential access of data. However, with appropriate definition of the tagging in XML, it can accommodate MARC data. Although XML is a verbose markup, that would not be an obstacle to its use for many applications. A strong aspect of XML is its broad adoption by the Web and the computing environments, which means many generalized tools that manipulate XML data are becoming available. If XML is not pushed offstage by another markup innovation it appears that MARC data could usefully be presented in an XML package as an alternative to the ISO 2709 package.

Experimentation is already taking place. The Library of Congress convened a meeting in 1995 of MARC and SGML experts to recommend an approach to take in developing an SGML DTD for MARC data, but even before 1995 a couple of projects experimented with MARC in SGML. Following that meeting a DTD was developed by the Network Development and MARC Standards Office, the office at Library of Congress charged with the maintenance responsibilities for MARC. In addition conversion scripts that transformed records from "classic" (ISO 2709) MARC structure to the MARC/SGML structure as defined in the new DTD were prepared. The DTD and the scripts were made publicly available and have been used for experimentation and for special purposes. By the time this work was complete, XML had become the popular structure so the SGML DTD was turned into an XML DTD (Library of Congress, 1997).

The XML DTD developed by the Library of Congress includes all the data in MARC 21, does not try to impose very much additional hierarchy on the data, and defines tagging in such a way that data elements can stand alone and still be fully identified. Validation of format compliance can be carried out with the DTD. But fulfilling these requirements for the extensive MARC 21 data element set required a very large DTD. There are other data models that could have been used for the MARC data and other DTDs have been developed that take other approaches, from extremely brief generic tagging to consideration of only a subset of MARC data. The Library of Congress MARC office is currently developing a revision of the DTD, as an XML schema, based on user comments and a study of data models used by others.

A pathway into XML appears not to be single threaded, but the library community will be able to use the new structures where applicable along with the classic structure until there is a clear way forward. The convergence of MARC formats to MARC 21 in the classic structure will be highly useful as MARC is permuted into new structures. Since bibliographic record files continually grow rather than ending and starting afresh, and integrated access to all records over time is valuable to the end user, the rapid change of the standards in the Web environment presents difficulties for the library community. Cataloging data created in the past cannot be left behind but must be brought along into the new structures. The broad use of XML and the rapidly developing tool support for it are good reasons, however, for continued work on a MARC XML transformation and perhaps eventual migration, recognizing that a multiplicity of formats may be a factor in the future. MARC was designed to be a communications format, but systems have handled internal MARC in different ways depending on the database management system employed. XML is also a communications format, and its use for databases is still being explored.

B. Content Designation or Markup

MARC 21 is a very large data element set. Over 30 years of use during which complex automated systems were developed, the format has taken on more and more roles that have different data needs involving resource discovery, use, and management. MARC's size is sometimes a barrier to adoption and use of MARC outside the library community, as the subset useful for these communities may be difficult to determine. Yet cultural institutions are actively pursuing integrated access to resources across museums, archives, and libraries. At the same time, a tremendous number of new resources that might potentially be cataloged using MARC are arriving at the library in electronic and digital form. In response, new initiatives have produced simple data sets such as the Dublin Core Metadata Element Set (Dublin Core Metadata Initiative, 1999) which is the opposite extreme from MARC, with only 15 elements that are at a high enough level that they can be used across cultural projects. One view of the situation is that community-specific formats, such as MARC in libraries and the Encoded Archival Description (EAD) DTD in archives, continue to bring out the level of specificity appropriate for detailed retrieval within the community, while a record that is general enough to be easily derived from community data, such as Dublin Core records, provides cross-community access.

Although the general level of Dublin Core does not adequately support library retrieval, its development and similar projects encourage inspection of the parsing of data in MARC to ensure that current subfielding is necessary and format changes reduce complexity. Content designation takes cataloger time to establish and maintain and serves as a barrier to use outside the library community.

C. Content

One of the most interesting events in the area of bibliographic content since the establishment of the "Paris Principles" for library cataloging in 1961 has been the rigorous development of a general data model for bibliographic data, using entity-relationship methodology. The model was completed by the International Federation of Library Associations and Institutions in 1997 and published as the *Functional Requirements for Bibliographic Records* (FRBR) (International Federation of Library Associations and Institutions, 1998). By 2002, it is beginning to influence various bibliographic content rules and conventions. At a simplified level, FRBR defines a four-tier hierarchy for document description—*work* (the most general), *expression, manifestation*, and *item*—and identifies the types of data that are appropriate for each. For example the *work Tom Sawyer* may be *expressed* as English language text or in other languages or media, one of these *expressions* may be published in a particular *manifestation* by a specific publisher, and a library may obtain a particular *item* or copy of this publisher's product. Over the decades, the bibliographic universe has devised various methods to bring together for the library patron different editions, performances, versions in different media, etc., anticipating that the patron is often seeking the work, not necessarily a particular version or manifestation of the work. The FRBR data model is a new and highly refined approach to the problem and has the potential to be used in a variety of ways to present bibliographic search results to users.

Following the completion of FRBR, a study was released in 1998 that analyzed data models inherent in the *Anglo American Cataloging Rules* (AACR), using the FRBR model: *The Logical Structure of the Anglo-American Cataloging Rules* (Delsey, 1998). These rules are used in several countries for cataloging and form the basis for other national cataloging codes. This is an initial step in some potential reorganization or refinement of AACR.

The content of a MARC 21 bibliographic record is defined by the cataloging rules used by the content providers, and the AACR are some of the more widely used rules among MARC users. Therefore the MARC 21 maintenance agency at the Library of Congress, the Network Development and MARC Standards Office, has had a study carried out that maps all the MARC 21 data elements onto the FRBR model and also onto the data models of the AACR/FRBR analysis cited above. This new study, available from the MARC 21 Web site, is the *Functional Analysis of the MARC 21 Bibliographic and Holdings Formats* (Delsey, 2002). That study was released in early 2002 and already individuals are working on analyses of actual MARC 21 records. Several agencies are exploring techniques for mining MARC records for the data applicable to the tiers defined in the FRBR model, with one focus being the generation of enhanced user presentations.

Although the MARC 21 record can accommodate a number of data models, the one that is used almost universally is the unit record model at the manifestation level. A target bibliographic entity is fully described in one record and, while there may be references and linkages to other entities more fully described in other records (e.g., name of the series of the target item), a full display can be made from the record in hand since the names and titles of related entities are also contained in the unit record for the target. Thus the linkages are not interdependencies. Interdependencies would require multiple records for display of bibliographic information about a single target entity. Many databases also hold the records in unit form but others take a more relational approach internally. The focus on the unit record by MARC

21 users also relates to the multiple uses of the bibliographic record. Union databases attach holdings to specific manifestations of a work, and catalogers need to be able to carry out copy cataloging for a specific manifestation.

VII. Conclusion

In summary, in the year 2002, MARC has had a remarkable impact on the library environment. Over the years, data sharing has propelled libraries toward a global approach both for record content and for data format with the AACR and MARC 21 as leaders. Now there are exciting new possibilities for data management and formats emerging for today's communications and computer technology. Librarians were ahead of technology when they developed MARC and are moving into the new environment both cautiously, in order not to lose the past, and creatively, as is evidenced by the experimentation and development with new technology occurring in libraries, with library system vendors, and at the large bibliographic utilities. Libraries have spent the past 20 years converting their pre-MARC data into machine-readable form, an enormous task that is largely complete. This will enable them to move in new directions with a stronger focus, perhaps, on using the new tools and models to transform their rich MARC records into more user-friendly and dynamic displays for library patrons.

References

American National Standards Institute (ANSI) (1971). *American National Standard Format for Bibliographic Information Interchange on Magnetic Tape* (ANSI Z39.2-1971). ANSI, New York. The standard has been reviewed and updated over the years and is now titled *Information Interchange Format* (ANSI/NISO Z39.2-1994 R2001). Available at http://www.niso.org/standards/resources/z39-2.pdf.

American National Standards Institute (ANSI) (1995). *Information Retrieval: Application Service Definition and Protocol Specification* (ANSI/NISO Z39.50-1995). Available at http://www.niso.org/standards/resources/z39-50.pdf.

Avram, Henriette D. (1975). *MARC Its History and Implications.* Library of Congress, Washington, DC. This publication contains a detailed description of the development of the format from the initiation of the MARC Pilot to the mid-1970s. It also contains an extensive bibliography early, related articles, and books.

Avram, Henriette D., Knapp, John F., and Rather, Lucia J. (1968). *The MARC II Format: A Communications Format for Bibliographic Data.* Library of Congress, Information Systems Office, Washington, DC.

British Library (2001). *British Library to Adopt MARC 21.* Available at http://www.bl.uk/.

Buckland, Lawrence F. (1965). *The Recording of Library of Congress Bibliographical Data in Machine Form; A Report Prepared for the Council on Library Resources, Inc.* Revised. Council on Library Resources, Inc., Washington, DC.

Delsey, Tom (1998). *The Logical Structure of the Anglo-American Cataloguing Rules.* Joint Steering Committee for Revision of AACR. Available at http://www.nlc-bnc.ca/jsc/aacr.pdf.

Delsey, Tom (2002). *Functional Analysis of the MARC 21 Bibliographic and Holdings Formats.* Network Development and MARC Standards Office, Library of Congress, Washington, DC. Available at http://www.loc.gov/marc/marc-functional-analysis/home.html.

Dublin Core Metadata Initiative (1999). *Dublin Core Metadata Element Set. Version 1.1.* Available at http://dublincore.org/documents/dces.

International Federation of Library Associations and Institutions (IFLA) (1977). *UNIMARC, Universal MARC Format.* IFLA International Office for UBC, London. The current edition of this format was published in looseleaf in 1994 by K. G. Saur, Munich.

International Federation of Library Associations and Institutions (IFLA) (1998). *Functional Requirements for Bibliographic Records, Final Report.* IFLA Study Group. K. G. Saur, Munich. Also available at http://www.ifla.org/VII/s13/frbr/frbr.pdf.

International Organization for Standardization (ISO) (1973). *Documentation—Format for Bibliographic Data Interchange on Magnetic Tape* (ISO 2709:1973). ISO, Geneva. The standard has been reviewed and updated over the years and is now available under the title *Format for Information Interchange* (ISO 2709:1996).

International Organization for Standardization (ISO) (1986). *Information Processing—Text and Office Systems—Standard Generalized Markup Language (SGML)* (ISO 8879:1986). ISO, Geneva.

International Organization for Standardization (ISO) (1998). *Information and Documentation— Information Retrieval (Z39.50)—Application Service Definition and Protocol Specification* (ISO 23950:1998). ISO, Geneva. ISO 23950 is equivalent to American National Standards Institute, 1995, which is available on the Web.

King, G. W. (1963). *Automation and the Library of Congress: A Survey Sponsored by the Council on Library Resources, Inc.* Library of Congress, Washington, DC.

Library of Congress (LC) (1997). *MARC DTDs (Document Type Definitions).* Network Development and MARC Standards Office, LC, Washington, DC. Available at http://www.loc.gov/marc/marcsgml.html.

Library of Congress (LC) (1999). *MARC 21 Format for Bibliographic Data.* 1999 edition and updates, looseleaf. Network Development and MARC Standards Office, LC, Washington, DC. Also available in a concise form at http://www.loc.gov/marc/bibliographic/.

Library of Congress (LC) (2002). *MARC Standards.* Network Development and MARC Standards Office, LC, Washington, DC. Available at http://www.loc.gov/marc/.

Licklider, J. C. R. (1965). *Libraries of the Future.* MIT Press, Cambridge, MA.

United National Educational, Scientific and Cultural Organization (UNESCO) (1984). *CCF: The Common Communications Format.* General Information Programme and UNISIST, UNESCO, Paris.

USEMARCON Plus, the Universal MARC Record Convertor (1998). Available at http://www.bl.uk/services/bibliographic/usemarcon.html.

High Touch or High Tech: The Collaborative Digital Reference Service as a Model for the Future of Reference

Diane Kresh
Library of Congress
Washington, DC 20540

I. Introduction and Background

The explosion of online information and the popularity of the Internet and commercial search engines have required librarians to look afresh at their profession. New demands and expectations have emerged from the overwhelming amount of information now available. The need to deliver information to the remote user has encouraged the creation of many innovative programs linking new technologies with traditional library services. Librarians now have an historic opportunity to adopt a new service paradigm and in so doing, demonstrate their relevance in the modern world. More importantly, they can use the new technology to provide a fundamental mission-based service that exceeds what might only have been dreamed of a mere 10 years ago, before the miracle of the World Wide Web. How do librarians build on their age-old status as trusted advisors and create services that will both meet these new demands and revitalize the profession? How do we take the reference desk to cyberspace? The Collaborative Digital Reference Service (CDRS), launched by the Library of Congress and partner libraries, is one such response. CDRS provides professional reference service to library patrons through an international digital network of libraries. This article explores how CDRS began, and what lies ahead for this and other innovative e-reference services.

Today's libraries are offering human-mediated reference over the Internet at an increasing rate. Research by Joe Janes and his colleagues (Janes, 2000) found that 45% of academic libraries and 12.8% of public libraries offer some type of digital reference service. These services, however, are often ad hoc and experimental. Highly publicized ventures such as "24/7 Reference," a collaboration of 13 public libraries in Southern California which provides

24/7 reference to anyone who initiates a search through one of the participating libraries, are evidence that such experiments are gaining traction as
librarians revolutionize their services in order to stay in business (Coffman
and McGlamery, 2000).

The image of the reference librarian is changing, too. Listservs broad-
cast queries from librarians seeking advice on how to set up 24/7 "live" reference services, job announcements search for "energetic," "dynamic," and
"highly motivated individuals" to lead teams in implementing "innovative
tools and services." Anne Lipow (Lipow, 1999) has warned that librarians had
better take notice of their shrinking clientele and begin providing "point of
need reference service to information seekers at the place where they are
when they have a question." Lipow suggests further that reference librarians
must provide service that is "obvious and as convenient to the remote user
as is access to the information itself"—what she provocatively describes as
"in-your-face reference."

The profession has heeded these warnings, and through a series of initiatives—early experiments with MOOS and MUDS, video conferencing, the
launch of the Internet Public Library (IPL), Stumpers, and now live chat—
has paved the way for federated services such as the Collaborative Digital
Reference Service (CDRS), which use new technologies to bring reference
and information services to patrons regardless of where they are located.
Overall, such efforts seek to evolve traditional services in an online environment without sacrificing quality or accuracy.

Libraries are not the only institutions undergoing profound change.
Higher education is also experiencing a sea change that could be a harbinger
of things to come for libraries and librarians, in terms of both the collections
they build and the communities they serve. As college course catalogs and
professional meetings signal, distance education is on the rise. According to
the National Center for Education Statistics, enrollments in distance education classes have more than doubled, increasing from 753,640 in the 1994–95
school year to 1,632,350 in 1997–98. As a result, it is harder for college and
university libraries both to define and then serve their primary clientele.
If students can come from anywhere, the physical boundaries that separate
institutions of higher learning from one another become meaningless.
Steve Coffman (Coffman, 2002) suggests that

> it is not hard to imagine the development of virtual libraries with well-selected electronic
> content coupled with online reference services to help students find their way around.
> Schools would "subscribe" to these libraries, just as they now subscribe to electronic
> databases. Instead of having a whole crew of reference librarians sitting at desks in the
> building, your reference librarians would be online where they could handle reference
> traffic from many institutions at once.

II. The Future Is Now

This is a watershed moment for libraries, an opportunity to create service visions that inspire and reflect the direction the profession must take to ensure that people continue to enjoy free access to information. This freedom is at the heart of their ability to participate fully in a democratic process. Libraries, along with schools, churches, civic associations, volunteer organizations, reading groups, and a host of other "communities," have an important role to play in shaping and sustaining the social fabric (Preer, 2001). History and technology have combined to provide libraries with a unique opportunity to extend their reach, unbound by time or place. History's greatest innovations have been about mass communication. The printing press linked communities and created a literary culture; the automobile linked urban and rural Americans and shrank the spaces between them; today, the World Wide Web has spawned a world community where, with a PC and a modem, a person can connect any time, anywhere with another human being to share information, seek advice, buy or sell a product—the opportunities are limitless. With leadership, the efforts of reference librarians can be pooled in a systematic way to provide the fulfillment of an important mission of every library—to serve the needs of its community.

It is worth remembering that a digital library program however, is not just a 21st-century equivalent of the 19th-century passive storehouse. Its potential is limited only by the imagination of its creators. The proliferation of Web sites and the explosion of e-commerce and other e-services all argue for dynamic library programs that will:

1. Employ technologies that make library collections and resources more widely accessible to patrons around the world and in so doing, shrink the digital divide
2. Collect and create significant publications in electronic formats so library and research collections continue to be universal and comprehensive
3. Build collaborations with both national and international institutions to create shared assets enabling libraries to store, preserve, provide access to, and expand their resources
4. Create a culture of technical and strategic innovation so libraries can fulfill both traditional and new initiatives.

Librarians should be heartened by the many efforts already under way to bridge the "digital divide" and make information freely available. The city of Houston, Texas (Swartz, 2000) will provide access to the Internet and to software for word processing and e-mail to all of its citizens through an arrangement with Houston-based Internet Access Technologies (IAT). IAT hopes to strike similar deals in up to 12 cities, including Chicago and Indianapolis, and may partner with Internet service providers such as AOL Time Warner and EarthLink. Houston's program is the latest to encourage Internet use among minorities, the poor, and people in rural areas.

The branch library concept has been taken to new heights as old meets new with the revitalization of e-library kiosks. E-library kiosks (Grenier, 2001) have sprung up in locales ranging from Baltimore, Maryland, to San Jose, California, offering everything from homework help to e-mail access, allowing people to reserve books and make reference queries. One innovative branch is part of a community gallery that displays artwork by local residents.

The challenges for librarians remain, however, as more and more users stream online. In the last half of 2000, 16 million new users gained access to the Internet, including notable increases in use by women, minorities, and families with modest incomes (The Pew Internet & American Life Project, 2000). Moreover, the public continues to turn to the Internet for a variety of information needs: recreation, shopping, health- and work-related research, online news, and financial information. Another recent study (The Pew Internet & American Life Project, 2000) verified what many of us already assumed to be the case, that the Internet has supplanted the library as a research tool for many online teenagers.

The picture is not all rosy for the Internet, however. Although more and more users are online, study after study confirms that the Internet is complex and hard to use. The best search engines cover only a third of the Web; the rest is "invisible"—hidden in databases that search engine spiders cannot penetrate (Price and Sherman, 2001).

Current research has shown that enormous expanses of the Internet are unreachable with standard Web search engines. Only 16% of Net-based information can be located using a general search engine. The other 84% is information stored in databases. Unlike pages on the visible Web, information in databases is generally inaccessible to the software spiders and crawlers that compile search engine indexes. As Web technology improves, more and more information is being stored in databases that feed into dynamically generated Web pages. Far from being superseded, librarians are needed more than ever to sift, sort, select, and serve information.

III. Imitation Is the Sincerest Form of Flattery

The Markle Foundation (Markle Foundation, 2001) found that 63% of all Americans, and 83% of those who go online, have a positive view of the Internet. The research further confirmed that the public identifies the Internet primarily as a source of information—with 45% saying their dominant image of the Internet is that of a "library" as opposed to 17% who compare it to a "shopping mall" or "banking and investment office." Despite the Internet's popularity, a significant portion of those surveyed feel that the authenticity of the Internet is of concern and that much of what is read on the Internet must be questioned. This is both good news and bad news for libraries—good news because libraries are compared favorably with something that is highly popular; bad news if librarians do not offer an effective alternative to the Internet and assert their role as trusted advisors.

The proliferation of the instant expert phenomenon has been well-documented. According to the *New York Times* (Guernsey, 2000) "an expert, it seems, is now an ordinary person sitting at home, beaming advice over the Internet to anyone who wants help." The creators of these sites argue that they are providing the missing link to millions of pages of information. What Internet users need, they say, is human intervention to locate answers quickly, answers that are personalized, easy to find, and free, at least for the time being. If it sounds familiar, it is because what they are describing sounds a lot like what happens in a library.

The story of the 15-year-old teenager who filled out a form and became an official legal expert for Askme.com represents the chilling downside of such entrepreneurial spirit. With "experience" gleaned from watching years of *Court TV*, the young man found himself ranked number 10 out of approximately 150 experts in AskMe.com's criminal-law division, many of whom were actual lawyers (Lewis, 2001).

If it is so easy to become an expert, is there a role for librarians in the Internet age? Yes, according to a CNN users poll, produced following an Associated Press article on the Library of Congress' Collaborative Digital Reference Service (Hopper, 2000). The poll overwhelmingly affirmed, with 90% of those surveyed, that users would prefer a library-based Web search tool over the commercial service they were already using.

IV. Differences between the World Wide Web and Libraries

The World Wide Web is growing—at this writing it hosts more than 7,399,000 sites. The Web also offers unprecedented opportunities for the creation and distribution of information in an unmediated and unrestricted environment. However, the breadth of freely available information on the Web gives the false impression that this material is easily accessible. The digital environment lacks the librarians, publishing houses, and traditions of peer review that regulate the print environment. Without such collaborative regulation, information seekers are forced to wade through mountains of disorganized data in the hopes of finding reliable, authoritative, historically significant and useful content. Edward Kerr (Kerr, 2001) summarizes what many of us have personally experienced, that search engines "may produce thousands of results, but often these are full of links to useless information, advertising banners and promotional garbage, and not to the information the person is looking for." Yahoo, although popular with library patrons, is seriously flawed (Cohen, 2001) as a reference tool. A large percentage of its listings are commercial Web sites and not of high research value. Convenience rules the realm of the commercial Ask-A services (Parsons, 2001). They perpetuate the illusion that all answers to questions may be found on the Internet by searching only what is available on the Internet, not the vast collections found in libraries nor the thousands of library online catalogs that describe and manage those collections.

In general, productive use of the Internet is undermined by several factors:

- The absence of traditional ways of cataloging (or organizing) information
- The collapse of distinctions between credible (or professional) and non-credible (or informal) knowledge producers
- The lack of high-quality, educational, diverse, and socially important content online
- The Web's ephemeral nature—how many times a day while browsing the Web do we encounter error 404: "file not found"?—Internet information is often here today and gone tomorrow

But libraries, too, are growing. According to *Bowker Annual 2000*, more than 806 million volumes are housed in academic libraries in the United States alone. Libraries, with their vast collections of artifactual knowledge, offer inestimable opportunities for information mining. Rather than rely on the labors of volunteers, libraries employ reference and subject specialists, whose knowledge is based on years of academic study and personal experience.

Libraries are different from the Internet in a number of other ways. For example, libraries:

- Organize information using controlled vocabularies and other standards tools to make materials accessible
- Evaluate materials carefully before selecting them according to documented policy statements and guidelines
- House print, nonprint, and digital formats
- Permit patron access in person, in writing, by phone and fax, and online by e-mail
- Evaluate the needs of the patron through the high-touch exercise of the reference interview

The hallmarks of libraries—structure and organization, in-depth subject expertise, sensitivity to the needs of patrons, community-vetted standards and best practices, and analog collections—contrast strongly with the universe of unstructured and unverified information on the Internet. And perhaps most important, unlike their online counterparts, libraries are built to last.

So how do we take the reference desk to cyberspace? The Collaborative Digital Reference Service (CDRS) is one such response. Launched by the Library of Congress in the spring of 2000, and with a growing membership of more than 150 libraries, CDRS enables libraries to help each other serve all of their users, no matter where the users are. Through this network of qualified professionals skilled in the art of locating, organizing, and authenticating information, CDRS combines the power and uniqueness of local collections with the diversity and availability of libraries and librarians everywhere, 24 hours a day, 7 days a week. The power of CDRS is made real every day as patrons gain access to some of the world's most prestigious libraries and collections and most knowledgeable subject experts.

V. The Vision for CDRS

The vision for CDRS began with the recognition that with all of the emphasis on creating digital collections, there had been little coordinated or collaborative focus on developing the public service potential of digital libraries. There was an increasing demand for public access to the Internet in libraries and for remote access to collections and expertise. In each case, the reference librarian was faced with determining how best to satisfy the needs of both the onsite and the remote library user, at a time when electronic resources were increasing at an astounding rate.

After a series of workshops and informal meetings with other professional colleagues, in 1998, the Library of Congress convened a conference called "Reference Service in a Digital Age," the first of its kind to address the public service issues directly. It was our goal to bring reference librarians together to discuss their services and needs at a time when predictions about the imminent demise of the book and printed reference sources (and by inference, libraries) were rampant. Many in the academic community worried aloud that students consulted only the Web for their research.

The conference resulted in an awareness among librarians that increased cooperation among libraries was essential to the future of reference service that integrated both electronic and print resources. Cooperation in the profession has always been strong. Libraries have cooperated to preserve collections, to catalog materials and make them accessible, and more recently, to create virtual libraries. They have borrowed collection items from one another and have shared service models. So why not share reference expertise online?

The Library of Congress began building CDRS in the spring of 2000. From the beginning, libraries of all types—national, academic, special, and public—joined the effort and each brought its special experience, knowledge of user behavior and needs, and subject expertise to bear. Indeed, the rapid development of CDRS is a direct result of the resourcefulness and prescience of its early member libraries.

A. CDRS Organization and Operating Assumptions

Sixteen libraries joined with the Library of Congress to create CDRS: The National Agricultural Library, the National Library of Australia, the National Library of Canada, the Smithsonian American Art Museum, the University of Texas at Austin, the University of Minnesota, Cornell University, Santa Monica Public Library, Morris County (NJ) Public Library, the Peninsula Library System of the Bay Area in northern California, the University of Washington, Vanderbilt University, the University of Southern California, Metropolitan Cooperative Library System (Los Angeles area), Ask ERIC, and The EARL Consortium (U.K.). They not only represented the range of types of libraries, but covered the entire continental United States and initiated the global expansion by covering 15 time zones.

The collaborative nature was in evidence from the start as we collectively defined the business rules and concept of operation by which CDRS would be developed and implemented. For example, we agreed that CDRS is a membership organization; the technology platform is built once to serve the membership as a whole and the "cost" is shared among the members; CDRS is an open service, meaning that members need only Internet access, a browser, and e-mail to use it; members are committed to quality, and service policies, membership certification and Service Level Agreements (SLAs) are enforced to ensure that the brand lives up to the market's expectations; CDRS is an international service and allows for the broadest participation among types of libraries; and the business model is flexible and ensures that no one library or group of libraries would bear all of the costs of establishing and sustaining CDRS. In summary, CDRS will:

- Provide access to global resources
- Collect knowledge for reference access
- Add value to information on the Internet
- Demonstrate flexibility in creating solutions
- Balance the needs of member libraries to ensure the broadest participation

These goals have fundamentally defined what CDRS is and what it is not, and as operating principles, they persist today.

Libraries and their local users are the main beneficiaries of CDRS. End users work through their local libraries, and questions that cannot be answered locally will be sent to CDRS. Membership Service Level Agreements (SLA) define the nature of the library's relationship. The SLA each library has with CDRS will be different and will be limited or expanded depending upon the strengths or limitations of the individual library. For example, a library may agree to ask and answer questions, only ask questions, ask or answer questions only during specified periods, serve as an editor for the knowledge base, or serve as the on-call library if the automatic request manager function is inoperable or if there are problems with the routing of questions and answers.

B. How Does CDRS Work?

CDRS is not an e-mail or "live chat" service, although it uses e-mail to notify members of incoming questions and answers and we are beginning to integrate "live chat" in part of the service. Experiments with the latter began in the fall of 2001. CDRS has two component parts: submission of questions and answers, and archiving of answers for future use. An end user requests information through a CDRS member institution and the member institution sends the query to the online Request Manager (RM) software for processing and assignment. The RM searches a database of CDRS Member institution profiles looking for the member institution best suited to answer the question. Matches are made on the basis of such data elements as hours of service, including time zones, subject strengths, scope of collections, and types of patrons served. The "matchmaking" happens in seconds. Once a match on an institution has been made, the query is sent to that institution for answering. After the query has been answered, it is routed back to the original CDRS requesting library via the RM to end the transaction and complete other administrative tasks.

A library's profile contains basic information about the library, including hours of service, collection strengths, staff subject and language strengths, education levels served, languages covered, geographic location of users served, whether there are special services provided and what they are—as many as 28 data fields. This information is captured in a table where it is used by the RM to sort, assign, and track incoming questions and to deliver answers to the end user. The answers are also edited and stored in a separately searchable archive. The participating library has complete control over the profile and can "code" itself as broadly or as narrowly as it chooses. Further, the profile tool is flexible enough to allow for regular updating to reflect staffing changes or special circumstances that would affect the automatic routing by the online RM. For example, if the astronomy specialist is on sabbatical for several months and no backup is available, the library might choose to remove that subject strength from its profile until the staff member returns.

CDRS uses Library of Congress Classification to classify the subject areas of the questions. More recently, we have been working to provide a Dewey Decimal classification crosswalk so that Dewey users can more easily code their questions and answers. To meet the needs of the medical library community, we are adopting use of Class W developed by the National Library of Medicine.

C. Pilot Tests

The implementation process began with a series of pilot tests of the technical solutions. Pilot 1 had two principal goals: to test the effectiveness of the library profiles and to test a Web form for submitting questions. Results indicated that more standardization of the data elements was needed. For example, we needed to reach agreement on use of a standardized tool to describe a library's subject strengths and for practical reasons, chose a truncated version of the Library of Congress Classification Schedule. All of the libraries contributed edited sample questions and answers which were sent through the system according to a scripted schedule.

In Pilot 2, we added more institutions worldwide, increased the number of questions asked of the system, revised the profile database, and began to experiment with software packages to serve as the Request Manager. On the administrative end of the project, we developed a variety of SLAs, identified training issues, and created an Advisory Board made up of volunteers from the participating libraries.

The first "live" question was posed on June 29, 2000. This reference inquiry—regarding ancient Byzantine cuisine—was sent by EARL Ask-A-Librarian, a participating public library consortium in the United Kingdom. The request, received by the CDRS server at the Library of Congress in Washington, was matched based on subject matter and time of day, and routed to the Santa Monica Public Library at 10:40 AM. Several hours later, a list of five books was on its way to London. So the "test" worked and we were on our way. During its first month of live testing, the member institutions exchanged more than 300 questions and answers, creating a virtual reference desk spanning three continents.

Pilot 3, which began in the late fall of 2000 and was to continue through the first quarter of 2002, focuses on scaling up the workflow, creating and implementing an online profiling tool, implementing a manual backup

system, the "on-call librarian," and developing and implementing a prototype of the knowledge base. New administrative features in the workflow
design permit a library to reject and redirect a question that was deemed to
be incorrectly assigned to another library and allow a library to be taken out
of service if its quota has been reached. The "on-call" librarian, implemented
in the summer of 2001, ensures that no question is lost in the system and
provides technical support if CDRS goes out of service. The "on-call" librarian monitors the system, keeps watch, and ensures that all is as it should be,
providing the high-touch sure hand in a high-tech environment.

D. Recycling Information: CDRS Knowledge Base

We demonstrated a prototype of the Knowledge Base (KB) at the annual
meeting of the American Library Association (ALA) in June 2001. As envisioned, the KB will provide librarians with access to a resource that is both
authoritative and peer-reviewed. It will also further cut down on duplicative
effort; librarians will be able to share commonly asked questions rather than
having to recreate the same answer an infinite number of times. The KB is
currently in test mode so questions and answers are not available to CDRS
members for browsing or searching. As we test the technical solution, we are
building the business rules for editing and managing the KB once it is in production. The KB, populated with the diverse and authentic information
provided by CDRS librarians, will ultimately serve as a front end to CDRS,
designed to "catch" and answer incoming questions if there is a ready match.
If there is no match on the knowledge base, the question will be routed
through the RM and assigned to a library.

In addition to populating the KB with data from questions and answers
generated in CDRS, we hope to include data from other sources outside of
CDRS: for instance, members' ready-reference files or databases of answered
e-reference questions. Or we may arrange to include content provided by
arrangement with a publisher. Disclaimers appear on the CDRS home page
and in all technical documents related to CDRS (e.g., the SLA) stating that
any question submitted is a potential candidate for the KB, and both the question and the answer will be stripped of personal information. A privacy statement is also posted. Finally, as with other aspects of CDRS, the primary
language of the KB is English. However, provisions have been made to
accommodate the bilingual needs of the National Library of Canada. We
know we have to add other language capabilities. Indeed, our marketing
research has identified the top six languages for development: Spanish,
Chinese, Russian, Japanese, French, and Italian.

Consistent with its collaborative nature, CDRS has sought editorial assistance from its membership not only to help with the actual editing of records

but also to serve as an ad-hoc editorial board. In general, the KB Editor is like a copy editor, who reviews records for bias and objectivity, provides quality control, and ensures that the format of particular types of data (such as URLs and bibliographic citations) conforms to standards. The ultimate objective of the editorial process is to enable better searching and browsing and overall usability of the database.

The current thinking is that the Editorial Review Board will set the standard for review of the questions. Editors will not be asked to make substantive changes or to correct content; rather, they will check for basic spelling and punctuation errors. If an editor determines that a record is so flawed that copy editing cannot fix it, it is set aside for further review or marked for deletion, making it unavailable to users of the KB.

In addition, some guidelines are being established to encourage CDRS members to adopt common data entry practices in order to add value to their answers *prior* to their inclusion in the KB: for example, the removal of personal information (such as patron family names, location or contact information, or any other identifying information) that appears in the question or answer text, or records containing information from licensed databases. In the latter case, if direct quotes from such databases are given, the editor will reconstruct the answers to provide a citation only, or to paraphrase the text from the database. No information will be directly copied from a licensed database and placed in the body of an answer.

All edited records will include the following basic information:

1. Administrative data relating to the question so that threads and links to related subject areas can be established
2. Key words, subject headings, and classification information
3. The date the record was entered into the system
4. Decisions about whether the record is to be updated and how often— for example, the answer to the question "Who was the third President of the United States?" will not change over time. But the answer to the question "Who *is* the President of the United States?" will change depending on when the question is asked
5. Source citations to include author, title, publisher, place of publication, date, unique ID (e.g., ISBN, LCCN, catalog number, or OCLC accession number)

Why create a knowledge base? A recent discussion on an e-ref listserv illuminated some of the challenges inherent in creating a reusable file of archived questions and answers for patron use. As one might imagine, the discussion was impassioned and went to the heart of the high-touch versus high-tech debate in reference service. Those less favorably disposed cited the diversity of questions asked, which would make it unlikely that the answers for highly specialized questions could be reused (Sloan, 2001). Others believe that factual questions are the exception, not the rule, in e-reference. Still others observed that our patrons merit some human contact in the information-seeking process—even if this contact is mediated by e-mail or Web contact center software. When patrons are sent to an online FAQ, librarians lose the opportunity to control the outcome, instruct the patron, and otherwise create a connection, all of which characterize a high-quality reference service.

On the flip side, still others allowed that although there are indeed few exact repeat questions, it is often true that our patrons are not exactly sure what they are asking for or what they need. So why not give them vetted Q&A related to their subject and let them decide if the information is useful? Such a resource might even cause them to reshape their thinking or see their topic in a new light. How often have we experienced the thrill of accidental discovery, browsing through the stacks and stumbling across the perfect book while the exact title that brought us to the stacks in the first place sits three books away on the shelf? And let's not forget the frenzy that surrounds current events phenomena that has all of us answering the same question over and over again (the impeachment, the millennium question, etc.) until the event recedes into the background. And what about the relevancy of our chosen profession? If we as a profession treat the product of our work as dispensable and not worthy of archiving, how are others to find it valuable?

E. Quality Is Job 1

Primary responsibility for quality review is currently borne by the participating institutions with periodic review by the system administrator (LC) and the "on call" librarian. Quality control issues under review include packaging of the question before it is routed (e.g., sources checked), content elements of the answer, turnaround time, and the appropriateness of the response given to an intended audience.

To begin to address quality control of the answers and information provided, the CDRS Home page links to *Facets of Quality for Digital Reference Services* (Virtual Reference Desk, 2000), a set of standards for creating and maintaining digital reference services participating in the Virtual Reference Desk (VRD) Network. VRD is a CDRS partner organization and this document is embraced as the standard for CDRS digital reference service, although we acknowledge that this is only a start. Indeed, the growing reference community has identified assessment of quality as a top research priority.

On behalf of CDRS, the Library of Congress agreed to participate in funding a study undertaken to develop methods to assess the quality of digital reference services. The study, begun in March 2001, is being conducted by the Information Use Management and Policy Institute at Florida State University under the direction of Dr. Charles R. McClure with the assistance of Dr. R. David Lankes and the Information Institute of Syracuse at Syracuse University. The study will produce a range of assessment techniques, measures of services, and quality standards for digital reference.

In the formal standards-setting arena, the Library of Congress hosted the National Institute Standards Organization (NISO) workshop on Networked Digital Reference Services in April 2001. The workshop attendees included a diverse group of stakeholders representing the library and information community, Ask-A service providers, and vendors. The workshop agenda addressed a range of questions including the following: What aspects of digital reference can benefit from standardization? Who are the stakeholders that would benefit from the standard? What existing work has been done that could be a starting point? What experimentation or research is needed for the development of the standard? And, what are the most appropriate next steps for possible standards development? A proposal to create standards for networked reference services resulted from this workshop. Details and description of next steps are available at http://www.niso.org/netref-report.html.

F. CDRS Administration: The Advisory Board

Governance of CDRS is achieved through an Advisory Board, which is composed of representatives from member institutions and approved by the membership. The Library of Congress and OCLC (the Online Computer Library Center in Dublin, Ohio) have permanent seats on the Board, which the Library of Congress chairs. The Advisory Board sets membership policies, including approval of new members, and charts future directions. All types of libraries are represented on the Board and at least two seats are occupied by international participants.

Business meetings with the membership are regularly held to elicit feedback, to raise and solve workflow problems, to discuss training and performance measures, and to build esprit de corps. Members routinely cite this aspect of the collaboration as the most valuable, in that it helps build professional relationships and professional acumen by working on reference questions from patrons all over the world.

The CDRS home page posts general information and news links, information for members, and project milestones. Rotating library logos co-brand the service with participating libraries and searching tips are provided by experts in the field. A listserv allows members to communicate freely and frequently with one another and get technical questions addressed.

G. Market Research

To help determine what potential members might pay for a service such as CDRS, the Library of Congress sponsored a series of interactive sessions and online surveys on cost models for library decision-makers. These sessions provided valuable information to the planners of CDRS—participants affirmed support for CDRS and its mission to have credentialed experts provide high-quality information, and expressed a willingness to pay for such a service.

The three market research activities conducted during 2001, were designed to:

- Understand industry trends, concerns, needs, and expectations that shape the direction of e-reference
- Identify the factors that speed or slow the adoption of e-reference services within libraries
- Determine the e-reference features that have the greatest importance to libraries and should be incorporated in CDRS
- Establish the preferred packaging of e-reference features and price support for CDRS

The combined research activities included a total of 625 participants representing libraries of all types (e.g., public, academic, national, special) from countries around the world. Information and opinions were gathered from participants through a series of interactive sessions—moderated workshops where participants cast electronic votes and discussed underlying issues—and an Internet survey. The market research activities were very productive and produced a number of major conclusions:

- Resources of libraries are being stretched thin as demand increases and expectations of patrons continue to rise
- Reference requests are becoming more specialized, detailed, and complex and require more effort to fulfill and access to resources beyond a library's walls
- There is strong agreement for collaboration among libraries to share resources and extend better services to patrons
- Interest in deploying e-reference services is very strong and will fundamentally change the profession of reference librarians
- Quality of information is the single most important performance attribute for CDRS
- Libraries are ready and willing to commit staff resources to CDRS

These conclusions will be used to guide the further development of CDRS.

H. The Whole Is Greater Than the Sum of the Parts

Maximum flexibility in developing the many component parts of CDRS is one of the service's fundamental precepts. For a library to want to participate in CDRS, CDRS has to be perceived to have value. Just as there are no "one size fits all" libraries, so, too, are there no "one size fits all" partnerships with CDRS. Libraries are structured and organized differently, they have different local audiences, and they have different policies and procedures for ensuring quality control. For the relationship to work, CDRS has to fill a service gap, e.g., a staffing need or a subject strength. In addition, many libraries have local, special collections that are unique to them. These specialized collections make a powerful contribution to CDRS overall, filling special niches that larger research institutions may not be able to fill. When the participating library defines the terms of the relationship with CDRS, that library will have greater incentive to make the arrangement work, for itself and for CDRS. We create the tools; the library decides for itself how to use them most effectively. Participation in CDRS allows libraries to:

- *Provide better service.* Members frequently see involvement in CDRS as an opportunity to implement their library's vision; extend service without adding more staff or increasing hours; increase the relevancy of their library in its community; or provide answers to questions they would not otherwise be able to answer.
- *Reach new patrons.* Libraries are using e-reference to good advantage as an outreach tool. CDRS member Cleveland Public Library recently launched KnowItNow and HomeworkNow, two live 24/7 online reference services which combine the reference expertise of librarians with the comprehensive resources of the CLEVNET libraries, and state-of-the-art technology to meet patron information needs. Librarians, like those at Cleveland Public and elsewhere, see technology as a means of reaching out to new patrons who don't visit the library, establishing new relationships with the younger generation on the Web, or supporting distance learning by using the Web to bring knowledge resources to their patrons.
- *Access valuable collections and resources.* This is frequently cited as the most exciting aspect of CDRS. Librarians appreciate having local access to remote collections and expertise. They also believe that participation in CDRS enables them to share resources in a more cost-efficient way and gives them the opportunity to extend access to knowledge even if their library's budget is declining. They find value in connecting with peers doing similar work around the world. It keeps their perspectives on and sensitivities to other cultures fresh and relevant, and builds understanding through access to new tools and resources.

I. Where Do We Go from Here?

In January of 2001, the Online Computer Library Center (OCLC) and the Library of Congress, on behalf of its member libraries, signed a cooperative agreement to guide CDRS through its next phase of development. According to the agreement, OCLC will provide technical and development support to CDRS by building and maintaining a database of profiles of participating institutions that will provide answers through CDRS; building and maintaining a question-and-answer database system that will enable CDRS participants to catalog answers and store them in a searchable and browsable database; and providing administrative support for CDRS, including marketing, registration of new members, training, and user support. Together, the Library of Congress and OCLC expect to develop a viable model for a self-sustaining digital reference service and promote CDRS in the library community.

Currently, libraries participating in CDRS connect with other libraries on behalf of end users so that libraries can define the parameters, determine what works and what does not work, and create a service that is scalable and maximally responsive to user needs. From the beginning, however, we have envisioned CDRS as a service that will be available directly to end users. We recognize that many individuals never go to their local library but still need information. And we want them to benefit from the power of a network of libraries that is dedicated to providing 24/7 reference service any time, anywhere. Over the next several months, CDRS will be developing a document delivery project to capture bibliographic information in the question/answer process that can be used to initiate an automatic interlibrary loan. This is the first step in building what we hope will be "one-stop shopping" for reference and information services.

CDRS delivers to a broad spectrum of users the direct benefits of quality reference service, including expert knowledge navigation, a searchable archive of authoritative answers, and increased visibility and support for libraries everywhere. Through CDRS, a library can extend its services without adding more staff or increasing hours, increase its relevancy in the community, and provide answers to questions that it might not otherwise be able to answer. CDRS affords a library the opportunity to reach out into the community in new and dynamic ways; reach patrons who don't visit the library; establish new relationships with the younger generation on the Web; support distance learning by using the Web to bring knowledge resources to its patrons; and provide global access to local collections, thereby extending access to knowledge even if a library's budget is declining.

As we build the service, we are performing a number of behind-the-scenes analyses to ensure the project's long-term sustainability, such as creating a marketing plan to attract new customers and determining the most cost-effective means of administering the network. We are continually examining and testing our technical solutions to ensure that we have the right ones to meet our mission, and that the tools we have created are easy for librarians to use. We are looking, too, at the length of time it takes to complete a transaction, developing criteria for determining when a library should use CDRS and when it should handle an inquiry within its own resources, devising how to thread the inquiry so that new information, if available, can be forwarded to the patron once the inquiry has been closed out.

J. Lessons Being Learned

CDRS is evolving and as it evolves, we continually check in with our participant libraries to ensure that we are developing a service that meets their needs. A number of them have voiced concerns that serve to remind us that there are many things we have yet to work out. For example, at the most basic level, successful implementation of CDRS in a library is dependent upon staff buy-in and buy-in from a library's governing body, e.g., a dean, a vice-president, a board. Every library is different and each will go about this task in a different way. Just as we market our services to patrons, so, too, must libraries market a service like CDRS to their staff and be certain that it is indeed something they need and will use.

Determining the appropriate and legal use of licensed databases is a question that all libraries will face and that, if not addressed, will undermine the ability of libraries to collaborate effectively. Librarians will need to work creatively and diligently with publishers of electronic resources to allow reasonable use of such services by those technically outside of the service parameters.

Many librarians have concerns about the questions that are sent to CDRS. Indeed, there may be many reasons why a library has elected to submit a question to CDRS—issues of staffing, the availability of various resources, a desire to practice using the software to work out workflow issues—and while it should be left to the discretion of the members when and how to use CDRS, use of an internal vetting and review process would help ensure that the receiving library won't feel it is doing someone's else's work. Librarians must take care to cite sources already searched not only to avoid duplication of effort but also to offer guidance on search strategy. CDRS online help documents are being created to assist members in making the most effective use of CDRS. For example, information is available on how to submit questions, complete a library profile, and perform a range of other procedures.

As CDRS looks to expand globally and become a true 24/7 service, there are many issues we must examine: service to local populations in their own languages; navigating cultural and political sensitivities; and e-commerce and trade agreements that may affect pricing models. It is sobering to realize that by 2003, non-English-language material will account for over half the content of the Internet. The solutions to these issues will determine the long-term success of CDRS.

K. Are We Ready for In-Your-Face Reference?

Libraries today are using technology to link those in need with credible and accurate resources. As I noted in the beginning of this article, CDRS is the latest in a series of innovative pilot projects designed to make information available faster and more effectively to meet more specialized demands.

This is undeniably a time for librarians to reinvent themselves, to adapt their skills to the demands of the protean universe of information, and to place themselves at the center of that universe. Technological advances have created new opportunities for libraries, information managers, researchers, and library patrons of all kinds. Indeed, the Internet has created a fundamental change in the way people collect information and acquire knowledge. Instead of making a trip to the library, researchers turn first to the Internet. Librarians, however, are still regarded as trusted advisors, knowledge navigators, keepers, interpreters, and mediators of information and knowledge. We perform this role because all people are entitled to equal access to information and knowledge. To keep current, we must adapt and not feel threatened by the pace of change, but embrace it and use it to imagine new and more responsive programs and services.

It is still early in this evolution from reference desk to cyberspace, and because we have not figured all of it out yet, apprehensions about e-reference services persist. Concerns about how they work, whether they will fit in a library, or whether they will meet the public's need are frequently voiced. Such concerns are a necessary part of the "thinking out loud" process that occurs on the listservs, at professional meetings, in training sessions, and at workshops, a process that must continue if we are to survive as a profession. The following sections discuss some common concerns.

1. The Benefits and Risks of E-Reference Are Unknown

There is a perception that e-reference is focused on short factual questions only. Our experience with CDRS to date has shown just the opposite. The range of topics queried has been broad, to say the least, everything from determining the transport and thermodynamic properties of ethylene glycol, through asking for a history of pop-up books, finding out what astronauts listen to in space, locating background information on the Rose McClendon Players (a black theater group during the Harlem Renaissance), defining "cheese head," or locating the Yiddish word for midget.

All of the excitement about "live chat" and its many features (e.g., co-browsing, page pushing, and complete transcripts of the transactions) underscores the belief that the profession needs to move well beyond e-mail to meet the needs of patrons. CDRS provides an online database of vetted and edited questions and answers for immediate access and assigns questions based on profiles of knowledge resources so that questions go to the right place. E-mail services do not typically do this.

Concern over quality of the answers is important. However, CDRS members are professionals, committed through Service Level Agreements to provide a high level of service. In addition, a certification program and a quality assurance program managed by the system administrator further ensure high quality.

2. E-Reference Services Such as CDRS Are Costly to Implement and Maintain

CDRS has been planned and implemented as a service any library can use and afford. The collaborative nature of the project and the use of Service Level Agreements that define the level of participation will determine the pricing models and how much a library will have to pay to be a member. In CDRS, many types of Service Level Agreements are possible and can be limited or expanded depending upon the strengths or limitations of the individual library. For example, a library may agree to ask and answer questions; only ask questions; ask or answer questions only during specified periods; serve as an editor for the knowledge base; or serve as the on-call library to troubleshoot system problems. This arrangement should make CDRS affordable for any library. The more important issue we should be asking ourselves is whether libraries can afford not to provide e-reference services to their patrons. Is it in the profession's best interest to abandon patrons to commercial, unmediated reference services that promise to deliver information to the desktop any time, anywhere, but don't promise high value or quality?

3. Some Librarians Are Reluctant to Learn and Use New Technology

Concerns that new technology will be too hard to learn and use are not insignificant. Further, there is a concern that libraries are falling prey to the latest gimmickry and will buy it whether or not it meets a service need. The technology base for CDRS is very simple and not hard to use. All a library needs to participate is a Web browser and Internet access. Information is collected on easy-to-use forms. If one can browse the Web, one can use CDRS. Also, there is an online training program and a variety of tools developed to help librarians understand and benefit from the full functional capabilities of CDRS. CDRS is also compatible with the various "live chat" services (e.g., 24/7, Convey, Q&A Café, LSSI) and each can be integrated to form a suite of online reference services that actively engages the patron in the search process. In CDRS, "live chat" may also be used to conduct the reference interview or to troubleshoot problems.

There is an underlying issue that relates to staff development. As libraries become increasingly involved in serving more users, many of whom expect to use electronic resources, and expect further that the resources will be delivered to their desktop, we will need to identify the skills needed to launch new programs without the comfort of the same old tools. Not everyone wants to or can think big. How do we teach creative thinking and innovation? Libraries will need to establish, if they have not already, a career development training program. Although we don't really know yet what catalogers or reference librarians or any staff will be doing in 5 years, many of the digital initiatives hold the keys to finding out just what the jobs might look like and what we need to do to get there from here.

4. Large Networks Such as CDRS Will Cut Out the Local Library

Some librarians have suggested that they don't need an e-reference service or need to collaborate with other libraries because they are able to answer all the questions they get. Can every library be sure that every question is being answered to the satisfaction of the patron and that the library will continue to perform at such a high level? If a reference staff is overworked, why not offload overflow questions to CDRS or another e-reference service?

We believe that CDRS strengthens the local library system because it not only adds resources, for an initial up-front investment of time, but also provides an opportunity for libraries to reexamine traditional ways of providing service. Such reexamination should prompt us to consider what today's patrons want from a digital reference service and begin to conduct the kinds of needs analysis sorely lacking to date (Assessing Quality in Digital Reference Services Study Bulletin 090101 What about the User?) that will result in user- rather than library-centric systems and solutions. Such analysis should not only help us define who uses digital reference services but also help us define services to meet their needs more effectively (Gray, 2000).

Through CDRS, there are libraries and partners to share the workload and software and databases to make reference work more efficient and timely.

Library patrons will have the opportunity to query institutions in remote locations for specialized information that would not otherwise be available to them. Library patrons will also be able to get an answer to a factual question when their local library is closed.

CDRS has the potential to get patrons to come back to libraries for their information needs. It is a tool for communication and for sharing resources. Rosemary Cooper, formerly of Boise Public Library, a CDRS member, observed recently that "CDRS has the potential to succeed beyond the efforts of Stumpers or even some regional reference center models, because it has the support of major institutions with some resources to contribute to the development and marketing of the project and can connect a wider range of participants and resources. CDRS can then also help position local libraries to become more meaningful resources to their communities. Local libraries have to articulate a need and commitment to the project for it to work as well. And getting the buy-in of reference staff is essential. It needs to truly be a collaboration and can't be perceived as anything less for it to work."

VI. Conclusion: Both/And

Most of us were drawn to the profession of librarianship because we liked the idea of helping others, serving the public good, and making a difference. Yet there is growing anxiety that the profession is becoming something many of us no longer recognize. Increased use of technology should not be an occasion to abandon the principles that brought us to the profession in the first place. Sensitively packaging information to serve patrons at the most appropriate level should still be an important goal.

The reference interview, historically the means through which we determined a patron's needs, now most often takes place sight unseen. It is still an essential component of library service, although perhaps more complicated to execute with no visual cues to prompt us. As we guide patrons through a live chat session, for example, time delays and keeping the patron interested while we search will not be insignificant challenges to overcome. We will need to check in more often with the patron: "I'm looking that up now" or "This search will take a couple of minutes." We will also have to remember that ending the transaction will take some extra steps.

We cannot leap to the conclusion that technology alone will do it all as we mentally flip on the elevator music and go about our real work. In other words, we must "not mistake a tool for a goal" (Katz, 2001). Wherever possible, through bibliographic instruction and the reference interview, we must educate patrons so that they can participate in the learning process and become more adept at searching. Decisions about uses of technology should be based on appropriateness, need, and network ability. If we are not already, we should be thinking about offering tiered services to meet differing needs and exploring ways to bring the library to where the users are.

It should be clear to each of us but perhaps bears repeating that with all this talk of technology, now is not the time to abandon our service values (Ferguson and Bunge, 1997). We still have an obligation to make the digital environment work effectively for all of the library's users. To that end, libraries must continue to ensure equity of access and customize our services to meet the needs of the patrons while exploring new service values such as integrating technologies, maintaining holistic computing environments, and collaborating across administrative lines both within and outside of our institutions. Up to now, the professional debate has focused on the wrong boolean operator: it is not high touch or high tech, but both high touch *and* high tech. As the geographic borders that define us disappear into wireless networks of interoperability that mitigate the effect of time zones, there is a greater likelihood that differences in cultural backgrounds and contexts will obscure information sending and receiving. The technical complexity of the global network will be far easier to overcome than will prevalent cultural and political prejudices and attitudes. And the assumptions we make in formulating answers—assuming patron proximity, for example, when the patron may be halfway around the world—may be false or we may give answers without appreciating or understanding the regional context. We know less about other regions than they know about us. Our Western culture is highly self-referential and our media are everywhere. It will take time, patience, and well-placed global partnerships before we can shed our blinders and interact responsibly with a world around us that is increasingly affecting each aspect of our daily lives.

CDRS helps fulfill the Library of Congress's mission to provide quality reference services through its international collections of broad subject, language, and format scope, as well as the traditional cataloging systems that support electronic reference. It continues a long LC tradition of collaboration with other libraries and a tradition of leadership in information services. But the Library of Congress does not and cannot do this alone. By engaging with librarians and libraries everywhere, LC and its partners can bring order and context to the global and diverse world of information.

The challenge for librarians is to leverage the excitement and power of new technology to create resources and services that researchers will return to again and again. Librarians would do well to remember the words of Librarian of Congress Ainsworth Rand Spofford, who wrote in an essay on "Aids to Readers": "Remember always, that readers are entitled to the best and most careful service, for a librarian is not only a keeper, but the interpreter of the intellectual stores of a library. It is a good and safe rule to let no opportunity of aiding a reader escape."

Current information about CDRS can be found at http://www.loc.gov/cdrs.

References

Coffman, Steve (2002). Distance Education and Virtual Reference: Where are we headed? *Computers in Libraries* **21**(4), 20.
Coffman, Steve, and McGlamery, Susan (2000). The Librarian and Mr. Jeeves. *American Libraries* **20**(5), 66–69.
Cohen, Laura B. (2001). Yahoo and the abdication of judgement. *American Libraries* **32**(1), 60–62.
Collaborative Digital Reference Service (CDRS), http://www.loc.gov/rr/digiref/news.html.
Ferguson, Chris D., and Bunge, Charles A. (1997). The shape of services to come: Values-based reference service for the largely digital library. *College & Research Libraries* **58**(3), 252–265.
Gray, Suzanne M. (2000). Virtual Reference Services directions and agendas. *Reference and User Services Quarterly* **39**(4), 365.
Grenier, Melinda Patterson (2001). E-branch library machines help to bridge digital divide. *Wall Street Journal*, July 12, 2001.
Guernsey, Lisa (2000). Suddenly everybody's an expert. *New York Times*, February 3, 2000.
Hopper, D. Ian (2000). New network links up libraries online. Associated Press, November 19, 2000.
Janes, J. (2000). Current research in digital reference: Findings and implications. Presentation at Facets of Digital Reference, the VRD 2000 Annual Digital Reference Conference, 17 October, 2000, Seattle, WA.
Katz, Stanley (2001). In information technology, "Don't mistake a tool for a goal." *Chronicle of Higher Education Review*, June 15, 2001, http://chronicle.com/free/v47/i40/40b00701.htm.
Kerr (2001). p. 8.
Lewis, Michael. Faking it: The Internet revolution has nothing to do with the Nasdaq. *New York Times Magazine*, July 15, 2001.
Lipow, Anne (1999). Strategies for the Next Millennium: Proceedings of the Ninth Australasian Information Online & On Disc Conference and Exhibition Sydney Convention and Exhibition Centre, Sydney, Australia, 19B21.
Markle Foundation (2001). Toward a Framework for Internet Accountability. July.
McClure, Charles, and Lankes, David (2001). What about the user? *Assessing Quality in Digital Reference Services, Study Bulletin* 090101.
McDonald, Tim (2001). Study: Internet rage hits the Information Highway. *NewsFactorNetwork*, April 9, 2001, http://www.newsfactor.com/perl/story/8806.html.
National Information Standards Organization (NISO), http://www.niso.org/netref-report.html.
OCLC, The WEB Characterization Project Web statistics, http://wcp.oclc.org/.
Parsons, Ann Marie (2001). Digital reference: How libraries can compete with Ask-A services. *Digital Library Federation Newsletter* **2**(1), http://www.diglib.org/pubs/news02_01/RefBenchmark.htm.
Perkins, Eva (2001). Johns Hopkins' tragedy: Could librarians have prevented a death?, http://www.infotoday.com/newsbreaks/nb010806-1.htm.
The Pew Internet & American Life Project, 2000 (2000). http://www.pewInternet.org/reports/toc.asp?Report=39.

Preer, Jean (2001). Where are libraries in bowling alone. *American Libraries* **32**, September, 60–62.

Price, Gary, and Sherman, Chris (2001). *The Invisible Web: Uncovering Information Sources Search Engines Can't See*. Information Today, Inc.

Sloan, Bernie (2001). Ready for Reference: Academic Libraries Offer Live Web-based Reference. Preliminary Report. Urbana, Champaign, IL, http://www.lis.uiuc.edu/~b-sloan/ready4ref.htm.

Spofford, Ainsworth Rand (1900). *A Book for All Readers, Designed as an Aid to the Collection, Use, and Preservation of Books, and the Formation of Public and Private Libraries*. G. P. Putnam's Sons, New York.

Swartz, Jon (2000). Houston citizens get free e-mail. Project attempts to close "digital divide." *USA Today*, August 20, 2000, p. 1A.

Virtual Reference Desk (2000). Facets of Quality for Digital Reference Services, Version 4. [Online], http://www.vrd.org/training/facets10-00.htm.

The Current State of Research on Reference Transactions

John V. Richardson, Jr.
UCLA Department of Information Studies
Los Angeles, California 90095-1520

I. Introduction: The Reference Transaction

So that the reader can understand the theoretical orientation of reference researchers, this chapter reviews what is known about reference transactions. Despite a relatively long history of writings dating from the latter part of the 19th century, the professional literature in general is rather too rich in merely descriptive articles; there are, however, several increasingly analytical models, and even some flowcharts presented in the later decades of the 20th century. Although we know most, if not all, of the component parts of the reference (i.e., question asking and answering) process, we do not yet understand the true influence of many variables on the process. Most of the previous work is based on simple bivariate models without any guiding theory. Perhaps this situation is due to the fact that no one has thoroughly synthesized all that we know about the process by analytically and evaluatively reviewing the previous research literature. To date there have been a handful of other attempts (e.g., Paisley, 1968; Dervin and Nilan, 1986; *Reference Assessment Manual*, 1995; Richardson, 1995; Julien, 1996; Palmquist, 1998; and Wang, 1999), but this chapter is the most extensive and most exhaustive analysis published in the open literature.

This chapter should be of interest to anyone wishing to build a testable model of the reference transaction, but this chapter should also be useful to library and information science educators as well as reference librarians who wish to improve their own professional practice using a research-based approach to the reference transaction.

II. Theoretical Constructs

Conceptually, the research literature can be characterized along several dimensions. Writing in 1992, Richardson suggested at least three dimensions:

reference materials, reference methods, and user characteristics of reference librarians. See his Table 1, columns 3–5.

A. Reference Materials, Methods, and User Characteristics

Indeed, 18 of the following studies have focused on the material tools necessary to answer reference questions successfully. In fact, it is really the oldest approach when one looks at the compilation of recommended reference tools at the end of the 19th century. Notable work in the 20th century identifying the useful tools has been undertaken by Bonk (1960, 1961, 1963, 1964), Larsen (1979), and Connell (1999).

The procedural approach to reference work (called the method perspective) is most strongly adovocated by Hutchins (1944) and many researchers (two-thirds; in fact) have adopted either an affective, behavioral, or cognitive approach (see later discussion for more on this tripartite scheme).

After an early start with DeJong in 1926, attention shifted to a more usercentric perspective in earnest with Perry (1961). In the main, these more sophisticated attempts have tried to model the user using stereotyping (Rich, 1979), a speech communication model (Gothberg, 1974), human information processing (White, 1983), or a sense-making model (Dervin, 1986). Nearly half (42%) of the studies have focused on the user.

B. Graphic Representations

Graphically, the various models which appear in the literature have also shown some increasing sophistication (see Table 1, column 6). The earliest representations started out as line drawings (see the one by Rees and Saracevic, 1963) and less often, but showing some quick progress to flowcharting (the earliest by Hayes and Carlson, 1964, followed by Jahoda *et al.*, 1968) or a flowsheet, a technique whereby detailed charting of the steps in the process takes place.

Despite the fact that the flowcharting technique was developed between 1915 and 1920 to study manufacturing processes, it has found a more general applicability (see Kuhlthau, 1989). Nevertheless, it does involve some distortions of reality by treating the reference interview as a discrete process rather than the continuous process that it is. In that respect, a flowchart represents reality as crisp rather than fuzzy. Such a model also assumes that the process is linearly progressive and composed of simple rather than complexly interdependent steps. The most complete representation as a flowchart, to date, is Richardson (1995).

Furthermore, much of the research literature adopts, either implicitly or explicitly, an input–process–output–feedback (IPOF) model when discussing

Table 1

Theoretical Constructs Presented in the Literature on the Reference Transaction

Entry	Author	Materials	Methods	Users	Use of Models	Affective	Behavioral	Cognitive
1	de Jong			1			1	
2	Conner	1						
3	Wyer		1				1	
4	Guerrier	1					1	
5	Alexander						1	
6	Hyers						1	
7	Hutchins						1	
8	Stone						1	
9	Cole	1					1	
10	Wood		1					
11	Delaney		1			1		
12	Maxfield		1		counseling	1		
13	Breed		1					1
14	Francillon	1					1	
15	Bonk	1					1	
16	Perry			1				
17	Univ. of Michigan SRC			1				
18	Taylor		1	1			1	1
19	Rees and Saracevic			1	graphic		1	1
20	Hayes and Carlson		1		flowchart			
21	Shera			1	graphic/decision theory			1
22	Bunge		1				1	
23	Goldhor		1				1	
24	Taylor			1	chart		1	1

177

Table 1
(Continued)

Entry	Author	Materials	Methods	Users	Use of Models	Affective	Behavioral	Cognitive
25	SUNY						1	
26	Crowley	1	1				1	
27	Jahoda et al.	1	1		flowchart		1	
28	Jestes and Laird		1					
29	Salton		1		chart			1
30	Crum		1	1			1	
31	Lubans		1	1			1	
32	Penland		1		counseling	1		
33	Vavrek			1			1	
34	King		1		Gallup q design/King adult eduction		1	
35	Stych		1				1	
36	Swope and Katzer			1			1	
37	Kronus			1	sociology of education		1	
38	Gothberg		1	1	speech comm/Rogers/Mehrabian		1	
39	Jennerich		1		counseling		1	
40	Benson and Maloney		1				1	
41	Boyer and Theimer		1					1
42	McFayden		1	1	Jones' common-sense		1	
43	Peck		1		counseling		1	
44	Boucher		1		nonverbal: Darwin, Birdwhistell, Ekman		1	
45	Powell	1	1				1	

No.	Author				Model / concept		
46	Lynch		1				1
47	Myers	1	1				1
48	Sandock			1			1
49	Eichman			1	modified Shannon-Weaver		1
50	Rettig		1				1
51	Bates		1				1
52	Belkin et al.			1		1	
53	Larsen	1					
54	Rich		1		stereotypes		1
55	Childers		1				1
56	Morgan			1			1
57	van House		1				1
58	White			1	human info processing/ Minsky's frames		wholistic
59	Hernon and McClure		1				1
60	Horne			1			
61	Kuhlthau et al.			1		1	
62	Markham et al.		1	1	Jourard's transparent self		1
63	Auster and Lawton		1	1			1
64	Neill		1		memory		
65	Patterson	1	1				1
66	Way		1				1
67	Brown	1					
68	Gers and Seward	1		1	sense making		1
69	Dervin and Dewdney		1	1			wholistic
70	Durrance		1	1			1

Table 1
(Continued)

Entry	Author	Materials	Methods	Users	Use of Models	Affective	Behavioral	Cognitive
71	Harris and Michell	1	1	1			1	
72	Hawley		1				1	
73	Saracevic et al.		1				wholistic	
74	Whitlatch		1	1				
75	Radford		1	1				
76	Richardson		1		data flow diagrams/ flowcharts			1
77	PGCMLS		1				1	
78	Childers	1	1				1	
79	Allen			1	Material and Emotional Satisfaction Models		1	
80	Applegate		1	1	user satisfaction models	1	1	
81	Dewdney and Ross		1	1			1	
82	Scherdin				MBTI			
83	Gross			1	Imposed query model			
84	RAM	1	1	1		1	1	1
85	ALA RASD		1				1	
86	Stalker			1			1	
87	Saxton	1	1	1	meta-analysis		1	
88	Connell	1					1	
89	Yoon	1		1	Roman Jakobson notion of topic		1	
90	Saxton	1	1	1	HLM			
	Totals	18	60	38	29	5	66	16
	Percentages	20.00%	66.67%	42.22%	32.22%	5.56%	73.33%	17.78%

the reference transaction. Relatively little attention has been devoted to the "activity . . . that transforms input data flow into output data flow," although one recent notable exception is Richardson (1998), who has tried to model reference transactions using a data flow diagram based on systems analysis techniques.

C. Affective, Behavioral, and Cognitive Approaches

As mentioned earlier, 56 of the following research pieces examined the mental processes of reference librarians; in general, these studies also adopt one of three particular viewpoints: (1) affective (only a handful of studies— about 6%—including Delaney, 1954; Maxfield, 1954; Penland, 1971; and Applegate, 1993); (2) behavioral (N = 66 or 73%, making it the overwhelming orientation in this tripartite scheme—see ALA's RUSA, 1996); or (3) cognitive aspects (N = 16 or 18% of the studies such as Breed, 1955; Kuhlthau, 1983; White, 1983; or Richardson, 1995) of the reference transaction. For more on these approaches, see Liza Wardell's "Information Seeking Behavior: The ABC's," MA thesis, UCLA, 2002.

D. Other Theoretical Perspectives

Nearly all of the 1000 books and articles on reference transactions that I examined during the preparation of this literature review are descriptive; for a complete bibliography of these titles, see http://purl.org/net/reference. Even relatively few of the research studies adopt an explicit theoretical perspective. Fortunately, some notable exceptions exist such as counseling approaches (for example, Penland, 1971; Peck, 1975; as well as Jennerich and Jennerich, 1997).

III. Analytical Review of Reference Research

The following section provides a chronological review of the major work that has been conducted on the reference transaction process; when more than one work per year appears, then the works are organized aphabetically by author within those years. Many scholars, notably Robert Taylor and Gerald Jahoda, have played an important part in advancing our understanding of the different steps in the question-answering process. Others such as Belkin *et al.* (1980), Kuhlthau *et al.* (1983), or Dervin (1986) seem to have reinvented the work of Taylor and Jahoda in some respects, though Belkin admits his "concept is not wholly original"; nonetheless, his work does show the shift from information need to a problem-oriented school of thought.

A. Late 19th to Early 20th Century

After S. S. Green's revolutionary proposal at the American Library Association in 1876, many libraries adopted his reader service concept. Yet, the
early literature shows little reflective thought—all of these early articles
are of the how-we-do-it-good sort. By the 1920s, however, librarians are
beginning to focus on counting questions, seasonal variations in question
asking, and calculating the time it takes to answer questions.

1. Mary De Jong (1926)

De Jong's 1926 analysis is one of the earliest studies of public library
reference questions to be categorized by the inquirer's characteristics. The
author reports on 1 month's inquiries at the Appleton Public Library (WI):
(1) study clubs (13 hours and 45 minutes to answer 20 questions); (2) general
public (13 hours and 30 minutes to answer 29 questions); (3) students (2 hours
and 25 minutes); (4) teachers (2 hours); and (4) other (39 reference questions
at the main desk and 12 questions over the telephone). Thirty-one hours were
spent with questions that took more than 10 minutes to answer.

2. Martha Conner (1927)

Designed to improve instruction in library schools, this study of 24,727
reference questions is the oldest based on the time period analyzed—i.e.,
the 4 months from September through December in the years 1905, 1910,
1915, 1920, and 1925 asked in the Reference Department of the Carnegie
Library of Pittsburgh; local questions were not tabulated or analyzed in this
study. Annual variations in questions occurred because of an election year
(i.e., 1920), and seasonal variations were reported as well (such as Halloween-,
Thanksgiving-, and Christmas-related questions). A cross tabulation with
Dewey classification numbers indicates a trend toward sociology (especially
the fields of government, education, and economics) followed by history and
literature.

B. Reference Transaction Work: The 1930s

During this decade, the first reference textbook appears. More studies repli-
cate the earlier work on question counting, using larger samples. The first
analytical studies of reference service appear.

1. James Wyer (1930)

Wyer is the first author to write a reference textbook. In his book, he
identifies the three essential elements of the paradigm: "... the reference

question completely and satisfactorily answered involves three factors: inquirer, reference librarian, sources or materials." His presentation suggests a straightforward linear process without many complications.

Wyer focuses on one of those dimensions, specifically the characteristics of successful reference librarians. By surveying 38 eminent librarians, Wyer found 27 mental traits important to success in reference work. In order of importance, his respondents identified intelligence, accuracy, judgment, professional knowledge, dependability, courtesy, resourcefulness, tact, alertness, interest in work, memory, mental curiosity, interest in people, imagination, adaptability, perseverance, pleasantness, cooperativeness, system, health, initiative, industriousness, speed, poise, patience, forcefulness, and neatness. Though based on informed opinion, such a descriptive identification of attributes does not address whether these factors directly influence success or in what order.

2. Edith Guerrier (1935)

In her study, Guerrier found that 33 branch libraries in major metropolitan areas reported an average of 20% of their time being spent answering reference questions. Her other findings give insight into the relative utility of various reference formats and specific titles. Analyzing 1000 questions asked at these branches, Guerrier found that 50% could be answered using (1) encyclopedias; (2) dictionaries; (3) atlases; (4) *World Almanac*; (5) *Statesman's Yearbook*; (6) *Reader's Guide*; (7) *Who's Who in America*; (8) *Who's Who*, and (9) debate and quotation books. She found that a list of 80-plus reference titles answered another 33% of the questions ($N = 333$) and the final 17% had to be answered with other titles. Anticipating later studies, she noted the profession's widespread assumption that "the correct answering of a reference question at a public library is taken for granted." Three decades later, research would cast serious doubts about the validity of the assumption.

3. Carter Alexander (1936)

At one time, Alexander's 1936 article was one of the most frequently cited studies of the reference process. A detailed stepwise approach to searching for the answer to an inquirer's question, this article represents one of the earliest analytical statements about the process. Alexander identifies six steps in the transaction:

   I. Find out precisely what the question really is.
   II. Decide which kind of library materials is most likely to have the answer to the inquiry.
   III. Decide which items in a given kind of library materials are most likely to have the answer, in order of likelihood.
   IV. Locate the chosen items.

V. Search in the chosen items in order of likelihood until the answer is found or you are sure it cannot be found there.

VI. If the answer is not found by the foregoing, go back over the previous steps and take next most likely sources.

The first step consists of two general procedures: "find out what the inquirer intends to do with the answer to his question" and "examine the question to see what clues to its answer it carries." It helps, he suggests, to classify the question into one of seven distinct types: (1) fact type including meaning type of fact, numerical or statistical type of fact, historical type of fact, exact wording type of fact, and proper name type of fact; (2) how to do type; (3) trends type; (4) supporting evidence type; (5) "all about" type; (6) evaluation of reference type; and (7) duplication of previous work type. By recommending analysis by type of reference format and then specific source within type (see steps II and III), his technique foreshadows the shift to the proceduralist approach articulated by Isadore Mudge and popularized by Margaret Hutchins.

4. Faith Hyers (1936)

Participating as part of Guerrier's study, the Los Angeles Public Library and its then 48 branches collected 1 week's worth of questions. Hyers's analysis reveals that 50,000 reference questions were asked during that period, averaging 11 questions per minute per 12-hour day. Using a tripartite scheme of bread-and-butter questions, technical or businesslike questions, and cultural questions, Hyers concludes (1) that individual differences exist among reference librarians in terms of the sources consulted to answer the same question; and (2) that there is a difference between knowing the subject and knowing the literature (i.e., the reference formats and their relative importance) of the subject. She also implicitly questions whether "the library should be able to answer any and every question." This question led other writers to examine the service policies of various libraries.

5. Margaret Hutchins (1937, 1944)

As a proceduralist, Hutchins makes an important distinction by differentiating between the clarification (i.e., question negotiation) and classification (a mental analysis technique) steps in the process. In the former, the reference librarian may need to clarify the inquirer's question further. For instance, "if the request seems peculiar a start may be made by restating it in a different way and asking if that is what is meant or would be satisfactory." Note that she is recommending a closed-ended question (i.e., one that requires a yes or no response) for this step in the clarification process.

Mentioning Wyer's earlier list of mental traits, Hutchins reorders the list, in presenting her top six: (1) memory; (2) imagination; (3) perseverance; (4) judgment; (5) accuracy; and (6) suitability to the reader. Again, the validity of this list has not been tested.

C. Reference Transaction Work: The 1940s

Another textbook, with its roots in the late 1930s, is published, detailing a procedural approach to reference work. For the first time, lists of unanswered questions are compiled. And, the type of users is examined in more detail than ever before.

1. Elizabeth Stone (1942)

In summarizing several methods of evaluating reference service, Stone encourages reference departments to compile questions that could not be answered. Such lists would be helpful in evaluating the reference collection, especially the identification of additional sources. Apparently, she did not consider the need for better training in answering questions or for better tools, per se.

2. Dorothy Cole (1943)

Cole collected 1026 questions from 14 public libraries in the Chicago area as well as in St. Louis and Billings, Montana. She analyzed these questions in four ways: by Dewey subject areas, inquirer's characteristics, time period of query, and level of complexity. Cole found that the social sciences, useful arts, and history accounted for 72% of the questions asked. Her occupational analysis indicated that students asked the most questions ($N = 356$, 35%), followed by unknown occupations ($N = 248$, 24%), professionals ($N = 210$, 21%), shopkeepers and salesmen ($N = 61$, 6%), and clerks and stenographers ($N = 59$, 6%). As for time periods, most inquiries concerned the immediate year ($N = 196$, 19%), followed by the 20th century ($N = 539$, 53%), modern era ($N = 153$, 15%), Middle Ages ($N = 12$, 1%), ancient times ($N = 20$, 2%), no single period ($N = 99$, 10%), and future events ($N = 7$, 1%). Cole's complexity analysis yielded the following results: (1) fact-type questions ($N = 565$, 55%); (2) general information about subjects ($N = 200$, 20%); (3) how-to information ($N = 105$, 10%); (4) supporting evidence ($N = 85$, 8%); (5) historical ($N = 35$, 3%); (6) trends ($N = 25$, 2%); and all others ($N = 11$, 1%). She concludes her thesis with a list of actual sources used in answering the 1026 reference questions.

D. Reference Transaction Work: The 1950s

In this decade, writers focus on what is the real question being asked by users. The role of question negotiation in getting to the "real question" is studied for the first time. For the first time, a theoretical perspective, that of psychology, is put forward by a researcher to help understand the process. And, what kind of knowledge is required to answer questions is also examined for the first time.

1. Raymund Wood (1952)

Based on his reference experience and on an analysis of actual questions, Wood asserted that clarification is often harder than finding the actual source to answer the question. It is a rare instance that the real question is asked immediately. Often, two or three exchanges are needed to define the reference question. He concluded with four illustrative examples of question negotiation.

2. Jack Delaney (1954)

Other researchers have included the work of Delaney in their literature reviews, although his article does not appear to be based on research or even first-hand reference experience. It is not documented; there are no footnotes or other references. Furthermore, the article does not even appear to be based on informed personal opinion; his position was identified as that of Order Librarian. No experience in reference work is claimed or represented.

Nevertheless, he focuses on the question negotiation process and offers "some interviewing errors common to librarians, {and} then we will consider twelve rules to help the library interviewer." These 12 common-sense rules about interviewing are not so numbered but can be sorted out in his brief narrative. These rules include:

(1) Find out what it is the patron wants. What he wants may not be what he asks for.... (2) The skill comes in finding out what the patron needs and what is best for him.... (3) Help the patron get what he wants or needs.... (4) Get to know as many steady patrons as possible because the more you know about a patron, the more effective your interview will be.... (5) Place your desk where you get a maximum of privacy.... (6) Put yourself in the other fellow's place.... (7) Keep your prejudices to yourself as much as possible. ... (8) If you are at ease, it will do much toward helping the patron feel the same way.... (9) Allow time enough for the patron to say what he must to make his needs clear, but do not let him waste time or wander on the subject.... (10) Make your questions short and do not put them in compound sentences.... (11) Beware the "halo effect" [i.e., Edward L. Thorndike's 1920 psychological concept]. That is, do not judge a patron's social, intellec-

tual, or financial level on his appearance, dress, or manners. . . . (and 12) The interview is most effective, not in getting facts but in giving away the attitude of the speaker.

His article raises an interesting ethical and philosophical question about needs versus wants.

3. David Maxfield (1954)

In one of the earliest efforts to do so, Maxfield draws upon the vast psychological literature, arguing for "more careful attention to . . . the individual person" and that the reference transaction be viewed as part of the "counseling process." Maxfield identifies four factors at work in the successful reference transaction: (1) acceptance and the importance of "suspending judgment"; (2) understanding through "tact and patience"; (3) communication built on asking "questions"; and (4) collaboration in the reader's efforts.

4. Paul Breed (1955)

After identifying the discrete steps in the general reference process, Breed categorizes the decision-making knowledge needed to accomplish each step according to a five-part scheme: (1) knowledge associated with a liberal arts education; (2) knowledge associated with library specialization (including experience); (3) personal knowledge; (4) knowledge gained in the search process; and (5) knowledge associated with subject specialization. Breed found that 81% of the decisions with his discrete steps required knowledge associated with library specialization.

Replication of his work, notably on the role or utility of an advanced subject degree, would come later.

5. Mary Francillon (1959)

Francillon provides valuable, and some of the earliest quantitative, information on the type of reference questions asked. Based on a sample of 956 reference questions asked in a special library between January and early December 1959, she categorized them into seven different types of questions, which she identified as A through G: (A) biographical sources and quotation sources, (B) dictionaries, (C) directories, encyclopedias, and handbooks, (D) bibliographies, catalogs, and indexes, (E) and (F) library catalogs, and (G) indexes. Three of her categories (i.e., types E and F; D; and C) include a mixture of different formats. Despite the fact that she used a mixed classification scheme, one can reconstruct the relative use of various reference formats. As such, it might serve as an indication of which formats to emphasize in schools of library and information science. A statistical manipulation of Francillon's (1959) Table One might serve as an indication of which formats to emphasize in schools of library and information science.

E. Reference Transaction Work: The 1960s

Several researchers undertake massive studies of reference tools. Detailed process descriptions appear. Researchers focus on query formulation and user perceptions of service. Computer simulations are written and decision theory is applied to the process. Toward the end of the decade, simple bivariate statistical models are proposed. This decade seems like the golden age of empirical research.

1. Wallace Bonk (1960, 1961, 1963, and 1964)

Starting in February 1959, Bonk asked other basic reference instructors in the United States about the reference titles they covered in class. He found that "all 25 schools agreed on only five titles out of a total of 1202": *Encyclopedia Americana, Encyclopedia Britannica, World Book, New English Dictionary*, and *Funk and Wagnall's New Standard Dictionary*. Overall, his survey of faculty found 50% agreement on 115 titles. Hence, he found it hard to make a prescriptive statement about what tools to study.

Desirous of a greater consensus on the core titles to be taught in library science programs, he surveyed 1090 secondary school libraries, public libraries, and college and university libraries to find the best titles based on actual use; he received 1079 usable returns (98.9% return rate). In actuality, reference librarians reported their perceptions of vital, recommended, and peripheral titles as well as titles not owned. Statistical manipulation of his data (calculating the mean scores and standard deviation for each format) reveals the most important formats along with the single title originally reported as most vital.

Interestingly, Bonk initially thought that "reference method" was more important than specific titles, but changed his mind several years later and started arguing that the reference core course's emphasis on technique and method ought to shift to principles, purposes, and policies, and, further, that instructors should "extend the range of titles as we drop away concern for pestiferous minutiae."

2. James Perry (1961, 1963)

Originally circulated in mimeograph form during 1961, Perry published the now-familiar four stages of query formulation as:

Q0 = some ideal "best" query to obtain information to deal with a given problem or situation

Q1 = the mental conception developed by some person as to needed information

Q2 = the statement of a query by a person without regard to a given IR [information retrieval] system

Q3 = the statement of a query by a person with regard to a given IR system.

The necessity of querying an IR system follows from his assumption that

Needed information = Information in mind + Information to be acquired.

3. University of Michigan SRC (1961)

One of the earliest and most rigorous studies of perceptions from the other side of the reference desk comes from Michigan's Survey Research Center (SRC). Respondents rated service on a three-point scale: excellent (54%), good (37%), and poor (only 1%). Quality must be seen from the user's point of view. Earlier studies of the Los Angeles Public Library, Columbia University, Indiana University, and the New York Public Library found similar high levels of reader satisfaction.

4. Robert Taylor (1962)

Perhaps the most sophisticated presentation yet of the inquirer's formation of a question, Taylor's work draws upon Shannon's Theory of Information, especially the concept of noise, and popularizes the earlier work of Perry. He also discusses question input, answer output, and the role of interim feedback. In passing, Taylor also points out that "filtering for the answer spectrum" involves a relevance judgment on the part of the inquirer.

Specifically, question formation based on the inquirer's informational need may be characterized as having four levels that move progressively from a kind of Platonic ideal question, which is psychological, abstract, complex, diffuse, ill defined, inchoate, and ambiguous, to a logical, more concrete, rigid, focused, and simplified state:

Q1 = the actual, but unexpressed, need for information (the *visceral* need)

Q2 = the conscious, within-brain description of the need (the *conscious* need)

Q3 = the formal statement of the question (the *formalized* need)

Q4 = the question as presented to the information system (the *compromised* need).

His article ends with a set of research questions and a plea to include the inquirer in the design of information retrieval systems, such as reference work and expert systems.

5. Allan Rees and Tefko Saracevic (1963)

Originally presented as a conference paper, this article is a descriptive statement of the 10 "evolutionary steps" in question asking and answering. Despite the fact that it contains no explicit statement of methodology (except that analysis of reference questions is analogous to subject analysis of documents), this piece is the most comprehensive and detailed description of the entire reference transaction to date. Furthermore, the authors are the first to represent it graphically with boxes, dotted lines, and solid lines with arrows.

The 10 steps are: (1) information problem and need; (2) initial formulation of question; (3) analysis by searcher; (4) negotiation between question analyst and questioner; (5) definition of question; (6) enumeration of concepts to be searched; (7) translation of search concepts into indexing language; (8) selection of search strategy; (9) conducting of search; and (10) formulation of alternate search strategies. Acceptable answers or responses from the librarian will be based on:

1. What the questioner needs . . .
2. What he thinks he wants . . .
3. What he wants . . .
4. What he is prepared to read . . .
5. How much of what he gets he is prepared to read . . .
6. How much time he is willing to devote to it all . . .
7. In what sequence he would like to read what he gets . . .
8. What value he will attach to what he gets . . .

6. Robert M. Hayes and Gary Carlson (1964)

This work is optimistic about the possibility of understanding human search behavior because the authors believe it is "really quite regular"; so, it is unfortunate that the literature has largely ignored this work up until now. Carlson proposes a computer simulation that then could be compared with human searching. He observed three librarians—one with 4 years of experience, one with 1 year, and another who had just started work; hence, there is some question whether they should have been considered expert librarians when two of them were, in fact, advanced beginners (see Richardson, 1995, p. 53). Nevertheless, this study is important because it examines what "librarians do, *not* what they *should* do." Using protocol analysis, one section of this report, "human search strategies," details the protocol of a search and then flow-charts it, while another part of the report flowcharts the process in much greater detail. Their work draws attention to the importance of considering the time and effort involved in the reference transaction: "at each branching point, these strategies serve to limit the search effort by providing estimates of the effort involved in following a particular choice and the likelihood of its leading to a satisfactory result."

7. Jesse Shera (1964)

Shera appears to have read Taylor's 1962 article and heard Rees and Saracevic's 1963 American Documentation Institute paper, and based part of his work on theirs without explicitly identifying his sources. However, the first half of his article is clearly original and devoted to establishing the proper role of decision theory and library automation in reference work; for instance, "the conviction that automation can raise the intellectual level of the reference librarian does not imply that a machine make a literature specialist out of a simple button pusher." The second half of his article proceeds from an explicit assumption:

> The fullest utilization of the potential of automation does necessitate a thorough study of the total reference process—from the problem that prompts the asking of a question to the evaluation of the response—for the very simple and obvious reason that machine simulation of that process cannot be accomplished without an understanding of the process itself.

He goes on to describe the "complex associative series of linkages, or events" in the process, which he views as a "communication flow." Echoing Taylor's work, one of his contributions is the explicit graphical recognition of the role of feedback in the process, or what he terms the "evaluation of pertinence" to the information need as well as the "evaluation of relevance" to the inquiry (i.e., its linguistic expression).

8. Charles Bunge (1967a,b, 1969)

For his doctoral work, Bunge began to inquire into the relationship between professional education and performance on the reference desk. He hypothesized that professionally trained reference librarians would outperform (based on the proportion of questions answered and the time it took) untrained staff members. Studying nine pairs of participants with 1 to 20 years of experience in seven different libraries, he found that the trained reference librarians were faster and more efficient than other staff. Among professionals, experience correlated with performance ($r^2 = 0.417$). Age alone and elapsed time from degree did not appear to be statistically significant predictors of success in the reference transaction.

Later, Bunge abstracted some information from his dissertation and made it more accessible by publishing his flowchart of "the major decisions and actions taken by the librarians in answering relatively simple 'fact' type questions." The underlying implicit theory of accuracy is that accuracy plus time is a function of the librarian and experience.

9. Herbert Goldhor (1967)

Following up an earlier study of a single public library, Goldhor submitted in writing 10 test reference questions to "the person in charge" at 12 public libraries in the Minneapolis area. Despite the fact that librarians took about 20 minutes per question on average (based on five libraries reporting the total time taken), the accuracy rate was only 51% correct. The underlying assumption is that accuracy is a combination of the librarian plus the collection. Along with Bunge's research, readers will recognize the now-familiar 50% rule.

10. Robert Taylor (1967, 1968)

This study is one of the most highly cited sources in the reference field. In the first part of his article, Taylor repeats his description of James W. Perry's four needs (i.e., Q1–Q4) almost verbatim. Taylor does provide an interesting chart of the prenegotiation decisions by the inquirer. However, the significant contribution to our understanding of the actual reference transaction is his detailed analysis of the process of question negotiation.

Based on personal interviews with 20 special librarians, he defines five "filters": (1) determination of subject; (2) objective and motivation; (3) personal characteristics of inquirer; (4) relationship of inquiry description to file organization; and (5) anticipated or acceptable answers. The second filter is the most important because it often reduces search time substantially and determines what constitutes an appropriate response.

11. The University of the State of New York (1967)

In a multiple-year study of public libraries, the Division of Evaluation found multiple reasons for poor performance despite strong local resources:

1. Inadequate awareness of collection
2. Trouble with technical questions
3. Acceptance of anything printed
4. Unawareness of other community resources
5. Lack of interviewing to clarify questions.

Nonetheless, reference librarians answered 70% of the questions correctly based on an inference drawn from the report's Table II.

12. Terence Crowley (1968)

Based on a study of 40 New Jersey public libraries using eight unobtrusive proxies as well as the PI, the author found that accuracy (based on 10 questions scored as correct or incorrect—see Chapter 4 for the questions) is not a function of the library's budget (which determines the kinds of librarians and collections present) where a high budget is defined as high expenditures and high per capita support. Although the six "high" libraries did answer more questions (36/60) than did six "low" libraries (29/60), no statistically significant difference was found at the 0.05 level. Although he admits the possibility of intervening variables, Crowley does not analyze "experience, training, age, interests, imagination, and tenacity" (p. 15).

F. Reference Transaction Work: The 1970s

This decade sees the introduction of more sophisticated theoretical concepts from a counseling perspective. The important role of question negotiation, especially nonverbal behaviors and asking open-ended questions, in making the question answering task easier for the professional and more successful for the end user. A shift to focus on the users and their needs occurs as well in this decade.

1. Gerald Jahoda et al. (1968, 1974, 1975, 1976, 1977, 1980, and 1981)

In their earliest work, Jahoda and Culnan studied 26 science and chemistry libraries for 1 month, but found only 47 unanswered questions. The reasons given for not answering these questions were categorized as: (1) no reference tool published to answer the question; (2) reference tool published but not in library; (3) existing reference tool not sufficiently up to date; (4) existing tool does not have adequate index; (5) existing tool does not have the information listed in a way to answer question; (6) answer probably in library— no time to answer; (7) question outside the scope of the library; (8) question not properly negotiated; and (9) other. This study echoes Stone's 1942 recommendation to compile questions that could not be answered.

Their latter research collapses the failure to answer the question into three general reasons: (1) 45% of the questions were unanswered because of reference tool limitations (i.e., categories 1, 3, 4, and 5); (2) 29% of the questions were unanswered because of library limitations (i.e., categories 2 and 7); and (3) 25% of the questions were unanswered because of personnel limitations (i.e., categories 6 and 8). Interestingly, Jahoda and Culnan recommend studying unasked questions in the future.

By 1974, Jahoda expresses pessimism about the success of machine searching in general reference work in contrast to Hayes and Carlson.

Nevertheless, he identifies nine steps in the machine searching process based on his analysis of 28 general reference questions in science and technology:

1. Selection of indexable information
2. Level of answer
3. Selection of types of reference tools to search
4. Types-of-reference-tools search sequence
5. Type of answer
6. Size of answer
7. Types of access points to search
8. Selection of specific titles of reference tools
9. Specific titles search sequence

In discussing point 4, he astutely observed that "Reference librarians have general guidelines but no specific rules for determining search sequence of types of reference tools." In his 1976 publication, Jahoda identifies eight situations when question negotiation may be necessary. For example,

1. The real query may not be asked.
2. Librarian is unfamiliar with the subject of the query.
3. Ambiguity or incompleteness of query statement.
4. Amount of information needed is not specified.
5. Level of answer is not specified.
6. The query takes more time than you can spend on it.
7. Answer to query is not recorded in the literature.
8. Language, time period, geography, or type of publication constraints need to be added to query statements.

Using 23 science and technical reference librarians, Jahoda's 1977 work rediscovers Hutchins's heuristic, but goes on to evaluate the reference process as a simpler six-step model: (1) message selection; (2) selection of types of answer-providing tools; (3) selection of specific answer-providing sources; (4) selection of search headings; (5) answer selection; and (6) negotiation and renegotiation.

Working with Judith Braunagel, Janice Fennell, Nice Figueiredo, Sims Kline, Miguel Menendez, Herbert Nath, William Needham, Afarin Shahravan, Lee Shiflett, and Vicki West, he developed and tested classroom modules in three reference courses, revising the modules based on faculty and student comments. His Table 2 provides a flowchart modeling the reference process; Table 4 is a useful tool-descriptor matrix of knowns and wanteds; and Table 5 identifies 12 formats [i.e., (1) atlases and maps; (2) biographical sources; (3) card catalogs and union lists; (4) dictionaries; (5) encyclopedias; (6) guides to the literature; (7) handbooks, manuals and almanacs; (8) indexes, bibliographies, and abstracts; (9) monographs and texts; (10) nonbiographical directories; (11) primary publications (dissertations etc.); and (12) yearbooks] that Jahoda thinks librarians consistently use.

Finally, Jahoda and Braunagel (1980) developed a checklist for determining whether questions are truly answerable based on: (1) clarity, (2) specificity, and (3) freedom from overly restrictive constraints such as language, time period, and geography.

2. Edward Jestes and David Laird (1968)

Jestes and Laird conducted a self-study of their own reference desk activities at the University of California, Davis. Only 21% of desk time was spent with users or on users' questions. Parenthetically, the actual time spent at the reference desk may be much smaller in public libraries, on the order of 6–8% of the time. Furthermore, they found that only 12.5% of the questions asked required professional training. Hence, they argue that the academic library should hire students to handle the more basic questions.

3. Gerard Salton (1968)

Writing from a computer science perspective, the author charts seven steps in an "information system capable of furnishing direct answers to input queries" as opposed to reference systems (see his Figure 10-1). After laying out the basic retrieval framework, the organization of the database, semantic interpretation, and extensions of the data base, Salton concludes that the outlook for such systems "in the foreseeable future is not good."

4. Norman Crum (1969)

Accepting Taylor's four needs as originally expressed, Crum points out that users present themselves at different Q stages. The librarian's responsibility is to work back through these stages to the informational need or problem. In the process, there are: (1) physical, (2) personality, (3) psychological, (4) linguistic, and (5) contextual barriers. He hypothesizes that the worst place to transact the interview is behind the reference desk; Crum recommends interviewing in the inquirer's territory (exactly as S. S. Green did in 1876). At the very least, though, it is a proactive, even aggressive, reference policy. Although he does not provide an itemized list of each barrier, he indirectly suggests some; for instance, personality barriers might include coolness, indifference, and withdrawal, while informal contacts, direct assignment, and wise choice of locations would reduce other barriers.

Finally, Crum recommends a second interview, a review process to check the results, as a kind of quality control assurance, just before the end of the transaction.

5. John Lubans (1971)

Focusing on the inquirer's recognition of the library as a possible source of information, Lubans surveyed nearly 3000 undergraduate college students in 1968. He found 8% nonusers and 37% occasional users of the library. Among all undergraduates, nonuse decreased during their 4 years in college. However, a 2-year follow-up still found a large number of nonusers, so Lubans conducted interviews with 20 of these students. He found: (1) 45% still nonusers, (2) nonusers had used other types of libraries, (3) 57% said that librarians were "helpful and effective," but (4) most would ask faculty for guidance first. Oddly, Lubans's abstract is not informative of the article's content, but contains 10 ways to convert nonusers into users based on information originally published in the Darnell Institute of Business newsletter (see section on inquirer below).

6. Patrick Penland (1971)

Influenced by Maxfield's work, Penland starts an entire school of thought regarding cross-disciplinary borrowing of concepts and concerns, that is, the field of counseling, or social service generally, which has developed relevant interviewing techniques. See the Jennerichs' work (later) for a fuller development of this school of thought.

7. Bernard F. Vavrek (1971)

Using content analysis on a set of 300 questions (i.e., 150 initial and then 150 negotiated questions), Vavrek establishes a significant difference between the number of elements in the inquirer's opening question (Taylor's Q4) versus the negotiated question. According to Vavrek's scheme, questions can contain up to nine elements: (1) personal or corporate references; (2) geographical references; (3) time/space references; (4) subject descriptors; (5) form of publication requested; (6) level of analysis requested; (7) specific title references; (8) number references; and (9) behavioral descriptors (i.e., motivational need). In fact, opening questions have 2.7 elements on average, while negotiated questions have 3.7 elements; indeed, the point of question negotiation is to elicit more information, and only 26% of the questions had the same number of elements after negotiation.

Vavrek found that initial questions commonly contained three elements: subject descriptors (56.7% of the time), form of publication (48.7%), and level of analysis (36%). After negotiation, subject descriptors increased (68.6%) as did level of analysis (52%). However, dramatic changes occurred in three other elements: behavioral descriptors increased 7.75 times (from $N=4$, 2.6%

to $N = 31$, 20.6%) and time/space references doubled (from $N = 11$ or 7.3% to $N = 22$ or 33%), while form of publication actually decreased. The last finding can be interpreted to mean that the requested informational package is not as important as the informational content of the recommended package.

8. Geraldine King (1972)

Focusing on the question negotiation process, King is influenced by Gallup's "Quintamentional Plan of Question Design" and F. W. King's adult education material, which encourage "general open-ended questions and [then] proceeds to close specific questions." King hypothesizes that open-ended questions help clarify the informational need in the inquirer's mind and provide more clues than do closed-ended questions. At the end of her article, she recommends that novices use the "'why' form of open-ended questions because the question 'why' facilitates understanding the request and the supplying of the information." Although King labels closed-ended questions "the tools of cross examination," and hence not particularly useful, one might assume that later in the classification process, closed-ended questions are more productive in confirming the likely match of potential formats with the inquirer's question.

9. F. S. Stych (1972)

In order to find "a logical basis for some of the choices and decisions which reference workers are called upon to make," Stych hypothesizes about the factors that will influence the librarian's question negotiation and subsequent search strategy. Strongly reminiscent of Taylor's five filters and Vavrek's structural elements in opening reference questions, Stych suggests four primary and five secondary factors: (1) subject field; (2) time; (3) space; and (4) language; as well as (5) level of inquiry; (6) amount of information required; (7) time available for search; (8) languages searcher can handle; and (9) languages acceptable to the inquirer. Stych attempts to rank order the top three: subject, space or language, and time. He believes that subject field is especially important in factual questions, and that geographical factors are significant in political and literary history; and he suggests consulting works published in the country of the inquirer's origin, but obviously, not consulting works published before an event has occurred.

10. Mary Jane Swope and Jeffrey Katzer (1972)

In their survey of library building users, Swope and Katzer found that 41% had questions, but fully 65% of them would *not* approach librarians. They conclude:

Since it is not the user, but the library and librarians who are being called upon ever more frequently to justify their budget in terms of services provided, the burden of responsibility falls ever more heavily on librarians to make whatever changes are necessary to communicate a different message to their potential users.

11. Carol Kronus (1973)

Adopting a sociology of education perspective, Kronus succinctly reviews the prior library user research, pointing out that much of it is based on simple correlations and hence confounded because of the nonindependence of variables. Thus, she argues the need for a more sophisticated approach, such as multiple regression and factor analytic studies.

Drawing upon a representative sample of 1019 Illinois residents, she found that all of the 14 variables previously identified by researchers resulted in mild correlations. However, Kronus found that use of public libraries in her regression and factor analytic study was dependent on three characteristics of the user, in order of importance: education (number of years and future plans), family life cycle (marital status, family size, and employment status), and urban residence. All told, she could explain about 20% of the variance in her study.

Finally, Kronus found that age, gender, and ethnicity were not statistically significant factors in public library usage when intervening variables were controlled.

12. Helen Gothberg (1974)

Gothberg reviews the extensive speech communications literature related to verbal and nonverbal transactions. She notes that Carl Rogers believed that empathy, warmth, and genuineness (or congruence) facilitated helping relationships and that Albert Mehrabian found that "total liking" of a person consisted of 7% verbal liking plus 38% vocal liking plus 55% facial liking.

Hence, she decided to study two reference librarians, one at the competent level and the other expert, in the Weld County Public Library of Greeley, Colorado, using a two-by-two factorial design, where the librarians role-played immediacy and non-immediacy (defined as directness and intensity measured by physical distance and body, especially head orientation and eye contact). She used Liebig's refinement of Frank and Anderson's instrument to rate user satisfaction.

Gothberg found that the "user was more satisfied with the reference interview when the reference librarian displayed immediate communication as opposed to non-immediate communication." It is interesting that users were not more satisfied with the actual information transferred. Her work is important because for the first time, a study defines satisfaction as a function of librarian's (nonverbal) behavior.

13. Elaine Jennerich and Edward Jennerich (1974, 1976, 1980, 1981, 1987, and 1997)

Using a rating sheet developed during her doctoral work, Jennerich suggested a five-point Likert scale of poor-to-excellent evaluating the reference librarian's nonverbal interviewing skills: (1) eye contact; (2) gestures; (3) relaxed posture; (4) facial expression as well as verbal skills; (5) remembering; (6) premature diagnosis; (7) reflect feelings verbally; (8) restate or paraphrase comments; (9) open questions; (10) encouragers; (11) closure; and (12) opinions, suggestions.

In discussing the ideal characteristics of reference librarians, the Jennerichs identify 11 attributes: (1) sense of humor; (2) dedication or commitment; (3) genuine liking for people; (4) good memory; (5) imagination; (6) creativity; (7) patience; (8) persistence; (9) energy; (10) stamina; (11) ability to jump quickly from one subject to another. Their work is important because it more fully develops Allen Ivey's microcounseling approach to the reference transaction, but fundamentally assumes "reference work in general is a creative art and that the reference interview in particular is a performing art."

Returning to this topic after more than 10 years, they add a new chapter on "angry and frustrated patrons" as well as Total Quality Management (TQM)—a customer service concept—to the second edition of their basic work.

14. James Benson and Ruth Maloney (1975)

Benson and Maloney's goal is "to analyze the [reference] search process, isolating the pertinent elements that make up a search and identifying the many decision points in the search process." Their three-element model reflects the 100-year-old paradigm identified by Richardson: (1) the query, (2) bibliographic bridge, and (3) system.

According to them, the query consists of three components: (1) type (i.e., known item, further subdivided by fact, document, or bibliography versus subject, further subdivided by general, specific, or research); (2) language (i.e., vocabulary); and (3) parameters (i.e., limitations). The "bibliographic bridge" consists of six steps: (1) clarify the query; (2) establish the search parameters; (3) identify the system; (4) translate the query; (5) conduct the actual search; and (6) deliver the information. One of their most important contributions is recognition that "failure to locate requested information may be system-related or searcher-related."

In the case of a searcher-related failure, failure analysis may consist of:

1. Looking for an expected answer, with failure to recognize what is actually found
2. Modifying the query to accommodate the searcher's prior knowledge of the system(s)
3. Misunderstanding the query
4. Relying upon the accuracy of the query
5. Relying upon the accuracy of the information within the system

To avoid these situations, Benson and Maloney recommend "a series of questions [which] can be applied to guide in the analysis: (1) Do I know what I am looking for? (2) Am I sure I have not found it? (3) At what points did I make decisions? (4) Taking each decision identified in order, were there alternative approaches I might have taken? (5) Having made the decision, did I proceed properly in following through on the decision made?"

15. Laura Boyer and William Theimer (1975)

Following Jestes and Laird's 1968 study recommending the use of students at reference desks, the authors surveyed a representative, stratified sample of 150 academic libraries to understand their local practices. Based on a return rate of 75%, they found that "in 69 percent of the reporting libraries, nonprofessionals *are* used at the reference desk."

A later study of a single library confirms that nonprofessionals can handle at least 62% of the questions asked, while two other libraries show significant differences in professionals' and nonprofessionals' capabilities.

16. Donald McFayden (1975)

Elaborating upon Taylor's four levels of need (along with passing reference to the work of Alan Rees and Helen Focke), McFayden relates Taylor's work to that of W. T. Jones on the inadequacy of common-sense language and finds that "experiential inquiries must therefore be matched by experiential, i.e., open-ended techniques of question-negotiation and search strategy." Technically, this work is more research agenda setting than research per se.

17. Theodore Peck (1975)

Peck assumes that reference librarians and counselors share similar tasks and that the former can learn from the latter. Drawing on the counseling psychology work of Delaney and Eisenberg as well as Krumboltz and Thoresen, Peck hypothesizes that certain characteristics of the reference librarian are especially important for successful transactions. According to his informed personal opinion, the three most important attributes are: (1) empathy, defined as the "ability to understand how his client feels"; (2) attentive behavior, including good eye contact, proper body position such as a pleasing smile, leaning forward, and open hands; and (3) content listening, defined as "the process of asking questions and repeating to the patron his question in his own words or similar terminology" including paraphrasing. Nonattentive behavior, notably body positions, includes stiffness (and hence aloofness or disinterest), while slouching or slumping may equate as boredom or fatigue. It may well be that the avoidance of these nonattentive behaviors contributes to higher user satisfaction and the adoption of these three attributes will facilitate users asking questions in the first place.

18. Virginia Boucher (1976)

Defining nonverbal communication as "the exchange of information through nonlinguistic signs," Boucher proposes "to explore the implications of nonverbal communication, particularly body movement, for the library reference interview." Drawing on the nonverbal communications research of Darwin, Birdwhistell, Ekman *et al.*, Scheflen, Harrison, and Key, Boucher implicitly hypothesizes that reference librarians fall into either a preoccupation mode or an availability mode that influences question receipt and subsequent success in the reference interview. Boucher identifies six characteristics of the preoccupation mode: "(1) Arms across chest (2) Downward gaze so no eye contact possible (3) Frown of concentration, firm mouth (4) Hands busy with books, papers, pencils, telephone (5) Turned or leaning away, head bent down [and 6] Behind desk." Then, she lists seven characteristics of the availability mode: "(1) Arms relaxed—not covering up body (2) Eyes ready to contact those who enter (3) Smile of greeting, relaxed mouth, eyebrows lifted in attention (4) Hands relaxed (5) Leaning forward, head up (6) Willingness to leave desk [and 7] Head nods . . . of positive reinforcement."

19. Ronald Powell (1976, 1978)

This study focuses on reference materials. Testing 60 reference librarians on 25 questions out of a set of 50 real, fact-type, ready-reference questions, Powell hypothesized that with a larger collection, reference librarians would be able to answer a larger number of questions. Performance (i.e., percentage of questions answered correctly) was significantly related: (1) nonlinearly to size of collection with diminishing returns at over 3500 reference titles, simple $r = 0.52$; (2) to librarian's perceived adequacy of reference collection, $r = 0.50$; (3) to librarian holding a professional degree, $r =$ not reported; and

(4) to the librarian's having taken a number of reference and bibliography courses, $r = 0.25$. Although age and professional experience were not statistically significant in determining success, the number of substantive reference questions received per week was ($r = 0.52$).

20. Mary Jo Lynch (1977 and 1978)

Examining the verbal aspects of the reference interview, Lynch seeks to answer three questions: (1) How often does the librarian negotiate the inquirer's initial question and does the frequency vary by (a) type of transaction? (i.e., holdings, substantive, or moving) or (b) when the librarian is less busy? (fewer than 11 questions per hour); (2) What information is sought?; and (3) Does the librarian use open- versus closed-ended questions?

She found that the level of negotiation did vary by type of transaction: 35% of the holdings transactions were negotiated, 53% of the substantive, and 78% of the moving, while the overall average was 49% of the time. She did not answer the second part of the first question. Parenthetically, others have attempted to deal with "busyness." Using content analysis reminiscent of Vavrek's work, Lynch did find significant differences in her study of question negotiation. As for open versus closed questions, Lynch found that librarians used open-ended questions only 8% of the time while closed-ended questions were asked 90% of the time. Furthermore, only 13% of the initial or original questions required a major reformulation to discover the real question. She argues, however, that if librarians are not using open-ended questions, they may be answering the initial, but not real, question in the case of substantive and moving transactions. Directional questions are probably what they appear to be.

In summary, Lynch found that reference librarians did not negotiate questions most of the time, and when they did, they used closed-ended questions, which do not elicit much additional information from the inquirer.

21. Marcia Myers (1977, 1980, 1983, and 1985)

Based on responses to telephone queries in a stratified random sample of 40 southeastern academic libraries during 1977, Myers found a 49% (±1.5%) accuracy at the 95% confidence level with 12 test questions, but "there was also evidence that even when the library owned the appropriate source, staff members either did not consult, did not know how to use, or misinterpreted the information given in the source. Additionally, staff members infrequently volunteered the source of their response." Parenthetically, a good recent example of this situation is *The Book of Answers* (Berliner *et al.*, 1990), which, while giving answers, does not cite sources either.

Librarians at universities did better than those at 4-year colleges with graduate degrees, who did better than librarians at 4-year colleges, who, in turn, did better than librarians at 2-year colleges (which is really an indirect measure of the library's size). Those institutions with more than 85,000 volume collections or more than 10,000 volume reference departments did the best. Hours open (an indirect measure of commitment to service), especially those open more than 80 hours, also correlated strongly with high-quality service. Implications are that LIS instructors need to teach novices and advanced beginners how to exploit the library's resources to the fullest.

22. Mollie Sandock (1977)

Studying a stratified random sample of every student enrolled during the Fall 1975 term at the University of Chicago, the author hypothesized that many students were unaware of such library services as reference. Based on telephone interviews, she found that 38% did not know where the reference department was located; other knowledge of other services ranged from 33% to 65%. Upon closer inspection, she discovered that most of these students who did *not* know the location were: (1) freshmen; (2) graduate students in the sciences; and (3) students in their first quarter of study at the University of Chicago. Hence, she concluded that a publicity campaign is necessary to ensure that such potential users are aware of reference department services. A similar study of Lake Forest College students is reported in the next decade, which found the percentage of correct answers about specific services ranged from 51% to 74% with an overall average of 65%.

23. Thomas Eichman (1978)

Drawing upon the Shannon–Weaver model of communication as modified by D. K. Berlo, Searle's speech acts, Leech's functional view of language, and Hellprin's threshold of stability, Eichman focuses on the inquirer's opening reference question. He hypothesizes that ease of access explains why inquirers ask their colleagues first; in passing, he also mentions Taylor's work on this point.

Eichman points out that several preparatory conditions must be present for a successful reference transaction; first, the inquirer's belief and sincerity, followed by the librarian's confidence. "The [inquirer's] speech act counts essentially as an attempt to elicit information from the hearer [the librarian]." In other words, in order for the inquirer to ask a question, he must have confidence in the librarian's ability to respond. And, furthermore the librarian must be empathetic throughout the exchange in order to maintain the inquirer's confidence.

Using Leech's five functions of language (i.e., the expressive, phatic, informational, aesthetic, and directive), Eichman argues that the inquirer's initial question must be general because it must perform several functions, notably the expressive, phatic, and informational, at once. Then, "if the librarian is also careful not to include in the initial response anything seriously challenging the motivational or other emotional aspects of the inquirer's opening speech act, the librarian's initial response rephrasing the proposition will also help satisfy the expressive function of the inquirer's speech act."

In summary, Eichman's work lays a foundation of a user's reference readiness theory and helps explain that the inquirer's initial phrasing of the question is often quite general because of the phatic function of language.

24. James Rettig (1978)

After a moderately extensive review of the literature, Rettig laments that the literature merely describes the process rather than presents a theoretical or conceptual approach that would explain why things proceed the way they do during the reference transaction. Rettig, then, proposes the necessity of adding feedback and background noise into any model of the reference process much like Taylor's drawing upon Shannon's theory.

Rettig raises the question "how message-receiving ability relates to the ability to provide the level of service a patron wants" without answering it. He does, however, relate effectively how Wyer's three levels of service (conservative, moderate, and liberal, or Rothstein's minimum, middling, and maximum policy) should vary according to the inquirer's information need. He observes that the American Library Association Reference and Adult Services Division's "A Commitment to Information Services" affirms his view.

25. Marcia Bates (1979)

Her objective was "to focus on and use the strengths and flexibility of human thinking processes" in order to identify short-term tactics used in four categories: monitoring, file structure, search formulation, and term. Monitoring tactics include: (1) check; (2) weigh; (3) pattern; (4) correct; and (5) record. File structure tactics encompass: (1) bibble; (2) select; (3) survey; (4) cut; (5) stretch; (6) scaffold; and (7) cleave. Search formulation tactics consist of: (1) specify; (2) exhaust; (3) reduce; (4) parallel; (5) pinpoint; and (6) block. Term tactics entail: (1) super; (2) sub; (3) relate; (4) neighbor; (5) trace; (6) vary; (7) fix; (8) rearrange; (9) contrary; (10) respell; and (11) respace.

In her article on idea tactics, Bates identifies 17 tactics based on a review of relevant literature: (1) think; (2) brainstorm; (3) meditate; (4) consult;

(5) rescue; (6) wander; (7) catch; (8) break; (9) breach; (10) reframe; (11) notice; (12) jolt; (13) change; (14) focus; (15) dilate; (16) skip; and (17) stop.

Like much of the previous professional literature, this work is based on "my own experience and thinking, from the literature, and from the comments of colleagues and students"—in other words, another armchair reflection of the reference process. No explicit research methodology is presented so that the study could be replicated by someone else. Although this work can be considered brilliant, synthetic, and intuitively correct, it has not been rigorously tested or validated to show that these tactics are actually used, as suggested by S. D. Neill (1984) later. As a facilitation and teaching model that may lead to testable hypotheses it remains provocative nonetheless.

26. Nicholas J. Belkin, and Robert N. Oddy (1979); Belkin, Helen M. Brooks, and Oddy (1979); Belkin (1980); and Belkin, Oddy, and Brooks (1982a,b)

Influenced by Robertson's 1979 work, Belkin's work focuses on document retrieval, but whose inadequacies lead to a cognitive communication system model of *information* retrieval. The ASK hypothesis is "that there is an anomaly in that state of knowledge with respect to the problem faced" by the user and the "inadequacies in a state of knowledge can be of many sorts, such as gaps or lacks, uncertainty, or incoherences, whose only common trait is a perceived 'wrongness' . . . depending on the level of the individual's knowledge of the topic and the nature of the person's situation." Although not "an innovative suggestion," the phrase ASK is certainly catchy and thus useful.

27. John Larsen (1979)

Following in Bonk's footsteps, Larsen surveyed the 63 accredited LIS programs, receiving usable responses from only 31 schools (a rather low 49.2% return rate). "Three additional schools do not discuss reference sources by type, format, or specific title, devoting the basic reference source to 'the communication process.'" The total number of titles presented to graduate students ranged from 61 to 615; the mode was 160, median 229, and mean 243.

Unfortunately, a statistical manipulation of Larsen's table to match Bonk's is impossible. "In the present survey, seven titles were listed by all thirty-one schools. They included two encyclopedias, *New Encyclopedia Britannica* (fifteenth edition), and *World Book Encyclopedia*; two biographical sources, *Current Biography* and *Dictionary of American Biography*; two indexes, *New York Times Index* and *Reader's Guide to Periodical Literature*; and one yearbook, *World Almanac*."

28. Elaine Rich (1979)

Writing from a computer science perspective, Rich raises the issue of how reference librarians can effectively use stereotyping behavior (i.e., "clusters of characteristics") based on a handful of visual cues (e.g., age, clothing, and gender) and aural cues (e.g., geographical origin and "self-assurance") from the inquirer. Stereotypes are similar to scripts, frames, and schemas. Her work has led to a new field called user modeling which distinguishes systems based on a canonical user or a truly individual user.

G. Reference Transactions: The 1980s

This decade witnesses more cumulative studies on the role of librarians' behavior in the process, closer examination of users, notably younger age groups, and increasing statistical sophistication.

1. Thomas Childers (1980)

Continuing his long-term interest in the evaluation of reference service, Childers reports on a 1977 study of 1110 unobtrusive queries by proxies at 57 public libraries in Suffolk County, New York. He included five types of test questions requiring: (1) factual information; (2) bibliographical information; (3) local government agency information; (4) further negotiation (which he called "escalator" questions); and (5) referral to nonlibrary resources.

Childers presents eight major findings: (1) an actual answer was offered 56% of the time; (2) 84% of these answers were correct or mostly correct; (3) 16% were wrong or mostly wrong; (4) only 17% of the time neither an answer nor a referral was given; (5) 66% of the referrals were to nonlibraries; (6) 66% of the nonlibrary referrals were correct; (7) 67% of the time librarians made no attempt to probe escalator-type questions; and so (8) only 20% got to the third and final step of these questions.

Childers raises issues such as when is it appropriate to negotiate further; when or how soon does one refer; how responsible is the library for its answers or referrals; and what constitutes a correct, mostly correct, or wrong answer. He also includes two brief, but informative, examples of failure to deal responsibly with legitimate reference questions.

2. Linda Morgan (1980)

Intrigued by architectural influences on reference service, Morgan examined user preferences for reference desks versus counters. She found that 72% of the users preferred the counter; they would even wait there when the reference desk was free. Her suggestions run counter to S. S. Green's no-reference-desk policy.

3. Nancy Van House DeWath (1981, 1984)

If for no other reason, this study is noteworthy for its methodological use of a panel of experienced reference librarians from outside the study area (i.e., California) to judge the quality of responses. They found that 79% of the responses were complete and correct, 15% mostly correct, 1% partially correct, 2% incorrect, and 4% yielded no answer. Test questions were mostly fact-type or broad requests, like requests for pictures or instructions. The average cost per reference question was $31, but this result and other factors such as time were not correlated with correctness. Her study is also one of the earliest to note cost.

4. Marilyn White (1981, 1983, and 1985)

In her earliest work on reference service, White found that pauses or the "pacing" of the reference interview significantly influenced the inquirer's responses. She found that either no pauses or pauses of more than 10 seconds had a negative influence on eliciting more information from the inquirer; the former meant that the inquirer could not get a word in edgewise, while the latter signaled lack of interest or termination of the transaction on the part of the reference librarian.

For her 1983 work, White draws upon human cognitive information processing and Minsky's concept of frames from AI research. She relates information about the role of memory, notably that the brain can remember only about seven items (cf. Vavrek's work on the number of elements in a typical reference question); that there is short-term memory loss after 30 seconds; transfers to long-term memory take 5 to 10 seconds; and simple question recognition may take 2 to 5 seconds. She believes that reference librarians use Minsky's frames to classify reference questions and are involved in a pattern-matching process.

White accepts Taylor's basic model, but illustrating it with three examples, she goes on to postulate a more complex interaction between Q1, Q2, Q3, and Q4 than the simple linear relationship that has previously been thought to exist. In particular, White argues that the librarian's motivation to move back to Q1 from Q4 is based on a concern for possible errors that may have crept in, while Q2 and Q3 may be influenced by the inquirer's problem-solving skills and knowledge of information sources.

Extending her original work, White proposes to evaluate the reference interview by looking for seven content topics: "(1) the problem behind the question, (2) the subject of the question, including its relationship to other areas, (3) the nature of the service to be provided . . . , (4) the internal constraints affecting the client's actual use of information . . . , (5) external constraints affecting use . . . , (6) prior search history, and (7) some assessment of the probability of a successful search." She also poses 11 indicators of good form: "(1) a positive, helpful attitude, (2) the absence of behavior that develops defensiveness in the client . . . , (3) the use of open questions when appropriate, (4) the use of probing or follow-up questions when necessary, (5) the use of closed questions when possible, (6) minimal interference in the flow of information for extraneous comments . . . , (7) sensitivity to the client's frame of reference . . . , (8) good, attentive listening, (9) a final summary . . . stating the characteristics of the acceptable answer, (10) use of other appropriate techniques of interviewing, and (11) no distracting personal mannerisms. . . ."

5. Peter Hernon and Charles McClure (1983)

Studying the reference service given in academic government document depository libraries in the Northeast and Southwest, Hernon and McClure found extraordinarily low success rates. Overall, only 37% of their unobtrusive questions were answered correctly, but that figure drops even lower when the day (i.e., 3% on Saturday and Sunday) or time of day (i.e., 15% in evening versus 42–43% during the morning or afternoon) is taken into consideration. Six factors including staff size, volumes held, depository items selected, and budget did not show any statistically significant relation to accuracy.

6. Esther E. Horne (1983)

In an experimental design, Horne studied the "inquiry process" or the "need 'to know'" of 198 LIS students asked to frame questions based on a text. Conceptually, she posits two types of questions (open or Kendon's "unsaturated" versus closed or what he called "saturated") and two types of acceptable answers: finite versus infinite alternative (based on Belnap and Steels' work). She hypothesized that the number of questions would vary directly or inversely with the information need. She found that "questioning behavior, while *idiosyncratic*, does present a pattern and a trend occurring within the constraints of a 'closed' problem situation."

7. Carol C. Kuhlthau (1983; 1985; 1987; 1988a,b,c; 1989; 1991; and 1993) and Robert J. Belvin (1989) and Betty Turock, Mary W. George, and Robert J. Belvin (1990)

Using a small exploratory sample of 26 East Coast advanced placement English high school students in 1981–1982, the author, as her doctoral dissertation, hypothesizes stages in their information search process. Method-ologically, she uses the students' journaling of two research papers, their search logs on the second paper, and results from six interviews done at different times and lasting 30 to 45 minutes each, along with an analysis of their time lines and flowcharts. Kuhlthau posits a six-stage sequential model of student searching along with affective content: (1) task initiation—receive assignment (uncertainty); (2) topic selection (optimism); (3) prefocus exploration (confusion/frustration/doubt); (4) focus formulation (clarity); (5) collect information or information focus (sense of direction/confidence); and (6) search closure—prepare to present (relief) (Kuhlthau 1985, 1988a, Table 1 and 1988c, p. 237; see Figures 1–7). She tests this so-called "emerging theory grounded in a real-life situation" by qualitative means and concludes that it is dynamic and complex, but "fit" with Kelly's personal constructs, Taylor's levels of need, and Belkin's ASK concept.

In 1986, the author attempts to verify (see Chapter 4 of her book-length work) and expand (see Chapter 5) her six stages (now labeled as initiation, selection, exploration, formulation, collection, and presentation). Next came larger scale verification using 147 students from six New Jersey high schools grouped by high achievers ($N = 34$), middle college-bound ($N = 73$), and lower-level achievers ($N = 40$). In 1989, Kuhlthau reports on the process survey that consisted of six questions administered at the beginning, middle, and end of the search to 107 students (the 40 low achievers had to be dropped). Two coders (no interscorer reliability reported) created a 10-point Likert confidence scale and a 9-point Thoughts Index while the teachers assessed their students' focus on a 5-point Likert scale. Although there was a gain in a student's confidence throughout the process and high-achieving students did receive higher grades, there was no statistically significant difference between the two groups of students nor in any variable including the number of sources consulted or the variety of sources cited. However, Kuhlthau does report weak correlations between letter grade and confidence ($r = 0.329$) and focus and confidence ($r = 0.228$).

In her longitudinal study 4 years later of the high-achieving or college-bound students, 20 responded to a 30-statement questionnaire. Analyzed with a t-test to determine whether there was a difference between their responses in high school and college, five differences emerged: (1) the college students were now more likely to agree that "I become more interested in a topic as I gather information" ($t = 2.574$, $p < 0.1$); (2) "A central theme evolves as I gather information on a topic" ($t = 1.759$, $p < 0.05$); (3) "My topic changes as I gather information about it" ($t = 3.340$, $p < 0.01$); (4) "I use periodicals when researching a topic" ($t = 3.842$, $p < 0.01$); and (5) less likely to agree that "The card catalog is the first place I check when researching a topic" ($t = 4.103$, $p < 0.01$). The article concludes with a set of five recommendations that do not appear to be based on the findings.

8. Marilyn J. Markham, Keith H. Stirling, and Nathan M. Smith (1983)

Using a modified form of Gothberg's questionnaire and influenced by Sidney M. Jourard's *The Transparent Self* (1964), this study concludes that librarian behavior influences satisfaction in some situations; specifically, this study correlated academic librarian self-disclosure and user satisfaction (measured on a 5-point Likert scale) using two professionals and two students who conducted 16 reference interviews (8 times using disclosure and 8 without) with a total of 64 patrons who were asked 17 questions about the reference interview. Using analysis of variance, there was no statistically significant difference ($p = 0.098$), although individual question analysis yielded the following: warm/cold (significance = 0.000), friendly/unfriendly (0.001), would you like to work with this reference librarian again (0.007), did you like working with the reference librarian (0.010), interesting/not interesting (0.011), how satisfied were you with the interview (0.031), did you feel the librarian asked enough of the right questions to clarify what you really wanted (0.040); the level of significance for the 10 other questions exceeded 0.050 (p. 371).

9. Ethel Auster and Stephen Lawton (1984)

One of the most sophisticated statistical studies of the reference process, this confirmatory study of White's earlier work involved a factor analysis of the types of questions (i.e., open versus closed), length of pauses (i.e., none or moderate), extent of inquirer's prior knowledge of the query, and the importance of the information problem as perceived by the inquirer.

Their findings indicate that the reference librarians' use of open questions leads to the inquirer learning more as well as being more satisfied. However, they also found that long pauses (i.e., 10 seconds or more) had a negative effect on quality, but that it might be due to their difficulty in training reference librarians to adopt this type of behavior. Finally, "those having a greater need for information are harder to satisfy than are those who have a lesser need."

10. S. D. Neill (1984)

Based on Lynch's and Dewdney's transcriptions of reference transactions, Neill illustrates three different types of memory devices. He calls these: (1) semantic memory, "which organizes things into lists and categories"; (2) episodic memory, which "points to the importance of experience and the usefulness of specific episodes"; and (3) schematic memory, organized spatially or temporally rather than categorically, which is based on prior experience and subsequent expectations. AI researchers such as Minsky and Schrank and Abelson have drawn heavily on this third category for their own work.

Neill asserts that the initial inquiry "will be more general than the question the patron has in mind."

11. Charles Patterson (1984)

Patterson attempts to answer Jahoda's 1981 questions about the necessary versus merely desirable traits for successful reference librarians. He believes the following traits are necessary: outgoing personality, logical mind, inquiring mind, and effectiveness on the job. He thinks that the following seven are desirable ones: good memory, judgment, imagination, thoroughness, orderliness, persistence, and accuracy. He believes that some, if not all, of these are unteachable, however. Rather, it is the instructor's responsibility to identify students with these innate traits and encourage them to go into reference work.

Another Jahoda question is whether students should know specific titles when they may be going into widely varying types and sizes of libraries. Patterson's informed opinion is that they should know specific titles, but he begs the rest of the question—whether the list of titles should vary by type and size of library.

12. Kathy Way (1984 and 1987)

In a telephone survey of two academic law depository libraries during different times of the day, Way found that sources were cited 74% of the time. Although the success rate was highest for MLS/JDs (75%), there was no statistically significant difference between them and MLS holders (69%) or nonprofessionals (53%). This fact may be due to the nature of the test questions, which were basic, fact-type questions that did not require the advanced, subject skills of the MLS/JD librarians.

13. Diane Brown (1985)

In this 1981 study of telephone reference in a medium-sized public library in Tennessee, the author categorized sought after answers (based on 429 general and informational and 219 subject-specific telephone questions) into four categories and then looked at the types of sources consulted. Not surprisingly, "answer format rather than subject is the factor determining the complexity of the question . . . there a low correlation between subject and sources used $[p = 0.01$, Cramer's $V = 0.26]$ . . . and there is some relationship between answer format and sources used $[p = 0.00$, Cramer's $V = 0.32$ overall, but especially for literature where $p = 0.04$, Cramer's $V = 0.65$], so that one expects a request for a document to lead to the card catalog; for a short answer, to the ready reference collections; for a description, to the ready or general reference collection; and for gathered information, to the general reference or circulating collections." The author also compares and contrasts her data on fields to Conner's early study, finding that science and technology, social sciences, geography and history, and general works are consulted most often.

14. Ralph Gers and Lillie Seward (1985)

With help from the University Research Foundation of the University of Maryland, the State Division of Library Development and Services in Maryland conducted a major study of inquirer perception of quality reference service. Using a modified version of the Crowley–Childers test, a set of 40 questions was asked in 60 branch libraries in 22 counties.

Findings indicated a statewide average of about 55% accuracy. Further analysis indicated that quality could be improved by: (1) getting the facts through an increased level of question negotiation; (2) setting the tone by the librarian communicating a higher interest level (e.g., more eye contact); (3) giving the inquirer more information by the librarian indicating an increased comfort level in the process (e.g., attentive comments, asking relevant questions); and (4) asking more follow-up questions (e.g., "Does this completely answer your question?"). Oddly, they found that accuracy increased only slightly during high-demand (i.e., busy) periods. The fourth behavior, asking more follow-up questions, was observed only 12% of the time, yet this one step "may be the single most important factor in the interview."

Interestingly, 87% of the reference questions asked in Maryland public libraries could be effectively answered with just seven titles: (1) *World Almanac*; (2) *Information Please Almanac*; (3) *World Book Encyclopedia*; (4) *Stevenson's Home Book of Quotations*; (5) *Reader's Guide to Periodicals*; (6) *Motor's* or *Chilton Auto Manual*; and (7) an unabridged dictionary.

15. Brenda Dervin and Patricia Dewdney (1986)

Based on 13 years of empirical research, Dervin and her coauthor propose that the inquirer's information need can be characterized as an attempt at "sense-making" that is "situationally bound." Specifically, they propose a tripartite model of information need that is composed of a situation, a gap or stoppages, and uses. Interviews with 17 public librarians about troublesome reference interviews substantiate Taylor's second filter (i.e., motivation and use objective) as the most important one, although without explicitly saying so or referring to his work at this point.

Although they identify the reference librarian's three options of closed, open, and neutral questions, they warn against the first because "all closed questions involve [a possibly premature] judgment already made by the librarian of what is relevant to the user." Instead, they provide a set of illustrative neutral questions for use in negotiations and strongly recommend these as opposed to leading, but open questions, although they do not use the term "leading" in their article.

In her doctoral study of 24 reference librarians in three Ontario public libraries, Dewdney found that the inquirer's initial satisfaction was already high, and that satisfaction with those librarians trained in Dervin's neutral questioning and Jennerich's micro-counseling skills actually decreased over time. However, those librarians trained in neutral questioning were rated higher on premature diagnosis, use of open questions, and closure. Dervin's work is important to understanding the reference process because it revitalizes research interest in applying communication theory.

16. Joan Durrance (1986)

Assuming that users of reference services are the best judges of quality service, Durrance and graduate students conducted 429 personal interviews with users of three Midwest academic libraries as they left the reference department during the morning, afternoon, evening, and weekend hours (note that the interviews, however, were weighted toward afternoons and evenings). Her objective was to examine factors affecting the client–librarian relationship. Her variables included: (1) "user knowledge of staff differentiation"; (2) recognition of staff members (including "the ability to identify library staff members by name"); (3) inclination to ask questions (including "the inclination to look for particular staff"); and (4) inclination to avoid staff members; and (5) "inclination to return." She found that: (1) 84% of the users thought that staff differences existed, but most did not know with any certainty; (2) more than half of the users used appearance (e.g., older) or environment (e.g., behind the desk) clues to establish to which category a staff member belonged; (3) "only 10 percent of all users look for particular staff," which the author interprets as a lack of a true client–librarian relationship; (4) most users had no criteria by which to select a librarian (including appearance, expertise, and personal knowledge); and (5) reasons given for avoiding certain staff included "negative style of the staff member, based on past experience or perception . . . [or] past experience unrelated to expertise."

17. Roma Harris and Gillian Michell (1986 and 1987)

The purpose of this experimental design (a $2 \times 2 \times 2 \times 2 \times 2$ fully crossed design) was to determine the effect of gender, appearance, and verbal and nonverbal behavior on the assessed quality of reference service where video-taped actors played the parts of librarians and users. The judges were 320 male and female users of a medium-sized public library randomly assigned to watch one of 16 videotapes.

Most viewers of the tapes found high levels of perceived competence in the "librarians" regardless of level of warmth or "inclusiveness" displayed based on a 24-item measure using the Newman–Keuls test when $p = 0.05$. Warmth was defined as "nonverbal behaviors including smiling, eye contact with the patron, warm voice tone, and open body posture" while inclusive-ness was defined as "the librarian explained how she was using the reference tools employed in searching for the answer to the patron's question" (p. 97). "A significant three-way interaction between sex of the observer, level of inclusion, and type of observer, $F (1127) = 3.91$, $p < 0.05$" emerged (p. 99).

Whereas reference librarians may count other attributes such as profes-sional expertise and knowledge of the library's collection highly, the users' judgment of the professionalism and competence of the reference librarian seem to depend more on communication skills: warmth and inclusiveness. Their follow-up study asked a total of 64 male and female librarians from dif-ferent types of libraries to view a subset of the same videotapes. Then com-parisons were drawn between the two groups (i.e., users and librarians). The authors found that: (1) "the librarians were harder to please than the library patrons with respect to competence in the reference interview"; (2) "female librarians who watched the tapes in which low inclusion was demonstrated gave lower perceived warmth ratings than the male and female patrons who watched the same condition," suggesting to the authors that female librari-ans may be out of touch with user reactions or that they have higher per-formance standards; (3) librarians, regardless of gender, thought the librarian who showed more warmth to be more competent, leading the authors to conclude that "the demeanor of the librarian toward the patron during the reference interview may be just as important as competently retrieving infor-mation." Other differences were based on the librarian's type of library and location.

Their most significant conclusion is that female librarians differ in their helping styles; they value "inclusiveness" and a teaching role in reference work, whereas female library users prefer warmth rather than being included. This serious conflict warrants further research; interested readers might pursue lines of thought presented in *You Just Don't Understand* (Tannen, 1990).

18. George Hawley (1987)

The objective of this Rutgers doctoral dissertation was "to identify factors that influence library referral." Referral includes in-house as well as out-of-building referrals to individuals, libraries, and other organizations. Structured interviews were conducted with 34 librarians (22 women and 12 men) at five academic and five public libraries in the Northeast.

His findings support Childers's finding that libraries infrequently provide referral, only about 17% of the time. Otherwise, his findings are purely descriptive; he identifies many possible factors, but does not provide a metric for measuring these factors or their interactions. Nonetheless, individual factors influencing referral include extent of training and experience; knowledge of outside resources and their strength (especially interaction with faculty for academic librarians); efficiency; equity; achievement motivation; empathy; tact; and independence. User or client factors are fourfold: physical; mental attitudes about distance and about travel information; attitudes about travel safety; monetary costs; and feedback (e.g., none, little, much, and organized). Institutional factors include interaction with the director; interaction with co-workers; activity level at reference desk; strength of collection; and the availability and use of referral tools. Factors related to the referral to an individual, library, or organization include helpful outside resources; ambiguous or unhelpful outside resources; and institutional policies toward outsiders.

19. Tefko Saracevic, Paul Kantor, Alice Y. Chamis, and Donna Trivison (1987 and 1988)

After an extensive 10-page literature review, this study examines 36 "outside searchers" along with three "project searchers" with the goal of testing a "model of question structure and the scheme for question classification" (p. 171). In particular, the 1988 study adopted D. A. Kolb's "learning style inventory" which is a four-stage process: concrete experience (CE), reflective observation (RO), abstract conceptualization (AC), and active experimentation (AE). In short, they found (where the t-value $= -2.39$) that searchers with "higher CE scores bring higher chances or odds for low precision or low chances for high precision" searching (p. 175).

20. Jo Bell Whitlatch (1987 and 1990)

Studying 257 reference transactions from five academic libraries in northern California, the author tested a model with eight independent variables including service orientation, feedback, and type of assistance, while the dependent variables included librarian, user evaluations of service rendered, and the user's success in finding the necessary material. Overall, her most significant conclusion is that the librarians' evaluation of service quality could substitute for the users' evaluation in 83% of the cases because their evaluations were the same or lower than the users' (echoing Harris and Gillian).

H. The Reference Transaction: The 1990s

In this decade, an increased clarity on measuring outcomes appears. Extensive work is undertaken to understand the decision-making of expert reference librarians. The earlier promise of artificial intelligence, especially knowledge-based systems, is explored in depth. The 50% rule is proved wrong by Saxton—the set of test questions used in most studies is not typical of actual questions, despite being so judged by a panel of experts. The most sophisticated statistical approach to date, hierarchical linear modeling, is employed as well.

1. Marie L. Radford (1989, 1993, 1996, and 1999)

Based on her 1993 doctoral dissertation at Rutgers University, her 1999 book presents qualitative findings related to four research questions (i.e., user and librarian perceptions about "the relational dimensions of the interpersonal aspects of reference interactions," p. 131) posed on page 5 of Chapter 1. A topical literature review is covered in Chapter 2 and the theoretical perspective (communication theory) in Chapter 3. Chapter 4 covers the methodology of the "pilot study conducted at a state-supported college in the Northeast" and the main study of nine librarians, three from each library (in a community college, a private university, and a public college). In her paired perceptions findings presented in Chapter 7, she notes, "The overall level of total agreement between eleven pairs of librarians and users (41%) is noteworthy, but there were ten pairs (37%) with partial agreement and six pairs (22%) who totally disagreed. The interviews showed that librarians and users can have different viewpoints and striking differences in their criteria for determining success" (p. 100).

Radford's major findings are:

- Interpersonal relationships and communication are of great importance in librarian and user perceptions of reference interactions.
- Library users in academic settings place a high degree of significance on the attitude and personal qualities of the librarian giving reference assistance.
- Some users valued interpersonal aspects more than their receipt of information.
- Librarians were more likely than users to evaluate the reference encounter from content dimensions that involve the transfer of information.
- Librarians also perceive relationship qualities to be important in the success of reference interactions (although to a lesser degree than users) (p. 104).

2. John V. Richardson Jr. (1989, 1995, 1998, and 1999)

Laying out a 10-year research agenda in this area starting in 1989, Richardson asks seven questions which must be answered for expert systems to play a strong role in the reference environment: (1) what is the proper scope of an expert system for answering reference questions; (2) can experts articulate their heuristics; (3) what is the best approach to implementing an expert system; (4) should expert systems model the reference process; (5) what had already been done; (6) what system validation has been undertaken; and (7) how shall we evaluate future efforts?

Comparing and contrasting the expert system Pointer (at SUNY, Albany) and the Government Documents Reference Assistant (Stanford), he and Rex Reyes provide a taxonomy of service quality based on an 8-point scale.

In Chapter 5 of his book, Richardson lays out a cognitive model of constructs (or architectural logic) used by librarians based on 300 reference interviews conducted by 24 expert reference librarians.

During his sabbatical year at OCLC's Office of Research, Richardson creates Question Master (http://purl.org/net/Question_Master) or QM, a Web-based decision support system for librarians. Consisting of 14 modules (the 8-level deep biographical and 4-level deep dictionary units were fully implemented using the architectural logic mentioned above), it tracks the user throughout the system from the initial question to the final resolution. In OCLC's usability laboratory, he finds that QM is "easy to use" (i.e., 4.5 on a 5-point scale where 1 is "very difficult" and 5 is "very easy to use"). Richardson further evaluates the biographical module against a test set of 10 questions. He find that QM can answer 66% of the questions put to it accurately (using a modified version of the service quality taxonomy above)— notably AltaVista and HotBot can only answer these questions accurately 30% and 20% of the time, respectively. This work explains why novices take longer to answer questions and suggests that the "half-right" reference results might be due to a "good enough" orientation to service (i.e., a resolution of rather than solution of information problems).

Adopting a systems perspective after becoming convinced that the expert model is too wide and too deep for successful adoption by most practitioners, Richardson posits a new model of the reference transaction using four data flow diagrams rather than traditional flowcharting techniques. Fifteen functional requirements are then identified: answering all questions; open-ended question negotiation; recording data related to questions; persistence of the system; closed-ended confirmation; determination of acceptable answer; obligatory data source; memory requirement; types of sources; complete, accurate answers; timely answers; system referrals; question logging; short-term customer satisfaction; and long-term customer satisfaction.

3. Prince George's County Memorial Library System, MD (1990)

Dedicated to the notion of continuous improvement of reference quality, this library system took the 1985 Maryland findings to heart, started a series of staff workshops, and worked hard to improve reference quality. By 1990, three of the 19 branches could report 95% accuracy in unobtrusive studies of reference service using a modified Childers–Crowley methodology. In fact, surveyors found an "unusual uniformity in the staff use of reference behaviors, and that the PGCMLS staff projected an image of cordiality, competence and professionalism in responding to their survey questions over the telephone." Overall, the 19 branches averaged 77.4% accuracy, while more than half the branches were above 80% accurate.

4. Thomas Childers (1993)

Based on 658 second-level reference questions from four California public library systems in 1990, the author adopts an extremely economically bivariate model to correlate difficulty ("actual" and "perceived" is measured on a seven-point Likert scale) with more than six variables: number of sources, types of sources, time spent, prior knowledge of subject, ease of access to answering sources, and library size. Given the normality violations and the fact that there were no data transformations as well as their use of Pearson as a descriptive statistic, they cannot generalize to make any inferences about the population. Nonetheless, he reports statistically significant Pearson correlations for the most important findings: (1) actual difficulty and time spent ($r = 0.61$); (2) actual difficulty and number of sources consulted ($r = 0.59$); and (3) actual difficulty and ease of access to sources ($r = 0.57$).

5. Mary Beth Allen (1993)

Based on a 52.7% sample ($N = 395$) of the 3401 international students at the University of Illinois at Champaign-Urbana, the author found previous use of library or other computers was a good predictor for no difficulty using the online catalog (chi-square = 8.6; $df = 2$; $p < 0.05$; Cramer's $V = 0.154$ and chi-square = 12.4; $df = 2$; $p < 0.01$; Cramer's $V = 0.184$, respectively). Similarly, use of computers, the library's or otherwise, also influenced the international students' perception of their preparedness to use U.S. libraries (chi-square = 10.2; $df = 2$; $p < 0.01$; Cramer's $V = 0.161$ and chi-square = 9.16; $df = 2$; $p < 0.01$; Cramer's $V = 0.153$).

6. Rachel Applegate (1993)

Summarizing more than a dozen works since the mid-1960s in library science, computer systems, marketing, and psychology, the author critiques three models of user satisfaction: the Material Satisfaction Model (MSM), the

Emotional Satisfaction Model–Simple Path (ESM-SO), and the Emotional Satisfaction Model–Multiple Path (ESM-MP). The ESM-MP model contains user organismic and user-acquired variables, which set expectations as well as product performance, which directly influences material satisfaction. Both expectations and material satisfaction feed disconfirmation while the latter also feeds emotional satisfaction, as does product setting. Finally, emotional satisfaction drives behavior, according to this model. Arguing that the former two models are inadequate and that only the latter can explain "more variance," the author concludes that this more complex model needs to be tested.

7. Patricia A. Dewdney and Catherine S. Ross (1994)

Using 77 University of Western Ontario MLIS students to collect data between 1992 and 1993, the authors studied the influence of librarian behavior (including friendliness, pleasantness, understanding, and helpfulness, each on 7-point Likert scales) on user satisfaction and the user's willingness to return (also on 7-point Likert scales) to public libraries ($N = 52$; 39 at main and 13 at branches), academic libraries ($N = 24$; 19 main and 5 departmental), and one apparently unidentified type of library. The objective was to focus attention on sources of the user's dissatisfaction and to identify statistically significant relationships. The two highest relationships were overall satisfaction and helpfulness ($r = 0.81$) and friendliness ($r = 0.71$); see their Table 2 for other statistical relationships, all of which are reported as significant.

8. Mary Jane Scherdin (1994)

Based on the Myers–Briggs Personality Type Indicator (MBTI), the author surveys 3500 ACRL members in 1992 and achieves a return rate of 58% ($N = 1600$ librarians), making this study the most reliable indicator of reference librarian personality type: most commonly ISTJ (16.5), INTJ (11.5), and INTP (9.1) of the 16 possible types (technically, the adult public services group of 489 librarians showed no statistically significant differences at the 0.001 level—see p. 137). Overall, "Sixty-three percent (63%) [of all librarians] have the Introversion preference. Sixty-nine percent (69%) of male librarians and 58% of female librarians have the Thinking preference. Fifty-nine percent (59%) are Intuitive types, and 66% are Judging types" (p. 211). Interested readers can try the free online "Temperament Sorter II" version by Keirsey, which appears to be reliable, at http://www.keirsey.com (accessed 1 December 2001).

9. Melissa Gross (1995)

Asserting that "The imposed query is a question that is given to someone else to transact or resolve" (p. 237), the author proposes a provocative, but untested, six-stage model (see her Figure 1). In addition, the author raises interesting, but unanswered questions about the frequency of imposed versus self-generated questions, the effect of imposed questions on later information-seeking behavior, relevancy judgments, and stereotyping in the question answering process.

10. Reference Assessment Manual (1995)

With the objective of providing access to "a wide range of evaluation instruments useful in assessing reference effectiveness," this extensive but unevenly annotated bibliography of approximately 540 items is designed to "encourage library administrators to support and promote evaluation of services." Organized into 15 chapters covering users and questions; material resources; human resources; reference process; and results (i.e., costs, outcomes, and reference effectiveness), this bibliography concludes by highlighting nine major survey instruments.

11. ALA RASD "Behavioral Guidelines" (1996)

In what is probably the pivotal professional document since S. S. Green's articulation of reference service in 1876, ALA's reference services division goes on record about what matters in providing standard professional service, based on informed professional opinion. The difficulty with their *Guidelines*, of course, is that it had not been tested until the appearance of Saxton and Richardson's *Understanding Reference Transactions* (2002).

12. John C. Stalker and Marjorie E. Murfin (1996)

At Ohio State University, the authors asked 41 upper division undergraduate journalism students (in three groups of 13, 13, and then 15 students) to answer eight moderately difficult questions (based on a question, taking a reference librarian 10 to 20 minutes to answer—see their Appendix A). The eight questions were drawn randomly from all of the substantial reference questions asked at the OSU Libraries' reference desk during a several-week period during the previous year. The first group ($N = 13$) was asked to search the eight questions in OSCAR, the online catalog, and two other groups used SOFI, an in-house computerized reference librarian's "source finder." Based on Nota Bene software, SOFI consisted of question units (i.e., sets of instructions for answering questions grouped according to cities, foreign languages, dates and chronologies, money and finance, government officials, tests and assessment, associations, and abbreviations). In this study, success was arbitrarily defined as 80% accuracy in locating and selecting the correct item by using one of three approaches: (1) keywords, (2) broad subjects, and (3) the direct answer method. Only 10.5% found an actual answer source in OSCAR whereas 58% of the second group found "the correct set of instructions for [answering] their question" in SOFI. In the second test of the revised SOFI, the third group found 78%.

13. Matthew Saxton (1997)

Applying a meta-analysis to 59 known studies of reference accuracy, the author was able to find only 12 studies where applicable variables ($N = 7$) could be added into a meta-analysis. The findings indicate that total library expenditures (Pearson $r = 0.61$), number of volumes added (0.55), size of service population (0.55), absolute change in the collection (0.51), number of volumes discarded (0.37), number of volumes in the library collection (0.22), and absolute change as a proportion of the total collection (0.13) correlate with accuracy. Because of the lack of generalizability, all subsequent researchers would do well to note his comments about the "lack of consistency regarding which variables are being examined and how they are being measured."

14. Tschera H. Connell and Jennifer E. Tipple (1999)

Using 60 ready-reference questions (see their Appendix 1) collected from the Upper Arlington Public Library (OH) between 10 and 16 October 1996, the authors entered these same questions to AltaVista's search engine. They scored the answers as correct (three points), mostly correct (two points), mostly wrong (one point), and wrong (zero points). Considering all of the pages returned ($N = 1160$), 64% "contained no answer (either correct or incorrect) at all. Correct and mostly correct answers were found 27.2 percent of the time, while wrong and mostly wrong answers were found 8.8 percent of the time. . . . However, a nearly 73 percent failure rate raises questions concerning the efficiency of using the Web for ready reference questions, especially if only one search engine is used" (p. 366). They do not compare and contrast their results using other search engines or meta-searching such as Copernic.

15. Kyunghye Yoon and Michael S. Nilan (1999)

The authors propose to investigate empirically the relationship between certainty (i.e., "what they perceive and how they employ it") and uncertainty (i.e., "what users do not know") in the information-seeking process. Using Roman Jakobson's notion of topic (i.e., an utterance related to aboutness— "what a person is talking about") and comment (i.e., an utterance that "relates or situates the topic to an individual perspective and context), data analysis of 171 useful utterances (see their appendix for sample interactions) from 19 (i.e., 7 university libraries, 6 public libraries, and 6 graduate students) user–source interactions yielded the fact that comment played the largest role in the specification of need (80.4%), but no statistically significant ($\chi^2 = 1.703\text{e-}45$) pattern between "classification of respondents' utterances by certainty/uncertainty and topic/comment" emerged.

16. Matthew Saxton (2000) and Matthew Saxton and John Richardson (2002)

Saxton argues that:

> The evaluation of reference service requires a multi-level research design that can account for the effects of intra-class correlation that arise as the result of gathering multiple observations from each library and librarian participating in the study. Few studies have ever tested for these effects that tend to diminish the value of the standard error, misleading the investigator into believing that a relationship between variables has been discovered which does not necessarily exist. Although many previous studies have focused on a single outcome variable, this study measures the influence of sixteen predictors on three outcomes: the accuracy of the information received by the library user, the utility of the information received by the user, and the inquirer's satisfaction with the reference process. Evidence suggested that in utility outcome measures about two-thirds of the variance is explained at the librarian level of the model and about one-third is explained at the library level of the model. The variance in accuracy and satisfaction measures is explained entirely at the librarian level of the model. Variables that predicted a significant effect on the outcome measures include the extent to which the librarian followed the RUSA Behavioral Guidelines, the difficulty of the query, the user's level of education, the user's familiarity with receiving reference service, and the librarian's job satisfaction. Variables that did not predict any significant effect on the outcome measures include the librarian's experience and education as well as the size and the service policies of the library.

Coauthored with Richardson, *Understanding Reference Transactions* (2002) is a major revision of Saxton's dissertation with additional chapters providing a systems analysis perspective as well as next steps for improving reference service. Quality reference service is defined in terms of three dimensions: accuracy, utility, and user satisfaction. These three outcomes appear unrelated, suggesting they are driven by different underlying factors. Consequently, users indicated they were satisfied even when they did not receive a useful response from the librarian. Also, users indicated they received useful information even when the information was inaccurate.

Typical "fact-type" queries used in previous accuracy studies are only representative of half of all queries received in this study; in other words, the so-called "55% rule" has not been tested against a truly representative field sample. In 90% of the cases in this study, a panel of reference experts determined that librarians recommended an accurate source or an accurate strategy in response to a user's query. Notably, the most important factor predicting accuracy was the difficulty of the query.

Users are more satisfied by those librarians who actively practice the reference skills outlined in the RUSA "Behavioral Guidelines" (1996): inviting queries, expressing interest, listening critically, and verifying user satisfaction. The probability of an individual finding useful and complete information not only is dependent on the librarian's reference skills, but also is predicted by the user's familiarity with the library and level of education.

Another important feature of the book is an appendix, listing the variables used by previous researchers.

IV. Conclusions

A clear consensus has emerged on what reference service or reference work is about, although confusion seems to exist on what the product is—information or the mediation itself. Another clear advance is the move from merely descriptive studies to those studies with more theoretical approaches and a clearly increasing methodological sophistication, usually quantitative, although a variety of methodological perspectives exist (e.g., quantitative versus qualitative). Regrettably, though, there is a strong lack of consensus on concepts and variables (notably operational definitions) and even competing models of the reference transaction.

As Matthew Saxton and I have said elsewhere: "The literature reveals two complementary lines of inquiry. The first line pertains to understanding how intermediaries seek and locate accurate information in response to the expressed needs of users. The second line pertains to understanding how those needs are recognized and how the response is expressed. Ultimately, research in both areas could lead to the development of a broader theory of intermediation."

Acknowledgments

Work on this project started in the late 1980s, when Kenneth D. Crews served as a research assistant on my reference evaluation project supported by UCLA's ASCOR; he published his findings as "The Accuracy of Reference Services: Variables for Research and Implementation," *Library and Information Science Research* 10 (1988): 331–355. An earlier version covering much of the literature from 1926 to 1990 appeared as "Modeling the Reference

Transaction," as part of Chapter 4 in my own *Knowledge-Based Systems for General Reference Work: Applications, Problems, and Progress* (Academic Press, New York, 1995). Since then, Matthew Saxton has worked as an ASCOR supported research assistant, undertaking to publish several items including his doctoral dissertation. During the 2001/2002 academic year, Marcia Schmitz has also worked as a research assistant on this long-term project. See http://purl.org/net/reference for a complete listing of the 1000 citations from which the preceding literature review is drawn.

References

Anonymous. (1990). Branches' unobtrusive survey results up from last year. *PGCMLS Staff Newsletter* **18**, 1, 5.

Alexander, C. (1936). The technique of library searching. *Special Libraries* **27**, 230–238.

Allen, M. B. (1993). International students in academic libraries: A user survey. *College & Research Libraries* **54**, 323–333.

American Library Association. Evaluation of Reference and Adult Services Committee (1995). *The Reference Assessment Manual*. Pierian Press, Ann Arbor, MI.

American Library Association. Reference and Adult Users Division (RASD). Ad Hoc Committee on Behavioral Guidelines for Reference and Information Services (1996). Guidelines for behavioral performance of reference and information services professionals. *RQ* **36**, 200–203.

Applegate, R. (1993). Models of user satisfaction: Understanding false positives. *RQ* **32**, 525–539.

Auster, E., and Lawton, S. B. (1984). Search interview techniques and information gain as antecedents of user satisfaction with online bibliographic retrieval. *Journal of the American Society for Information Science* **35**, 90–103.

Baldwin, E., and Marcus, W. E. (1941). *Library Costs and Budgets: A Study of Cost Accounting in Public Libraries*. Bowker, New York.

Bates, M. J. (1979a). Information search tactics. *Journal of the American Society for Information Science* **30**, 105–214.

Bates, M. J. (1979b). Idea tactics. *Journal of the American Society for Information Science* **30**, 280–289.

Belkin, N. J. (1980). Anomalous state of knowledge as the basis for information retrieval. *The Canadian Journal of Information Science* **5**, 133–143.

Belkin, N. J., and Oddy, R. N. (1979). *Design Study for an Anomalous State of Knowledge Based Information Retrieval System*. British Library, London.

Belkin, N. J., Brooks, H. M., and Oddy, R. N. (1979). Representation and classification of anomalous state of knowledge and information for use in interactive information retrieval. Paper presented at the IRFIS 3: Proceedings of the 3rd International Research Forum in Information Science, Oslo.

Belkin, N. J., Oddy, R. N., and Brooks, H. M. (1982a). ASK for information retrieval: Part I. Background and theory. *Journal of Documentation* **38**, 61–71.

Belkin, N. J., Oddy, R. N., and Brooks, H. M. (1982b). ASK for information retrieval: Part II. Results of a design study. *Journal of Documentation* **38**, 145–164.

Benson, J., and Maloney, R. K. (1975). Principles of searching. *RQ* **15**, 316–320.

Berliner, B., Corey, M., and Ochoa, G. (1990). *The Book of Answers; The New York Public Library Telephone Reference Service's Most Unusual and Entertaining Questions*. Prentice Hall Press, New York.

Bonk, W. J. (1960). *Composite List of Titles Taught in Basic Reference by 25 of the Accredited Library Schools*. University of Michigan Department of Library Science, Ann Arbor.

Bonk, W. J. (1961). Core curriculum and the reference and bibliography courses. *Journal of Education for Librarianship* **2**, 28–33.

Bonk, W. J. (1963). *Use of Basic Reference Sources in Libraries*. University of Michigan Department of Library Science, Ann Arbor, MI.

Bonk, W. J. (1964). Core reference course. *Journal of Education for Librarianship* **4**, 196–208.

Boucher, V. (1976). Nonverbal communication and the library reference interview. *RQ* **16**, 27–32.

Boyer, L. M., and Theimer Jr., W. C. (1975). The use and training of non-professional personnel at reference desks in selected colleges and universities. *College and Research Libraries* **36**, 193–200.

Breed, P. F. (1955). An analysis of reference procedures in a large university library. Ph.D. dissertation, University of Chicago.

Bunge, C. A. (1967a). *Professional Education and Reference Efficiency*, Springfield, IL.

Bunge, C. A. (1967b). Professional education and reference efficiency. Ph.D. dissertation, University of Illinois, Champaign-Urbana.

Bunge, C. A. (1969). Charting the reference query. *RQ* **8**, 245–250.

Carlson, G. (March 17, 1964). *Search Strategy by Reference Librarians; Part 3 of the Final Report on the Organization of Large Files*. Hughes Dynamics, Advance Information Systems Division, Sherman Oaks, CA.

Childers, T. (1980). The test of reference. *Library Journal* **105**, 924–928.

Childers, T. (1983). *Information and Referral: Public Libraries*. Ablex, Norwood, NJ.

Childers, T. (1993). *A Reference Evaluation Pilot*. California State Library, Sacramento, CA.

Cole, D. E. (September 1943). An analysis of adult reference work in libraries. MA thesis, University of Chicago.

Coney, D., *et al.* (1940). *Report of a Survey of the Indiana University Library for Indiana University*. American Library Association, Chicago.

Connell, T. H., and Tipple, J. E. (1999). Testing the accuracy of information on the World Wide Web using the AltaVista search engine. *Reference and User Services Quarterly* **38**, 360–368.

Conner, M. (1927). What a reference librarian should know. *Library Journal* **52**, 415–418.

Crowley, T. (1971). The effectiveness of information service in medium size public libraries. In: *Information Service in Public Libraries: Two Studies* (T. Crowley and T. Childers, eds.). Scarecrow Press, Metuchen, NJ.

Crum, N. J. (1969). The librarian–customer relationship: Dynamics of filling requests for information. *Special Libraries* **60**, 269–277.

De Jong, M. (1926). Where does the reference librarian's time go? *Wisconsin Library Bulletin* **22**, 7–8.

De Wath, N. Van House (1981). *California Statewide Reference Referral Service: Analysis and Recommendations*. King Research, Rockville, MD.

Delaney, D. J., and Eisenberg, S. (1972). *The Counseling Process*. Rand McNally, Chicago.

Delaney, J. (1954). Interviewing. *Wilson Library Bulletin* **29**, 317–318.

Dervin, B., and Dewdney, P. (1986). Neutral questioning—A new approach to the reference interview. *RQ* **25**, 506–531.

Dewdney, P. (1982). *Query Negotiation in Public Libraries: A Content Analysis of Filtering Techniques Used by Reference Librarians in the Process of Clarifying the Inquirer's Information Need*. School of Library and Information Science, University of Western Ontario.

Dewdney, P. (August 1986). The effects of training reference librarians in interview skills: A field experiment. Ph.D. dissertation, School of Library and Information Service, University of Western Ontario.

Dewdney, P., and Ross, C. S. (1994). Flying a light aircraft: Reference service evaluation from a user's viewpoint. *RQ* **34**, 217–230.

Dion, K. K., Berscheid, E., and Walster, E. (1972). What is beautiful is good. *Journal of Personality and Social Psychology* **24**, 285–290.

Durfee, L. J. (1986). Student awareness of reference services in a liberal arts college library. *Library Quarterly* **56**, 286–302.

Durrance, J. C. (1986). The influence of reference practices on the client–librarian relationship. *College and Research Libraries* **47**, 57–67.

Eichman, T. L. (1978). The complex nature of opening reference questions. *RQ* **17**, 212–222.

Fitzgerald, J., Fitzgerald, A., and Warren D. Stallings, J. (1987). *Fundamentals of Systems Analysis*. Wiley, New York.

Francillon, M. (1959). Information retrieval: A view from the reference desk. *Journal of Documentation* **15**, 187–198.

Gers, R., and Seward, L. J. (1985). Improving reference performance: Results of a statewide study. *Library Journal* **110**, 32–35.

Goldhor, H. (1960). Reference service analysis. *Illinois Libraries* **42**, 319–322.

Goldhor, H. (1967). *A Plan for the Development of Public Library Service in Minneapolis-Saint Paul Metropolitan Area*. State of Minnesota, Department of Education, Library Division; with a chapter by Wesley C. Simonton. Minneapolis, MN: Department of Education, Library Division, 1967; reprint ed., Washington, DC: ERIC Document Reproduction Service ED 1977, 1967, St. Paul, MN.

Gothberg, H. M. (August 1974). User satisfaction with a librarian's immediate and nonimmediate verbal–nonverbal communication. Ph.D. dissertation, University of Denver.

Green, S. S. (1876). Personal relations between librarians and readers. *American Library Journal* **1** (November 1876), 74–81.

Gross, M. (1995). The imposed query. *RQ* **35**, 236–243.

Guerrier, E. (1935). Measurement of reference service in a branch library. *ALA Bulletin* **29**, 632–637.

Halldorsson, E. A., and Murfin, M. E. (1977). The performance of professionals and non-professionals in the reference interview. *College & Research Libraries* **38**, 385–395.

Halperin, M. (1977). Waiting lines. *RQ* **16**, 297–299.

Harris, R. M., and Michel, B. G. (1986). The social context of reference work: Assessing the effects of gender and communication skill on observers judgments of competence. *Library and Information Science Research* **8**, 85–101.

Harris, R. M., and Michell, B. G. (1987). Evaluating the reference interview: Some factors influencing patrons and professionals. *RQ* **27**, 95–105.

Hawley, G. S. (1987). *Referral Process in Libraries: A Characterization and an Exploration of Related Factors*. Scarecrow Press, Metuchen, NJ.

Hayes, R. M. (30 April 1964). *The Organization of Large Files-Introduction and Summary; Part 1 of the Final Report on the Organization of Large Files*. Hughes Dynamics, Advance Information Systems Division, Sherman Oaks, CA.

Haygood, W. C. (1938). *Who Uses the Public Library: A Survey of the Patrons of the Circulation and Reference Departments of the New York Public Library*. University of Chicago Press, Chicago.

Hernon, P., and McClure, C. R. (1983). Testing the quality of reference service provided by academic depository libraries: A pilot study. In: *Communicating Public Access to Government Information* (P. Hernon, ed.), pp. 109–123. Greenwood Press, Westport, CT.

Horne, E. E. (1983). Question generation and formulation: An indication of information need. *Journal of the American Society for Information Science* **34**, 5–15.

Hutchins, M. (1937). The artist-teacher in the field of bibliography; an application of modern educational theories and techniques to the teaching of the first-year library school. *Library Quarterly* **7**, 99–120.

Hutchins, M. (1944). *Introduction to Reference Work*. American Library Association, Chicago.

Hyers, F. H. (1936). Librarians: Savants or dilettantes? *Pacific Bindery Talk* **8**, 87–89.

Jahoda, G. (1974). Reference question analysis and search strategy development by man and machine. *Journal of the American Society for Information Science* **25**, 139–144.

Jahoda, G. (1975). *Progress Report: The Process of Answering Reference Questions-A Test of a Descriptive Model* (Report Number Contract/Grant Number OEG-0-74-7307). Florida State University, Tallahassee.

Jahoda, G. (January 1977). *The Process of Answering Reference Questions; A Test of a Descriptive Model*. Florida State University School of Library Science; reprint ed. (Bethesda, MD: ERIC Document Reproduction Service, ED 136 769, 1977), Tallahasse, FL.

Jahoda, G. (1981). Some unanswered questions. *The Reference Librarian* **1/2**, 159.

Jahoda, G., and Braunagel, J. S. (1980). *The Librarian and Reference Queries: A Systematic Approach*. Academic Press, New York.

Jahoda, G., and Culnan, M. (1968). Unanswered science and technology questions. *American Documentation* **19**, 95–100.

Jahoda, G., Braunagel, J., and Nath, H. (1977). The reference process: Modules for instruction. *RQ* **17**, 7–12.

Jennerich, E. Z. (1974). Microcounseling in library education. Ph.D. dissertation, University of Pittsburgh, Pittsburgh, PA.

Jennerich, E. Z. (1980). Before the answer: Evaluating the reference process. *RQ* **19**, 360–366.

Jennerich, E. Z. (1981). The art of the reference interview. *Indiana Libraries* **1**, 7–18.

Jennerich, E., and Jennerich, E. J. (1976). Teaching the reference interview. *Journal of Education for Librarianship* **17**, 106–111.

Jennerich, E. Z., and Jennerich, E. J. (1987). *The Reference Interview as a Creative Art*. Libraries Unlimited, Littleton, CO.

Jennerich, E. Z., and Jennerich, E. J. (1997). *The Reference Interview as a Creative Art* (2nd ed.). Libraries Unlimited, Englewood, CO.

Jestes, E. C., and Laird, W. D. (1968). A time study of general reference work in a university library. *Research in Librarianship* **2**, 9–16, 77.

Jourard, S. M. (1964). *The Transparent Self*. Van Nostrand, Princeton, NJ.

Julien, H. (1996). A content analysis of the recent information needs and uses literature. *Library and Information Science Research* **18**, 53–65.

Kaam, A. L. V. (1959). Phenomenal analysis: Exemplified by a study of the experience of "really feeling understood." *Journal of Individual Psychology* **15**, 66–72.

King, G. B. (1972). The reference interview: Open and closed questions. *RQ* **12**, 157–160.

Kronus, C. L. (1973). Patterns of adult library use: A regression path analysis. *Adult Education* **23**, 115–131.

Krumboltz, J. D., and Thoresen, C. E. (1969). *Behavioral Counseling: Cases and Techniques*. Holt, New York.

Kuhlthau, C. C. (1983). The research process: Case studies and interventions with high school seniors in advanced placement English classes using Kelly's theory of constructs. Ph.D. dissertation, Rutgers University, New Brunswick, NJ.

Kuhlthau, C. C. (1989). The information search process of high-, middle-, and low-achieving high school seniors. *School Library Media Quarterly* **17**, 224–226.

Kuhlthau, C. C., Belvin, R. J., and George, M. W. (1989). Flowcharting the information search process: A method for eliciting user's mental maps. Paper presented at the Proceedings of the American Society for Information Science 52nd Annual Meeting.

Kuhlthau, C., Turock, B. J., George, M. W., and Belvin, R. J. (1990). Validating a model of the search process: A comparison of academic, public and school library users. *Library and Information Science Research* **12**, 5–32.

Larsen, J. C. (1979). Information sources currently studied in general reference courses. *RQ* **18**, 341–348.

Los Angeles. Bureau of the Budget and Efficiency. (1949–1950). *Organization, Administration and Management of the Los Angeles Public Library*. The Bureau, Los Angeles.

Lubans, J. Jr. (1971). Nonuse of the academic library. *College and Research Libraries* **32**, 362–367.

Lynch, M. J. (1977). Reference interviews in public libraries. Ph.D. dissertation, Rutgers University, New Brunswick, NJ.

Lynch, M. J. (1978). Reference interviews in public libraries. *Library Quarterly* **48**, 119–142.

Markham, M. J., Stirling, K. H., and Smith, N. M. (1983). Librarian self-disclosure and patron satisfaction in the reference interview. *RQ* **22**, 369–374.

Maurice Tauber, *et al.* (1958). *The Columbia University Libraries: A Report on Present and Future Needs*. Columbia University Press, New York.

Maxfield, D. K. (1954). Counselor–librarianship: A new departure. *Occasional Papers, No. 38* entire issue.

McClure, C. R., and Hernon, P. (1983). *Improving the Quality of Reference Service of Government Publications*. American Library Association, Chicago, IL.

McFayden, D. (1975). The psychology of inquiry: Reference service and the concept of information/experience. *Journal of Librarianship* **7**, 2–11.

Morgan, L. (1980). Patron preference in reference service points. *RQ* **19**, 373–375.

Myers, M. J. (1979). The effectiveness of telephone reference/information services in academic libraries in the Southeast. Ph.D. dissertation, Florida State University, Tallahassee.

Myers, M. J. (1980). The accuracy of telephone reference services in the Southeast: A case for quantitative standards. In *Library Effectiveness: A State of the Art*. American Library Association, Chicago, IL.

Myers, M. J. (1983). Telephone reference/information services in academic libraries in the Southeast. In: *The Accuracy of Telephone Reference/Information Services in Academic Libraries* (M. J. Myers and J. M. Jirjees, eds.). Scarecrow Press, Metuchen, NJ.

Myers, M. J. (1985). Check your catalog image. *Reference Librarian* **12**, 39–47.

Neill, S. D. (1984). The reference process and certain types of memory: semantic, episodic, and schematic. *RQ* **23**, 417–423.

New York State Department of Education. (1967). *Emerging Library Systems: The 1963–66 Evaluation of the New York State Public Library Systems*. University of the State of New York, Albany.

Paisley, W. J. (1968). Information needs and uses. In *Annual Review of Information Science and Technology*, pp. 1–30. Encyclopedia Britannica, Chicago, IL.

Palmquist, R. A., and Kim, K.-S. (1998). Modeling the users of information systems: Some theories and methods. *The Reference Librarian* **60**, 3–25.

Patterson, C. D. (1983). Personality, knowledge and the reference librarian. *Reference Librarian* **9**, 167–172.

Peck, T. P. (1975). Counseling skills applied to reference services. *RQ* **14**, 233–235.

Penland, P. (1970). *Interviewing for Counselor and Reference Librarians* (preliminary ed.). University of Pittsburgh, Pittsburgh, PA.

Perry, J. W. (1961). *Defining the Query Spectrum—The Basis for Designing and Evaluating Retrieval Methods*.

Perry, J. W. (1963). Defining the query spectrum: The basis for developing and evaluating information-retrieval methods. *IEEE Transactions on Engineering Writing and Speech* **6**, 20–27.

Powell, R. R. (1976). An investigation of the relationship between reference collection size and other reference service factors and success in answering reference questions. Ph.D. dissertation, University of Illinois, Urbana.

Powell, R. R. (1978). An investigation of the relationships between quantifiable reference service variables and reference performance in public libraries. *Library Quarterly* **48**, 1–19.

Rees, A. M., and Saracevic, T. (1963). Conceptual analysis of questions in information retrieval systems. Paper presented at the Automation and Scientific Communication, Topic 8: Information Storage and Retrieval, Annual Meeting of the American Documentation Institute, Part II.

Rettig, J. (1978). A theoretical model and definition of the reference process. *RQ* **18**, 19–29.

Rich, E. A. (1979). Building and exploiting user models. Ph.D. dissertation, Computer Science, Carnegie Mellon University, Pittsburgh, PA.

Richardson, J. V. (1992). Teaching general reference work: The complete paradigm. *Library Quarterly* **62**, 55–89.

Richardson, J. V. (1998). Question naster: An evaluation of a Web-based decision-support system for use in reference environments. *College and Research Libraries* **59**, 29–37.

Richardson, J. V. (1999). Margaret Hutchins (1884–1961). *American National Biography* **11**, 589–590.

Richardson, J. V. (2002). Half right reference is wrong. *Library Journal* **105** (15 April 2002), 41–42.

Richardson, J. V., and Reyes, R. (1995). Expert systems for government information: A quantitative evaluation. *College and Research Libraries* **56**, 235–247.

Robertson, W. D. (1980). A user-oriented approach to setting priorities for library services. *Special Libraries* **71**, 345–353.

Salton, G. (1968). Automatic question answering systems. In: *Automatic Information Organization and Retrieval* (G. Salton, ed.) pp. 392–413. McGraw-Hill Book Company, New York.

Sandock, M. (1977). A study of university students' awareness of reference services. *RQ* **16**, 284–296.

Saxton, M. L. (1997). Reference service evaluation and meta-analysis: Findings and methodological issues. *Library Quarterly* **67**, 267–289.

Saxton, M. L. (2000). Evaluation of reference service in public libraries using a hierarchical linear model: Applying multiple regression analysis to a multi-level research design. Ph.D. dissertation, UCLA.

Saxton, M. L., and Richardson, J. V. (2002). *Understanding Reference Transactions: Turning an Art into Science.* Academic Press, New York.

Scherdin, M. J. (1994). *Discovering Librarians: Profiles of a Profession.* American Library Association, Chicago, IL.

Shera, J. (1964). Automation and the reference librarian. *RQ* **3**, 3–7.

St. Clair, J. W., and Aluri, R. (1977). Staffing the reference desk: Professionals or nonprofessionals. *Journal of Academic Librarianship* **3**, 149–153.

Stalker, J. C., and Murfin, M. E. (1996). Why reference librarians won't disappear: A study of success in identifying answering sources for reference questions. *RQ* **35**, 489–503.

Stone, E. O. (1942). Methods of evaluating reference service. *Library Journal* **67**, 296–298.

Stych, F. S. (1972). Decision factors in search strategy: Teaching reference work. *RQ* **12**, 143–147.

Swope, M. J., and Katzer, J. (1972). {Silent Majority:} Why don't they ask questions? *RQ* **12**, 161–166.

Tannen, D. (1990). *You Just Don't Understand: Women and Men in Conversation.* William E. Morrow and Company, New York.

Taylor, R. (1968). Question–negotiation and information seeking in libraries. *College and Research Libraries* **29**, 178–194.

Taylor, R. S. (1962). The process of asking questions. *American Documentation* **13**, 391–396.

Taylor, R. S. (1967). *Question–negotiation and Information-seeking in Libraries*. Center for the Information Sciences, Lehigh University, Bethlehem, PA.

University of Michigan. Social Research Center (1961). *Faculty Appraisal of a University Library*. University of Michigan Library, Ann Arbor.

Van House, N. A., and Childers, T. (1984). Unobtrusive evaluation of a reference referral network: The California experience. *Library and Information Science Research* **6**, 305–319.

Vavrek, B. (1971). *Communications and the Reference Interface*. University of Pittsburgh, Pittsburgh.

Wang, P. (1999). Methodologies and methods for user behavioral research. *Annual Review of Information Science and Technology* **34**, 53–99.

Way, K. A. (1984). Measurement and evaluation of telephone reference/information service in law school depository libraries in the greater Los Angeles, California area: A quantitative study. Masters thesis, UCLA.

Way, K. A. (1987). Quality reference service in law school depository libraries: A cause for action. *Government Publications Review* **14**, 207–219.

White, M. D. (1981). The dimensions of the reference interview. *RQ* **20**, 373–381.

White, M. D. (1983). The reference encounter model. *Drexel Library Quarterly* **19**, 38–55.

White, M. D. (1985). Evaluation of the reference interview. *RQ* **24**, 76–84.

Whitlatch, J. B. (1987). Client/service provider perceptions of reference service outcomes in academic libraries: Effects of feedback and uncertainty. Ph.D. dissertation, University of California, Berkeley.

Whitlatch, J. B. (1990). Reference service effectiveness. *RQ* **30**, 205–220.

Wood, R. F. (1952). What exactly do you wish to know? *California Librarian* **13**, 213, 245.

Wyer, J. I. (1930). *Reference Work: A Textbook for Students of Library Work and Librarians*. American Library Association, Chicago, IL.

Yoon, K., and Nilan, M. S. (1999). Toward a reconceptualization of information seeking research: Focus on the exchange of meaning. *Information Processing and Management* **35**, 871–890.

Discourse Fashions in Library Administration and Information Management: A Critical History and Bibliometric Analysis

Mark T. Day
Indiana University Libraries
Bloomington, Indiana 47405

I. Introduction

The contentious, fragmented nature of contemporary managerial knowledge presents serious difficulties for anyone who wants to evaluate organization and management theories and use them to improve the practice of library administration (Burrell, 1996; Clegg and Palmer, 1996; Koontz, 1961, 1980; March, 1965; Reed, 1996). Over the past several decades, a multitude of conflicting research paradigms for the study of organizations and management have been produced by the academic community (Burrell and Morgan, 1979; Clegg *et al.*, 1996b; Collins, 1994; Frost *et al.*, 2000; Perrow, 1985, 1986; Pugh and Hickson, 1996; W. R. Scott, 1992; Reed, 1992). This phenomenon has been paralleled in the management practitioner community by an even greater proliferation of popular management fads and fashions (Carson *et al.*, 2000; Eccles *et al.*, 1992; Frank, 2000; Hilmer and Donaldson, 1996; Micklethwait and Wooldridge, 1996; O'Shea and Madigan, 1997; Ramsey, 1996; Shapiro, 1996).

Exacerbating both of these trends has been the continued existence of "a considerable gap between organizational research findings and management practices" (Rynes *et al.*, 2001, p. 340). Although the causes and consequences of this gap have not received a great deal of empirical study, a growing body of evidence suggests that managers do not consult academics or rely on academic research to inform their decision making (Abrahamson, 1996; Mowday, 1997; L. W. Porter and McKibbon, 1988). Nor do researchers consult practitioners in designing and interpreting their research (Rynes *et al.*, 1999; Sackett and Larson, 1990). Indeed, some studies indicate that,

ADVANCES IN LIBRARIANSHIP, VOL. 26

unlike the idealized model of scholarly communication in which organizational researchers develop scientific theories, which are then communicated to managers who apply them to local conditions, the flow of influence tends to be in the opposite direction with the business community setting the agenda for the research community (Abrahamson and Fairchild, 1999; Argyris, 1996; Barley et al., 1988; Galbraith, 1980; Rynes et al., 2001).

The research reported on in this article represents one approach to exploring this management knowledge wilderness in a way that may provide guidance for those who have to travel through it. The specific methods used arose from a convergence of two needs. On the one hand, the Comparative Library Organization Committee (CLOC), of which the author is a member, needed a way to select important texts for a bibliography of influential works aimed at improving professional communication and managerial practice. On the other hand, the author needed a methodology for selecting influential texts that represented the full range of managerial and organizational topics dealt with in the library and information science literature. Data about these texts would be used to further test his hypotheses about the rise to prominence of "transformational discourse" as a dominant managerial ideology (Day, 1998). That research had been based on a qualitative rhetorical analysis of all texts found in the academic library and information science literature that dealt with the topic of organizational change.

A suggestion by a member of CLOC that it publish a list of top 20 works relevant to library organization eventually provided the stimulus for the comparative, bibliometric approach outlined in this paper. Initially, however, the suggestion simply stimulated a great deal of discussion about how to define and select such a set of "top" works. Did we want to emphasize current "hot" topics and produce yet another ephemeral publication that further contributed to the already faddish nature of management knowledge? Did we want to emphasize management "classics" and reproduce the work of existing textbooks and anthologies? Did we want to emphasize "critical" works that placed the existing conflicted nature of management knowledge in perspective? Alternatively, did we simply want to emphasize the most "influential" works? How would we identify what was hot, classical, critical, or influential? Should we use our collective, professional, but subjective judgment to select titles as exemplified by the controversial *Required Reading: Sociology's Most Influential Books* (Clawson, 1998)? Could we use some more objective, empirical means to identify best sellers or highly cited materials?

Ultimately, it was decided that citation counts from *Social Science Citation Index* would be used to generate two lists of influential works. The first list would contain the top 20, most highly cited works published outside of the professional library literature, and the second list would contain the top 20 works published within that literature. A comparison of the resulting lists provides one way to gauge the extent of the gap between organizational theory and management practice. The resulting lists also exhibit several important limitations. First, although the procedure of counting citations from *SSCI* is "almost certainly the most common form of efforts to quantify influence, [it] is far more appropriate as a measure of article than of book influence" (Clawson and Zussman, 1998, p. 8). Because librarianship, like sociology, is distinguished by the existence of a book and an article culture, lists of books and articles produced from counts using the *SSCI* can reliably indicate influence only in the article culture, not the book culture. Second, because librarianship is further distinguished, like management, by the existence of a scholarly, research and a popular, practitioner culture, the focus of the *Social Science Citation Index* on the scholarly, research literature prevents its being used to reliably indicate influence in the practitioner culture. In addition, although citation analysis of *SSCI* data is a quantitative, empirical method, the various imperfections and inconsistencies in the data often make the process "subjective and inhospitable to standardization" (Cronin, 1981, p. 17). Finally, bibliometric analysis tends to ignore the communicative context within which a work has been cited so that without examining the actual content of the citing source, the interpretation of citation patterns remains rather abstract and arbitrary.

The close rhetorical analysis of the discourse fashions which have been identified in this study will be the subject of the next stage of the author's research. The current study primarily aims to provide a reasonably comprehensive and comprehensible description of the contested management knowledge terrain from a critical historical and a bibliometric perspective. In addition, CLOC members are annotating the titles in each list from the perspective of professional practice. The resulting annotated bibliography is being published in two parts in *Library Administration & Management* as "Required reading for library administrators: An annotated bibliography of influential authors and their works." The first part will appear in the Summer 2002 issue of Volume 16.

II. A Brief History of Modern Management Discourse

A. The Social Construction of Management in the United States

Social scientists define modern formal organizations, exemplified by government bureaucracies and business corporations, as "social entities that are goal-directed, deliberately structured activity systems with an identifiable boundary" (Daft, 1986). Such organizations gradually developed as part of the overall modernization and rationalization project of Western civilization that began during the Late Middle Ages with the creation of the juristic "corporate person" as a bourgeois counterweight to the authority of the Church and the State (Cheney and McMillan, 1990, p. 96). However, their current dominance as a primary means for the social control of economic and political activity can be traced to the 19th century and the crucial role that formal organizational procedures took in solving the "control crises" created by the industrial revolution (Beniger, 1986).

The resulting expansion of large-scale industrial production in the last two decades of the 19th century supported by the growth of highly routinized organizations radically changed the basis for the social organization of work in the United States. "As the twentieth century began, . . . a society structured by the frontier, personal community relationships and local institutions was being replaced by one structured by big business, big government, big labor, a 'culture of professionalism' and science" (Jacques, 1996, p. 96). "In the emerging order, a discourse of objectivity, pronounced by university-certified 'experts' and grounded in ideally value-free science, would provide a new basis for order . . . one requiring a new 'common sense,' and new subjects: the *manager*, the *employee*, the *professional*, and the *consumer*" (Jacques, 1996, p. 61).

This new discourse and its new subjects became established during the 1920s, which saw the growth of the "Management Movement" (Jacques, 1996, pp. 136–145) and ushered in the "Managerial Age" (W. G. Scott, 1992, pp. 9–24) celebrated by management scholars such as Alfred Chandler (1977), Peter Drucker (1950, 1954), Herbert Simon (1947), and Dwight Waldo (1948). The terms of this discourse have formed the foundation for management knowledge and practice ever since. Within this discourse the manager became "a special form of *l'employé*, one charged with representing the interests of ownership to other employés [*sic*]" (Jacques, 1996, p. 87). In this sense, the term manager may be treated as synonymous with the term administrator, whose pedigree according to the *Oxford English Dictionary* goes back to the medieval stewards employed "to minister" (ad+minister), i.e., to act as a minister or servant for others. Both terms include the sense of carrying out duties and directing affairs, but the term manager became the dominant term for the practice of running modern organizations in which the problem of breaking in, handling, and training employees becomes a central concern (Hood and Jackson, 1991; Jacques, 1996; Scarbrough and Burrell, 1996). The term derives from the Italian term *il maneggio*, which means someone who is a skillful handler or trainer of horses (Hood and Jackson, 1991, p. 160; Jacques, 1996, pp. 86–88; Scarbrough and Burrell, 1996, p. 174).

Several important features of horse handling made it an ideal vehicle for describing the new position of "manager." Scarbrough and Burrell (1996) point out the initial low status of managers. They note that *maneggiare*, meaning "management" in Italian, refers primarily "to the role of the ostler and not the horseman," and that the equivalent French word, *ménager*, "denotes the direction and control of domestic services" (1996, p. 174). In addition, associating managers with horse handlers implies that workers resemble wild horses who need to be broken in and domesticated to their new role as employees. This reflects the early development of management within the context of direct shop floor supervision and the need to turn a mass of previously independent workers into disciplined company employees.

This metaphorical transfer of the duties and status associated with horse handling to those associated with bureaucratic, corporate authority thus was part of the historical process by which the new social roles of employee, manager, and consumer were socially constructed. By the beginning of World War II, the meanings and behaviors assigned to these roles had become deeply imbedded in American culture, social institutions, legal systems, and public discourse categories. They continue today to constitute the largely unquestioned categories used in management discourse to describe what the organizational world is like. They form the core "grammar of motives" (K. Burke, 1969a) for the more specific "rhetoric of motives" (K. Burke, 1969b) that we find in contemporary discourses about organizations and their management.

Management fashions, which the current study investigates, can thus be said to represent the topics of these discourses. Although these topics, as we shall see, focus on turbulent environments, radical change, and technological innovation, the underlying institutional structures and action motives of corporate capitalism remain remarkably constant (Abrahamson, 1997; Barley and Kunda, 1992; Eccles *et al.*, 1992; Guillén, 1994; W. G. Scott and Hart, 1989). Thus, we may ask along with Jacques—with all our talk about the new postcapitalist, postindustrial, information age and the new postbureaucratic, postmodern organization—are we really "managing for the next century—or the last" (Jacques, 1996, pp. 1–9)? We may also legitimately study management rhetoric to investigate why it continually recycles old concepts and to what extent it ever introduces truly new concepts (Eccles *et al.*, 1992, pp. 17–37).

Management discourse, in addition to defining the nature of its core concepts such as the consumer, employee, manager, and professional, also defines the basic nature of the corporate capitalist environment within which these social roles are enacted. That environment is characterized by what Schumpeter called "creative destruction," in which heroic capitalistic entrepreneurs apply innovative technology to continuously reengineer production and create new consumer markets, thereby increasing wealth and promoting progress (Simonetti, 1996; Schumpeter, 1991). That nearly all popular management theorists subscribe to this view not only is evident from the nature of their arguments, but is often explicitly stated, as in Peter Drucker's acknowledgement in the preface to his early best seller on *The Practice of Management* (1954, p. viii) of the debt that he owed to Schumpeter. Drucker begins this book with the claim that the "manager is the dynamic, life-giving element in every business" (1954, p. 3). Managers who avidly consume the works of theorists such as Drucker not surprisingly find this to be an appealing self-image and tend to see themselves in the role of a decisive, heroic leader even when their actual room for action remains highly constricted (Hansen, 1996; W. G. Scott, 1992). Carson *et al.* (2000) review fashion discourse studies and offer their own comprehensive study of management fashion cycles over the past 30 years. The results of their study support the hypothesis that these structural and rhetorical patterns lead managers to seek rational and progressive fashions (Abrahamson, 1996), which are used in a capitalist economy to enable organizations to "outcompete" each other (Kieser, 1997).

Because we live in an imperfect world, all social inventions exhibit fundamental internal contradictions that give rise to a variety of unanticipated consequences. Thus, while resolving some of the major problems created by the transition to a highly industrialized society, the construction of the modern formal organization created new problems. Foremost among the fundamental contradictions built into such organizations is their need to create unity out of diversity. A primary dilemma thus becomes how to motivate each employee to identify with the organization as a whole and to work hard to improve organizational performance, while at the same time respecting the individuality of each employee as a skilled, autonomous agent. This requires managers to treat each employee as a "human resource," i.e., to simultaneously treat him or her as an individual person and as an economic factor of production.

This dilemma is exacerbated by the sophisticated division of expert labor which complex organizations require but which creates a diverse social structure of multiple interests and differential power that conflicts with the managerial need to coordinate and control this social structure in the interest of common goals. In addition, the destructive creativity of modern, global capitalism creates a constantly changing environment that puts pressure on organizations to continuously modify their institutionalized structure of authority—often in radical ways such as reengineering or downsizing. Such modifications tend to destroy the very stability and trust that organizations need if they are to function in the predictable manner demanded of a rational social instrument. This paradoxical negative effect of management rhetoric intended to improve organizational life has been noted in many studies on the implementation of management fashions (du Guy, 1996; Easton and

Jarrell, 2000b; Eccles *et al.*, 1992; Kaboolian, 2000; Kochan and Rubinstein, 2000; Micklethwait and Wooldridge, 1996; O'Shea and Madigan, 1997; Ramsey, 1996; Staw and Epstein, 2000; Tuckman, 1994; Sandkull, 1996).

B. Organizational Paradigms and Management Rhetoric

Given the nature of modern formal organizations and the accompanying logic of modern management discourse, it is not surprising to find that American administrative theories have cycled between rational, scientistic and norma- tive, humanistic rhetorics of control—between "structural, contingent" and "human relations, organizational culture" approaches (Abrahamson, 1997; Guillén, 1994; Barley and Kunda, 1992; Eccles *et al.*, 1992; Lynch, 1985). The rationalistic tradition may be traced from the theory of "scientific man- agement" initiated by Frederick Taylor (1911), through the so-called classi- cal theory of "administrative principles," exemplified by the work of Henri Fayol (1916, 1949), to the wide variety of contemporary structural "contin- gency theories" derived from work done in the 1960s by researchers such as Tom Burns and G. M. Stalker (1961), Alfred Chandler (1962, 1977), and the Ashton Group under Derek Pugh (Pugh and Hickson, 1997, pp. 9–17). According to the advocates of contingency theory, earlier principles which prescribed the "one best way to structure an organization or manage it" needed to be "replaced by the systems theory principle . . . that more than one means of reaching a desired state exists" (Howard, 1984, p. 479). "Suc- cessful managers have to identify correctly the contingencies they are dealing with," such as environmental stability, organizational size, and appropriate technologies; "having done that they can adopt the organization design that best fits these contingencies, according to contingency theory research" (Clegg and Palmer, 1996, p. 13).

The normative tradition may be traced from the "industrial betterment" movement which flourished from 1870 to 1900 (Barley and Kunda, 1992, pp. 365–368), through the well-known "human relations" movement initiated by Elton Mayo and the Hawthorne plant studies (Mayo, 1933), to the wide variety of contemporary "organizational development and change" efforts derived from work begun in the late 1950s by organizational consultants such as Chris Argyris (1957), Richard Beckhard (1997), Warren Bennis (1969), Robert Blake and Jane Mouton (1964), Douglas McGregor (1960), and Herbert Shepard (1960). According to the advocates of organization devel- opment, improving organizational effectiveness requires "a planned process of change in an organization's culture through utilization of behavioral science technology and theory" (W. W. Burke, 1987, p. 53). Although "there is no single, all-encompassing theory of OD" (W. W. Burke, 1987, p. 53), the practice of organization development was founded on the belief that the "present need is for modes of organization which permit rapid adaptation to changing circumstances; the search is for ways in which people can organize for innovative, unprogrammable activities [which requires] a more humanistic organization theory [and] more humanistic means of dealing with members of organizations" (Shepard, 1965, pp. 1142–1143).

C. The Professionalization of Management Science and Library Administration

Both the rational and normative approaches to management have always relied heavily on scientific research to provide evidence in support of their various theories. In addition, both management and librarianship undertook what Macdonald calls "professionalization projects" (1995, pp. 8–14), which were part of the general "rise of the professions" accompanying the process of industrialization (Abbott, 1988; Larson, 1977; Winter, 1988). An important rhetorical objective of these projects was to demonstrate that the members of the professionalizing occupation possessed a body of what Murphy calls "formally rational, abstract utilitarian knowledge" (1988, p. 245). Such projects necessarily entailed heavy reliance on the new "discourse of objectivity, pronounced by university-certified 'experts' and grounded in ideally value-free science" (Jacques, 1996, p. 61). Thus, the founding issues of the *Harvard Business Review* (1922) and the *Library Quarterly* (1931) were both associated with prestigious university programs and advocated respectively the application of social scientific methods to the study of business management and library administration.

However, it was only in the 1950s that broadly based and well financed attempts were made to create academic disciplines focused on the systematic, social scientific study of formal organizations and their administration. These attempts were part of a "strongly positivistic, neo-Lockean intellectual trend" that dominated the period from 1945 to 1960 (Bender and Schorske, 1997, p. 8). This trend entailed "the establishment of the primacy of analytical method and a quest for epistemological certainty not only within each discipline but across the whole spectrum" (Bender and Schorske, p. 8) and resulted in a major transformation of American academic culture. Thus, the founders of "administrative science" assumed that there were indeed scientific laws of organizational behavior, which social scientists could discover and which managers could apply to improve organizational performance, although they recognized that "the building will not be easy" (Thompson, 1956, p. 103).

The basic idea was to develop a research-based, experimentally validated scientific theory of administration, whose propositions could be used to guide managerial decisions in place of what Herbert Simon initially called "The

Proverbs of Administration" (1946) and what Wallace B. Donham, Dean of Harvard's Graduate School of Business, had earlier referred to as "rules of thumb" (1922, p. 1). Simon used this phrase to refer to existing administrative principles, such as the need for unity of command, because he believed that such principles were merely rhetorical justifications and that "for almost every principle one can find an equally plausible and acceptable contradictory principle [and] there is nothing in the theory to indicate which is the proper one to apply" (Simon, 1946, p. 53; 1976, p. 20).

The fields of librarianship and documentation were transformed during this period into library and information science by these same academic trends, as were the subfields of library administration and information management. One result of this transformation was a renewed attempt to strengthen the claim that managers in general and library administrators in particular were true professionals who possessed expert, scientifically validated knowledge. Participating in this renewed professionalization project, the Library Administration and Management Association (LAMA) started life as the Library Administration Division (LAD) in 1956. This was the very same year in which the *Administrative Science Quarterly*, which has become the premier journal for the discipline of administrative science, was founded.

Although a variety of organizational forms have arisen throughout the development of modern society in response to the changing environment of industrial capitalism, the bureaucratic form remains basic. Along with free markets, in which expert knowledge has been embodied in commodities (technology), and occupations, in which expert knowledge has been embodied in professionals (persons), formal organizations (bureaucracies) represent the third of three major logical means by which modern society embodies expert knowledge to control collaborative human endeavors (Abbott, 1991; Beniger, 1990; Freidson, 2001; Scarbrough, 1996). Thus, to the extent that their claims of expertise are persuasive, both the management and the library professions can claim increased authority within their realm of expertise. It was based upon such claims that management achieved the status that Drucker attributed to it and that librarians were able to achieve higher status within the organizations in which they worked (Day, 1997). It should not surprise us, therefore, that the crises of authority and stability that both librarianship and management currently are undergoing have occurred within a social environment dominated by market ideologies and the introduction of powerful new information technologies. Nor, given the underlying assumptions about the entrepreneurial and progressive nature of American society, should it surprise us that most contemporary management discourse criticizes the competing bureaucratic and professional forms of control and recommends their radical restructuring in order to adapt to the environment demands of market forces and customer desires.

The task of encouraging the production, dissemination, and use of scientific knowledge relevant to professional practice was from the beginning a major function of LAMA and is incorporated into LAMA's overall mission statement and into the specific charges given LOAMS and CLOC (American Library Association, 1978, 1999a,b,c,d). However, it was not until the 1980s that this process was institutionalized with the creation of specialized professional journals such as *The Journal of Library Administration* in 1980, *Advances in Library Administration and Organization* in 1982, and LAMA's own *Library Administration and Management* in 1987. Since then, a sizable literature has grown up in which library administrators with formal training in organizational studies have applied the theories produced by administrative scientists to library practices, or more often have summarized those theories, recommended their application, and called for more research (Birdsall, 1995; Howard, 1984; Jones, 2000; Klingberg, 1990; Lynch, 1985, 1990; Lynch and Smith, 2001; Lynch and Verdin, 1983; Mittermeyer, 1990; Moran, 1980).

However, researchers interested in advancing administrative science and general organization theory have seldom found libraries interesting or profitable locales for testing their theories and almost no literature on library topics has been produced by social scientists (Day, 1969; Estabrook, 1984; Gatten, 1991; Reeves, 1980). In practice, the major influence of administrative theories on the practice of library management probably has occurred through the incorporation of organizational development techniques into projects officially sponsored by professional library organizations. A prime example of such influence can be seen in the work of the Association for Research Libraries. This includes its creation of the "Office of Management Studies (OMS)" in 1970, now called the "Office of Management Services." One of its first projects was to develop and promote the Management Review and Analysis Program (MRAP) (Johnson and Mann, 1980). Since then it has continued to disseminate information through its various *SPEC Kits* about popular management fashions such as quality improvement (Siggins and Sullivan, 1993), strategic planning (Clement, 1995), and library restructuring (Eustis and Kenney, 1996). More recently the ARL has developed and heavily promoted the "LibQUAL+" library service assessment tool (Association for Research Libraries, 2000).

D. The Rise of Information Science and Bibliometrics

Although statistical methods had been applied to the study of literature for over a century (Pritchard and Wittig, 1981), the modern field of "bibliometrics" arose in the 1960s as one of the many scientific disciplines, professional organizations, and information technologies invented to understand and control the post–World War II explosion of scientific research and technological innovation. The field shared the same positivistic and paradigmatic assumptions noted previously in regard to the founding of new academic disciplines in the post–World War II period. In attempting to create a disciplinary knowledge base, it drew on three specific developments.

In the first of these developments, empirical studies in bibliography, communication, linguistics, and literature led to the formulation of several statistical "laws" that exhibited impressive explanatory and predictive power. The classical works that helped define the field were those of Lotka (1926), Bradford (1934), and Zipf (1949), concerning, respectively, the high productivity of a relatively small cadre of scientific authors; the concentration of highly cited documents in a few core sources; and the uneven but relatively stable frequency distribution of letters and words in any set of texts. All of these statistical patterns reflect a general rule that the usage of elements in any set of literary data (from individual letters and words to individual authors and works) is uneven, with relatively few elements being frequently used and most elements being infrequently used. Most library administrators are probably more familiar with this statistical pattern in terms of Trueswell's (1969) 80/20 rule that "a small portion [20%] of a library's inventory satisfies most [80%] of the library's requests" (Diodato, 1994). An important corollary of the general rule states that the actual content of the various proportions depends upon the type, size, and time period of the population sampled. A well-known example within academic librarianship concerns the differential patterns of usage among the various disciplines. At one extreme the physical sciences tend to use current journal articles almost to the exclusion of monographs and older materials, while at the other extreme, the humanities utilize materials published over a much broader date range and use monographs more heavily than journal articles.

The application of these theories to help solve the practical problems of scholarly communication was motivated and made possible by the second and third developments. Motivation came from the rapid expansion of the scientific community, the proliferation of specialized disciplines within that community, and the concomitant explosion of scholarly publications. This well-known "information explosion" created a great demand for ways to manage this information. It also created extensive document sets that could be used for research into scholarly communication, but that remained cumbersome to manage and tedious to analyze in printed formats. The third development, advances in computer technology, finally made it possible to facilitate research by automating significant portions of the process by which the information was created, stored, processed, and accessed. The end result of these three developments was the provision of large, high-quality, publicly available bibliographic and full-text databases, including the citation databases produced by the Institute for Scientific Information (ISI) and begun by the company's founder, Eugene Garfield, in 1961 (Institute for Scientific Information, 2000a).

E. Management Knowledge and Fashions in an Age of Transformational Discourse

Despite all these attempts to enlighten managerial practice with administrative theory, the very possibility of treating the study of formal organizations as a science and their administration as a matter of rational design has become increasingly controversial. In fact, using the terminology made popular by Thomas Kuhn's *The Structure of Scientific Revolutions* (1970), most observers agree that the burgeoning disciplines of administrative and organization science still haven't developed into "normal sciences" whose work is disciplined by a dominant research "paradigm" (Burrell, 1996; Frost *et al.*, 2000; Hood and Jackson, 1991; Howard, 1984). Instead, a proliferation of competing viewpoints and methods has occurred. Many researchers and practitioners welcome this diversity and see a positive benefit in using multiple frameworks (Bolman and Deal, 1997; Burrell and Morgan, 1979; Clegg *et al.*, 1996a; Palmer and Dunford, 1996; Van Maanen, 2000; Weick, 1979, 1989, 2000). Others worry about paradigm proliferation and suggest that an official paradigm is needed in order to advance the accumulation of knowledge by organization science, to defend its disciplinary boundaries, and to secure its scientific status (Donaldson, 1985, 1996a,b, 1999; Pfeffer, 2000; Reed, 1990).

Similarly, the movement to professionalize organizational development still hasn't succeeded in establishing for itself the traditional defining features of a professional discipline: "1) A Common Body of Knowledge; 2) A graduate level of education; 3) Agreed upon conditions for entry into the field" (Varney *et al.*, 1999). Library administration appears to be in a similar situation. Mittermeyer and Houser, in their 1979 study of "The Knowledge Base for the Administration of Libraries," found that "theory-based research literature on the management and administration of libraries is minimal" (p. 255), and in 1990, Susan Klingberg still found "little evidence to suggest that library managers do make use of theory or research in seeking solutions" (p. 101). Numerous articles in the library literature continue to complain about the detrimental influence of management fads and fashions on library administrative practice (Fisher, 1996; Lubans, 2000). Overall, this fluid theoretical and professional environment appears every bit as turbulent and confusing as the economic, social, and technical environments which challenge our organizations, and which administrative theories and professional disciplines are supposed to help us understand and control.

Organizational theorists who have recorded what managers actually do note that the life of practicing managers is exceedingly fragmented, dominated by a heavy work load, and oriented to personal communication (Mintzberg, 1973, 1975). The result is that little time or energy remains to undertake research or to systematically review and apply sophisticated management science techniques and theories as reported in the academic literature (Offermann and Sprios, 2001; Terpstra and Rozell, 1997). Rather, with the rise of "market populism" (Frank, 2000), new management theories and techniques have become knowledge commodities—produced and marketed by a new class of "idea entrepreneurs" (Abrahamson and Fairchild, 2001) and communicated via consulting firms, the popular press, practitioner literature, and personal networks (Micklethwait and Wooldridge, 1996; O'Shea and Madigan, 1997; Ramsey, 1996; Vyborney, 1992). The development of these theories and techniques tends to be driven by practical needs and by action research designed to solve specific organizational problems (Barley *et al.*, 1988; Lynch, 1985, 1990; McClure, 1989, 1991; Stenson, 1987).

At the same time, "the nature of computer technology, the uses to which it has been put, and the effects of popularization have combined to give computers claim to special status as a 'transformative' or 'defining technology'" (Vyborney, 1992, pp. 19–20). Talk about the radical, transformational effects of information technology permeates public discourse. Contemporary discourse about management theories and techniques tends to focus on the emergence of a radically new "post-industrial, information society" (Castells, 1996; Duff, 2000; Harris *et al.*, 1998; Webster, 1995, 2000) and the need to adapt to this changed environment by creating radically new organizational forms (Barley, 1996; Heyderbrand, 1989; Hodson and Parker, 1988; Travica, 1998; Wallace, 1989).

It is often claimed that, within an expanding commercial sphere characterized by fierce global corporate competition, information has replaced physical labor and material capital as a primary source of value. Within such an environment, those organizations that will prevail in the new age will be "learning organizations," and those men and women who will prevail will belong to the rising new class of "information professionals," "knowledge workers," and "knowledge managers." Librarians and library administrators may or may not belong to this class (Abbott, 1988, 1998). Not surprisingly, over the past two decades, a profuse variety of management fads and fashions has evolved to meet the rising demand for administrative nostrums to handle the bewildering array of unanticipated organizational problems. In these circumstances, management knowledge has come to appear to be "less a science and more like cookbook knowledge: it is knowledge of recipes and their applications" (Clegg and Palmer, 1996, p. 4). Cookbooks, of course, just like popular management books, represent a ubiquitous and potentially profitable information commodity. Both are subject to similar types of market forces and fashion cycles. Thus, rather than contributing yet another cookbook of management recipes for the harried organizational chef, this article provides a comparative bibliometric review of trends in management cuisine in order to help potential management consumers make more knowledgeable judgments about the ease of preparation and the nutritional value of various recipes.

III. Using Citation Analysis to Select Influential Authors and Their Works

A. Extracting Bibliometric Data from *Social Science Citation Index*

The ISI *Social Science Citation Index* (*SSCI*) database, in the online *Web of Science* version beginning with 1987, was used to generate the list of articles and citations from which lists of highly cited authors and their works were constructed. At the time the records were extracted, only those records published between January 1987 and March 2000 were available online to the author. Nevertheless, for the purposes of this project, the data collected were more than adequate. The primary purpose was to provide a solid empirical foundation for reviewing the state of library administrative knowledge and to focus that review on enduring issues, core works, and basic principles. Using the *Social Science Citation Index* database made it possible to undertake such a project, although the nature of ISI citation databases also placed important limitations on the nature of the results achieved.

ISI citation databases are designed primarily to improve scholarly communication among scientific disciplines and are constructed to represent the core journal literature for those disciplines as defined by Bradford's Law (Institute for Scientific Information, 1998). This approach allows ISI to select, from the large number of journals published each year, a relatively small sample of prestigious and productive sources in which the bulk of important articles and citations appear. However, this approach treats every area of study and practice as if it were a formal, scientific discipline in which all important communication is documented in a core set of current, scholarly journal articles. In addition, ISI citation indexes are designed to provide comprehensive, multidisciplinary, up-to-date coverage and therefore rely heavily on automated scanning and indexing routines, which normalize citations through a process of abbreviation and truncation, while at the same time preserving bibliographic and typographical errors contained in the original. Overall, this approach allows ISI to provide, in a very timely manner, a database that indexes all articles and all citations included in the selected source journals. Unfortunately, the lack of controlled subject terms makes it difficult to reliably search for specific topics. Likewise, given the abbreviated and inconsistent format of many citations, this approach makes it difficult to reliably retrieve all references to a particular cited author or work without a great deal of manual review.

These characteristics of the data in *SSCI* constrained the current study in several ways. As suggested in Section II, the profession of library administration and management has not developed into a scholarly discipline with a core literature that obeys Bradford's Law. As an applied social science with strong humanistic and pragmatic components, a significant proportion of its literature appears in book rather than periodical formats, and so is not included in the ISI citation databases. In addition, none of the journals specifically focused on the field of library administration and management have been indexed by ISI—presumably because they do not fit the rigorous criteria for inclusion (Institute for Scientific Information, 1998). Nevertheless, ISI does fully index all the major "Information Science & Library Science" journals—although the specific list of journal titles included changes from year to year depending upon a continuing evaluation of each journal's importance (Institute for Scientific Information, 1998). Although ISI groups both information science and library science journals under a single category heading, it recognizes that this category "covers journals on a wide variety of topics" (Institute for Scientific Information, 2000b). In fact, studies of journal cocitation practices point to the existence of

> three largely autonomous subdisciplines. *C&RL* is the leader of library science, which focuses on research-oriented studies of practice and policy and applications of new information technologies. . . . The *Journal of the American Society for Information Science (JASIS)* is the leader of the second subdiscipline, information science, which focuses on information retrieval, theoretical aspects of information technologies, and bibliometrics. . . . *Library Journal* is the leader of the third subscipline, librarianship, which focuses on nonacademic libraries, practitioner reports, and professional news (Schwartz, 1997, pp. 25–26).

Given the strengths and weaknesses of the *SSCI* data, the following procedures were used to produce the most comprehensive and representative results possible. First, a list was made of all 78 *SSCI* source journals categorized as "Information Science & Library Science" (which will be abbreviated as "LIS" for the remainder of this article) anytime during the period 1979–1999. Based upon the cocitation studies of Rice (1990) and Schwartz (1997), these 78 titles were divided into three groups of 17 core information science journals, 32 core combined library science and librarianship journals, and 29 noncore LIS journals. Next, 11 additional journals dealing with library and information related topics were identified. Altogether 89 library and information science source journals were selected. An extended online search was then undertaken which identified and downloaded all records from LIS journals on administrative topics. The process had to be done in stages. At each stage, small sets of related titles from the list of 89 source journals were

Table I
SSCI Sets Used to Construct Database of Articles on Library Administration and Information Management

SSCI journals searched: Total Database of Mutually Exclusive Sets	No. of journals	No. of authors of articles	No. of articles	Estimated no. of citations	No. of citations/ articles
Core Information Science	17	1,624	1,451	25,182	17.35
Core Library Science & Librarianship	32	2,945	3,352	35,421	10.57
Other titles classed as LIS by *SSCI* 1977–1998	29	2,904	2,140	54,668	25.55
Other titles about information, libraries, and knowledge	11	187	101	3,220	31.88
Titles with articles citing 1 or more of 5 library admin. and mgt. serials	18	31	22	1,189	54.05
Subtotals (including duplicate authors and citations)	107	7,691	7,066	119,680	16.94
Totals (unique authors and citations)	107	7,279	7,066	111,307	15.75

combined first with one and then with a second set of topic terms. These topic terms come from source article titles and abstracts plus the few key words sometimes assigned. The first group of terms (usually truncated to the most meaningful stem) dealt with administration, corporations, management and organizations. The second group dealt with more specific contemporary management topics such as leadership, reengineering, and TQM. Finally, a search was made for all articles in any *SSCI* source that included citations to any of the five major library administration and management journals not indexed by *SSCI*. This was done on the assumption that any source article citing these journals had some connection to library administration as a topic. Combining all of these sets resulted in a final database of 7066 unique records from 107 different journals (Table I).

B. Identifying Highly Cited Authors and Their Works

These records contained an estimated 111,307 citations (an automatically generated precise count is not possible given the current format of the *SSCI* data). At this point, a decision had to be made about how to rank these citations in order to obtain lists of the most influential works on library administration and management. The data had been downloaded using the ProCite bibliography management program and this allowed experimental manipulation of the data to be undertaken on a personal computer. However, the format of the citations does not allow easy identification of individual works or automatic ranking of them. Hand counting of the citations from a print-out was required. This would have been an impossible task to undertake for the entire 111,307 citations. Sample counts indicated, moreover, that quite different rankings resulted—as would be expected—when different subdiscipline populations were used. In addition, the data clearly indicated that the information science and technology literature over the period from 1987 to 2000 had come to dominate the library science and librarianship literature, so that any composite LIS ranking would be heavily biased toward information science concerns.

Because the initial focus of this project was on the *library* as a formal organization and on *library* administration as a professional practice, rather than on information science and library science as academic disciplines, an *ad hoc* grouping of source journals was created which consisted simply of all those journals with the word "library" in some form in their titles. Journals retaining the "L" word in their titles were presumed to be concerned with the library as a valued institution and with library management as a valued professional practice. This created a group of 35 journals to which was added the journal *Libri*. All of the citations from the 3152 articles about library administration topics in these 36 journals were then printed out and the total number of citations per cited author was counted. Those authors who had been cited 10 or more times were then identified. This produced a list of 332 authors, of which 42 were found to have published primarily outside the professional LIS literature and 290 within that literature (Table II). To the extent that bibliographic citations represent actual influence on the citing authors, these 332 highly cited authors clearly form a core group of authors who have had a major impact on professional LIS discourse about library administration and information management.

Since the original purpose of this bibliography was to provide ready access to a core set of significant works, not just to identify the most influential authors, the next problem was to identify the most highly cited titles by these authors. To accomplish that, it was decided to return to the entire database in order to extract all the articles that included one or more citations to any of these influential authors. The resulting ranking of works includes sources from the entire information science and technology literature indexed in the *SSCI*. Including citations from all sources should help to provide a better indicator of the overall impact each work has had on the entire LIS literature. However, given the tedious manual editing and review needed to verifiably identify specific titles in the online *SSCI*, the potential number of articles citing the 290 LIS authors cited 10 or more times would have been excessive. Therefore, that number was reduced to 83 by selecting

Table II

Distribution of Highly Cited LIS and Non-LIS Authors

Source data: Databases extracted from main database to identify highly cited authors and works	No. of journals	No. of authors of articles	No. of articles	Estimated no. of citations	No. of citations/ articles
Subset of all journals with the stem "Librar" in their titles	36	2,871	3,152	34,774	11.03
Percent of total database	37%	39%	45%	31%	—
List of 332 authors who were cited 10 or more times in "librar*" subset (manually selected)	N/A	N/A	N/A	N/A	N/A
Set of all articles in the full database of 7066 records that cited the 42 non-LIS authors who appeared in the "librar*" list of 332 authors					
Core Information Science	15	304	221	9,402	42.54
Core Library Science & Librarianship	21	372	328	9,606	29.29
Other titles classed as LIS by *SSCI* 1977–1998	22	934	617	27,361	44.35
Other titles about information, libraries, and knowledge	7	67	35	1,432	40.91
Titles with articles citing 1 or more of 5 library admin. and mgt. serials	5	6	5	534	117.4
Subtotals (including duplicate authors and citations)	70	1,683	1,206	48,335	40.12
Totals (unique authors and citations)	70	1,613	1,206	45,181	37.46
Percent of total database	65%	22%	17%	41%	—
Set of all articles in the full database of 7066 records that cited the 83 LIS authors who were cited 20 or more times in the list of 332 authors					
Core Information Science	17	417	332	13,126	39.54
Core Library Science & Librarianship	31	1,044	933	22,880	24.52
Other titles classed as LIS by *SSCI* 1977–1998	22	250	148	5,569	37.63
Other titles about information, libraries, and knowledge	2	4	2	42	21
Titles with articles citing 1 or more of 5 library admin. and mgt. serials	9	15	12	728	60.67
Subtotals (including duplicate authors and citations)	81	1,730	1,206	42,345	29.67
Totals (unique authors and citations)	81	1,634	1,427	39,582	27.74
Percent of total database	76%	22%	20%	36%	—

only those LIS authors from the subset of 36 "librar" journals who were cited 20 or more times.

C. Identifying Works by Library and Information Science (LIS) and Non-LIS Authors

The procedures just described provided a large number of citations to each author from which it was possible to identify more clearly the various works cited. Specifically, 1206 articles were extracted that cited any of the top 42 non-LIS authors and 1427 articles were extracted that cited any of the top 83 LIS authors (Table II). The downloaded *SSCI* records for each of these articles were then copied from the master ProCite database of 7066 article records into 125 individual databases—one for each of the highly cited authors—and two larger databases of all 42 non-LIS authors and 83 LIS authors. The databases were then analyzed using ProCite's grouping, subject bibliography, indexing, and counting capabilities, with each SSCI citation being treated as an indexed subject heading. This analysis helped to generate the detailed data in Table II. In addition, the database of non-LIS authors was used to rank its 42 authors by total number of citing sources and the database of LIS authors to rank its 83 authors. Table III lists all 42 non-LIS authors in alphabetical order, with each author's ranking given before the entry for that author. Similarly, Table IV lists all 83 LIS authors. Finally, individual HTML formatted lists of all citations to each author were output using ProCite's subject bibliography output function. These files are available to interested readers by contacting the author.

Before ranked lists of highly cited works could be generated, additional manual editing was required. Typographic and bibliographic errors found in the *SSCI* data were corrected, citations to different editions of the same title were treated as citations to the same work, and citations to different pages of the same title were identified. A separate ProCite record was then created for each author's most highly cited work and the number of times it had been cited was recorded. These records were then copied and consolidated into two additional databases of highly cited works by non-LIS authors and those by LIS authors. The titles in each database were separately ranked and lists generated for the top 20 most highly cited titles in each category (Tables V and VI). Full bibliographic information about these 40 titles is contained in the references for this article.

D. Some Prominent Bibliometric Features of the Highly Cited Authors and Their Works

Certain prominent features and trends in the LIS literature on library administration appear when we review the entire list of authors and works. Within

Table III

Non-LIS Primary Authors Cited 10 or More Times with Ranking by Author Citation Count

# 34. Abbott, Andrew	# 29. Naisbitt, John
# 17. Allen, Thomas J.	# 40. Nelson, Theodor H.
# 11. Argyris, Chris	# 28. Ouchi, William G.
# 33. Bennis, Warren G.	# 8. Peters, Thomas J.
# 41. Berry, Leonard L.	# 10. Pfeffer, Jeffrey
# 42. Blake, Robert R.	# 1. Porter, Michael E.
# 27. Bush, Vannevar	# 23. Price, Derek J. de Solla
# 22. Cameron, Kim S.	# 6. Rogers, Everett M.
# 37. Crane, Diana	# 16. Schein, Edgar H.
# 3. Daft, Richard L.	# 25. Schön, Donald A.
# 36. Damanpour, Fariborz	# 39. Schrage, Michael
# 30. Deming, W. Edwards	# 19. Senge, Peter M.
# 4. Drucker, Peter F.	# 7. Simon, Herbert A.
# 32. Hage, Jerald	# 24. Strauss, Anselm L.
# 35. Hall, Richard H.	# 26. Toffler, Alvin
# 5. Hammer, Michael	# 14. Tushman, Michael L.
# 18. Handy, Charles	# 38. Walton, Mary
# 13. Kanter, Rosabeth M.	# 9. Weick, Karl E.
# 20. Kotler, Philip	# 31. Zeithaml, Valarie A.
# 21. Kuhn, Thomas S.	# 15. Zuboff, Shoshana
# 12. March, James G.	
# 2. Mintzberg, Henry	

the top 20 non-LIS works, 16 (75%) are books and only 4 (25%) are articles. For the top 20 LIS works, 13 (65%) are monographs and 7 (35%) articles. This pattern of dominance by printed monographs is commonly found in situations where authors within a primary discourse community cite materials outside their own areas of specialization and in disciplines with a strong humanistic tradition.

Bibliometric theory predicts that the bulk of citations in any field will come from a few high-impact journals located in the most influential subdisciplines. A simple descriptive analysis of the source articles supports this prediction. A total of 1206 source articles (17% of the 7066 articles in the entire database) from 70 source journals (65% of the 107 journals in the database) generated all of the citations to works by the 42 most highly cited non-LIS authors. However, the bulk of these articles came from a small number of high-impact journals in the fields of information technology management and information science: *MIS Quarterly* contributed 134 articles (11%); *Infor-*

Table IV
LIS Primary Authors Cited 20 or More Times with Author Citation Ranking

# 18. Atkinson, Ross	# 20. Griffiths, José-Marie	# 1. McClure, Charles R.
# 72. Baker, Sharon L.	# 62. Hamaker, Charles A.	# 83. McElderry, Margaret K.
# 64. Battin, Patricia	# 54. Harris, Roma M.	# 78. Mech, Terrence F.
# 63. Boss, R. W.	# 21. Hayes, Robert M.	# 35. Metz, Paul
# 81. Brandon, A. N.	# 31. Heim, Kathleen M.	# 48. Moran, Barbara B.
# 74. Broadus, R. N.	# 4. Hernon, Peter	# 79. Neal, James G.
# 34. Broering, N. C.	# 69. Hewitt, J. A.	# 46. Oberg, Larry R.
# 6. Buckland, Michael K.	# 29. Intner, S. S.	# 43. Okerson, Ann S.
# 33. Budd, John M.	# 32. Johnson, Peggy	# 73. Olsgaard, John N.
# 37. Burrell, Q. L.	# 50. Kantor, Paul B.	# 68. Osburn, Charles B.
# 27. Cargill, Jennifer S.	# 10. Koenig, Michael E. D.	# 56. Powell, Ronald R.
# 30. Chen, C. C.	# 5. Lancaster, Frederick W.	# 76. Putnam, H.
# 40. Childers, Thomas	# 61. Lewis, David W.	# 19. Riggs, Donald E.
# 59. Chrzastowski, T. E.	# 24. Lindberg, D. A. B.	# 23. Shaughnessy, Thomas W.
# 13. Cox, R. J.	# 14. Line, Mauric B.	# 52. Sherea, J. H.
# 36. Crawford, Walt	# 70. Lowry, Charles B.	# 82. Sieverts, E. G.
# 42. Creth, Sheila D.	# 38. Lynch, Beverly P.	# 28. St. Clair, Guy
# 3. Cronin, Blaise	# 9. Lynch, Clifford A.	# 7. Taylor, Robert S.
# 60. Cummings, Anthony M.	# 55. Lynch, M. J.	# 22. Tenopir, C.
# 65. D'Elia, George P.	# 58. Marchant, Maurice P.	# 75. Trueswell, R. W.
# 8. Dervin, Brenda	# 45. Marshall, Joanne Gard	# 57. Tuttle, M.
# 12. Dougherty, Richard M.	# 44. Martell, Charles R.	# 11. Van House, Nancy A.
# 47. Drake, Miriam A.	# 77. Martin, M. S.	# 25. Veaner, Allen B.
# 49. Euster, Joanne R.	# 80. Martin, Susan K.	# 41. Weingand, Dalene E.
# 53. Feather, J.	# 66. Matarazzo, J. M.	# 2. White, Herbert S.
# 71. Fine, Sara F.	# 39. Matheson, N. W.	# 51. Wiegand, Wayne A.
# 16. Garfield, Eugene	# 67. McCabe, Gerald B.	# 17. Woodsworth, Anne
# 15. Gorman, Michael	# 26. McCain, Katherine W.	

mation & Management provided 127 articles (10.5%); the *International Journal of Information Management* contained 110 articles (9%); and *JASIS*, plus its earlier title *Journal of Documentation*, donated a combined total of 66 articles (5%). The next largest number of articles came from high-impact journals in the fields of library science and librarianship: *Library Trends* contributed 74 articles (6%); the *Journal of Academic Libraries* provided 36 (3%); and *C&RL* contained 27 (2%). Altogether, these seven journals, representing only 6.5% of the total contributing journal titles, produced 47% of the source articles (569).

As with the non-LIS authors, a small number of high-impact journals produced most of the citations to the most highly cited LIS authors. Thus, 1427 source articles (20% of the entire database of 7066 articles) from 81 journals (76% of the 107 journals) generated the citations to all works by the

Table V

Top 20 Non-LIS Management Titles

Rank	Primary author	First edition	Title
1	Porter	1985	"How Information Gives You Competitive Advantage"
2	Rogers	1983	*Diffusion of Innovations*
3	Hammer	1993	*Reengineering the Corporation*
4	Zuboff	1988	*In the Age of the Smart Machine*
5	Daft	1986	"Organizational Information"
6	Mintzberg	1973	*The Nature of Managerial Work*
7	Senge	1990	*The Fifth Discipline*
8	Weick	1969	*The Social Psychology of Organizing*
9	Drucker	1988	"The Coming of the New Organization"
10	Kuhn	1962	*The Structure of Scientific Revolutions*
11	Peters	1982	*In Search of Excellence*
12	Allen	1977	*Managing the Flow of Technology*
13	Argyris	1978	*Organizational Learning*
14	Kanter	1983	*The Change Masters*
15	March	1958	*Organizations*
16	Simon	1947	*Administrative Behavior*
17	Pfeffer	1981	*Power in Organizations*
18	Bush	1945	"As We May Think"
19	Strauss	1990	*Basics of Qualitative Research*
20	Abbott	1988	*The System of Professions*

top 83 LIS authors. However, the influence of the information and library science fields was reversed in this case, with the bulk of the articles coming from a small number of high-impact journals in the field of library science: *Library Trends* contributed 112 articles (8%); *C&RL* contained 105 articles (7%); the *Journal of Academic Libraries* provided 101 articles (7%); and the *Bulletin of the Medical Library Association* donated 78 articles (5%). The next largest number of articles came from high-impact journals in the field of information science: *JASIS*, plus its earlier title *Journal of Documentation*, donated a combined total of 108 articles (7.5%); the *Proceedings of the American Society for Information Science* provided 38 (3%); and *Information Processing and Management* contained 35 (2.5%). Altogether, these seven journals, representing again only 6.5% of the total contributing journal titles, produced 40% of the source articles (577).

Bibliometric theory also predicts both that the bulk of citations in any field will be to a small number of prestigious authors and that the rate of cita-

Table VI
Top 20 LIS Management Titles

Rank	Primary author	First edition	Title
1	Taylor	1986	*Value-Added Processes in Information Systems*
2	Cummings	1992	*University Libraries and Scholarly Communication*
3	Matheson	1982	"Academic Information in the Academic Health Sciences Center"
4	Van House	1982	*Output Measures for Public Libraries*
5	Dervin	1986	"Information Needs and Uses"
6	Baker	1977	*The Measurement and Evaluation of Library Services*
7	Johnson	1991	*Automation and Organizational Change in Libraries*
8	McClure	1987	*Planning and Role Setting for Public Libraries*
9	Crawford	1995	*Future Libraries: Dreams, Madness & Reality*
10	Oberg	1992	"The Emergence of the Paraprofessional in Academic Libraries" and "The Role, Status, and Working Conditions of Paraprofessionals"
11	Buckland	1991	*Information and Information Systems*
12	Marshall	1992	"The Impact of the Hospital Library on Clinical Decision-Making"
13	Lindberg	1993	"The Unified Medical Language System"
14	Veaner	1990	*Academic Librarianship in a Transformational Age*
15	Lancaster	1997	*Technology and Management in Library and Information Services*
16	Cronin	1991	*Elements of Information Management*
17	Lynch	1983	"Job Satisfaction in Libraries"
18	Battin	1984	"The Electronic Library—A Vision for the Future"
19	Hernon	1987	*Federal Information Policies in the 1980s*
20	Cargill	1988	*Managing Libraries in Transition*

tion depends upon how long ago the work was published. Generally, unfamiliar new materials have low citation rates. These rates gradually rise, peak, and then fall off as time passes. In some fields, particularly in humanistic disciplines dominated by monographic publications, a significant number of classics will continue to be cited for an extended period. Looking at the list of top 20 non-LIS titles (Table V), we find that the bulk of the titles (9 or 45%) were first published in the 1980s. The most recent title (Hammer and Champy's *Reengineering the Corporation*) was first published in 1993 and the two oldest titles (Bush's "As We May Think" and Simon's *Administrative Behavior*) were first published in 1945 and 1947. The popularity of the reengineering movement has just begun to die down, and the latter two works are classics that helped define the fields of information science and administrative science. Looking at the list of LIS titles (Table VI) we find a similar pattern, with the same number of titles (9 or 45%) first published in the 1980s and only one title being published after 1993 (Lancaster's 1997 *Technology and Management in Library and Information Service*). There is one classic (Baker's *The Measurement and Evaluation of Library Service*), which was first published in 1977 with Lancaster as the lead author.

IV. The Bibliometric Study of Discourse Fashions

A. The Social Scientific Study of Management Fashions

Sociologists have been interested in fads and fashions as an object of scientific study from the beginning of the discipline (Simmel, 1957), but it has not formed a major topic for research. In 1957, Meyersohn and Katz suggested that the study of fads and fashions might "serve the student of social change much as the study of fruit flies has served geneticists: neither the sociology nor the geneticist has to wait long for a new generation to arrive" (p. 594). In 1968 Blumer outlined the basic nature of fashions and fads. His definition of the phenomena bears repeating:

> Fads and fashions are related yet fundamentally different social phenomena. Fashion is the more important of the two. Its general nature is suggested by the contrasting terms "in fashion" and "outmoded." These terms signify a continuing pattern of change in which certain social forms enjoy temporary acceptance and respectability only to be replaced by others more abreast of the times. This parade of social forms sets fashion apart from custom, which is to be seen as established and fixed. The social approbation with which fashion is invested does not come from any demonstration of utility or superior merit; instead, it is a response to the direction of sensitivities and taste.
>
> Although conspicuous in the area of dress, fashion operates in a wide assortment of fields. . . .
>
> Areas amenable to fashion are those that have been pulled into an orbit of continuing social change. The structuring of social life in such areas tilts away from reliance on established social forms and toward a receptiveness to novel ones that reflect new concerns and interests; thus, these areas are open to the recurrent presentation of prospective models of new social forms that differ from each other and from prevailing social forms. These models compete for adoption, and opportunity must exist for effective choice among them. Most significant in this selective process are prestigeful personages who through their advocacy of a model give social endorsement or legitimacy to it. Means and resources must be available for the adoption of the favored models (pp. 341–342).

Only recently have students of organizational life begun to seriously and systematically study management fashions, led by the work of Eric Abrahamson (1991, 1996, 1997) and by Abrahamson in collaboration with several colleagues (Abrahamson and Fairchild, 1999, 2001; Abrahamson and Fombrun, 1994; Abrahamson and Rosenkopf, 1993). His research builds on the seminal work of Barley *et al.* (1988) and Barley and Kunda (1992) and has been supplemented and critiqued by several other scholars (Carson *et al.*, 2000; Kieser, 1997; Ramsey, 1996; Shapiro, 1996; Staw and Epstein, 2000; Worren, 1996).

For the purpose of identifying the existence and prevalence of management fashions, many of these studies have relied in part on what Staw and Epstein term "informational measures" (2000, p. 532). Often the use of these measures involved a content analysis or citation analysis of influential publications. In many cases, the use of informational measures involved counting the citations in commercial indexing databases to specific management topics, organizations, and authors. Databases used included *ABI Inform* (Abrahamson and Fairchild, 1999); the *Business Periodicals Index* (Carson *et al.*, 2000; Abrahamson, 1997); the *Industrial Arts Index* and the *Index of Applied Science and Technology* (Abrahamson, 1997); and the *Nexis News Library* (Staw and Epstein, 2000).

The nature and results of these management fashion studies complement similar bibliometrically based studies that analyze scholarly discourses in the fields of organizational behavior and librarianship (Culnan *et al.*, 1990; Estabrook, 1984; Gatten, 1991; Guillén, 1994; Houser and Sweanery, 1979; Mittermeyer and Houser, 1979; Schwartz, 1997; Üsdiken and Pasadeos, 1995; March, 1965). Publications and databases used in these studies have included *Administration Science Quarterly* and *Organization Studies* (Üsdiken and Pasadeos, 1995); *Library Literature* (Mittermeyer and Houser, 1979; Houser and Sweany, 1979); and the *Social Science Citation Index* (Culnan *et al.*, 1990; Schwartz, 1997).

The core findings in all of these studies support the claim that through the use of extensive, representative data sets, the bibliometric study of formal discourse can reveal meaningful intertextual patterns that reflect the intellectual and communication structure of identifiable social groupings (Borgman, 1990). In addition they support the idea that "like products and industries, management fashions follow a bell-shaped curve [and] typically progress through an established life cycle [of] (1) invention, . . . (2) acceptance, . . . (3) disenchantment, . . . and (4) decline" (Carson *et al.*, 2000, p. 1145). Finally, the results obtained by most of the citation studies of management fashions do correlate reasonably well with results obtained by other measures and have been used in combination with such measures to empirically test a wide variety of hypotheses about the "effects of popular management techniques on corporate performance, reputation, and CEO pay" (Staw and Epstein, 2000), and about management fashion "lifecycles, triggers, and collective learning processes" (Abrahamson and Fairchild, 2001).

However, these results remain controversial and subject to diverse inter-pretations since the relationship between a specific public discourse and a par-ticular private meaning will always remain a highly subjective matter. Worren, for example, suggests that swings in management discourse fashions merely represent swings in the labels that we attach to "the underlying principles and structures that companies are implementing" (1996, p. 613). Thus, the fact that fashion discourse and fashion adoption appear to coevolve does not in itself explain the reasons for using a particular discourse and for adopting a particular fashion. It is also clear that different selection criteria and differ-ent databases tend to identify different bibliometric patterns and social groupings.

Both the positive findings from bibliometric studies of management fashion and the caveats about their validity, reliability, and explanatory power highlight the need to put the results of any single bibliometric study into comparative context, supplemented by critical historical and rhetorical analy-sis. It was for this reason that the initial project of producing a list of highly cited works was supplemented first by a brief history of modern management discourse and then by the following two complementary bibliometric proj-ects. The first complementary project collected data on management dis-course fashion cycles in the LIS literature as a way of documenting the mimetic nature of these cycles arising in response to their earlier appearance in the business literature. The author of the current study first documented this dependent relationship in his 1969 review of management models dealing with "The Library as an Organization." The second complementary project extracted cocitation data from the two sets of highly cited authors produced by the initial project as a way of mapping the intellectual relationships among writers on organizations and management as perceived by authors publish-ing in the field of LIS discourse.

B. Extracting Bibliometric Data from *Library Literature, Library and Information Science Abstracts*, and *Social Science Citation Index*

The first task was to identify as comprehensive a set of management fashions as possible that had been validated and analyzed in the existing literature. The recent work by Carson *et al.* (2000) provided a solid base from which to begin. It drew on a number of published studies "with the intent of offering a com-prehensive, operational explanation of management fashion" which would distinguish it both from more ephemeral management fads and more insti-tutionalized management customs (p. 1143). On that basis, management fash-ions were defined as organizational interventions that are: (1) subject to social contagion; (2) perceived to be innovative, rational, and functional; (3) aimed at encouraging better organizational performance; (4) motivated by a desire to correct a deficiency or capitalize on an opportunity; and (5) considered of transitory value because research has not been able to legitimize their long-term utility and generalizability (pp. 1143–1144). Using this definition Carson *et al.* reviewed three distinct sources in order to produce a comprehensive list of modern management fashions. These sources included: (1) academic and popular publications on the topic; (2) consulting firm reports and lists of fashions; and (3) the *Harvard Business Review* supplement published in September–October "on seminal ideas, events, and publications during the years 1922–97" (Carson *et al.*, 2000, pp. 1148–1149). Eventually, 16 management fashions were identified, with many possible candidates being eliminated because they had not appeared in the *Harvard Business Review* supplement or had not warranted a major heading in the *Business Periodicals Index* (*BPI*) within a decade of their introduction into the management discourse domain (Carson *et al.*, 2000, p. 1149). These 16 fashions were then tracked from 1955 to 1995 via a bibliometric analysis of articles cited in the *BPI*.

Beginning with these 16 fashions, the author of the current study reviewed the library and information science literature to locate treatments and lists of these specific fashions, such as those by Lubans (2000) and by King (1994), as well as of management theories and concepts in general such as that by Khalil (1984). Experimental searches were then done in the online versions of *Library Literature* and *Library and Information Science Abstracts* (*LISA*), including a careful review of the online thesaurus used by *LISA*. These searches revealed what terms were used in LIS discourse to describe the various management fashions and also gave a rough estimate of how, when, and to what extent these fashions had penetrated that discourse. A final list of 28 fashions was compiled and ranked by the total number of citing articles found in a comprehensive search of *LISA* for the period from 1967 to 1999 (Table VII). This list was generated using LISA, because that database provides the most controlled subject access, offers the most extensive coverage of exclusively LIS literature, and covers a longer period of time in its online version than any other database. The list itself represents a more complete and less tightly defined list of fashions than that used by Carson *et al.* in order to provide a more comprehensive initial look at how management fashions have been treated in the LIS literature.

C. A Comparative Analysis of Dominant Discourse Patterns and Fashion Cycles

"Management Information Systems" and "Knowledge Management" represent the two most highly cited discourse fashions in the list of 28 and illustrate the degree to which contemporary LIS discourse has come to be

Table VII
Distribution of Management Fashions in the LISA Database

Total no. articles	Fashion	First cited	Last cited
834	Management Information Systems (MIS)	1968	2000
673	Knowledge Management	(1975)[a] 1981	2000
625	Performance Measures	1968	2000
592	Strategic Planning	1975	2000
529	Personnel Management	1976	2000
373	Systems Analysis	1969	2000
335	Total Quality Management	1968	2000
302	Reengineering	(1972) 1992	2000
231	Change Management	1990	2000
165	Leadership	1977	2000
160	Corporate Culture	1981	2000
154	Planning Programming Budgeting System (PPBS)	1969	2000
152	Competitive Advantage	1984	2000
150	Staff Empowerment	1970	2000
100	Teamwork	1976	2000
93	Operation Research	1968	2000
73	ISO 9000	1992	2000
71	Management by Objectives (MBO)	1973	2000
70	Benchmarking	1993	2000
56	Core Competencies	1990	2000
54	Scientific Management	1972	2000
53	Vision	1988	2000
23	Program Evaluation Review Technique and Critical Path Method (CPM-PERT)	1975	1998
14	Quality Circles	1983	2000
13	Quality of Worklife Programs	1980	2000
12	Horizontal (Flatter) Organizations	(1969) 1992	1998
6	Agile Strategies	1996	2000
4	Sensitivity Training and T-Groups	1974	1996
5917			

[a] Dates in parentheses indicate a single, earlier article with a long hiatus between its appearance and the next citation, which begins a more closely spaced and generally increasing series of citations. The first use of the term "knowledge management" in the LISA database, for example, occurred in an article on copyright (Henry, 1975) and the article's abstract puts the term in quotation marks. Similarly, the first article cited on "Reengineering" occurred in an article "On Database Management System Architecture" by Michael Hammer (1979), who is the acknowledged founder of the movement that rose rapidly in popularity after he published *Reengineering the Corporation* in 1993.

dominated by the discourses of information technology and the information society. However, because these are not terms commonly treated as management fashions outside of the LIS literature and because their rapid growth and high number of citations overwhelms any other fashionable topics with which they might graphically be represented, it was decided to simply point out the importance of these two fashions and focus on a more detailed analysis of the other 12 fashions represented in *LISA* by 100 or more citing articles. Figure 1 provides a line graph tracing the cycle of the next six most highly cited fashions. It clearly indicates what we might have inferred from the two lists of top 20 titles. The six dominant discourse topics are focused on what Eccles *et al.* call the "management basics" of strategy, structuring, and performance measurement (1992, pp. 87–167), to which may be added the core topic of personnel administration. The LIS titles tend to represent the more customary, institutionalized, and rationalized approaches to these basics, whereas the non-LIS titles focus more upon fashionable and radical approaches such as TQM and reengineering.

Given the documented rapid rise to dominance of TQM and reengineering in recent management fashion discourse, a more detailed analysis of these two fashions was undertaken. As a beginning, fashion cycles were graphed for the next six most highly cited management fashions in *LISA* (Fig. 2). All six of these fashions focus on issues of organizational transformation and have been associated with the broader "quality movement" (Boelke, 1995; Cole and Scott, 2000; O'Neil, 1994). The Programming Planning Budgeting System (PPBS) fashion, with 154 citing sources in *LISA*, did not seem to fit with the other fashion sources graphed in Fig. 2 and so was not included. Mintzberg analyzes PPBS in some detail as a founding model for strategic planning (1994); PPBS has not been treated in the management fashion literature; and it clearly represents the type of overly rationalized mode of management to which quality advocates were reacting. The citation patterns graphed in Fig. 2, like those in Fig. 1, clearly follow the general trends described in other studies of management fashions and exhibit similar discourse life cycles.

The next step was to evaluate how the total quality and reengineering fashions were differentially treated in *Library Literature*, *LISA*, and *SSCI* and to compare the results with how these same fashions were treated in the business and organization literature. Only one study was found that contained comparable, high-quality data on these two movements (Abrahamson, 1999). That study was based upon a rigorous search of *ABI Inform* and produced citation data for the period from 1965 to 1995 on four related fashions: job enrichment, quality circles, total quality management, and business process reengineering. The data were given in the form of a line graph, so that the exact citation counts had to be estimated from Abrahamson's "Figure 3"

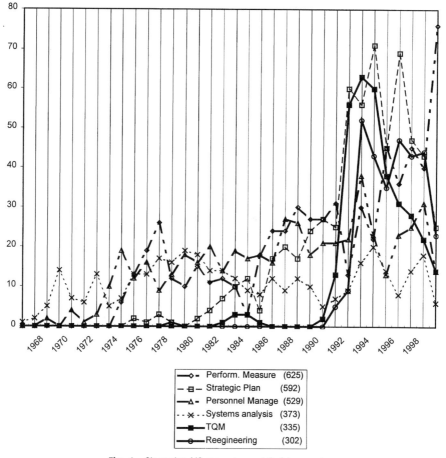

Fig. 1 Six major LIS management fashion cycles.

(p. 723) for use in the current study. These estimates were then entered into a spreadsheet along with the data obtained from searches of *Library Literature*, *LISA*, and *SSCI*. Two line graphs with data tables were then generated for each of the two fashions. Figure 3 presents the fashion cycle of quality management articles in *ABI Inform*, *Library Literature*, *LISA*, and *SSCI*, while Fig. 4 presents a similar graph of the fashion cycle for reengineering. These graphs clearly support the hypotheses that LIS management fashion discourse is dependent for its innovative ideas on idea entrepreneurs external to itself, that these ideas are incorporated after a short lag period, and that they follow a similar life cycle.

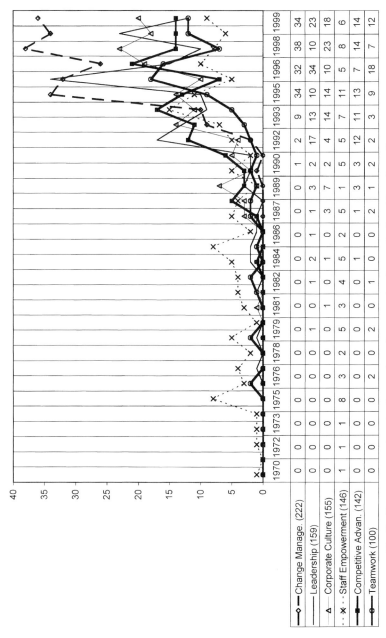

	1970	1972	1973	1975	1976	1978	1979	1981	1982	1984	1986	1987	1989	1990	1992	1993	1995	1996	1998	1999
Change Manage. (222)	0	0	0	0	0	0	0	0	0	0	0	0	0	1	2	9	34	32	38	34
Leadership (159)	0	0	0	0	0	0	1	0	1	2	1	1	3	2	17	13	10	34	10	23
Corporate Culture (155)	0	0	0	0	0	0	0	1	0	1	0	3	7	2	4	14	14	10	23	18
Staff Empowerment (146)	1	1	1	8	3	2	5	3	4	5	2	5	1	5	5	7	11	5	8	6
Competitive Advan. (142)	0	0	0	0	0	0	0	0	0	1	0	1	3	3	12	11	13	7	14	14
Teamwork (100)	0	0	0	0	2	0	2	0	0	0	0	2	1	2	2	3	9	18	7	12

Fig. 2 Six management cycles focused on discourse about organizational transformation.

261

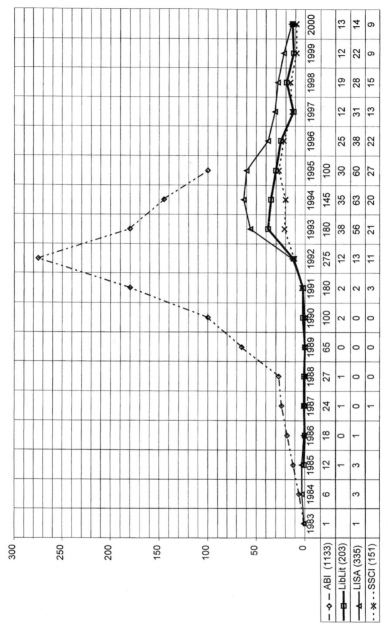

Fig. 3 Fashion cycle of quality management articles in business and LIS literatures.

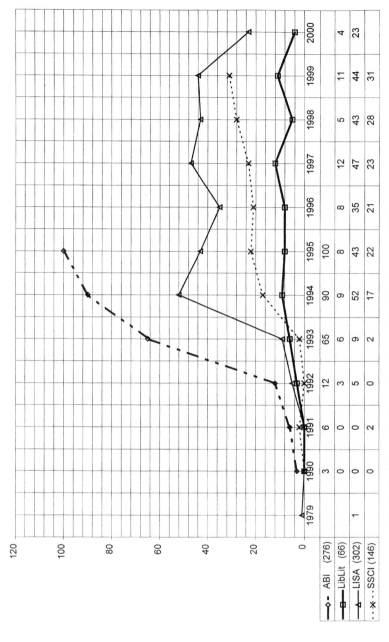

Fig. 4 Fashion cycle of reengineering articles in business and LIS literatures.

	1979	1990	1991	1992	1993	1994	1995	1996	1997	1998	1999	2000
ABI (276)		3	6	12	65	90	100					
LibLit (66)		0	0	3	6	9	8	8	12	5	11	4
LISA (302)	1	0	0	5	9	52	43	35	47	43	44	23
SSCI (146)		0	2	0	2	17	22	21	23	28	31	

263

Data was then extracted on which journals provided the most source citations for the TQM fashion and thus might be considered as having a high impact on the transmission of TQM fashions into LIS discourse (Fig. 5). Because each of the three LIS sources indexes a different, if overlapping, set of journals, it is not possible to produce a full comparison of the three sources. Thus, both *Library Literature* and *LISA* miss the high degree of influence that journals such as *MIS Quarterly* and the *International Journal of Information Management* have come to have within LIS, just as *SSCI* misses the influence of more popular management publications such as *Library Management and Administration*. However, the data clearly indicate that the ranking of each journal within all the databases is roughly comparable. It also is remarkable, but predicted by previous bibliometric research, that the same group of high-impact journals arises as were discovered in the analysis of highly cited titles. The continued dominance of medical and research librarianship in the production of article discourse is clear, whereas some of the most highly cited LIS titles came out of public librarianship. For the purpose of tracking fashion discourse trends, the journal *Library Trends* seems to be living up to its name.

D. Cocitation Maps and the Interdisciplinary Communication of Management Fashions

The bibliometric technique of cocitation analysis was developed during the early 1980s as a relatively objective way to help explore the intellectual structure of a particular body of literature as revealed in its network of citations (White, 1990a,b). It results in various graphical and tabular displays that can be "identified with subject areas, research specialties, schools of thought, shared intellectual styles, or temporal and geographic ties" (McCain, 1990, p. 433). The technique consists first of identifying a set of prominent, representative authors within a literature and counting the number of source documents that have cited any given pair of these authors. For this analysis, the existing sets of 42 non-LIS and 83 LIS authors were used. Cocitation frequency counts were retrieved by using ProCite's searching facility to construct search statements of the form "Keywords BEGINS WITH ARGYRIS C" AND "Keywords BEGINS WITH DRUCKER P." The resulting counts were then entered into an MS Excel worksheet to create two matrices of cocitation frequencies, one for each set of authors.

This matrix was then used to select out the most highly cocited authors. In this case selecting authors with 100 or more cocitations produced a group of 20 highly cocited non-LIS authors and a group of 27 LIS authors. Individual cocitation matrices for each of these groups were then extracted. This process, of course, changed the total numbers of cocitations, since each

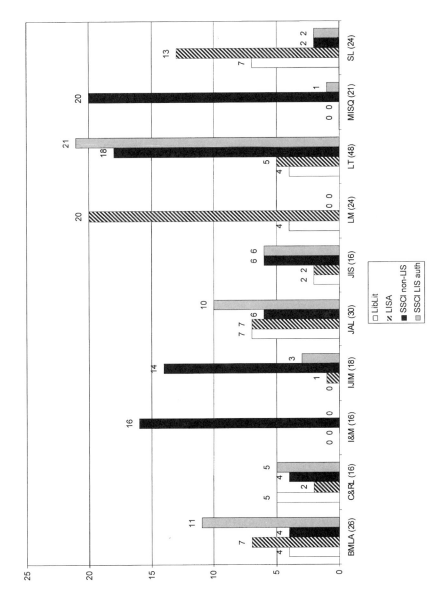

Fig. 5 Distribution of articles on quality management in the top ten LIS journals among major LIS databases.

265

author was now being compared only with the smaller number of extracted authors. However, comparison with the master matrix revealed that the relative percentages of cocitations received by each author—a rough measure of that author's influence within a particular intellectual space—remained the same. The matrix in Fig. 6 illustrates how the raw reciprocal citing data for the 20 most highly cocited non-LIS authors was assembled into rows and columns that were identically ordered by author name. The cells going diagonally from the top left to the bottom right corner represent each author's overall citation count, i.e., total number of source articles citing each author. For the purposes of the current study, that count was subtracted in the row entitled "minus self-cites," so that each "total cocites" count represents only the number of source articles that jointly cite each author with another author in the set.

Two methods were then used to present for analysis the data contained in the various matrices: (1) bar graphs of total cocitation counts; and (2) cocitation networks of cocited authors. The bar graph in Fig. 7, for example, shows the relative total cocitation counts of the top 27 most highly cocited LIS authors. The two matrices of 20 non-LIS and 27 LIS authors were then combined to produce the bar graphs in Figs. 8a and 8b. These graphs illustrate which authors were most influential within an interdisciplinary context and can help us answer the question: are there any LIS authors commonly cocited with non-LIS authors? Some interesting patterns can also be revealed when we compare this list of highly cocited authors with the lists of highly cited works discussed in Section III.

Of the 20 non-LIS authors in Fig. 8, 16 are identical with those listed in Table III. Four authors from the top 20 works list (Abbott, Bush, Kuhn, and Strauss) drop out, to be replaced by Handy, Naisbitt, Schein, and Tushman. This seems to have happened because the high standing of the first four authors in the LIS literature results from a high citation rate for a single work in a field relevant, but peripheral, to management. Thus, Abbott's work concerns the information professions, Bush deals with information technology, Kuhn focuses on scientific communication, and Strauss outlines the methodologies of qualitative research. None of the four authors is cited consistently with any of the other 42 non-LIS authors.

The divergence is much greater when we compare the 27 LIS authors in Fig. 7 and in Fig. 8 with the 20 LIS authors in Table IV. There are only 12 identical authors, leaving 8 unique authors of highly cited works (Battin, Cummings, Crawford, Dervin, Lindberg, Marshall, Matheson, and Oberg) and 15 unique highly cocited authors (Atkinson, Budd, Childers, Dougherty, Gorman, Griffiths, Hayes, Koenig, Line, C. A. Lynch, Metz, Riggs, Shaughnessy, H. S. White, and Woodsworth). As with non-LIS authors, the eight authors of highly cited LIS works mostly likely do not appear in the list

Authors:	Allen	Argyris	Daft	Drucker	Hammer	Handy	Kanter	March	Mintzberg	Naisbitt	Peters	Pfeffer	Porter	Rogers	Schein	Senge	Simon	Tushman	Weick	Zuboff
Allen	51	2	11	3	2	1	7	7	10	0	1	1	2	10	2	2	1	13	8	0
Argyris	74	126	12	12	9	8	12	13	14	5	16	5	8	7	13	17	17	3	12	9
Daft	11	12	126	12	7	4	9	18	37	3	11	19	16	10	7	7	14	28	32	6
Drucker	3	12	12	157	24	17	22	6	27	11	30	12	22	8	8	18	10	8	10	15
Hammer	2	9	7	24	132	12	9	5	20	4	16	6	20	4	8	11	5	7	6	18
Handy	1	8	4	17	12	57	10	3	14	4	14	4	7	2	5	9	7	4	2	7
Kanter	7	12	22	9	9	10	75	8	16	7	17	6	8	15	15	7	7	8	9	4
March	7	9	18	6	5	3	8	64	19	2	7	12	8	6	4	4	22	14	12	7
Mintzberg	10	14	37	27	20	14	16	19	172	5	22	20	34	9	11	12	20	16	26	12
Naisbitt	0	5	3	11	4	4	7	7	5	33	13	3	4	1	5	5	2	3	3	4
Peters	1	16	11	30	16	14	17	7	22	13	91	6	13	4	6	13	5	8	11	11
Pfeffer	2	5	5	12	6	4	6	7	20	3	6	76	14	6	5	3	12	17	11	9
Porter	2	8	16	22	20	7	8	8	34	4	13	14	182	6	6	5	14	10	2	5
Rogers	10	7	10	8	8	2	15	6	9	1	4	6	6	120	4	2	4	12	1	4
Schein	2	13	7	8	8	5	15	4	11	5	6	5	6	4	60	8	5	5	6	6
Senge	7	17	7	18	11	9	7	4	12	5	13	3	5	4	8	57	8	0	6	10
Simon	1	17	14	10	5	5	7	22	20	2	5	12	10	4	8	8	95	7	1	2
Tushman	13	3	28	8	7	4	8	14	16	3	8	17	10	1	5	0	7	67	12	5
Weick	8	12	32	10	6	2	9	12	26	3	11	11	2	1	6	6	13	12	81	8
Zuboff	0	9	6	15	18	7	4	7	12	4	11	9	5	4	6	10	2	5	8	79
Subtotal cocites:	134	389	389	432	325	189	271	241	516	117	315	248	386	235	189	203	268	247	271	221
Minus self-cites:	-51	-126	-126	-157	-132	-57	-75	-64	-172	-33	-91	-76	-182	-120	-60	-57	-95	-67	-81	-79
Total cocites:	83	263	263	275	193	132	196	177	344	84	224	172	204	115	129	146	173	180	190	142

Fig. 6 Cocitation matrix of top twenty cocited non-LIS authors.

267

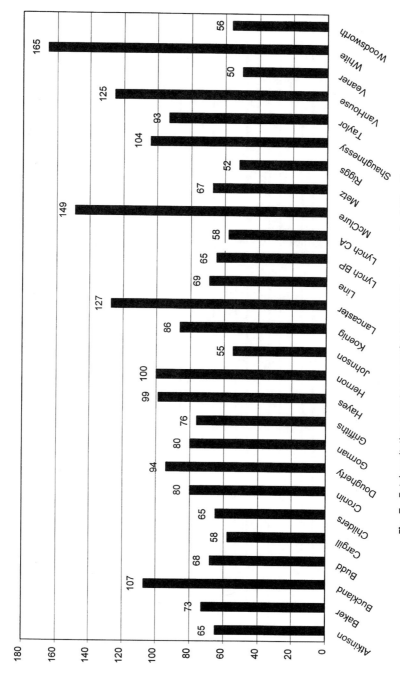

Fig. 7 Total cocitation counts among the top twenty-seven cocited LIS authors.

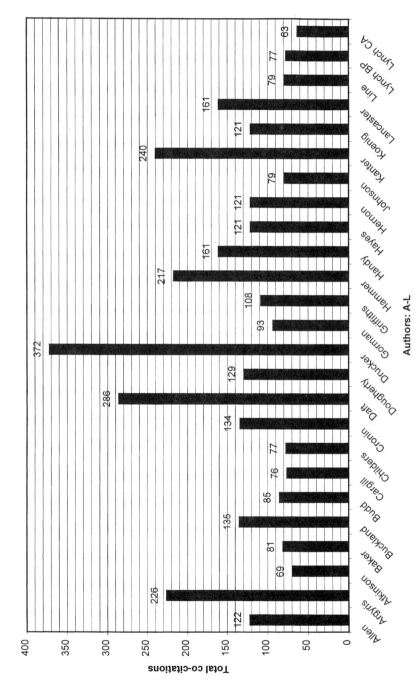

Fig. 8a Cocitation counts for combined sets of twenty non-LIS and twenty-seven LIS authors, selected from authors who had ten or more citations and one hundred or more cocitations: (a) Authors with last names from A–L.

269

270

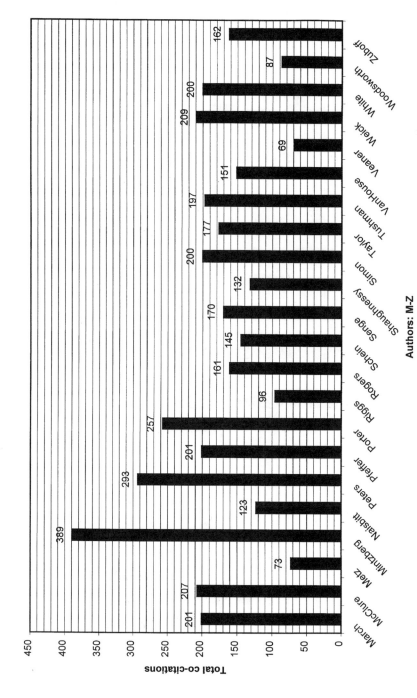

Fig. 8b (b) Authors with last names from M-Z.

of highly cocited authors because the high citation rates for their works come from a single work (Battin, Cummings, and Crawford), from focusing on an approach or topic uniquely identified with them (Dervin and Oberg), or from working in a highly technical subspecialty (Lindberg, Marshall, and Matheson).

The matrix of 20 non-LIS authors was then used to produce a cocitation network for these authors (Fig. 9) and the combined matrices of 20 non-LIS and 27 LIS authors were used to produce a cocitation network for these two sets of authors (Fig. 10). The lines of varying strength between each set of two authors represent the relative amount of cocitation. The number of lines and their strength then determines where each author is placed, so that authors with many, strong cocitation links come to the center of the network and those with fewer, weaker links drift to the outside. Similarly, sets of authors who are often cited together tend to cluster into groups. In order to make such networks readable, the principle of focusing only on those biblio-metric entities of apparent high impact was followed once again. Including all links of only one cocitation, for example, would make the networks totally unreadable and would not communicate any useful information. In fact, only a small number of line types of varying strength can be used and that number will vary depending upon the number of sources and authors selected. After reviewing the data, three levels of cocitation were selected for the set of non-LIS authors: 16–20 cocites, 20–25 cocites, and 26–37 cocites. The resulting network contains 16 of the original set of 20 authors. For the combined set of LIS and non-LIS authors, four levels were selected: 5 cocites, 6–7 cocites, 8–13 cocites, and 22–30 cocites. The resulting network includes a total of 5

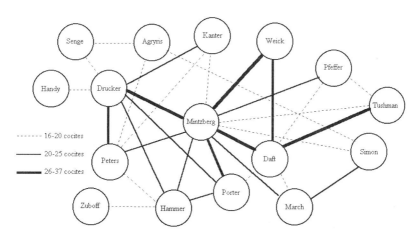

Fig. 9 Cocitation network for top twenty cocited non-LIS authors.

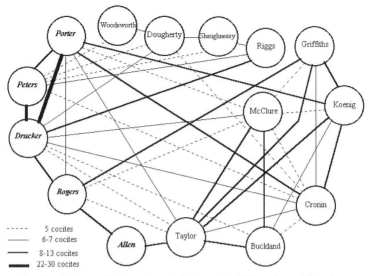

Fig. 10 Cross-cocitation network for top cited LIS and non-LIS authors.

non-LIS authors and 10 LIS authors. It is interesting to note that all 5 of the non-LIS authors also were on the list of most highly cited non-LIS titles, whereas only 4 of the 10 LIS authors also wrote one of the 20 most highly cited LIS works.

Prior cocitation studies of similar sets of management theorists support the characterization made by many writers that organization research is very loosely structured with a profusion of divergent perspectives (Culnan *et al.*, 1990; March, 1965; Üsdiken and Pasadeos, 1995). Attempts in these studies to group authors have tended to produce a pattern in which each author can legitimately be placed in many different categories, although a general distinction has been found between "micro authors" focused on organizational psychology and "macro authors" focused on organizational sociology, as well as between American and European authors (Culnan *et al.*, 1990; Üsdiken and Pasadeos, 1995). The cocitation patterns found in Figs. 9 and 10, of course, do not represent a citation network produced by those same authors as is usually the case in cocitation studies. Rather, they represent relationships among writers on organizations and management as perceived by authors writing within the field of library and information science. They suggest, therefore, which management and organization authors and fashions are of specific concern to LIS authors. Of course, to adequately interpret these citation networks in terms of those concerns, we have to refer to our previously acquired knowledge about the history and nature of modern management discourse, about the content of specific LIS and non-LIS discourses, and about the bibliometric trends in that discourse.

A review of Fig. 9 suggests the following interpretation of its groupings. Mintzberg stands at the center of the network and serves as the node for many different groups. His book on *The Nature of Management* (1973) was the sixth most heavily cited work of the 20 highly cited non-LIS titles. In addition, he is one of the few management gurus to have written about and continually defended the uniqueness of nonprofit public institutions such as universities and libraries and to have carefully analyzed many of them as "professional bureaucracies" (Mintzberg, 1989, 1993). The 1980s "saw the great success of Mintzberg, a McGill professor. The popularity of his ideas was characterized by the massive utilization of his books on management courses, and the adoption of his typology of organization by professors, consultants and managers" (Chanlat, 1996, p. 133). He has written on the entire gamut of management topics.

Peter Drucker represents another, quite predicable, central node. It can be argued that Drucker was the first modern management consultant, the original "guru's guru" (Micklethwait and Wooldridge, 1996, p. 63) who served as a model for all others. Since the production of his first management best seller on *The Concept of the Corporation* in 1946 (which arose out of his contract to write a history of GM), "Drucker has either invented or influenced virtually every part of management theory" (Micklethwait and Wooldridge, 1996, p. 68). For example, Drucker's concept of "decentralization" first adumbrated in his 1946 book has been credited with moving the majority of Fortune 500 companies to radically decentralized forms (Micklethwait and Wooldridge, 1996, p. 69). He invented "Management by Objectives" (Drucker, 1954, p. 121; Micklethwait and Wooldridge, 1996, p. 71), coined the term "knowledge worker" in 1959 (Drucker, 1993, p. 6; Micklethwait and Wooldridge, 1996, p. 70), and in writing *The Age of Discontinuity* (1969) initiated the idea and movement of "privatization" (Micklethwait and Wooldridge, 1996, p. 72). In fact, if one reads *The Practice of Management* (1954) closely, one finds reference, often in the exact same terminology, to almost every management fashion that has arisen since. See for example: continuously improving performance (p. 5); management by objectives (p. 12); leadership (p. 13); customer focus (p. 37) and values (p. 54); asking what is or should be our business (p. 194); reorganizing by business process (p. 205); using teams (p. 220); automation making possible flatter organizations (p. 221); willingness to accept change (p. 268); achieving peak performance (p. 289); worker participation (p. 304); informing the worker (p. 306); managerial vision and corporate culture (p. 307); new management information tools (p. 346); and operations research and systems analysis

(p. 366). The mostly highly cited title by Drucker, it should be noted, was an article in the *Harvard Business Review* on "The Coming of the New Organization" (1988).

Located on the left side of the network one finds those writers, primarily connected through Drucker, who are devoted to promoting the view that we live in a *turbulent age of discontinuity* (Drucker, 1969, 1980) and *unreason* (Handy, 1989) that requires managers to strive for *excellence* (Peters and Waterman, 1982) and to become *change masters* (Kanter, 1983) who use tools such as the *fifth discipline* of systems thinking (Senge, 1990), *organizational learning* (Argyris and Schön, 1978), business process *reengineering* (Hammer and Champy, 1993), and *smart machines* (Zuboff, 1988) to create the *new organization* (Drucker, 1988), which will be infused with *information* and thereby give us a *competitive advantage* (L. W. Porter and Millar, 1985).

Located on the right side of the network, one finds a second group of six writers with Daft forming the node. Although they are writing on the same topics of organizational innovation and information technology as the other group, they do so in a much more academic and technical tone. Michael Tushman's *Winning Through Innovation: A Practical Guide to Leading Organizational Change and Renewal*, written with Charles O'Reilly and published by the Harvard Business School Press in 1997, is the work that most clearly resembles the works written by authors in the first group. Unlike that group, none of the authors in this group can be considered management gurus. Perhaps most interestingly, their heavy citation counts come almost entirely from the information science and technology literature, with almost no citations in most cases from the library science and librarianship literature. This fact is not, unfortunately, immediately obvious from the network diagram itself, but requires going back to the original databases of *SSCI* source records that were created for each author. Finally, it is interesting to note that the two founding fathers of organization science and administrative science (March and Simon), whose continued collaborative work keeps them forever linked in cocitation networks like Siamese twins, remain among the top group of highly cited and cocited authors. However, as the laws of bibliometrics would predict, the direct bibliometric influence of these writers and their classic works has begun to diminish.

The cross-disciplinary links in Fig. 10 present a network that is clearly divided into two groups, with five highly cocited non-LIS authors on the left and 10 highly cocited LIS authors on the right. The non-LIS authors form a chain with Drucker once again functioning as a central link. The LIS authors are further broken up into two major groupings, a small group of 4 authors linked through Dougherty and a larger group of 11 authors clustered around McClure and Taylor. The authors in the Dougherty group primarily represent the interests of academic research libraries and have been concerned in their most highly cited writings with strategic planning (Dougherty and Hughes, 1991, 1993; Riggs, 1984), with the integration of librarianship and information technology management (Woodsworth, 1991), and with promoting total quality management (Shaughnessy, 1993). Of the five links between Peters and the LIS authors, four are to the members of this group, with the strongest being to Riggs, who also has the strongest link (8–13 cocites) with Drucker. In fact the trio of Dougherty, Riggs, and Shaughnessy seem to have acted as major LIS implementers, interpreters, and propagators of contemporary popular management fashions. Dougherty, with Heinritz, for example, wrote the first definitive book on the *Scientific Management of Library Operations* (Dougherty and Heinritz, 1966) and wrote an early editorial on "TQM: Is it the real thing?" (1992). In 1997 he wrote "Repositioning Campus Information Units for the Era of Digital Libraries" with McClure. More recently, after retirement, he has become a management consultant and writes about "Being Successful (Nimble and Agile) in the Current Turbulent Environment" (2001). Shaughnessy has written a large number of articles on reengineering, total quality management, and its associated fashions such as benchmarking and organizational culture (1987, 1988, 1993, 1995, 1996). Riggs has promoted total quality management in a number of publications (1992a,b, 1993) and has favorably reviewed the major fashions of the last two decades as "new management and leadership techniques" (1997, p. 3).

In the second group of LIS authors, the strongest cross-disciplinary links are with Porter and Rogers, rather than with Peters and Drucker. This suggests a split in the LIS literature similar to that which appears in Fig. 9 between a group focused on the practical implementation of popular techniques and a group focused on a more scholarly and technical analysis of the issues. In fact, the authors in the second group are mostly researchers in variously named departments of information and library science. However, as was noted about management research in general, the research agendas of these authors appear to be dominated by the concerns of practitioners, along with a focus on information management and the education of "The New Information Professional" (Griffiths, 1998, pp. 8–12). Koenig's most highly cited work, for example, is a review article on that ubiquitous topic of "Strategic and Long Range Planning in Libraries and Information Centers" (Koenig and Kerson, 1983). Buckland's most highly cited work is his 1991 guide to *Information and Information Systems*. McClure is noted for his advocacy of action research (1989, 1991) and his most highly cited work, which was prepared for the Public Library Development Project, is about *Planning and Role Setting for Public Libraries* (1987). His position as a major network node seems to derive from the broad range of his interests and many collaborative publications.

Taylor's similar orientation to practical discourse is illustrated by his work on *Value-Added Processes in Information Systems* (1986), whose popularity as the single most highly cited LIS work may be ascribed to its treatment of information as a market-driven commodity. The strong interdisciplinary links from Cronin to Porter, Peters, and Drucker, plus his intradisciplinary links to Taylor, Koenig, and Griffiths, demonstrate Cronin's aggressive advocacy (Cronin, 1986, 1995; Cronin and Davenport, 1988, 1991) of "information as a competitive advantage" (M. E. Porter and Millar, 1985) and of using information science schools to produce knowledge workers who can successfully compete in the "system of professions" described by Abbott (1988). A review of the original data files for this group of authors indicates that the citing sources show a strong preference for journals linked to information science and technology, but that these sources are much more broadly distributed throughout the LIS literature than are the sources citing the more technical and scholarly works by non-LIS authors.

E. Identifying Causes, Consequences, and Mechanisms

Recalling the definition by Carson *et al.* of management fashions, it is important to reiterate the fact that managers who seek out and select the latest such fashions do so because they are attempting to solve managerial problems and to encourage better organizational performance with the most innovative and effective means possible. That is, they are attempting to make rational choices, usually defined in modern economic terms as "choosing the alternative whose consequences have the greatest utility" (Simon, 1968, p. 77). In fact, however, "physical, psychological, social, informational, and environmental circumstances prevent people from maximizing their utilities" (W. G. Scott, 1992, p. 98). "Herbert Simon received credit for labeling this construct 'bounded rationality,' which more accurately described an idea that Barnard named 'limited choice'" (W. G. Scott, 1992, p. 98). In Simon's now classic work, *Administrative Behavior: A Study of Decision-Making Processes in Administrative Organization*, which was first published in 1947 and for which Barnard wrote the foreword, the author had not yet actually labeled the concept, but merely discussed the "limits to rationality . . . which bound the area of rationality" (Simon, 1947, pp. 40–41).

Since Barnard and Simon first adumbrated this concept, a great deal of research has been done on the nature of bounded rationality and its consequences for organizational behavior (B. D. Jones, 2001). This research suggests that human beings have evolved a variety of abilities and behaviors and have socially constructed a variety of artifacts, customs, and structures as decision-making mechanisms to compensate for the human condition of bounded rationality. Studies of management fashions represent one prong of this research salient, treating the very existence of such fashions as one modern mechanism that managers use to assist them in making rational choices about organizational interventions under extreme social pressure to conform and to perform within a constantly changing area of divergent possibilities and ambiguous outcomes.

Paradoxically, in attempting to find innovative organizational interventions and to justify those innovations with the rhetoric of scientific rationality, professional expertise, or market pressures, managers often appear to become social conformists and to make their choices not on the basis of technical or economic criteria but on the basis of the prevailing institutional norms and fashions of their industry. Research on this topic is part of a broader research field about the relative influence of choices driven by criteria of technical and economic utility versus choices driven by institutional norms. The two main contending theories are rational choice theory and institutional theory (Archer and Tritter, 2000; Barley and Tolbert, 1997; Cole, 2000; Jones, 2001; W. R. Scott and Christensen, 1995; Tolbert and Zucker, 1996). According to institutional theorists, by selecting and implementing fashionable techniques, management seeks to improve the reputation of its organization as one that strives for excellence and follows the most innovative, best practices in its industry. Reputation thus provides a vehicle to gain legitimacy and to improve the cultural support and resources available to the organization. It remains a moot question as to whether a firm that seeks to improve its reputation by the adoption of popular management techniques also experiences "a reduction in the technical or economic performance of the firm" (Staw and Epstein, 2000, p. 526). Staw and Epstein designed their research project to test this proposition on companies associated with implementing three fashions (quality, teams, and empowerment). They found that such companies did not achieve higher economic performance, but did see an increase in their reputations and in the pay of their CEOs (Staw and Epstein, 2000). On the other hand, Easton and Jarrell (2000a) found that companies that had made a sustained attempt to implement TQM did show an increase in their economic performance. Similarly, Huselid (1995) found that the firms who adopted high performance human resource practices improved their turnover, productivity, and financial performance.

Much of the deviance among such studies can be ascribed to the many persistent "Problems in the measurement of organizational effectiveness" (Steers, 1975). Some deviance can be explained, however, by more detailed studies of how organizations actually implement management fashions. These studies often reveal the continuing influence of institutionalized behavior and cultural norms, when managers are faced with turbulent environments, unanticipated opportunities, or unexpected competition. The study by Carson *et al.* (2000) revealed that contemporary fashion cycles are getting shorter, but that managers are adopting those very fashions that are the most difficult to implement and that require the greatest long-term commitments. In such cases, managers often use radical rhetoric about the need to develop innovative organizational forms, yet make very traditional choices about strategic directions and have great difficulty in actually implementing the innovative techniques that they do attempt (Abrahamson and Fombrun, 1994; Dhillon and Orton, 2001).

Under these circumstances, many management gurus have gotten more shrill in their rhetoric and more radical in their recommendations, with the series of books by Tom Peters—going from *In Search of Excellence* (1982), through *Thriving on Chaos* (1987), to *Liberation Management* (1992) and beyond—being the prime example cited by many critics (Eccles *et al.*, 1992; Frank, 2000; Micklethwait and Wooldridge, 1996). In another phase of their research on the implementation of TQM by major American companies, Easton and Jarrell (2000b) found that many of the companies who attempted to implement TQM had begun their programs under the influence of the consultant Philip Crosby. Cole notes that Crosby's 1979 book *Quality Is Free* "probably did more to raise top manager's awareness of quality as a major issue linked to financial performance than any other event or publication during the early 1980s" (Cole, 2000, p. 81). That book has often been favorably cited in the LIS literature as an important resource for library managers interested in implementing a quality program (O'Neil *et al.*, 1993; O'Neil, 1994). The problem with relying on Crosby's approach was that it "is fatally fundamentally flawed. In fact, the data from this sample of companies suggest that a Crosby approach is virtually certain to stall after 3 years [as] appears to be true of all the guru-based approaches" (Easton and Jarrell, 2000b, p. 104). However, "even though Crosby's approach is flawed, the system has a logic and a coherence that results in effective improvement over the short term" (p. 105). Unless an organization experiences too much disillusionment when the program ultimately fails, those companies who persisted illustrate that "a Crosby approach can be evolved into an advanced quality management system" (p. 105).

Looking now at causes, rather than consequences, we might ask: what leads managers to seek out and attempt to implement quality fashions in the first place? We have already discussed what Abrahamson calls "endogenous triggers" (1999) of fashion cycles that are created by the underlying structures and processes of linguistic behavior and of modern capitalist society. That is to say, norms of progress and rationality continually generate a demand for new and improved management techniques, which demand is supplied by the invention and production of innovative techniques by knowledge entrepreneurs (Abrahamson, 1999; Abrahamson and Fairchild, 2001).

In addition, because management fashion discourse is a species of linguistic behavior, its published forms should obey the major bibliometric laws and exhibit patterns similar to those manifested by other discourse communities. We now need to discuss the more immediate causes of management fashion cycles, or what Abrahamson calls " exogenous triggers" (1999). These are the immediately perceived environmental forces that suggest a need to rectify an organization's performance and improve its competitive position. In the American business community, the exogenous triggers for the rise of the quality movement seem to have been the threat of foreign competition and Japanese management techniques in the context of economic hardship and a turbulent environment (Abrahamson, 1999; Barley *et al.*, 1988; Cole, 2000). In the American nonprofit community, within which most libraries reside even if only as nonprofit centers within larger corporate bodies, the exogenous triggers for seeking out innovative management fashions have been the threat from private information companies using business techniques in the context of drastically reduced financial support and a perceived turbulent environment (du Guy, 1996; Kaboolian, 2000). The pressure was, and still is, to do more with less and to do it better.

Since the 1980s, financial capital has come to dominate the American economy, supported by an ideology of "market populism" (Frank, 2000). This ideology teaches that free market consumer choices not only always result in more rational decisions and better organizational choices, but also produce decisions that are more democratic than those reached by bureaucratic, political, professional, or traditional means. Thus, there exist strong cultural norms for managers to adopt the techniques and slogans of private enterprise. Specifically, managers are told to treat users as "customers" and information as a "commodity" (Budd, 1997); to embrace the "entrepreneurial imperative" as a requirement for "advancing from incremental to radical change" (Neal, 2001); and to "reinvent" government (Osborne and Gaebler, 1992); higher education (Johnson and Rush, 1995); and libraries (Branin, 1996; McCoy, 1993; Stoffle *et al.*, 1996; Sweeney, 1994, 1997).

It should be noted in this regard that the managerial justification for radical organizational interventions, as a response to a radically changed, "turbulent" environment, itself represents a discourse fashion. As reported by Mintzberg (1994, pp. 204–209), managers and consultants have been claiming since 1970 that the organizational sky was falling as a result of the uniquely turbulent society in which we live. The planning literature in particular, with its obsession with control, has continually stressed the need to adopt formal planning procedures as a prophylactic (Mintzberg, 1994, pp. 201–203). Library discourse has not been immune to this rhetoric (Clement, 1995; Koenig and Kerson, 1983; McClure, 1987; Riggs, 1984). Strategic planning, it will be recalled, ranked as the fourth most cited management fashion in the *LISA* database (Table VII). It still seems to be very popular among library managers as a means for controlling library organizations "in these times of rapid change" (McClamroch *et al.*, 2001).

The initial idea of a turbulent economic environment "stemmed from two articles of the 1960s, one by Emery and Trist in 1965 and the other by Terreberry in 1968" (Mintzberg, p. 204). Alvin Toffler then popularized the idea in his series of utopian writings about the wondrous radical changes occurring in the new postindustrial, information society (1970, 1980, 1990). Igor Ansoff was another important popularizer who also was a founder of strategic planning and promoted it as a means for dealing with uncertainty and economic turbulence (1965, 1979, 1988).

V. Discussion and Conclusions

A. Finding Our Way Through the Management Fashion Jungle

This paper began by noting the confused, contentious state of discourse about management and organizations in both the academic and practitioner communities. It documented how the original promise of administrative science to clear up this confusion has not been realized. Thus, contemporary critics echo Herbert Simon's original complaint about the "proverbs of administration" (1946) that "the real problem with management theory is that it is pulling institutions and individuals in conflicting directions" (Micklethwait and Wooldridge, 1996, p. 15).

However, this paper has also shown how the careful historical, rhetorical, and social scientific study of this phenomenon can help us in "clearing a path through the management fashion jungle" (Carson *et al.*, 2000). The current study has not attempted to use sophisticated statistical tests to prove or disprove specific scientific theories about the production, adoption, and implementation of management fashions by library administrators and information managers. Rather, it first reviewed social scientific studies of management knowledge and fashion, then applied the most relevant studies and fruitful theories to analyze discourse fashions in library administration and information management. That analysis has been supported by an extensive set of empirically derived descriptive bibliometric statistics. These statistics contain primarily qualitative data in which each individual "observation is a word or code that represents a class or a category" (Witte, 1993). Thus, *authors' last names* were used to represent the total set of their works that had been cited or cocited; *journal names and abbreviations* were used to represent the total set of articles in each journal that had cited a particular author or topic; and *topical phrases* were used to represent the total set of articles about a particular management fashion in which the phrase (or others defined as synonymous) had appeared.

The sets of authors and titles used in the analysis were initially selected by a process that Strauss and Corbin call "theoretical sampling . . . on the basis of concepts that have proven theoretical relevance" (1990, p. 176). This primary selection criterion was supplemented by the collection of a sample as comprehensive as possible from as many relevant sources as were conveniently available. The resulting bibliographic records extracted from the online versions of *SSCI*, *Library Literature*, and *LISA* produced several large and varied data sets, which provided the opportunity to discover important patterns and to make valid internal and external comparisons. Within the limits of this methodology, the data strongly support and expand most of the expectations and interpretations presented by the author in his study of transformational discourse (Day, 1998).

B. Mapping the Theoretical Terrain

Discourse about library administration and information management does seem to follow the typical patterns associated with other bibliometric research on scholarly communication (Tables I–VI) and with research on management fashions (Table VII and Figs. 1–5). Thus, a small number of only 42 influential non-LIS authors received 41% of all citations and 83 influential LIS authors received 36%. Similarly, 7 journals representing only 6.5% of the total produced 47% of the articles citing the top 42 non-LIS authors and a slightly different combination of 7 journals produced 40% of the articles citing the top 83 LIS authors.

The fashion cycle data in Figs. 1–4 illustrate how the LIS literature about management tends to revolve around the same topics and to follow the same cyclical patterns as the business literature, but with a slight temporal lag. This clearly supports the thesis that the flow of influence is almost entirely from the business management and organizational studies communities to LIS and not vice versa. The high ranking in LIS discourse of topics such as management information systems and knowledge management possibly indicates a unique aspect of LIS discourse. It would be very enlightening to study how such topics have been treated in the business and organizational studies literature to see if perhaps the influence does run in the other direction in this case.

The cocitation data clearly reveal the differential influence of certain authors and fashions of LIS discourse communities. Figure 9, for example, is populated primarily by management gurus 10 of whom out of the 16 are explicitly treated as such by Micklethwait and Wooldridge (1996). These popular management authors group together toward the left side of the network, excluding Daft, March, Simon, Tushman, and Pfeffer, who group together on the right. The dominance of management gurus in Fig. 9, as well as in the list of most highly cited non-LIS authors (Table V), strongly supports the contention that transformational discourse about organizational change in libraries has been dominated by the most popular management fashions. The only surprise was to find that Mintzberg formed the central node of the network in Fig. 9. Although often treated as a guru, this author does not appear at the top of most guru lists. Most practicing librarians, in this author's experience, have never heard of him. However, his high profile in the management education community, coupled with the comprehensive range of his published research and his iconoclastic support of professional and nonprofit forms of organization threatened by market populism, may explain his centrality in the LIS literature.

The split between a popular, guru-dominated literature associated with authors on the left side of Fig. 9 and a more academic, technical literature associated with authors to the right side seems to reflect the underlying split found by other cocitation studies between the library and information science communities. This hypothesis finds additional support from an analysis of the source articles, which shows that most of the citations to authors on the left come from library journals and almost all of the citations to authors on the right come from information science and technology journals. The hypothesis is also supported and given a more precise interpretation when data from Fig. 10 are taken into account. Two groups and two subgroups stand out in this cross-cocitation network: (1) a small group of the management gurus consisting of Porter, Peters, and Drucker; (2) an even smaller group of more technical non-LIS authors consisting of Rogers and Allen; (3) a small cluster of authors primarily associated with academic research library administration and consisting of Woodsworth, Dougherty, Shaughnessy, and Riggs; and (4) the largest group of authors primarily associated with information science and consisting of Griffiths, Koenig, Cronin, Buckland, Taylor, and McClure. It becomes clear from the links between these groupings that the academic research administrator's community serves as a primary vehicle for the dissemination of popular management fashions such as TQM and reengineering. Similarly, the majority of links from Rogers and Allen connect to members of the information science community. What might explain these differential patterns?

Most obviously, there is a simple mapping of authors into shared topical spaces, with information scientists being interested in theories about *Managing the Flow of Information* (Allen, 1977) and the *Diffusion of Innovations* (Rogers, 1995). Less obvious, but perhaps more decisive, may be the fact that the two LIS groups each are identified with a different social institution that serves sometimes complementary, but often diverging, interests. On the one hand, information science professors have a vested ideological interest in promoting the value of information itself and in promoting their occupational status as researchers and that of their students as potential information workers. On the other hand, academic library administrators have a vested ideological interest in maintaining their own managerial authority and in promoting the organizational reputation and survival of the institutions that they control.

The fashion cycle patterns for the quality movement in Fig. 3 and reengineering in Fig. 4 reveal some small differences between how these two fashions have been received in the LIS literature. Taking into account the fact that these graphs have been drawn to represent raw citation counts and thus do not compensate for differences in total articles indexed over time or among databases, the graphs of articles on these two fashions indexed in the *SSCI* represent a pattern commonly found in the reception of popular ideas by scholarly communities. The slope does not exhibit any sudden surges but tends to pick up the fashions somewhat more gradually and then to let go of them more slowly. Such a pattern would seem to reflect the more analytical and skeptical norms of scholarly communication. However, the citation patterns graphed for the articles from *LISA*, which covers a higher percentage of information science materials than does *Library Literature*, seem to mimic the more radical changes of slope found in the business databases, particularly in regard to reengineering.

C. The Path Not Taken

Perhaps by this point in our journey through the management fashion jungle, we will have learned to identify the intellectual flora and fauna that inhabit this virtual environment. This should help us clear a path that will avoid the more dangerous species, while not destroying the ecological balance of the environment that necessarily sustains the practice of management and the study of organizations. Along the way, we may even have found some edible varieties that we might want to collect for use in our favorite mixed-metaphor management recipes. Perhaps, also, some of the underlying ecological principles that favor the luxurious and exuberant growth of these jungle forms will have become clear. Although a number of interacting principles and forces operate to generate this profusion of management discourse and to create those disciplinary communities who explore it, a broadly accepted, but probably seriously outdated, common map is usually used for navigating through it.

The literature on library administration and information does not appear to provide many alternative paths through the jungle. A few examples of resistance to the dominant discourse do appear; for example, Crawford and

Gorman's *Future Libraries: Dreams, Madness & Reality* (1995) appears as the ninth most cited title. However, as participants in the debate between *Librarianship and the Information Paradigm* (Apostle and Raymond, 1997) about which approach should dominate the system of professions, Crawford and Gorman present their vision for the profession in a very ideological style (Budd, 2001, pp. 512–513). In this context, an ideological style is one in which the author's intent appears to be that of dominating discourse so as to rule out options (Budd, 2001). Not surprisingly, Blaise Cronin (1995) is one of Crawford and Gorman's most tenacious adversaries, whose rhetorical practice also strongly tends toward the ideological (Budd, 2001, pp. 510–511). Although Cronin's ideological works are cited fairly often in the database and his interest in promoting a particular vision of library and information science education may account for his nodal position in Fig. 10's cocitation network, his most cited work, with Davenport, is the much more technical and practical *Elements of Information Management* (1991).

What stands out in the production of management fashion discourse and its appropriation within LIS discourse is the fact that nearly all of it exhibits this ideological style. Budd, for example, also analyzes the ideological nature of Stoffle *et al.* (1996), a well-known leader of the reengineering movement in academic librarianship. The ideological nature of most managerial discourse probably should not surprise us given the social and economic forces producing it and the primary rhetorical need of managers to create organizational unity out of diversity (Cheney and McMilan, 1990; Czarniawska-Joerges, 1997; Day, 1998, pp. 639–640; Eccles *et al.*, 1992). However, this means that most library administrators and information managers only follow the ideological superhighways that have been ripped through the management theory jungle. A writer such as Budd, who often attempts to take a more nuanced, critical approach to fashionable ideas, is seldom cited—although his relatively large output of work on mainstream topics has placed him on the list of 83 top cited authors (Table IV). For non-LIS writers, the exceedingly well cited and cocited Mintzberg may be thought of as providing an alternative path through the ideological jungle. However, his continual iconoclastic defense of traditional organizational and professional forms and his refusal to promote a particular technique as the answer to every manager's prayer mean that his works tend to be used analytically and are seldom cited as justification for radical change. In this sense, Mintzberg may be playing the role of Crawford and Gorman within the non-LIS writers in resisting radical change and reinforcing traditional institutional customs.

For the past 30 years management discourse has described the American organizational environment as turbulent, and the majestic corporate bodies that float upon this ocean as in danger of sinking from the massive waves created by the storms of innovative technological change. Beneath those waves of change, and the high-pitched rhetorical winds describing them, have flowed incredibly strong and steady currents of discourse assumptions and social customs: about how organizations do and should behave in a free-market, capitalist economy; about the role of entrepreneurship, information, and technology in promoting rational social progress; and about the roles appropriate for customer–consumers and employee–managers. Discourse about managing organizations in such an environment thus exhibits those paradoxical features typical of a fashion-driven discourse whose participants have "been pulled into an orbit of continuing social change" (Blumer, 1968, p. 342). In particular, transformational discourse based upon these foundational assumptions argues that this environment of unprecedented, discontinuous (but somehow perpetual) environmental change requires radical, discontinuous (but somehow continual) organizational improvement. Examples abound in the literature of library administration and information management throughout the entire period studied. Thus, in 1981 Helen Howard wrote that there "is widespread agreement among organizational theorists and researchers that, for organizations to survive and be viable with a distinct role to play, they need to be flexible and able to meet the challenges of a changing environment." She then cites Drucker's 1969 book on *The Age of Discontinuity* in support of her contention, plus his 1980 book *Managing in Turbulent Times* (Howard, 1981, p. 427). In 1997, Ray McBeth uses the same paradigm to argue that those managing in the information age need new rules for a new reality: "Traditional managerial problem-solving methods do not work because the industrial era assumptions on which they are based, no longer apply" (p. 165); therefore "traditional management activities must change as a result of [this] paradigm shift from an industrial to an information-based society . . . if organizations are to survive" (p. 168). The ideological consistency of managerial rhetoric over the past three decades, and the influence of popular management authors in shaping this rhetoric, clearly appears in these examples. It is not at all clear, however, whether, the promotion of such discourse has improved the reputations of libraries and increased their legitimacy in the eyes of those who provide cultural and financial support for them. Nor is it clear whether the increased adoption of business management fashions has had a positive or negative effect on organizational performance.

References

Abbott, A. (1988). *The System of Professions: An Essay on the Division of Expert Labor*. University of Chicago Press, Chicago.

Abbott, A. (1991). The future of professions: Occupation and expertise in the age of organization. *Research in the Sociology of Organizations* **8**, 17–42.

Abbott, A. (1998). Professionalism and the future of librarianship. *Library Trends* **46**, 430–443.

Abrahamson, E. (1991). Managerial fads and fashions: The diffusion and rejection of innovations. *Academy of Management Review* **16**, 586–612.

Abrahamson, E. (1996). Management fashion. *Academy of Management Review* **21**, 254–285.

Abrahamson, E. (1997). The emergence and prevalence of employee management rhetorics: The effects of long waves, labor unions, and turnover. *Academy of Management Journal* **40**, 491–533.

Abrahamson, E., and Fairchild, G. (1999). Management fashion: Lifecycles, triggers, and collective learning processes. *Administrative Science Quarterly* **44**, 708–740.

Abrahamson, E., and Fairchild, G. (2001). Knowledge industries and idea entrepreneurs: New dimensions of innovative products, services, and organizations. In *The Entrepreneurship Dynamic: Origins of Entrepreneurship and the Evolution of Industries* (C. B. Schoonhoven and E. Romanelli, eds.), pp. 147–177. Stanford University Press, Stanford, CA.

Abrahamson, E., and Fombrun, C. J. (1994). Macrocultures: Determinants and consequences. *Academy of Management Review* **19**, 728–755.

Abrahamson, E., and Rosenkopf, L. (1993). Institutional and competitive bandwagons: Using mathematical modeling as a tool to explore innovation diffusion. *Academy of Management Review* **18**, 487–517.

Allen, T. J. (1977). *Managing the Flow of Technology: Technology Transfer and the Dissemination of Technological Information within the R&D Organization*. MIT Press, Cambridge, MA.

American Library Association (1978). Library Administration Division. In *The ALA Yearbook*, pp. 172–173. American Library Association, Chicago.

American Library Association (1999a). LAMA Library Organization and Management Section, http://www.ala.org/lama/committees/loms/index.html.

American Library Association (1999b). LAMA LOMS Comparative Library Organization, http://www.ala.org/lama/committees/loms/clo.html.

American Library Association (1999c). Library Administration and Management Association. In *ALA Handbook of Organization 1999–2000*, pp. 98–103. American Library Association, Chicago.

Ansoff, H. I. (1965). *Corporate Strategy*. McGraw-Hill, New York.

Ansoff, H. I. (1979). *Strategic Management*. Macmillan, London.

Ansoff, H. I. (1988). *The New Corporate Strategy*. Wiley, New York.

Apostle, R. A., and Raymond, B. (1997). *Librarianship and the Information Paradigm*. Scarecrow Press, Lanham, MD.

Archer, M. S., and Tritter, J. Q. (2000). *Rational Choice Theory: Resisting Colonization* (Critical realism—interventions). Routledge, London, New York.

Argyris, C. (1957). *Personality and Organization: The Conflict between System and the Individual*. Harper, New York.

Argyris, C. (1996). Unrecognized defenses of scholars: Impact on theory and research. *Organization Science* **7**, 79–87.

Argyris, C., and Schön, D. A. (1996). *Organizational Learning, Vol. 2: Theory, Method, and Practice* (Addison-Wesley OD series: Addison-Wesley series on organization development). Addison-Wesley, Reading, MA.

Association for Research Libraries (2000). LibQUAL+Project, http://www.arl.org/libqual/.

Baker, S. L., and Lancaster, F. W. (1991). *The Measurement and Evaluation of Library Services*, 2nd ed. Information Resources Press, Arlington, VA.

Barley, S. R. (1996). *The New World of Work*. British–North American Committee, London.

Barley, S. R., and Kunda, G. (1992). Design and devotion: surges of rational and normative ideologies of control in managerial discourse. *Administrative Science Quarterly* **37**, 363–399.

Barley, S. R., and Tolbert, P. S. (1997). Institutionalization and structuration: Studying the links between action and institution. *Organization Studies* **18**, 93.

Barley, S. R., Meyer, G. W., and Gash, D. C. (1988). Cultures of culture: academics, practitioners and the pragmatics of normative control. *Administrative Science Quarterly* **33**, 24–60.

Barnard, C. I. (1938). *The Functions of the Executive*. Harvard University Press, Cambridge, MA.

Battin, P. (1984). The electronic library—a vision for the future. *Educom Bulletin* **19**, 12–17, 34.

Beckhard, R. (1997). Foreword. In *Organization Development Classics: The Practice and Theory of Change—the Best of the OD Practitioner* (D. F. Van Eynde, J. C. Hoy, and D. C. Van Eynde, eds.), pp. xi–xii. Jossey-Bass, San Francisco.

Bender, T., and Schorske, C. E. (1997). Introduction. In *American Academic Culture in Transformation: Fifty Years, Four Disciplines* (T. Bender and C. E. Schorske, eds.), pp. 3–13. Princeton University Press, Princeton, NJ.

Beniger, J. R. (1986). *The Control Revolution: Technological and Economic Origins of the Information Society*. Harvard University Press, Cambridge, MA.

Beniger, J. R. (1990). Conceptualizing information technology as organization and vice versa. In *Organizations and Communication Technology* (J. Fulk and C. Steinfield, eds.), pp. 29–45. Sage Publications, Newbury Park, CA.

Bennis, W. G. (1969). *Organization Development: Its Nature, Origins, and Prospects* (Addison-Wesley series: Organization Development). Addison-Wesley, Reading, MA.

Birdsall, D. G. (1995). The micropolitics of budgeting in universities: Lessons for library administrators. *The Journal of Academic Librarianship* **21**, 427–437.

Blake, R. R., and Mouton, J. S. (1964). *The Managerial Grid*. Gulf Publishing Co., Houston.

Blumer, H. G. (1968). Fashion. In *International Encyclopedia of the Social Sciences*, Vol. 5, pp. 341–345. Macmillan, New York.

Boelke, J. H. (1995). Quality improvement in libraries: Total quality management and related approaches. *Advances in Librarianship* **19**, 43–83.

Bolman, L. G., and Deal, T. E. (1997). *Reframing Organizations: Artistry, Choice, and Leadership*, 2nd ed. (The Jossey-Bass Business & Management Series: The Jossey-Bass Higher and Adult Education Series). Jossey-Bass Publishers, San Francisco.

Borgman, C. L. (1990). *Scholarly Communication and Bibliometrics*. Sage Publications, Newbury Park.

Bradford, S. C. (1934). Sources of information of scientific productivity. *Engineering* **137**, 85–86.

Branin, J. J. (1996). *Managing Change in Academic Libraries* (Journal of Library Administration No. 22, Issue 2/3). Haworth Press, New York.

Buckland, M. K. (1991). *Information and Information Systems*. Praeger, New York.

Budd, J. M. (1997). A critique of customer and commodity. *College & Research Libraries* **58**, 310–321.

Budd, J. M. (2001). Instances of ideology in discursive practice: Implications for library and information science. *Library Quarterly* **71**, 498–517.

Burke, K. (1969a). *A Grammar of Motives*. University of California Press, Berkeley, CA.

Burke, K. (1969b). *A Rhetoric of Motives*. University of California Press, Berkeley, CA.

Burke, W. W. (1987). *Organization Development: A Normative View* (The Addison-Wesley Series on Organization Development). Addison-Wesley, Reading, MA.

Burns, T., and Stalker, G. M. (1961). *The Management of Innovation*. Tavistock, London.

Burrell, G. (1996). Normal science, paradigms, metaphors, discourses and genealogies of analysis. In *Handbook of Organization Studies* (S. R. Clegg, C. Hardy, and W. R. Nord, eds.), pp. 642–658. Sage Publications, Thousand Oaks, CA.

Burrell, G., and Morgan, G. (1979). *Sociological Paradigms and Organisational Analysis: Elements of the Sociology of Corporate Life*. Heinemann, London.

Bush, V. (1945). As we may think. *The Atlantic Monthly* **146**, 101–108.

Cargill, J. S., and Webb, G. M. (1988). *Managing Libraries in Transition*. Oryx Press, Phoenix.

Carson, P. P., Lanier, P. A., Carson, K. D., and Guidry, B. N. (2000). Clearing a path through the management fashion jungle: Some preliminary trailbrazing. *Academy of Management Journal* **43**, 1143–1158.

Castells, M. (1996). *The Rise of the Network Society* (Information Age: Economy, Society and Culture No. 1). Blackwell, Malden, MA.

Chandler, A. D. (1962). *Strategy and Structure: Chapters in the History of the Industrial Enterprise.* (MIT Press Research Monographs.) MIT Press, Cambridge, MA.

Chandler, A. D. (1977). *The Visible Hand: The Managerial Revolution in American Business.* Belknap Press, Cambridge, MA.

Chanlat, J.-F. (1996). From cultural imperialism to independence: Francophone resistance to Anglo-American definitions of management knowledge in Québec. In *The Politics of Management Knowledge* (S. R. Clegg and G. Palmer, eds.), pp. 121–140. Sage Publications, Thousand Oaks, CA.

Cheney, G., and McMillan, J. J. (1990). Organizational rhetoric and the practice of criticism. *Journal of Applied Communication Research* **18**, 93–114.

Clawson, D. (ed.) (1998). *Required Reading: Sociology's Most Influential Books.* University of Massachusetts Press, Amherst, MA.

Clawson, D., and Zussman, R. (1998). Canon and anti-canon for a fragmented discipline. In *Required Reading: Sociology's Most Influential Books* (D. Clawson, ed.), pp. 3–17. University of Massachusetts Press, Amherst, MA.

Clegg, S. R., and Palmer, G. (1996). Introduction: producing management knowledge. In *The Politics of Management Knowledge* (S. R. Clegg and G. Palmer, eds.), pp. 1–18. Sage Publications, Thousand Oaks, CA.

Clegg, S. R., Barrett, M., Clarke, T., Dwyer, L., Gray, J., Kemp, S., and Marceau, J. (1996a). Management knowledge for the future: Innovation, embryos and new paradigms. In *The Politics of Management Knowledge* (S. R. Clegg and G. Palmer, eds.), pp. 190–235. Sage Publications, Thousand Oaks, CA.

Clegg, S. R., Hardy, C., and Nord, W. R. (eds.) (1996b). *Handbook of Organization Studies.* Sage Publications, Thousand Oaks, CA.

Clement, R. W. (1995). *Strategic Planning in ARL Libraries: A SPEC Kit* (SPEC kit No. 210). Association of Research Libraries, Office of Management Services, Washington, DC.

Cole, R. E. (2000). Market pressures and institutional forces: The early years of the quality movement. In *The Quality Movement and Organization Theory* (R. E. Cole and W. R. Scott, eds.), pp. 67–87. Sage Publications, Thousand Oaks, CA.

Cole, R. E., and Scott, W. R. (eds.) (2000). *The Quality Movement and Organization Theory.* Sage Publications, Thousand Oaks, CA.

Collins, R. (1994). *Four Sociological Traditions.* Oxford University Press, New York.

Crawford, W., and Gorman, M. (1995). *Future Libraries: Dreams, Madness & Reality.* American Library Association, Chicago.

Cronin, B. (1981). The need for a theory of citing. *Journal of Documentation* **37**, 16–24.

Cronin, B. (1986). Towards information-based economies (Samuel Lazerow Memorial Lecture No. 3). Indiana University, School of Library and Information Science, Bloomington, IN.

Cronin, B. (1995). Shibboleth and substance in North American library and information science education. *Libri* **45**, 45–63.

Cronin, B., and Davenport, E. (1988). *Post-Professionalism: Transforming the Information Heartland.* Taylor Graham, London.

Cronin, B., and Davenport, E. (1991). *Elements of Information Management.* Scarecrow Press, Metuchen, NJ.

Cronin, B., and Tudor-Šiloviä, N. (1992). *From Information Management to Social Intelligence: The Key to Open Markets.* ASLIB, The Association for Information Management, London.

Crosby, P. E. (1979). *Quality Is Free: The Art of Making Quality Certain*. New American Library, New York.

Culnan, M. J., O'Reilly, C. A., and Chatman, J. A. (1990). Intellectual structure of research in organizational behavior, 1972–1984: A cocitation analysis. *Journal of the American Society for Information Science* **41**, 453–458.

Cummings, A. M., White, M. L., Bowen, W. G., Lazarus, L. O., and Ekman, R. H. (1992). *University Libraries and Scholarly Communication: A Study Prepared for the Andrew W. Mellon Foundation*. Published by the Association of Research Libraries for the Andrew W. Mellon Foundation, Washington, DC.

Czarniawska-Joerges, B. (1997). *Narrating the Organization: Dramas of Institutional Identity*. University of Chicago Press, Chicago.

Daft, R. L. (1986). *Organization Theory and Design*, 2nd ed. West Publishing Co., St. Paul.

Daft, R. L., and Lengel, R. H. (1986). Organizational information requirements, media richness and structural design. *Management Science* **32**, 554–571.

Day, M. T. (1969). The library as an organization: A critical overview of concepts and approaches. Master's thesis. University of Chicago, Chicago.

Day, M. T. (1997). Challenges to the professional control of knowledge work in academic libraries: A proposed agenda for organizational research and action. In *Choosing Our Futures: Proceeding of the 8th ACRL National Conference*. Association of College and Research Libraries, Chicago, http://www.ala.org/acrl/paperhtm/c24.html.

Day, M. T. (1998). Transformational discourse: Ideologies of organizational change in the academic and information science literature. *Library Trends* **46**, 635–667.

Dervin, B., and Nilan, M. (1986). Information needs and uses. *Annual Review of Information Science and Technology* **21**, 3–33.

Dhillon, G., and Orton, J. D. (2001). Schizoid incoherence, microstrategic options, and the strategic management of new organizational forms. *M@n@gement* **4**, 229–240, http://www.dmsp.dauphine.fr/management/.

Diodato, V. P. (1994). *Dictionary of Bibliometrics* (Haworth Library and Information Science). Haworth Press, New York.

Donaldson, L. (1985). *In Defence of Organization Theory: A Reply to the Critics* (Management and Industrial Relations Series No. 9). Cambridge University Press, New York.

Donaldson, L. (1996a). *For Positivist Organization Theory: Proving the Hard Core*. Sage Publications, Thousand Oaks, CA.

Donaldson, L. (1996b). The normal science of structural contingency theory. In *Handbook of Organization Studies* (S. R. Clegg, C. Hardy, and W. R. Nord, eds.), pp. 57–76. Sage Publications, Thousand Oaks, CA.

Donaldson, L. (1999). *Performance-Driven Organizational Change: The Organizational Portfolio*. Sage Publications, Thousand Oaks, Calif.

Donham, W. B. (1922). Essential groundwork for a broad executive theory. *Harvard Business Review* **1**, 1–10.

Dougherty, R. M. (1992). TQM: Is it the real thing? *The Journal of Academic Librarianship* **18**, 3.

Dougherty, R. M. (2001). Being successful (nimble and agile) in the current turbulent environment. *The Journal of Academic Librarianship* **27**, 263–267.

Dougherty, R. M., and Heinritz, F. J. (1966). *Scientific Management of Library Operations*. Scarecrow Press, Metuchen, NJ.

Dougherty, R. M., and Hughes, C. (1991). *Preferred Futures for Libraries: A Summary of Six Workshops with University Provosts and Library Directors*. The Research Libraries Group, Inc., Mountain View, CA.

Dougherty, R. M., and Hughes, C. (1993). *Preferred Library Futures II: Charting the Paths*. The Research Libraries Group, Inc., Mountain View, California.

Dougherty, R. M., and McClure, L. (1997). Repositioning campus information units for the era of digital libraries. In *Restructuring Academic Libraries: Organizational Development in the Wake of Technological Change* (C. A. Schwartz, ed.), pp. 67–80. Association of College and Research Libraries, American Library Association, Chicago.

Drucker, P. F. (1946). *The Concept of the Corporation*. The John Day Company, New York.

Drucker, P. F. (1950). *The New Society: The Anatomy of the Industrial Order*. Harper and Row, New York.

Drucker, P. F. (1954). *The Practice of Management*. Harper & Row, New York.

Drucker, P. F. (1969). *The Age of Discontinuity*. Harper & Row, New York.

Drucker, P. F. (1980). *Managing in Turbulent Times*. Butterworth–Heinemann, London.

Drucker, P. F. (1988). The coming of the new organization. *Harvard Business Review* **66**, 45–53.

Drucker, P. F. (1993). *Post-Capitalist Society*. HarperCollins, New York.

du Guy, P. (1996). Making up managers: Enterprise and the ethos of bureaucracy. In *The Politics of Management Knowledge* (S. R. Clegg and G. Palmer, eds.), pp. 19–35. Sage Publications, Thousand Oaks, CA.

Duff, A. S. (2000). *Information Society Studies* (Routledge Research in Information Technology and Society). Routledge, London.

Easton, G. S., and Jarrell, S. L. (2000a). The effects of total quality management on corporate performance: An empirical investigation. In *The Quality Movement and Organization Theory* (R. E. Cole and W. R. Scott, eds.), pp. 237–270. Sage Publications, Thousand Oaks, CA.

Easton, G. S., and Jarrell, S. L. (2000b). Patterns in the deployment of total quality management: An analysis of 44 leading companies. In *The Quality Movement and Organization Theory* (R. E. Cole and W. R. Scott, eds.), pp. 89–130. Sage Publications, Thousand Oaks, CA.

Eccles, R. G., Nohria, N., and Berkley, J. D. (1992). *Beyond the Hype: Rediscovering the Essence of Management*. Harvard Business School Press, Boston, MA.

Emery, F. E., and Trst, E. L. (1965). The causal texture of organizational environments. *Human Relations* **18**, 31–32.

Estabrook, L. (1984). Sociology and library research. *Library Trends* **32**, 461–476.

Eustis, J. D., and Kenney, D. J. (1996). *Library Reorganization & Restructuring: A SPEC Kit* (SPEC kit No. 215). Association of Research Libraries, Office of Management Services, Washington, DC.

Fayol, H. (1916). *Administration Industrielle Générale*. Durod, Paris.

Fayol, H. (1949). *General and Industrial Management*. Translated by Constance Storrs. Pitman, London.

Fisher, W. H. (1996). Library management: The latest fad, a dismal science, or just plain work? *Library Acquisitions-Practice and Theory* **20**, 49–56.

Frank, T. (2000). *One Market under God: Extreme Capitalism, Market Populism, and the End of Economic Democracy*. Anchor, New York.

Freidson, E. (2001). *Professionalism: The Third Logic*. University of Chicago Press, Chicago.

Frost, P. J., Lewin, A. Y., and Daft, R. L. (2000). *Talking about Organization Science: Debates and Dialogue from "Crossroads"* (Organization Science). Sage Publications, Thousand Oaks, CA.

Galbraith, J. R. (1980). Applying theory to the management of organizations. In *Frontiers in Organization and Management* (W. M. Evan, ed.), pp. 151–167. Praeger, New York.

Gatten, J. N. (1991). Paradigm restrictions on interdisciplinary research into librarianship. *College & Research Libraries* **52**, 575–584.

Griffiths, J-M. (1998). The new information professional. *Bulletin of the American Society for Information Science* **24**, 8–12.

Guillén, M. F. (1994). *Models of Management: Work, Authority, and Organization in a Comparative Perspective*. University of Chicago Press, Chicago.

Hammer, M., and Champy, J. (1993). *Reengineering the Corporation: A Manifesto for Business Revolution.* Harper Business, New York.

Hammer, M., and McLeod, D. (1979). *On Database Management System Architecture.* MIT, Cambridge Laboratory for Computer Science, Cambridge, MA.

Handy, C. (1989). *The Age of Unreason.* Arrow Books, London.

Hansen, K. P. (1996). The mentality of management: Self-images of American top executives. In *The Politics of Management Knowledge* (S. R. Clegg and G. Palmer, eds.), pp. 36–45. Sage Publications, Thousand Oaks, CA.

Harris, M. H., Hannah, S. A., and Harris, P. C. (1998). *Into the Future: The Foundations of Library and Information Services in the Post-industrial Era,* 2nd ed. (Contemporary Studies in Information Management, Policy, and Services). Ablex, Greenwich, CT.

Henry, N. (1975). *Copyright, Information Technology, Public Policy. Part I: Copyright—Public Policies.* Marcel Dekker, Inc., New York.

Hernon, P., and McClure, C. R. (1987). *Federal Information Policies in the 1980s: Conflicts and Issues.* Ablex, Norwood, NJ.

Heyderbrand, W. V. (1989). New organizational forms. *Work and Occupations* **16**, 323–357.

Hilmer, F. G., and Donaldson, L. (1996). *Management Redeemed: Debunking the Fads That Undermine Corporate Performance.* Free Press, New York.

Hodson, R., and Parker, R. E. (1988). Work in high-tech settings: a review of the empirical literature. *Research in the Sociology of Work* **4**, 1–29.

Hood, C., and Jackson, M. W. (1991). *Administrative Argument.* Dartmouth Pub. Co., Aldershot, Hants, England.

Houser, L. J., and Sweanery, W. (1979). Library administration literature: A bibliometric measure of subject dispersion. *Library Research* **1**, 359–375.

Howard, H. (1981). Organizational structure and innovation in academic libraries. *College & Research Libraries* **42**, 425–434.

Howard, H. (1984). Organizational theory and its application to research librarianship. *Library Trends* **32**, 477–493.

Huselid, M. A. (1995). The impact of human resource management practices on turnover, productivity, and corporate financial performance. *Academy of Management Journal* **38**, 635–672.

Institute for Scientific Information (1998). The ISI database: The journal selection process, http://www.isinet.com/hot/essays/199701.html.

Institute for Scientific Information (2000a). Corporate timeline: ISI, http://www.isinet.com/isi/about/timeline.

Institute for Scientific Information (2000b). Social Science Citation Index scope notes: Information science & library science, http://www.isinet.com/products/citation/scope/ssci96b.html.

Jacques, R. W. (1996). *Manufacturing the Employee: Management Knowledge from the 19th to 21st Centuries.* Sage Publications, Thousand Oaks, CA.

Johnson, E. R., and Mann, S. H. (1980). *Organization Development for Academic Libraries: An Evaluation of the Management Review and Analysis Program* (Contributions in Librarianship and Information Science No. 38). Greenwood Press, Westport, CT.

Johnson, P. (1991). *Automation and Organizational Change in Libraries* (Professional Library Series). G. K. Hall, Boston.

Johnson, S. L., and Rush, S. C. (1995). *Reinventing the University: Managing and Financing Institutions of Higher Education.* John Wiley and Sons, New York.

Jones, B. D. (2001). *Politics and the Architecture of Choice: Bounded Rationality and Governance.* University of Chicago Press, Chicago.

Jones, P. J. (2000). Individual accountability and individual authority: the missing links. *Library Administration and Management* **14**, 135–145.

Kaboolian, L. (2000). Quality comes to the public sector. In *The Quality Movement and Organization Theory* (R. E. Cole and W. R. Scott, eds.), pp. 131–153. Sage Publications, Thousand Oaks, CA.

Kanter, R. M. (1983). *The Change Masters: Innovation and Entrepreneurship in the American Corporation.* Simon & Schuster, New York.

Khalil, M. (1984). Modern theories and concepts of management: Their relevance and application to libraries. *Library Focus* 2, 1–25.

Kieser, A. (1997). Rhetoric and myth in management fashion. *Organization* 41, 49–74.

King, W. R. (1994). Process reengineering: The strategic dimensions. *Information Systems Management* 11, 71–73.

Klingberg, S. (1990). Library reorganization: The role of theory and research. *Library Administration & Management* 4, 101–104.

Kochan, T. A., and Rubinstein, S. (2000). Human resource policies and quality: From quality circles to organizational transformation. In *The Quality Movement and Organization Theory* (R. E. Cole and W. R. Scott, eds.), pp. 387–399. Sage Publications, Thousand Oaks, CA.

Koenig Michael, E. D., and Kerson, L. (1983). Strategic and long range planning in libraries and information centers. *Advances in Library Administration and Organization* 2, 199–258.

Koontz, H. (1961). The management theory jungle. *Journal of the Academy of Management* 4, 174–188.

Koontz, H. (1980). The management theory jungle revisited. *Academy of Management Review* 5, 175–187.

Kuhn, T. S. (1970). *The Structure of Scientific Revolutions*, 2nd enl. ed. (International Encyclopedia of Unified Science: Foundations of the Unity of Science; Vol. 2, No. 2). University of Chicago Press, Chicago.

Lancaster, F. W., and Sandore, B. (1997). *Technology and Management in Library and Information Services.* University of Illinois Graduate School of Library and Information Science, Champaign, IL.

Larson, M. S. (1977). *The Rise of Professionalism: A Sociological Analysis.* University of California Press, Berkeley, CA.

Lindberg, D. A. B., Humphreys, B. L., and McCray, A. T. (1993). The unified medical language system. *Methods of Information in Medicine* 32, 281–291.

Lotka, A. J. (1926). The frequency disstribution of scientific productivity. *Journal of the Washington Academy of Sciences* 16, 317–323.

Lubans, J. (2000). "I borrowed the shoes, but the holes are mine": Management fads, trends, and what's next. *Library Administration and Management* 14, 131–134.

Lynch, B. P. (1985). Introduction. In *Management Strategies for Libraries: A Basic Reader* (B. P. Lynch, ed.), pp. x–xiii. Neal-Schuman, New York.

Lynch, B. P. (1990). Management theory and organizational structure. In *Academic Libraries: Research Perspectives* (M. J. Lynch, ed.), pp. 213–234. American Library Association, Chicago.

Lynch, B. P., and Smith, K. R. (2001). The changing nature of work in academic libraries. *College & Research Libraries* 62, 407–420.

Lynch, B. P., and Verdin, J. A. (1983). Job satisfaction in libraries: Relationships of the work itself, age, sex, occupational group, tenure, supervisory level, career commitment and library department. *Library Quarterly* 53, 434–447.

Macdonald, K. M. (1995). *The Sociology of the Professions.* Sage Publications, Thousand Oaks, CA.

March, J. G. (1965). Introduction. In *Handbook of Organizations* (J. G. March, ed.), pp. ix–xvi. Rand McNally, Chicago.

March, J. G., and Simon, H. A. (1958). *Organizations.* Wiley, New York.

Marshall, J. G. (1992). The impact of the hospital library on clinical decision-making: The Rochester study. *Bulletin of the Medical Library Association* 80, 169–178.

Matheson, N. W., and Cooper, J. A. (1982). Academic information in the academic health sciences center: Roles for the library in information management. *Journal of Medical Education* **57**, 1–93.

Mayo, E. (1933). *The Human Problems of an Industrial Civilization*. Macmillan, New York.

McBeth, R. (1997). Managing in the information age: New rules for a new reality. *Advances in Library Administration and Organization* **15**, 165–185.

McCain, K. W. (1990). Mapping authors in intellectual space: A technical overview. *Journal of the American Society for Information Science* **41**, 433–443.

McClamroch, J., Byrd, J. J., and Sowell, S. L. (2001). Strategic planning: Politics, leadership and learning. *Journal of Academic Librarianship* **27**, 372–378.

McClure, C. R. (1987). *Planning and Role Setting for Public Libraries: A Manual of Options and Procedures*. American Library Association, Chicago.

McClure, C. R. (1989). Increasing the usefulness of research for library managers: Propositions, issues, and strategies. *Library Trends* **38**, 280–294.

McClure, C. R. (1991). Communicating applied library/information science research to decision makers: some methodological considerations. In *Library and Information Science Research: Perspectives and Strategies for Improvement* (C. R. McClure and P. Hernon, eds.), pp. 253–266. Ablex, Norwood, NJ.

McCoy, J. (1993). Re-engineering academic and research libraries: Technology continues to change the nature of our jobs. *College & Research Libraries News* **54**, 333–335.

McGregor, D. M. (1960). *The Human Side of Enterprise*. McGraw-Hill, New York.

Meyersohn, R., and Katz, E. (1957). Notes on the natural history of fads. *American Journal of Sociology* **62**, 594–601.

Micklethwait, J., and Wooldridge, A. (1996). *The Witch Doctors: Making Sense of the Management Gurus*. Times Books, Random House, New York.

Mintzberg, H. (1973). *The Nature of Managerial Work*. Harper & Row, New York.

Mintzberg, H. (1975). The manager's job: Folklore and fact. *Harvard Business Review* **53**, 49–61.

Mintzberg, H. (1989). *Mintzberg on Management*. Free Press, New York.

Mintzberg, H. (1993). *Structure in Fives: Designing Effective Organizations*. Prentice Hall, Englewood Cliffs, NJ.

Mintzberg, H. (1994). *The Rise and Fall of Strategic Planning: Reconceiving Roles for Planning, Plans, Planners*. Free Press, New York.

Mittermeyer, D. (1990). Libraries as "complex" organizations: A concept in need of an operational definition. *Library & Information Science Research* **12**, 231–249.

Mittermeyer, D., and Houser, L. J. (1979). The knowledge base for the administration of libraries. *Library Research* **1**, 255–276.

Moran, R. F. (1980). Improving the organizational design of academic libraries. *Journal of Academic Librarianship* **6**, 140–143.

Mowday, R. T. (1997). Presidential address: Reaffirming our scholarly values. *Academy of Management Review* **22**, 335–345.

Murphy, R. (1988). *Social Closure: The Theory of Monopolization and Exclusion*. Oxford University Press, New York.

Neal, J. G. (2001). The entrepreneurial imperative: Advancing from incremental to radial change in the academic library. *Portal: Libraries and the Academy* **1**, 1–13, http://muse.jhu.edu/journals/portal_libraries_and_the_academy/v001/1.1neal.html.

O'Neil, R. (1994). *Total Quality Management in Libraries: A Sourcebook*. Libraries Unlimited, Englewood, CO.

O'Neil, R., Harwood, R. L., and Osif, B. A. (1993). A total look at total quality management: A TQM perspective from the literature of business, industry, higher education, and librarianship. *Library Administration and Management* **7**, 244.

O'Shea, J. E., and Madigan, C. (1997). *Dangerous Company: The Consulting Powerhouses and the Businesses They Save and Ruin*. Times Business, New York.

Oberg, L. R. (1992). The emergence of the paraprofessional in academic libraries: Perceptions and realities. *College & Research Libraries* **53**, 99–112.

Oberg, L. R., Mentges, M. E., McDermott, P. N., and Harusadangkul, V. (1992). The role, status, and working conditions of paraprofessionals: A national survey of academic libraries. *College & Research Libraries* **53**, 215–238.

Offermann, L. R., and Spiros, R. K. (2001). The science and practice of team development: Improving the link. *Academy of Management Journal* **44**, 376–392.

Osborne, D., and Gaebler, T. (1992). *Reinventing Government: How the Entrepreneurial Spirit Is Transforming the Public Sector*. Addison-Wesley, Reading, MA.

Palmer, I., and Dunford, R. (1996). Interrogating reframing: Evaluating metaphor-based analyses of organizations. In *The Politics of Management Knowledge* (S. R. Clegg and G. Palmer, eds.), pp. 141–154. Sage Publications, Thousand Oaks, CA.

Perrow, C. (1985). The short and glorious history of organization theory. In *Management Strategies for Libraries: A Basic Reader* (B. P. Lynch, ed.), pp. 232–247. Neal-Schuman, New York.

Perrow, C. (1986). *Complex Organizations: A Critical Essay*, 3rd ed. Random House, New York.

Peters, T. J. (1987). *Thriving on Chaos: Handbook for a Management Revolution*. Macmillan, London.

Peters, T. J. (1992). *Liberation Management: Necessary Disorganization for the Nanosecond Nineties*. Fawcett Columbine, New York.

Peters, T. J., and Waterman, R. H. (1982). *In Search of Excellence: Lessons from America's Best-Run Companies*. Harper & Row, New York.

Pfeffer, J. (1981). *Power in Organizations*. Pitman Publishers, Marshfield, MA.

Pfeffer, J. (2000). Barriers to the advance of organization science: Paradigm development as a dependent variable. In *Talking about Organization Science: Debates and Dialogue from "Crossroads"* (P. J. Frost, A. Y. Lewin, and R. L. Daft, eds.), pp. 39–61. Sage Publications, Thousand Oaks, CA.

Porter, L. W., and McKibbon, L. E. (1988). *Management Education and Development: Drift or Thrust into the 21st Century*. McGraw-Hill, New York.

Porter, M. E., and Millar, V. E. (1985). How information gives you competitive advantage. *Harvard Business Review* **63**, 149–161.

Pritchard, A., and Wittig, G. R. (1981). *Bibliometrics: A Bibliography and Index, 1874–1959*. AALM Books, Watford, U.K.

Pugh, D. S., and Hickson, D. J. (1996). *Writers on Organizations*. Sage Publications, Thousand Oaks, CA.

Ramsey, H. (1996). Managing skeptically: A critique of organizational fashion. In *The Politics of Management Knowledge* (S. R. Clegg and G. Palmer, eds.), pp. 155–172. Sage Publications, Thousand Oaks, CA.

Reed, M. I. (1990). From paradigms to images: The paradigm warrior turns postmodern guru. *Personnel Review* **19**, 35–40.

Reed, M. I. (1992). *The Sociology of Organizations: Themes, Perspectives and Prospects* (Studies in Sociology). Harvester Wheatsheaf, New York.

Reed, M. I. (1996). Organizational theorizing: A contested terrain. In *Handbook of Organization Studies* (S. R. Clegg, C. Hardy, and W. R. Nord, eds.), pp. 31–56. Sage Publications, Thousand Oaks, CA.

Reeves, W. J. (1980). *Librarians as Professionals: The Occupation's Impact on Library Work Arrangements*. Lexington Books, Lexington, MA.

Rice, R. E. (1990). Hierarchies and clusters among communication and library and information science journals, 1977–1987. In *Scholarly Communication and Bibliometrics* (C. L. Borgman, ed.), pp. 138–153. Sage Publications, Newbury Park, CA.

Riggs, D. E. (1984). *Strategic Planning for Library Managers*. Oryx, Phoenix, AZ.

Riggs, D. E. (1992a). Strategic quality management in libraries. *Advances in Librarianship* **16**, 93–105.

Riggs, D. E. (1992b). TQM: Quality improvement in new clothes. *College & Research Libraries* **53**, 481–483.

Riggs, D. E. (1993). Managing quality: TQM in libraries. *Library Administration & Management* **7**, 73–78.

Riggs, D. E. (1997). What's in store for academic libraries: Leadership and managment issues. *The Journal of Academic Librarianship* **23**, 3–8.

Rogers, E. M. (1995). *Diffusion of Innovations*, 4th ed. Free Press, New York.

Rynes, S. L., Bartunek, J. M., and Daft, R. L. (2001). Across the great divide: Knowledge creation and transfer between practitioners and academics. *Academy of Management Journal* **44**, 340–355.

Rynes, S. L., McNatt, N. B., and Bretz, R. D. (1999). Academic research inside organizations. *Personnel Psychology* **52**, 869–898.

Sackett, P. R., and Larson, J. R. (1990). Research strategies and tactics in industrial and organizational psychology. In *Handbook of Industrial and Organizational Psychology*, 2nd ed., Vol. 1 (M. D. Dunnette and L. M. Hough, eds.), pp. 419–489. Consulting Psychologists Press, Palo Alto, CA.

Sandkull, B. (1996). Lean production: The myth which changes the world? In *The Politics of Management Knowledge* (S. R. Clegg and G. Palmer, eds.), pp. 69–79. Sage Publications, Thousand Oaks, CA.

Scarbrough, H. (1996). *The Management of Expertise*. St. Martin's Press, New York.

Scarbrough, H., and Burrell, G. (1996). The axeman cometh: the changing roles and knowledges of middle managers. In *The Politics of Management Knowledge* (S. R. Clegg and G. Palmer, eds.), pp. 173–189. Sage Publications, Thousand Oaks, CA.

Schumpeter, J. A. (1991). *The Economics and Sociology of Capitalism*. Princeton University Press, Princeton, NJ.

Schwartz, C. A. (1997). The rise and fall of uncitedness. *College & Research Libraries* **58**, 19–29.

Scott, W. G. (1992). *Chester I. Barnard and the Guardians of the Managerial State*. University Press of Kansas, Lawrence, KS.

Scott, W. G., and Hart, D. K. (1989). *Organizational Values in America*. Transaction Publishers, New Brunswick, NJ.

Scott, W. R. (1992). *Organizations: Rational, Natural, and Open Systems*, 3rd ed. Prentice Hall, Englewood Cliffs, NJ.

Scott, W. R., and Christensen, S. (1995). *The Institutional Construction of Organizations: International and Longitudinal Studies*. Sage Publications, Thousand Oaks, CA.

Senge, P. M. (1990). *The Fifth Discipline: The Art and Practice of the Learning Organization*, 1st ed. Doubleday/Currency, New York.

Shapiro, E. C. (1996). *Fad Surfing in the Boardroom: Managing in the Age of Instant Answers*. Addison-Wesley, Reading, MA.

Shaughnessy, T. W. (1987). The search for quality. *Journal of Library Administration* **8**, 5–10.

Shaughnessy, T. W. (1988). Organizational culture in libraries: Some management perspectives. *Journal of Library Administration* **9**, 5–10.

Shaughnessy, T. W. (1993). Benchmarking, total quality management, and libraries. *Library Administration & Management* **7**, 7–12.

Shaughnessy, T. W. (1995). Total Quality Management: Its application in North American research libraries. *Australian Academic and Research Libraries* **26**, pp. 1–5.

Shaughnessy, T. W. (1996). Lessons from restructuring the library. *The Journal of Academic Librarianship* **22**, 251–256.

Shepard, H. A. (1960). Three management problems and the theories behind them. In *An Action Research Program for Organization Improvement*, pp. 1–6. Foundation for Research on Human Behavior. Ann Arbor, MI.

Shepard, H. A. (1965). Changing interpersonal and intergroup relationships in organizations. In *Handbook of Organizations* (J. G. March, ed.), pp. 1115–1143. Rand McNally, Chicago.

Siggins, J., and Sullivan, M. (1993). *Quality Improvement Programs in ARL Libraries: A SPEC Kit* (SPEC kit No. 196). Association of Research Libraries, Office of Management Services, Washington, DC.

Simmel, G. (1957). Fashion. *American Journal of Sociology* **62**, 541–558.

Simon, H. A. (1946). The proverbs of administration. *Public Administration Review* **6**, 53–67.

Simon, H. A. (1947). *Administrative Behavior: A Study of Decision-Making Processes in Administrative Organization*, 3rd ed. Macmillan, New York.

Simon, H. A. (1968). Administrative behavior. In *International Encyclopedia of the Social Sciences*, Vol. 1, pp. 74–79. Macmillan, New York.

Simon, H. A. (1976). Some problems of administrative theory. In *Administrative Behavior: A Study of Decision-Making Processes in Administrative Organization*, 3rd ed. (H. A. Simon, ed.), pp. 20–44. Free Press, New York.

Simonetti, R. (1996). Technical change and firm growth: "Creative destruction" in the *Fortune* list, 1963–87. In *Behavioral Norms, Technological Progress, and Economic Dynamics: Studies in Schumpeterian Economics* (E. Helmstädter and M. Perlman, eds.), pp. 151–181. University of Michigan Press, Ann Arbor, MI.

Staw, B. M., and Epstein, L. D. (2000). What bandwagons bring: Effects of popular management techniques on corporate performance, reputation, and CEO pay. *Administrative Science Quarterly* **45**, 523–556.

Steers, R. M. (1975). Problems in the measurement of organizational effectiveness. *Administrative Science Quarterly* **20**, 546–558.

Stenson, P. F. (1987). Current management literature for technical services. *Illinois Libraries* **69**, 95–103.

Stoffle, C. J., Renaud, R., and Veldof, J. (1996). Choosing our futures. *College & Research Libraries* **57**, 213–225.

Strauss, A. L., and Corbin, J. (1990). *Basics of Qualitative Research: Grounded Theory Procedures and Techniques*. Sage Publications, Newbury Park, CA.

Sweeney, R. T. (1994). Leadership in the post-hierarchical library. *Library Trends* **43**, 62–94.

Sweeney, R. T. (1997). Leadership skills in the reengineered library: Empowerment and value added trend implications for library leaders. *Library Administration & Management* **11**, 30–41.

Taylor, F. W. (1911). *The Principles of Scientific Management*. Norton, New York.

Taylor, R. S. (1986). *Value-Added Processes in Information Systems* (Communication and Information Science). Ablex, Norwood, NJ.

Terpstra, D. E., and Rozell, E. J. (1997). Sources of human resource information and the link to organizational profitability. *Journal of Applied Behavioral Science* **33**, 66–83.

Terreberry, S. (1968). The evolution of organizational environments. *Administrative Science Quarterly* **12**, 590–613.

Thompson, J. D. (1956). On building an administrative science. *Administrative Science Quarterly* **1**, 102–111.

Toffler, A. (1970). *Future Shock*. Random House, New York.

Toffler, A. (1980). *The Third Wave*. Morrow, New York.

Toffler, A. (1990). *Powershift*. Bantam, New York.

Tolbert, P. S., and Zucker, L. G. (1996). The institutionalization of institutional theory. In *Handbook of Organization Studies* (S. R. Clegg, C. Hardy, and W. R. Nord, eds.), pp. 175–190. Sage Publications, Thousand Oaks, CA.

Travica, B. (1998). Information aspects of new organizational designs: Exploring the non-traditional organization. *Journal of the American Society for Information Science* **49**, 1224–1244.

Trueswell, R. W. (1969). Some behavioral patterns of library users: the 80/20 rule. *Wilson Library Bulletin* **43**, 458–459, 461.

Tuckman, A. (1994). The yellow brick road: total quality management and the restructuring of organizational culture. *Organization Studies* **15**, 727–751.

Tushman, M. L., and O'Reilly, C. A. (1997). *Winning Through Innovation: A Practical Guide to Leading Organizational Change and Renewal*. Harvard Business School Press, Boston, MA.

Üsdiken, B., and Pasadeos, Y. (1995). Organizational analysis in North America and Europe: A comparison of co-citation networks. *Organization Studies* **16**, 503–526.

Van House, N. A., and Zweizig, D. (1987). *Output Measures for Public Libraries: A Manual of Standardized Procedures*, 2nd ed. American Library Association, Chicago.

Van Maanen, J. (2000). Style as theory. In *Talking about Organization Science: Debates and Dialogue from "Crossroads"* (P. J. Frost, A. Y. Lewin, and R. L. Daft, eds.), pp. 63–82. Sage Publications, Thousand Oaks, CA.

Varney, G., Worley, C., Darrow, A., Neubert, M., Cady, S., and Guner, O. (1999). Guidelines for entry level competencies to organization development and change: Presented to ODC Division, Academy of Management, August, 1999, http://www.aom.pace.edu/odc/report.html.

Veaner, A. B. (1990). *Academic Librarianship in a Transformational Age: Program, Politics, and Personnel* (Professional Librarian Series). G. K. Hall, Boston.

Vyborney, W. M. (1992). Computer reasons and human power: Epideictic strategies in popularized scientific discourse on the nature and potential of computer technology. Dissertation, University of Minnesota, Ann Arbor, MI.

Waldo, D. (1948). *The Administrative State*, 2nd ed. Ronald Press, New York.

Wallace, M. (1989). Brave New Workplace: Technology and work in the new economy. *Work and Occupations* **16**, 363–392.

Webster, F. (1995). *Theories of the Information Society* (International Library of Sociology). Routledge, London.

Webster, F. (2000). Information: A sceptical account. *Advances in Librarianship* **24**, 1–23.

Weick, K. E. (1979). *The Social Psychology of Organizing*, 2nd ed. (Topics in Social Psychology). Addison-Wesley, Reading, MA.

Weick, K. E. (1989). Theory construction as disciplined imagination. *Academy of Management Review* **14**, 516–531.

Weick, K. E. (2000). Quality improvement: A sensemaking perspective. In *The Quality Movement and Organization Theory* (R. E. Cole and W. R. Scott, eds.), pp. 155–172. Sage Publications, Thousand Oaks, CA.

White, H. D. (1990a). Author co-citation analysis: Overview and defense. In *Scholarly Communication and Bibliometrics* (C. L. Borgman, ed.), pp. 84–106. Sage Publications, Newbury Park, CA.

White, H. D. (guest ed.) (1990b). Perspectives on author cocitation analysis. *Journal of the American Society for Information Science* **41**, 429–468.

Winter, M. F. (1988). *The Culture and Control of Expertise: Toward a Sociological Understanding of Librarianship* (Contributions in Librarianship and Information Science No. 61). Greenwood Press, New York.

Witte, R. S. (1993). *Statistics*. Harcourt Brace College Publishers, Fort Worth, TX.

Woodsworth, A. (1991). *Patterns and Options for Managing Information Technology on Campus*. American Library Association, Chicago.

Worren, N. A. M. (1996). Management fashion. *Academy of Management Review* **21**, 613.

Zipf, G. K. (1949). *Human Behavior and the Principle of Least Effort*. Addison Wesley, Cambridge, MA.

Zuboff, S. (1988). *In the Age of the Smart Machine: The Future of Work and Power*. Basic Books, New York.

A Rush to Serve: Digital Reference Services and the Commitment to 24/7

Michael G. Jackson
Rockefeller Library
Brown University
Providence, Rhode Island 02912-9101

I. Introduction

Since the mid-1990s, librarians in academic, public, and special libraries have been excitedly discussing the future of digital reference services. Seen as the logical next step to achieving the dream of creating a network of virtual libraries "without walls," digital; reference services appear within reach. New technologies, such as e-mail reference, reference "chat," online tutoring, videoconferencing, and call messaging, are making it possible for librarians to serve their users when they need it, with no need for the users to come to a specific structure such as a library building.

There is a real atmosphere of excitement and impending change in the library profession. Things will not be the same. Ferguson and Bunge presciently noted in 1997 that computer networks have had "a revolutionary impact on the entire Weltanschauung of academic librarianship" compelling librarians to seek "new alliances," "radically change" their views on user needs, and "transform" how they organized themselves in meeting user needs. The incontestable fact is that libraries will be "highly digital and probably largely digital" with a shift away from the model of library as place or central locus for research activity (Ferguson and Bunge, 1997, pp. 252–253).

Huge changes in Internet usage patterns are taking place. In the United States, alone, more than 45 million households were connected to the Internet by 1999, an increase of 15 million since 1996; personal use of the Internet averaged 27 hours per year in 1997, projected to climb to 192 hours a year by 2003; and teenagers and children constituted the fastest growing population of Internet users (Kresh, 2000, pp. 1–2).

Anne Lipow put it bluntly: if librarians do not jump on the digital bandwagon and provide real-time, fully interactive services to users, we will "witness the disappearance of reference service by librarians," with commer-

ADVANCES IN LIBRARIANSHIP, VOL. 26
Copyright © 2002, Elsevier Science (USA). All rights of reproduction in any form reserved.
0065-2830/02 $89.95

299

cial groups coming in to fill the void (Lipow, 1999, p. 50). Judy Horn declared that there is no time to wait, for "the future is now" regarding reference services in the electronic era (Horn, 2001, p. 1). This trend is generating intense coverage in the library literature (Janes *et al.*, 1999; Tenopir and Ennis, 1998; Ferguson, 2000; Gray, 2000; Lankes *et al.*, 2000).

Surveys suggest that libraries have been responding to the call with investments not only in more electronic resources, but also in digital reference services. Tenopir described the results of a questionnaire sent out to 70 academic libraries; complementing traditional reference services, 99% of these libraries offer e-mail reference; 96% offer research consultations by appointment; and real-time virtual reference services were offered by 20 out of 70 libraries (29%) (Tenopir, 2001, p. 1). It was reported that as of April 2001, more than 270 libraries had put a chat reference service in place, of which 77% were implemented because of consortia agreements with other libraries (Ellis and Francoeur, 2001). Janes found in 2000 that 45% of American libraries and nearly 13% of public libraries offered some kind of digital reference service (McClure and Lankes, 2001, p. 2).

Indeed, even another rattle-the-cage article by Jerry Campbell, which deplored the "55% success rate of reference," declining reference statistics, librarian denial about the ramifications of the electronic revolution, the migration of learning into the "asynchronous environment," and the reality of the digital revolution and "dot.coming" of educational practice, has not sparked heated calls of outrage from librarians as some of his publications have elicited in years past (Campbell, 2000). It is almost as if Campbell is now preaching to the converted.

A major part of the excitement also has to do with a corollary point: not only to give library users access to electronic collections around the globe, but to have reference librarians be able and willing to answer inquiries for information in real time, 24 hours a day, 7 days a week. Comments from librarians have been extremely positive. Tennant fully supports all "digital, global, 24/7 reference efforts" (Tennant, 2000); (Constantine, n.d.) argued that "users expect digital services 24/7"; Diane Kresh described how electronic discussion lists are crammed with inquiries from librarians about how to set up "24/7 live reference and chat services" and how libraries have to "expand globally and become a true 24/7 service" (Kresh, 2001, pp. 1, 4). Tracy Strobel of Cleveland Public Library's Web site approvingly stated, "We're out there looking for ways to maintain a place in today's society. . . . People are out there 24/7 using the Web, and we wanted to be there for them" (Flagg, 2001, p. 1). As Oder observed, "The year 2000 brought the advent of live reference" and the possibility of providing 24/7 reference services (Oder, 2001, p. 47). Users who search a database on the weekend or after library hours should not have to wait days, or hours, to be assisted with their informational and research needs. Assistance should be given in hours, minutes, or *instantly*, in real time, with a real expert helping them. Strong supporters of 24/7 argue that this expert should be a reference librarian.

What is striking in the literature about this issue is how uncritical much of the analysis is. As the preceding quotations convey, there is a tone of absolute rightness about the idea of being on call, 24/7. It will represent the epitome of our librarian public service commitment, providing a service which an information-needy public craves. There is a sense that if a sizable number of users are conducting their online searching of full-text databases and electronic journals between the hours of 11 PM and 8 AM, when most libraries are closed, these users might be in great need of reference services during this period. It is not enough for libraries to just give users the option of forwarding their questions by e-mail to a reference librarian. Comments from proponents of 24/7 strongly imply that if this service is not made available, commercial providers will step in to fill the gap, leaving the library out of the loop. In surveying the library literature about 24/7, one finds little sense of limits or caution. It is portrayed as an unmitigated good.

Competition from commercial providers such as Ask Jeeves has especially galvanized the push to 24/7 digital reference. Coffman described how information services such as these have become wildly popular. For example, Ask Jeeves in 2000 grew from serving 1.3 million people per month with fewer than 500,000 questions per day to more than 5 million people per month with more than 2 million questions per day; usage statistics grew at the rate of 46% per quarter; with more than 485 million queries in 12 months. This was over 70% more than the 284.96 million reference transactions handled by all public libraries in the United States in 1996 (Coffman and McGlamery, 2000, p. 1).

There is a sense that librarians must directly compete with commercial services such as Ask Jeeves. As Kresh noted, "The founders of these sites argue that they are providing the missing link to the millions of pages of information." It is thought that because the quality of answers on commercial sites may be limited, libraries can fill this niche, and must do so. According to Kresh, "the growth of the Internet is exploding: it is located everywhere and is open for business 24/7" (Kresh, 2000, p. 2).

This article will survey, not so much the revolution in digital reference services (it is here to stay and properly so), but its supposed logical conclusion, that a librarian *must* be on call 24/7 in order to effectively serve the users of any library, whether it is public, academic, or special. The goal being promoted is not just access (which many users already have) but the capacity for users to directly interact with librarians anytime, anywhere, any day. The origins of this idea, how it is currently being implemented, its impact on library staff and professionalization, and most importantly, how it is being evaluated will be explored. For an argument that is so ubiquitous, there is little rigorous assessment of their assertion that users want this kind of service from libraries after regular hours. The pluses and minuses of "round-the-clock service" will be examined, along with an analysis of user populations, their demographics, and what their information-seeking behaviors appear to be.

II. The Current Face of 24/7 Services

The idea of 24/7 has been around awhile. One has only to look at the existence of numerous "night owl" telephone after-hours reference services, usually in public libraries. However, it was around 1998 that the vision of 24/7 really began to take off. The major push behind it was the introduction of the Collaborative Digital Reference Service Project from the Library of Congress (CDRS). Groundbreaking in scope, it is a pilot project with the goal of providing professional library reference service to users through a collaborative international digital network of libraries. This partnership of libraries ". . . will be the first of its kind to connect users with accurate, timely and credible information anytime anywhere." Libraries that are participating include Library of Congress, Santa Monica Public Library, AskERIC, National Library of Australia, Brown University, Cornell University, University of Southern California, and many others (Library of Congress, 2000, p. 1). As explained by Kresh, "By linking libraries for reference services, the CDRS would combine the power of local collections and staff strengths with the diversity and availability of libraries and librarians everywhere, 24 hours a day, 7 days a week" (Kresh, 2000, p. 3). With CDRS, there will always be a librarian to provide high-value reference service, anytime and anywhere.

Other examples of major 24/7 hour reference service projects include the following:

The Virtual Reference Desk (VRD). This is a project that is dedicated to the promotion of digital reference services. The U.S. Department of Education sponsors it. Its goal is the startup of Web-based information services that connect users with subject experts who can rapidly answer their questions. VRD is part of "AskA" services, which are popular and widespread. It includes a searchable database of high-value K–12 AskA services, with supporting incubator software, instruction and support, and research and development. VRD staff has been very active in conferences and highly visible with their message about digital reference services.

Metropolitan Cooperative Library System (MCLS) 24/7 Project Reference Service. MCLS is an association of public and academic libraries in the greater LA basin. Working in collaboration, these libraries have developed a centralized Web-based call center that can, after regular library hours, transfer inquiries to a centralized service point. Their calling software facilitates the answering of reference questions, scripting, routing of calls, and live, real-time collaborative browsing over the Web, allowing librarians to "push" the patron's browser to relevant Web sites. Staff can also work in remote locations away from library building itself.

Ready for Reference Service—Alliance Library System in Illinois. The Ready for Reference service is a collaborative 24/7 live reference service. Eight academic libraries are providing it in the Alliance Library System in Illinois.

There are increasing examples of libraries offering 24/7 digital reference services independent of consortia. They include the Digital Reference Service at the Georgia Institute of Technology, the "Ask a Question" at the University of California, Irvine, the University of North Texas Libraries Online Reference Help Desk, and others (Lankes *et al.*, 2000).

There is no question that both consortia and individual libraries are making investments in the 24/7 concept of reference service. In fact, North Carolina State University has been taking it to the extreme, with real librarians staffing public service desks around the clock, along with real-time electronic reference (Anderson *et al.*, 2000); Boyer, 2001). Innovations in software packages are also encouraging the movement for real-time, live reference interactions, such as Virtual Reference Services (VRD) from Library Systems & Services (LSSI) (Broughton, 2001, pp. 2–4).

As previously mentioned, comparisons with commercial providers have been used to rally support for librarians to adopt the technology for 24/7 digital reference services. A closer look at this key assumption and others is in order, though.

III. Competition, Reference "Declinism," and Service Values

The reality of commercial competition has been cited as a prime rationale for the adoption of 24/7. In general, according to Suzanne Gray, "The 24/7 availability of the network has added fuel to the trend of around-the-clock-support. . . . Users can call a number of catalog clothing companies and place orders anytime; J. Crew customers . . . can contact dedicated e-mail customer service representatives twenty-four hours per day. Even the IRS implemented a twenty-four-hour customer service line last year" (Gray, 2000, p. 371). Her strong implication is that libraries should follow the lead of commercial sites.

Many other commercial sites besides Ask Jeeves are available to the user. Sites include Answer-Point (part of Ask Jeeves), Exp.com (bids for answers from "experts"), Kasamba (users have access to experts in many categories), AskAnything.com (users can get answers to all questions), and BumperBrain (puts people in contact with experts). These Web information providers are visited by millions of users annually.

Indeed, compared to data about digital reference hits received in library 24/7 services, there is no contest between the two. Gross, McClure, and Lankes report that their survey of academic libraries indicated that only 26 to 56 questions were received per month; for public libraries, the volume of digital reference questions was reported at "a mean of 5.6 e-mail reference questions per week; the model or most frequent response was 3 questions per week" (Gross *et al.*, 2001, p. 7). The numbers are not impressive. These figures could support the argument that there are millions of users waiting to be served by librarians. If libraries do not initiate aggressive proactive policies to reach out to them on the competitive 24/7 information battlefield, libraries will become even more irrelevant to most seekers of information.

Upon first thought, this seems a persuasive argument. However, several questions should be asked. What is it that users are really getting from commercial services such as Ask Jeeves? Is the type of information they are getting the same as that provided by librarians and libraries on their own 24/7 services? Would it be better if reference librarians could link products with customers as the commercial sites do? Or, is it a false challenge for libraries to compete for this market? Should commercial sites be the yardsticks to measure our own efforts?

Most librarians know very well that the quality of the information on Ask Jeeves and others is very questionable and of poor quality, according to our own standards. Compared to common reference strategies of finding information, the system of commercial providers can lead to bad outcomes in accuracy and effectiveness. A consortia system in Northern California informally tested Ask Jeeves by forwarding to it 12 questions libraries in its system had answered. These were typical, standard questions. The results? Ask Jeeves came up short; it could not answer any of the questions (Kresh, 2000, p. 2).

But, is it possible that the type of question received by libraries, whether public or academic, is qualitatively different? Janes concluded that digital reference "best" serves users who ask ready reference questions, who are regular library users, or who deal with popular culture. To Janes, digital reference most "poorly" handles research questions, questions from children, or questions of a personal or private nature (Janes, 2000, RUSA presentation). Is it possible that users know that Ask Jeeves is a better source to go to get information about J. C. Crew or vacations than 24/7 library services? Indeed, that they are aware that what library information services provide is very different from what they expect to get from Ask Jeeves and other sites? Much more research needs to be conducted to see what these millions of users are actually needing and finding on commercial sites, and whether libraries want to compete for these kinds of questions and make the high-value investments to establish a 24/7 infrastructure to answer them.

Another supposed reason for 24/7 digital reference is the phenomenon of declining reference transactions, talked about by many librarians and being increasingly documented. With declining reference statistics, the argument is that users find the trouble of going to static sites such as reference desks or buildings to be a waste of time; what they need is instant access in real time to what they are unwilling to do in person. This decline does appear to be taking place. Tennant recently wrote,

> Statistics collected by the Association of Research Libraries indicate that the number of reference queries handled per professional staff member has gone down over the last two years at a number of ARL libraries. . . . One can only conjecture as to the reason, but my money is on the Internet (Coffman, 2000, p. 66).

Steve Coffman reported that according to the National Center for Education Statistics, reference statistics for all academic libraries fell by almost 10% from 2.1 million per week in 1994 to 1.9 million per week in 1996, the exception being for public libraries, which had a 2% increase (Coffman, 2000, p. 66).

Current statistics bear out this trend. Checking the latest figures from the Association of Research Libraries (ARL), from 1999–2000, median reference transactions per library in 1991 were 133,022. They reached a peak of 158,294 by 1997, then declined steadily to 117,027 by 2000 (Association of Research Libraries, 2001, p. 7). Are users flocking to the Internet for their answers, with no need for mediation at the reference desk? And, as Coffman puts it, "Can Librarians afford to work 9-to-5 when the Internet offers reference service that never closes?" (Coffman, 2000, p. 66). Thus, 24/7 is advanced by some as a solution to the question of how to recover lost transactions at the reference desk.

Yet, as with the competition argument, a closer analysis is needed of the trend.

Do we really know for sure that not being open or offering 24/7 reference service is the primary reason for the decline? As we all know, librarians have a tendency to measure success by numbers, quantitative measures of library visits, circulation figures, collections volume, and reference transactions. As Kena put it, ". . . administrators seeing falling reference enquiry numbers may tend to see this as an indication of falling demand and therefore falling performance" (Kena, 1999, p. 3). But does this logic follow? Are we victims of our own success instead of performance failure?

ARL's own analysis of the trend bears some scrutiny; patrons may indeed make less use of the reference desk because of the availability of online catalogs, e-journals, electronic indexing/abstracting tools, and other electronic services. Yet,

Often, though, those people who do approach reference librarians require more assistance than before. At the same time, virtual reference services are adding another dimension to the growing complexity of responding to reference questions. Libraries have instituted initiatives with a deliberate emphasis on direct contact between subject specialists and users (shifting research consultation activity away from desk-based service). Thus, a simple count where each reference questions gets a single "tally" cannot capture the varying dimensions and growing complexities of reference services.

Though total figures for reference transactions have experienced a slight decline, ". . . the overall numbers are still substantial, about 117,000 per year for the median ARL library" (ARL, 2001, p. 7).

In other words success, at least in academia, may be taking place at locations other than the reference desk. Surveys show group presentations and library instruction are up, an increase from 518 in 1991 to 731 in 2000; a typical ARL library offered more than 730 teaching sessions in 1999/2000 (ARL, 2001, p. 7). Perhaps as result of information literacy efforts there is less traffic at the reference desk, facts that have little to do with the lack of 24/7. More analysis of figures such as these is crucially needed. The current point of view may be too pessimistic; what may be needed is not more around-the-clock reference help, but better access to electronic products, instruction, and information literacy programs.

Another assumption for 24/7 seems to spring from librarian service values and our public service ethic. Librarians want to serve our users, as much as possible. As Tennant states,

> Imagine, if you will, an American university student needing reference assistance at 3 a.m. Why can't a librarian on duty in Perth, Australia provide some essential front-line help? Meanwhile, librarians in the American university could in turn help students in Perth in the middle of the night (Hohmann, 2000, p. 3).

This idea of reference service across time zones, with collaborative arrangements with our global colleagues, excites many professionals in the field. It seems like an excellent idea. Yet, why should a librarian in Perth be better able to answer a question after hours about the "Big Dig" excavation project in Boston than a librarian in the United States? By waiting a few hours, the user could connect with a real specialist in the field, who would instantly know what the Big Dig was. If all our Australian colleagues had to use was their own resources, these might presumably be limited to sources specific to Australia or the Pacific Rim. And, even if they could "push" the patron to systems in the United States, how would a patron be able to access subscription databases such as Lexis-Nexis if they had no affiliation with the library, which has Lexis-Nexis? What about the myriad licensing agreements that publishers insist upon? Plus, do they have a primary obligation to serve their own users or others around the world? How much real effort could one expect from others? Would the quality be good and consistent or spotty and uneven? Granted, CDRS is doing just this with their pilot project. There should be a thorough assessment of reference answers "globally" to determine their patterns and quality.

IV. Who Are These Users? What Do They Want? And When?

Upon first thought, 24/7 would appear to perfectly complement the information needs of Internet users. Not surprisingly, surveys suggest that students expect to have *all* their research needs met online. One librarian stated, "The biggest change is increased user expectations. Increasingly, users expect to be able to find everything online, full text. Technology lets us do much more, but it also increases expectations about what we can do" (Gray, 2000, p. 365). This statement should not surprise any library reference professional. By every indicator, users want their information in electronic format and in full text. A study conducted at Duke University tried to find what users want for their information. Their responses? They wanted information that was accessible, fast, labor saving, free, computerized, networked with other libraries, comprehensive, and linked to available expertise (Rader, 2000, p. 28).

The Pew Center's "Pew Internet & American Life" project also offers interesting facts about Americans and their usage of the Internet. In March 2001, 65% of people with Internet access searched on the job at least once a day; many reported that they did so several times during the working day. Of Internet users, 49% have access only at home; 8% only at work; 39% at both home and work; and the remaining in other areas such as schools. Daily surfing is the norm, with high rates at work. Pew reports that there is an increase in those who use it at work and a drop for those at home.

Whereas in March 2000, about 49% logged in after 5 PM, this proportion was down to 40% a year later. Pew conjectured that repeated visits at work may be "taxing people's stamina for surfing in the evening or that some leisure surfing is taking place during the workday." Users are spending less time overall on the Internet, with a 7-minute dropoff in session times from 90 minutes to 83 for the average session. Pew states that some users report less searching because they didn't have the time, or because "some say they don't find using the Internet as appealing as they did before." Interestingly enough, in terms of getting information, there were increases in that category of behavior, with the bulk of it focused on health care information, news, and financial information and product information (Pew Center, 2002).

Although this is far from conclusive, there are some interesting connections to the 24/7 debate. If Pew is right, librarians are preparing to serve a population after hours that may be beginning to reduce its use of the

Internet because of either fatigue or lack of time. In fact, those who do appear to be searching seek out medical information, news, finance, and product information subjects. These subjects may be qualitatively different from those of many of the ready reference and research questions librarians are used to providing.

Moreover, as Gross, McClure, and Lankes concluded in their major overview of quality of digital reference services in 2001, the few statistics that have been compiled by librarians on the use of digital reference and 24/7 services are mixed at best. "The majority of the evaluation attempts reported are anecdotal, suffer from weak methods, and provide only a limited analysis of the service" (Gross *et al.*, 2001, p. 18). The volume of reference inquiries is not overwhelming—26 to 56 queries per month on average. So far, according to their survey of what studies exist, the "volume of questions received is minimal" (Gross *et al.*, 2001, p. 18). Moreover, the majority of questions received from users are of a ready reference nature or come from a library's usual population of patrons—for example, in academia, faculty, students, and staff. Users report that they like it, but repeat use "appears to be minimal" (Gross *et al.*, 2001, p. 18).

In 2001, Sloan began an extensive evaluation of the Ready for Reference Services 24/7 project under development by the Alliance Library System in Illinois. The results seem to challenge the argument for comprehensive around-the-clock service. His report showed that 50% of all activity took place between the hours of 8 AM and 5 PM and 80% of the activity took place during "typical" library operating hours—8 AM to 10 PM. For 1 AM to 6 AM, there was not much activity (10 sessions in 13 weeks, or about 2.2% of total activity). Sloan observed, "The data . . . might lead one to conclude that 24-hour-a-day service may not be a necessity" (Sloan, 2001, p. 2).

At a minimum, these first surveys should give the profession pause regarding 24/7. Of course, some institutions report success with their 24/7 services. Temple University with its TalkBack and TalkNow live digital reference services reported great satisfaction with results (Stormont, 2001, p. 1). Other articles in the literature, though, reveal interesting facts about off-hours usage. One noted that Clevnet's 24/7 services, in its first 18 days, garnered 1334 questions. The busiest period was between noon and 3 PM (368 questions); the lowest, from 3 to 6 AM (11 questions received). From MCLS in 2001, 200 questions were received daily in the spring, but only between 75 and 100 were currently being received; between 1 and 5 AM the service "only receives five or so questions, usually one or two are from librarians in other parts of the world, such as Japan or Sweden" (Flagg, 2001, p. 2).

These survey results are provocative. Is there a public out there that really expects librarians to provide top-shelf reference services around-the-clock? Naturally, these figures can be challenged by several counterarguments. For example, more promotion and marketing is needed to make the public aware that an alternative to Ask Jeeves is available. Or, once more sophisticated software and hardware packages are online, the public will readily use 24/7 services. Another is that the low usage reflects the newness of the projects and the fact they are just getting off the ground. Nevertheless, a question needs to be asked. Is the assumption that there is a vast pool of night-owl users wanting librarians to serve them really accurate? Or is it a reflection of what we want to believe?

Another major point about shifting reference services to a 24/7 electronic priority model concerns the question of information "haves" and "have-nots" among users. According to a study by Congressional Quarterly Researcher, "The wealthy are 20 times more likely to have Internet access than the poor, according to a recent Commerce Department study. And single parents, rural residents, Native Americans, Hispanics and blacks also lag behind in computer ownership and Internet access. . . ." The "digital divide" has turned into a "racial ravine" when one looks at who has access to the Internet. According to the Commerce Department, "The Internet-access gap between blacks and whites grew 53 percent between 1997 and 1998, and 56 percent between Hispanics and whites" (Koch, 2000, pp. 2–3). Joe Morehead also has addressed the issue of "Information Apartheid" (Morehead, 2000, p. 135) and describes it as a major problem. Those who plan for 24/7 services, especially at the public library level, must not forget this digital divide in access; it would be tragic if the assumption grew that all Americans were wired into the Internet when in fact it is not true.

V. Impact of 24/7 on Reference Practices

As noted earlier, reference transactions have declined since the mid-1990s. However, librarians have reported those questions "takes longer on average to answer," or that "reference questions have generally become more complex and sophisticated." Users only come to the reference librarian after first trying Internet sites and coming up short, and they have higher expectations from reference librarians (Tenopir and Ennis, 1998, pp. 2, 3, Online Pagination Source. They feel unsettled. Many staff members feel as though the "goal posts are moving" (Tenopir, 1998, p. 1).

Feelings among librarians are mixed. Some are very enthusiastic about 24/7; others are unsure of what it means. The reality and requirements of real-time reference are sending mixed signals to librarians about service and how to perform it. For example, we have been taught the primacy of the direct reference interview; you could see and hear users' verbal, nonverbal, and visual cues. In a face-to-face interview, "Tones of voice, patterns of speech, facial expressions, and eye contact can give important clues about the course of an encounter." Short of real-time videoconferencing, this is not available in electronic interviewing. The electronic interview is not dependent upon a face-to-face interview. New interviewing skills will be needed (Straw, 2000, p. 376). There can be uncertainty about what this implies for reference work.

These mixed signals are taking place when reference librarians are being told that users do not want face to face, and that they want their information now, instantly on demand, and will not brook any inconvenience in their research demands. 24/7 is predicated upon speed of response and timeliness; it is a core virtue. The following is a tongue-in cheek illustration of the problem:

> Why isn't there an article about . . . any event that has occurred within the last five hours? Why do I have to get up from the computer to get that information? (Smith, 2000, p. 3).

The idea that users should be taught that not everything is available on the Web, that information literacy requires the ability to shift and synthesize differing formats of information (print, electronic, microform), and that we must teach critical thinking is being subtly weakened. Moreover, if as some surveys indicated there is a consensus that chat reference has to be performed in space away from the reference desk or off-site from the library (in the home or in another office), librarians know they cannot offer the full spectrum of formats to answer many of the questions that will be posed to them. In short, we may be adopting what we have fought against for years—the idea that all information *is* on the Web and is free to those who can be guided to it by 24/7 experts, in our drive to supply information instantly in real time. In fact, we may ourselves be encouraging in our users misconceptions and false promises about the primacy of the Internet. One Florida legislator recently declared that no money should be spent for the state's university library system because he believed that "Harvard University's entire collection is now digitized and available for free" (Hathorn, 1997, p. 3). Could it be that elements of the 24/7 imperative are encouraging this idea that all information can be found on the Web?

VI. Deprofessionalization Issues

There are other manifestations of unease in the profession about the wholesale and precipitous adoption of 24/7. Certainly there are concerns about new training protocols, or how to serve a new type of user who is "individualistic" and "egalitarian" and not wanting hierarchical interactions with reference staff (Wilson, 2000, p. 388). What about keyboard strain and stress? Also worrisome are very positive forecasts by some key advocates of 24/7 that the library as place will be permanently gone. Indeed, according to them, most of our roles and jobs will disappear, too.

For example, Steve Coffman takes an extremely benign and optimistic view of the 24/7 future. To Coffman,

> online reference services would allow us to radically change the way those physical libraries are staffed, so that instead of having a whole crew of reference librarians sitting at desks in the building, your reference librarians would be online where they could handle reference traffic from many institutions at once.

Coffman continues in this train of speculation.

> The role of the physical library might change to more of a warehouse for books (although it could still be a very nice-looking warehouse, with comfortable reading rooms, etc.) and you staff it mostly with student assistants and paraprofessionals who would take care of checking items in and out, reshelving, and helping people find what they needed on the shelves.

As for any reference questions beyond the "routine" (which the students and paraprofessionals in the warehouse could handle, "She (user) could walk over to a reference terminal and work with a librarian online." A librarian would be accessible online inside the building, "but he would also be accessible from the student's desktop later that evening when she got back home, began working on her paper, and found she had another question" (Coffman, 2001, pp. 4–5).

Coffman calls it a "pretty compelling future on a number of counts." Students and faculty would love it because of more convenient access to sources and services.

Most importantly, though, since most academic libraries spend around 60 to 65% of their budgets on staff, by treating the physical building more like a warehouse and outsourcing most of the professional functions, virtual reference could allow organizations to realize tremendous savings in staff costs (Coffman, 2001, p. 5). It is not at all clear that librarians would welcome this future and consequent downgrading of their jobs and status, let alone being outsourced.

Karen Schneider also strongly buys into this new vision of the 24/7 professional model of the future. She, too, favors outsourcing from local library sites. Which librarians would participate in this new arrangement?

> Think of a world where there are far fewer reference librarians, but they earn much, much more than the average salaries today . . . the word on the street is that the starting salary at the LSSI reference center will be $60,000 MJ. Finally, professional pay for professional work! (Schneider, 2000, p. 2).

The question of downsizing and "deprofessionalization" of the majority of reference librarians cannot be a pleasing prospect to most librarians. If this were the future which 24/7 implies, it is not at all certain that most in the profession would welcome this radical change. Lancaster noted some of these worries. "Librarians perceive technology to be glamorous. Some believe the path of technology will improve the librarian's image, status and perhaps even salary. But little evidence exists that this has actually occurred." Concentration on technology may cause other expertise to deteriorate with the danger of "deprofessionalization." Tennant advocated the following skills for the "new millennium": imaging, markup languages abilities, indexing and database technology, programming, and Web technology. But, as Lancaster noted, he makes no mention of knowledge of user needs and behaviors, interpersonal skills or public service ethics (Lancaster, 1999, pp. 49–50).

VII. Conclusions

It is not the purpose of this chapter to offer a sweeping analysis of the phenomenon of 24/7; rather, it offers an alternative point of view to the generally highly positive treatment of the issue in the literature. Nor is it the purpose, Luddite-like, to argue that reference professionals do not utilize the full range of tools available with new digital products. Indeed, the potential of these products to help us with our mission to provide accurate information and research instruction is truly great. What is intended, though, is a call for a more critical look at some of the major assumptions underlying the argument for 24/7 reference service, anywhere, anytime. The major points are:

1. It is questionable whether librarians should use the commercial model of Ask Jeeves as the "north star" for our own efforts. More research has to be conducted to ascertain the nature of their users' information needs, and whether libraries provide a qualitatively different, and valued, type of information/reference service to our users.
2. Should the library be available for 24-hour reference service online, every day, and all the time? Key library surveys suggest that the numbers using these services after hours have been minimal. Is there really a need here that needs to be filled? Should high-value investments be made in staffing, training, and promotion for electronic "night owl" services? Breeding makes a good point: "But while the opportunity is there, launching a virtual reference operation doesn't necessarily involve a commitment to offering it 24 hours a day" (Breeding, 2001, p. 3). Perspective is needed here before jumping into this kind of service.

3. It is crucial that rigorous guidelines for adoption and implementation of 24/7 reference services be made. Do an institution's users need or want it? Sloan poses some tough questions that should be asked: what services are being talked about; will they be ready reference, in-depth information, basic or comprehensive; and what is realistic planning for them, in an era of continuing tight budgets? Questions about personnel and training and infrastructure issues must be addressed in a tough-minded fashion. For example, "There's no point planning video reference service if the campus network ... has insufficient bandwidth to support quality video images (or the users lack the software and hardware cameras to make use of it)" (Sloan, 1998, pp. 2, 3).

4. It is doubtful whether reference librarians can fully expect to answer research inquiries only from Internet-based sources, be they public domain or by subscription. Indeed, if you are working in a 24/7 offsite service after hours, you may not be able to address a reference question with all your tools. "Until such time as a critical mass of resources are available online, it is crucial that librarians handling electronic reference services be situated near the reference collection. The virtual reference librarian still needs to be tethered to the physical reference collection." We are a long way from achieving that "critical mass" in e-resources (Sloan, 1998, p. 3). Online Pagination Source And, if online patrons really only want direct copy sent to them, "pushing" them to other Web sites will only add to their frustration and be perceived by them as ineffective.

5. In our drive for 24/7 all the time, anywhere, anyplace reference services, we must make sure that key values and commitments do not fall by the wayside. Many librarians have signed on to Information Literacy standards. According to the January 2000 ACRL Information Literacy Competency Standards for Higher Education, five standards exist. They are: determine the nature and extent of information needed; access the needed information effectively and efficiently; evaluate information and its sources critically and incorporate selected information into one's knowledge base; use information effectively to accomplish a specific purpose; understand many of the economic, legal and social issues surrounding the use of information and access and use information ethically and legally. If this goal is viable and worthy of achieving, how does the 24/7 imperative for speed and instant copy affect librarians' ability to meet these goals and values in reference encounters that value speed? Indeed, they may be in great conflict with another (Ellis and Francoeur, 2001, pp. 3–4).

Jennifer Mendelsohn's insightful qualitative analysis of what good reference service is stressed the element of time:

> Quality service is only feasible within reasonable time frames. Time is identified as key by all the participants and is frequently referred to in connection with quality service.... Time is needed to make the patron feel comfortable, to connect, assess, act, meet the need, and teach (Mendelsohn, 1997, p. 15).

6. Professional and working conditions must also be taken into account. What incentive is there to sign on to a course of action which, as some of its strongest advocates speculate, will lead to libraries becoming warehouses, staffed by student assistants, and outsourcing of librarians who never come into direct contact with users? Indeed, those few librarians who survive the weeding process of who can be a real cybrarian might make more money, but at what a Pyrrhic price to the profession. To many librarians, this is not an appealing vision (and clashes with our own perceptions of who our users are and what they need—and, indeed, who we are). One strong advocate described 24/7 reference and said in approving tones,

> In an online reference session, as long as you have a user, you and your busy fingers are constantly working for the entire period on the virtual reference desk. Mental and physical exhaustion come very quickly, and staff can't do anything else during the session (Schneider, 2000, p. 1).

> Only a few years ago, librarians were lamenting the fact that we could not be everything to everyone, with many questions of conflicting duties, expectations, stress, and so on. Are these other tasks really going to disappear as we transform ourselves into "computarians" as Susan Perry described (Rapple, 1997, p. 7)?

One shoe may not fit all reference feet. Exciting work is being accomplished regarding 24/7 initiatives. Nevertheless, tough and thoughtful evaluation must be done to make sense of user statistics and the effectiveness of the services. "What financial models support digital reference, especially if offered twenty-four hours a day? ... What are the trademarks of quality digital reference and can they be measured? What kind of statistics document digital reference?" (Koyama, 1998, p. 2). These are excellent questions that need to be addressed.

The enthusiasm for around-the-clock digital reference should also be tempered with some skepticism. "A lack of information resources for practitioners of digital reference ... has allowed many AskA services to online without a clear understanding of either the process of digital reference itself or how to develop and manage such services effectively" (Wasik, 1999, p. 3).

A rush to serve 24/7, anytime, anywhere, is noble and within our traditional service commitment belief system. As Lankes notes, "If people can buy books, search for Websites, and even check their stocks at 2 a.m. (anywhere in the world), why can't they at least submit a question to their local library?" (Lankes, 2000, pp. 6–7); but it must be matched with capabilities, hard data, and a realistic appraisal of where we want to go.

References

Anderson, E., Boyer, J., and Ciccone, K. (2000). Remote reference services at the North Carolina State University Libraries. Paper presented at The Virtual Reference Desk—2nd Annual Digital Reference Conference, Seattle, Washington, October 16–17.

Association of Research Libraries (2001). ARL Statistics: 1999–2000. Association of Research Libraries, Washington, DC.

Boyer, J. (2001). Virtual reference at North Carolina State: The first one hundred days. *Information Technology & Libraries* **20**(3), 122–128. Retrieved from OCLC FirstSearch.

Breeding, M. (2001). Providing virtual reference service. *Information Today* **18**(4), 42–43. Retrieved from OCLC FirstSearch.

Broughton, K. (2001). Our experiment in online, real-time reference. *Computers in Libraries* **21**(4), 26–31. Retrieved from OCLC FirstSearch.

Campbell, J. D. (2000). Clinging to traditional reference services: an open invitation to Libref.com. *Reference & User Services Quarterly* **39**(3), 223–227. Retrieved from OCLC FirstSearch.

Coffman, S., and McGlamery, S. (2000). The Librarian and Mr. Jeeves. *American Libraries* **31**(5), 66–69.

Coffman, S. (2001). Distance education and virtual reference: where are we headed? *Computers in Libraries* **21**(4), 1–6. Retrieved from http://www.infotoday.com/cilmag/apr01/coffman.htm.

Constantine, P. J. How digital reference works in one academic library. Retrieved from http://www.loc.gov/rr/digiref/source/constantine.ppt.

Ellis, L., and Francoeur, S. (2001). Applying information competency to digital reference. Paper presented at the 67th IFLA Council and General Conference, August 16–25.

Ferguson, C. D. (2000). "Shaking the conceptual foundations," too: integrating research and technology support for the next generation of information service. *College & Research Libraries* **61**(4), 300–311. Retrieved from OCLC FirstSearch.

Ferguson, C. D., and Bunge, C. A. (1997). The shape of services to come: values-based reference service for the largely digital library. *College & Research Libraries* **58**(3), 252–265.

Flagg, G. (2001). Libraries launch 24/7 E-reference service. *American Libraries* **32**(7), 16–17. Retrieved from OCLC FirstSearch.

Gray, S. M. (2000). Virtual reference services: directions and agendas. *Reference & User Services Quarterly* **39**(4), 365–375.

Gross, M., McClure, C. R., and Lankes, R. D. (2001). Assessing quality in digital reference services: overview of key literature on digital reference. Syracuse University, Information Institute of Syracuse, Syracuse, New York.

Hathorn, C. (1997). The librarian is dead, long live the librarian. *PreText Magazine*. Retrieved from http://www.pretext.com/oct97/features/story4.htm.

Hohmann, L. K. (2000). Providing reference services over the Internet. *Colorado Libraries* **26**(2), 16–18. Retrieved from OCLC FirstSearch.

Horn, J. (2001). The future is now: reference service for the electronic era. Paper presented at ACRL 10th National Conference. Denver, Colorado, March 15–18.

Janes, J. (2000). Associating continually with curious minds: the evolution of reference. Paper presented at RUSA President's Program—Reference 24/7: High Touch or High Tech? American Library Association, Chicago.

Janes, J., Carter, D. S., Memmott, P. (1999). Digital reference services in academic libraries. *Reference & User Services Quarterly* **39**(2), 145–150.

Kena, J. (1999). Performance indicators for the electronic library. Retrieved from http://members.ozemail.com.au/~jkena/perf.html.

Koch, K. (2000). The digital divide. *Congressional Quarterly*, Washington, DC. From Congressional Quarterly Researcher, January 28, 2000. Retrieved from CQ Online.

Koyama, J. T. (1998). http://digiref.scenarios.issues. *Reference & User Services Quarterly* **38**(1), 51–53. Retrieved from OCLC FirstSearch.

Kresh, D. N. (2000). Offering high quality reference service on the web: The collaborative Digital Reference Service (CDRS). *D-Lib Magazine* **6**(6).

Kresh, D. N. (2001). From Sshh to search engine: reference.net on the Web. *Information Technology & Libraries* **20**(3), 139–142. Retrieved from OCLC FirstSearch.

Lancaster, F. W. (1999). Second thoughts on the paperless society. *Library Journal* **124**(15), 48–50.

Lankes, R. D., Collins, J. W., III, and Kasowitz, A. S., eds. (2000). *Digital Reference Service in the New Millennium: Planning, Management, and Evaluation*. Neal Schuman, New York.

Library of Congress. (2000). Reference 24/7: libraries test Collaborative Digital Reference Service. Library of Congress Information Bulletin **59**(10), 229. Retrieved from OCLC FirstSearch.

Lipow, A. G. (1999). "In your face" reference service. *Library Journal* **124**(13), 50–51.

McClure, C. R., and Lankes, R. D. (2001). Assessing quality in digital reference services: a research prospectus. OCLC, Dublin, OH. Retrieved from http://quartz.syr.edu/quality/Overview.htm.

Mendelsohn, J. (1997). Perspectives on quality of reference service in an academic library. *Reference & User Services Quarterly* **36**(4), 544–557. Retrieved from http://www.ala.org/rusa/rusq/99mendelsohn.html.

Morehead, J. (2000). Information haves and have nots: small thoughts on large themes. *The Reference Librarian* **71**, 131–143.

Oder, N. (2001). The shape of E-reference. *Library Journal* **126**(2), 40–46.

Pew Internet and American Life Project (2002). Summary of findings. Retrieved from http://www.pewinternet.org/reports.report.

Rader, H. B. (2000). Information literacy in the reference environment: preparing for the future. *The Reference Librarian* **71**, 25–33.

Rapple, B. A. (1997). The electronic library: new roles for librarians. *Cause/Effect* **20**(1), 45–51. Retrieved from http://www.educause.edu/ir/library/html/cem971a.html.

Schneider, K. G. (2000). The distributed librarian: live, online, real-time reference. *American Libraries* **31**(10), 64. Retrieved from OCLC FirstSearch.

Sloan, B. (1998). Electronic reference services: some suggested guidelines. *Reference & User Services Quarterly* **38**(1), 77–81. Retrieved from OCLC FirstSearch.

Sloan, B. (2001). Ready for reference: academic libraries offer live web-based reference—evaluating system use. Retrieved from http:alexia.lis.uiuc.edu/~b~sloan/r4r.final.htm.

Smith, K. R. (2000). Great expectations: or, where do they get these ideas? *Reference & User Services Quarterly* **40**(1), 27–31. Retrieved from OCLC FirstSearch.

Stormont, S. (2001). Going where the users are: live digital reference. *Information Technology & Libraries* No. 3, 129–134. Retrieved from OCLC FirstSearch.

Straw, J. E. (2000). A virtual understanding: The reference interview and question negotiation in the digital age. *Reference & User Services Quarterly* **39**(4), 376–379.

Tennant, R. (2000). Digital reference: issues, implications, & impressions. Paper presented at RUSA President's Program—Reference 24/7: High Touch or High Tech? American Library Association, Chicago.

Tenopir, C. (1998). *Library Journal* **123**, 39–40. Retrieved from OCLC FirstSearch.

Tenopir, C. (2001). Virtual reference services in a real world. *Library Journal* **126**(12), 38–40. Retrieved from OCLC FirstSearch.

Tenopir, C., and Ennis, L. A. (1998). Reference services in the new millennium. *Online* **25**(4), 40–45. Retrieved from OCLC FirstSearch.

Wasik, J. M. (1999). Building and maintaining digital reference services. *ERIC Digest*. Retrieved from ERIC.

Wilson, M. C. (2000). Evolution or entropy? Changing reference/user culture and the future of reference librarians. *Reference & User Services Quarterly* **39**(4), 387–390.

Index